ORGANIZATIONAL COMMUNICATION IN THE PERSONAL CONTEXT

ORGANIZATIONAL COMMUNICATION IN THE PERSONAL CONTEXT

From Interview to Retirement

Mark Hickson, III
University of Alabama at Birmingham

Don W. Stacks
University of Miami

with

Marilyn Padgett-Greely
University of Alabama at Birmingham

Allyn and Bacon
Boston • London • Toronto • Sydney • Tokyo • Singapore

Vice President, Editor in Chief: Paul A. Smith
Series Editor: Karon Bowers
Editorial Assistant: Leila Scott
Marketing Manager: Kris Farnsworth
Editorial–Production Administrator: Donna Simons
Editorial–Production Service: Matrix Productions, Inc.
Composition and Prepress Buyer: Linda Cox
Manufacturing Buyer: Suzanne Lareau
Cover Administrator: Jenny Hart

Copyright © 1998 by Allyn & Bacon
A Viacom Company
160 Gould Street
Needham Heights, MA 02194

Internet: www.abacon.com
America Online: keyword: College Online

Library of Congress Cataloging-in-Publication Data

Hickson, Mark.
    Organizational communication in the personal context : from interview to retirement / Mark Hickson III, Don W. Stacks with Marilyn Padgett-Greely.
      p.   cm.
    Includes bibliographical references and index.
    ISBN 0-205-19775-2
    1. Career development.   2. Communication in organizations.
3. Interpersonal communication.   4. Interpersonal relations.
I. Stacks, Don W.   II. Padgett-Greely, Marilyn. III. Title.
HF5381.H45   1998
650.14—dc21   97–44740
                                       CIP

Printed in the United States of America

10 9 8 7 6 5 4 3 2 1   02 01 00 99 98 97

CONTENTS

Preface   **xi**

1   **The New Organization**   **1**
Analytic Elements   *3*
The Organization   *5*
   The Old Organization: Agrarian to Industrial   5
   The Post-World War II Organization   6
   Pre-Automation   7
The New Organization   *11*
Where Do We Go from Here?   *12*
Summary   *13*
Questions for Thought   *13*
References   *14*

2   **Communicating as Individuals in Organizations**   **15**
Content Research   *16*
   Selectivity in Content Knowledge   20
   Gaining Knowledge through Research   20
   Setting a Base for Organizational Knowledge   21
Types of Knowledge   *22*
   Economic Knowledge   22
   Political Knowledge   23
   Religious Knowledge   24
   Aesthetic Knowledge   24
   Social Knowledge   24
   Intellectual Knowledge   25
   Review   25

Communication Dialogue   25
    Dialogue as Learning   26
Client Analysis   29
    Homophily   30
    Credibility   31
    Interpersonal Attraction   34
    Messages Form Relationships   35
Summary   36
Questions for Thought   36
References   37

3   **Researching in the New Organization   38**
Why Conduct Research?   40
Information Collection: Initiating Research   41
    Documentary Evidence
        (Reviewing the Literature)   41
    Research Questions   44
    Selecting a Method   44
Formal Methods of Research: Collecting Information   47
    Quantitative Methods   48
    Qualitative Methods   55
Analyzing and Utilizing the Data   56
Informal Observation and Organizational Performance   57
Summary   57
Questions for Thought   58
References   59

4   **Preparing for Organizational Communication   60**
The Career Choice/Job Search   63
    Analyzing Skills   63
Career Planning   65
    Content Research: The Corporation   66
    Establishing the Initial Contact   67
Résumés and Cover Letters   69
    The Cover Letter   69
    The Professional Résumé   71
The Job Interview   77
Summary   81
Questions for Thought   81
References   82

5   **Socialization in Organizational Communication   83**
Anticipation   84
    Formal and Implied Contracts   84
    Managing Self-Concept   86

Organizational Structure and Anticipation   87
Researching the Organizational Structure   92
Encounter   94
Analyzing the Organizational Encounter   94
Identification   100
Summary   101
Questions for Thought   102
Notes   102
References   103

6   Individuality in Apprenticing for Leadership   105
Asserting Individuality in the Organization   107
Individuality Types and Roles   108
Personality Types   108
Personality Orientation   110
Communication Roles
   in the Organization   111
Traits and Roles   111
Communication Cues and Individuality   112
Verbal Messages   112
Nonverbal Messages   114
Review   116
Socialization and Mentoring   116
Choosing a Mentor   118
Number of Mentors   121
Career Impact   121
Summary   123
Questions for Thought   124
Notes   124
References   124

7   Supervising and Motivating Others   126
Supervision   128
What Is a Supervisor?   128
The Optimal Supervisor   130
Supervisory Content Research   131
Motivation   131
Maslow's Hierarchy of Needs   132
Herzberg's Two-Factor Model   134
Japanese or "Theory Z"   136
Strategic Communication Models   136
Power   137
Communication Climates   140
Homans' Exchange Theory   140
Message-Centered Strategies   141

Summary   145
Questions for Thought   145
References   146

8   Leading Work Groups   147
Small Group Communication in the Organization   149
What Is a "Group"?   149
Task and Social Groups   152
Group Dynamics   153
Decision Making in the Group   155
Approaches to Problem Solving   157
Leadership   157
Descriptive Leadership Approaches   159
Leadership Contingency   160
Leadership Adaptability   161
Leadership through Empowerment   163
Communication Strategies   164
Summary   165
Questions for Thought   166
References   167

9   Adapting to Change   168
Frederick Taylor's Scientific Management   169
Bureaucratic Machines   170
Information Machines   173
Review   176
Elton Mayo's Human Relations Approach   176
Review   179
Chester Barnard and Herbert Simon's
    Analytic Framework   179
The Small Group Approach   179
James March and Herbert A. Simon   180
Review   180
New Theories of Organizing   180
Systems Theory   181
Review   185
Ouchi's Theory Z
    (Japanese Theory)   185
Review   186
Total Quality Management (TQM)   186
Summary   187
Questions for Thought   188
References   188

**10 Organizational Communication and
    Professional Conduct   190**
    Professional Competence   192
        Hiring   194
        Employee Evaluations   197
        Firing   200
        Review   202
    Daily Legal Concerns   203
        Alcohol and Drug Addiction   204
        Workplace Safety and Product Quality   205
        Confidential Information   205
        Marketing and Advertising Issues   206
        Financial Accounting   207
        Computer-Based Information Systems   207
        General Legal Issues   207
    Ethical Conduct   208
    Professional Etiquette   210
    Summary   211
    Questions for Thought   212
    References   212

11 Organizational Change and Innovation   213
    Types of Organizational Change   215
        External Change   216
        Technological Change   216
        Information/Knowledge Change   217
        Economic Change   218
        Political Change   218
        Cultural Change   219
        Demographic Change   220
        Social Change   221
        Task Change   222
        Personnel Changes   222
        Structural Change: Formality, Complexity, and Size   225
    Implementing Organizational Change   227
    Assessing Organizational Change   230
    Summary   231
    Questions for Thought   232
    References   232

12 Women and Minorities in the Workplace   233
    Discrimination   234
    The New Culture   236

A Comparison   237
Moving Ahead   238
Sexual Harassment   *240*
Racial Harassment   *246*
Non-Discriminatory Language   *247*
Other Human Factors in the Workplace   *248*
Employees with Disabilities   248
Religion in the Workplace   249
Internationalism in the Workplace   249
Age Discrimination   250
Summary   *251*
Questions for Thought   *251*
References   *252*

13 **Separation from the Organization   253**
The Psychological Pattern of Separation   *256*
Types of Organizational Separation   *257*
Involuntary Termination   *258*
Firing   258
Downsizing   259
The Early Retirement: Involuntary and Voluntary   *260*
Involuntary Retirement: The Buyout as Downsizing   260
Voluntary Separation   263
Starting a Business or Changing Careers   *264*
Avoiding the Inevitable   *267*
Summary   *267*
Questions for Thought   *268*
References   *269*

14 **Summary and Conclusions   270**
Goal Orientation in the Workplace   *271*
Social Interaction in the Workplace   *273*
The Process of Organizational Communication   *275*
The Future of Organizational Communication   *276*
Social Aspects of the New Organization   *278*
Summary   *279*

Index   281

PREFACE

In recent years, there has been a hue and cry concerning the evolution of "Corporate America." Profit-making organizations and their institutions appear to be more and more concerned about their missions of *gaining* on their competitors. Because gains are based on *profits*—and profits are based on higher prices and/or lower costs—there has been only one real solution: reduce the costs (products, services, information, and so forth) associated with production. *Internationalism,* once thought of as a corporate savior, has actually decreased the possibility of higher prices. Therefore, to be competitive, businesses have been forced to lower their costs, resulting in most cases in a reduction in the workforce. Despite governmental statements to the contrary, most of the newly-created positions have been relatively low-wage jobs. Workers who have been working for decades have either lost their jobs or fear that they will.

In our own cases, each of us has known friends who have encountered this troublesome situation. Many ask, "What did I do?" or "What didn't I do?" The answers tend to vary significantly, but in this text we hope to provide some answers to people who are *seeking* positions or who simply want to stay where they are.

Our experience with most organizational communication textbooks is that they not only do not accomplish this purpose, but that few even attempt to do so. Many textbooks take the *organizational* or *managerial* viewpoint, characterizing the reader as being among those executive decision makers who can or will operate the organization as some "pie in the sky" club.

Our intention is not to be negative or cynical, but to be *realistic.* Using this as our basic premise, we provide information about how to enter an organization, as well as how to maintain one's position there and move ahead. "From interview to retirement" not only provides the general plan for the book, but also emphasizes the importance of organizational *transitions* for the organization and the individual *member* him- or herself.

We would like to express our appreciation to a number of people for their assistance with this book. First, and foremost, we would like to thank our families: Nancy Dorman-Hickson, Brennan Hickson, Joshua Hickson, Robin Stacks, Stacy Stacks, Katie Stacks, Meg Stacks, and Tate Greely. They have always supported us. But we especially appreciate their allowing us the time to complete this project. Second, we have had some professors who have influenced our thinking on the topic of organizational communication. They should not be blamed for our ideas in the book, but they have provided us some insight. They include: the late William S. Smith (Auburn University, Emeritus Professor), Thomas J. Pace (Southern Illinois University, Emeritus Professor), Gordon Welty, and Russell W. Jennings. We would also like to thank some of the bosses that we have had, who appeared to encompass the thoughts that we have herein: Paul Reehling (WFPM Radio), the late Frank B. Davis (Auburn University, Professor Emeritus), Edward L. McGlone (Emporia State University, Professor), Michael S. Hanna (University of South Alabama), Donald K. Wright (University of South Alabama), and Edward F. Pfister (University of Miami). We would like to express our appreciation to our many students over the years who have also helped us think our way through organizational communication. Especially we would like to thank Kathy Evans, Michael Gazlay, Scott Jones, Tim Mahoney, and Stephanie Shoults for their help on the interviewing chapter; Brenda Klask (for a final and complete proofing of the initial manuscript) and Gavin Williams (for tracking down those troublesome citations and publisher addresses), both of the University of Miami; we would also like to thank the Placement Service of the University of Alabama at Birmingham for help with that same chapter.

Finally, we would like to thank the staff at Allyn and Bacon for their able assistance and the reviewers of this book: Margaret Fitch-Hauser, Auburn University; William Kennan, Radford University; Jerie McArthur, University of Minnesota; John Stewart, University of Washington; Dudley Turner, University of Akron; and Rita Kirk Whillock, Southern Methodist University.

Despite all of these influences on our lives and on this book, we take full responsibility for the final outcome.

MLH
DWS
MAP-G

1

THE NEW ORGANIZATION

Analytic Elements

The Organization
 The old organization: Agrarian to industrial
 The post-World War II organization
 Pre-automation

The New Organization

Where Do We Go from Here?

Objectives

By the end of this chapter you should be able to

1. Define and differentiate between the "old" and "new" organization.
2. Distinguish three analytical elements in organizational communication.
3. Explain how organizations have evolved over time.
4. Differentiate between how the "old" and the "new" organization approaches communication.
5. Explain why an organization's ability to adapt its communication may dictate organizational success or failure.

Organizations are collectives of individuals established to pursue specified multiple objectives on a more or less continuous basis (Hickson & Jennings, 1993). In the broadest sense, and based on their objectives, there are many types of organizations: bridge clubs, governmental agencies, religious groups, industrial corporations, and academic institutions, to name but a few. The organizations discussed in this book, however, are ones in which the individuals are paid for time spent working for the organization to achieve its purpose.

These are primarily profit-making enterprises, though some are legally not-for-profit and some may be governmental. Many of the non-profit and governmental organizations model themselves after profit-making institutions.

Because our purpose is to understand organizational communication, we focus our discussion on institutions that are collectives. Thus, sole proprietorships are specifically excluded; even two-person partnerships are not generally considered as collectives. In addition, the organizations we examine involve individuals; often we will find a natural conflict between the notions of "collective" and "individual." Thirdly, organizations have multiple purposes, one of which, as Hickson (1971) noted, is to "keep on keeping on." Finally, there is an assumption that organizations operate on a more or less continuous basis. That is, they are not constructed for a temporary purpose—as is a political campaign organization—they have perceived permanence. Central to our definition of organization, then, are "collectives," "individuals," "multiple objectives," and "more or less continuous basis."

As Hammer and Champy (1993) have suggested, the organizational principles "laid down more than two centuries ago [have] shaped the structure, management, and performance of American businesses throughout the nineteenth and twentieth centuries" (p. 1). Their book, *Reengineering the Corporation*, emphasizes the point that those "traditional" principles will no longer be effective as we enter the twenty-first century. Many of Hammer and Champy's early principles have been highly valued by previous writers on the subject of organizational communication.

The twilight of the twentieth century, though, brings with it certain fears and a lot of uncertainty about corporate America. Boyett and Boyett (1995), for example, state that

> In the last five years, almost everything about working in America has changed. The places where Americans work, the way they work, the relationship they have with their boss and peers, the security of their jobs— all of these things and many, many more have changed (p. xi).

According to *Beyond Workplace 2000*, many people in today's organizations perceive that the revolution into the next century is over, that the modern organization has evolved from the problems associated with the past two decades. Boyett and Boyett argue, however, that the revolution has just begun; its survivors are those who understand what has happened and who adapt to the new principles of the New Organization.

In this chapter we will outline how the traditional organization functioned up until about 1990. This chapter will be followed by a number of researchers' views on the New Organization. We will present the types of communication activities pertinent to the New Organization, those not based on *goals,* but instead based on *roles.* While this book may not alleviate one's fears of the new workplace, it should provide some assurance that knowledge leads to advantages for those who possess it. Throughout the text, we will enumerate how, from the initial job interview to retirement, knowledge of the new organizational communication will assist and can be used to predict strategies for career success.

Organizational communication is an important element in any organization. Organizations are complex sets of human relationships. Such relationships are built on episodes (Pearce, 1976). An episode may be defined as "any part of human life, involving one or more people, in which some internal structure can be determined" (Harre & Secord, 1973, p. 153). An episode may also be defined as a series of conversations about the same or similar topics. Conversations are composed of messages. Messages are translated ideas or feelings exchanged between people for some purpose. Thus, messages make conversations; conversations make episodes; episodes form relationships; and relationships are the core of organizations. Organizational communication makes the New Organization what it is.

There have been scores of books written about organizational communication. Some have been concerned with the history of the subject. Many have focused on communication audits (much like an accountant's business audit); others have focused almost exclusively on theory. While such factors are important—and will be covered as we explore the New Organization—other factors may be even more significant and may help us better understand how the New Organization works.

Another characteristic of most traditional organizational communication textbooks is a top-down or top management viewpoint on communication. That is, traditional analysis of the organization is seen through management's eyes. The New Organization is as much about the employee as it is about the manager, but if one expects to advance in the New Organization, she must plan her move from the ranks of the managed to the office of the manager. Unfortunately, in today's world, most people, even those with advanced academic degrees, do not start at the top. Thus, it is our view to begin at the beginning—with the preparation required for the first job interview in the profession.

ANALYTIC ELEMENTS

Throughout this book, we will focus on three essential elements that help us unravel the mysteries of the New Organization. Not surprisingly, each deals with communication knowledge, how that knowledge is acquired, and how that knowledge is best utilized, as follows:

- Content Research
- Client Analysis
- Communication Dialogue

Content research is undertaking the task of discovering knowledge about one's own (or potential) organization, its competitors, and the industry in general, as well as the general status of the culture, economy, and work. Content research requires knowledge of both historical perspective and current events. It is formal and informal: formal in the sense that it can be undertaken through academic-type research (in the library, through online databases, and through interviews with others) and informal through a daily reading of newspapers and magazines. Perhaps the most frequent informal research is undertaken by actively participating in the organizational experience.

Client analysis deals with an understanding of the audiences with whom we communicate. It allows the individual to find out about those with whom she interacts: customers, co-workers, managers, shareholders, the competition, the government, and others. Like content research, its knowledge is gained through both formal means (surveys, polls, content analysis) and informal means (talking on the job and with others off the job). Audience analysis allows us to prepare our messages to be maximally persuasive, something the New Organization requires.

Communication dialogue involves learning about the processes of communication in all possible contexts, including those not available or understood at the time. It explores not only how the message is created, but also how transmission of that message affects reception, processing, and acceptance. The New Organization communicates in many ways that were unheard of or not expected to impact much on organizational communication just ten years ago: cellular telephones, personal computer networks, e-mail, and fax transmission. To understand the potential of the future as a New Organization member, you must continually update your knowledge of how communication is being processed and transmitted.

The key to the New Organization, then, is *adaptation*. Adaptation, however, only comes about when the individual understands the organization, its members, and how they communicate within, among, and between their various audiences. Using this knowledge allows us to predict how an organization might change (and whether we want to be a part of that change), as well as how to adapt to the organization once it has changed. Peters (Peters, 1987; Peters & Waterman, 1982) has noted that the "excellent" organization of the 1980s had to change, to adapt, to meet the 1990s.

In his book, *In Search of Excellence,* Peters noted that excellent organizations found their niche. However, just a few years later, in *Thriving on Chaos,* Peters argued that, in order to survive, only those organizations that were willing to change their niches, to adapt to new ideas or markets, actually survived. In other words, organizational survival—whether at the company or employee level—requires an ability to understand what is needed for survival and then adapt to make the pertinent changes. Adaptation, then, is successful organizational change, and organizational change is a function of human communication.

There is no way to prioritize these elements. At various points in time, one will be more important than another. But all of them are always important, for they both interact with and influence each other. As an example, let's examine the process of job seeking.

To be hired for any position one must first be a competent candidate for the job. What is important here is the concept of *credibility*. There are many people seeking the same job, often hundreds for one position, each of them having a different background, with different skills and outlooks. Only one will be chosen, and that is the one the interviewer believes is most credible. Credibility helps you establish dialogue with others.

To be successful, you must determine first what a credible candidate is. How important is education? How important is experience? What other elements might be important in establishing initial credibility? A letter of recommendation? An impressive résumé? How important is it to dress appropriately for the interview? How important is it to research the company where you are applying? Already, the content research element (information about the organization) has become intertwined with communication and client research.

THE ORGANIZATION

The organization has evolved over time. To understand the New Organization better we must first examine the "old" organization. This form of content research helps us better predict, based on past experience, how the new organization will operate and thus how best to communicate within it. After examining the "old" organization, we will turn to what has made the American experience unique: the free enterprise system. Finally, we will look at what the New Organization is about and prepare for an extended examination through the rest of the book.

The Old Organization: Agrarian to Industrial

A brief history of the United States illustrates that early on we were an agrarian, self-sufficient society. In 1850, 60 percent of the population was engaged in farming; today that has shrunk to less than 3 percent (Rifkin, 1995, p. 110). Farmers grew and raised their own food products. From the surplus, they were able to pay for their equipment, stock, crops, and land. Each individual or family was responsible for life's essentials. The few who were hired were selected because of some particular expertise or for their ability to engage in physical labor. Expertise could have involved artistry, education, or some other individual skill limited to a few people. Thus, in early America, wages and salaries were associated with the "labor supply."

Through the Industrial Revolution, work became more and more complex. As machines were invented, expertise to operate them became a valuable commodity. The emphasis was on transforming the raw materials of nature into more usable commodities that could be purchased by others.

Thus, industrial workers manufactured clothing, preserved food products, created machines, and created machines that produced machines. This "new" organizational way of operating (and thinking) allowed people to specialize. Some of those who used to have to grow their own food and manufacture their own tools and clothes now focused instead on the demands of their industrial livelihood.

History brought wars between national powers. A major industry in this country was producing war products so that we could protect ourselves from warring nations. The assembly line process created by Ford in the late nineteenth century to construct automobiles also constructed tanks and other weapons of war. World War II created particular problems for the labor force because the mostly white, European, North American male could no longer produce enough to satisfy the demand during a time of war and still defend the nation. Women and minorities suddenly, and in an almost revolutionary way, became part of the industrialized labor force.

The Post-World War II Organization

By the end of World War II, the United States was undoubtedly the most industrialized nation in the world. The end of the conflict produced a need for *increased* industrialization. When soldiers returned from Europe and Asia, there was a need to build housing. A new "GI Bill" afforded the soldier an education as never before and new college campuses were needed. In addition, the war machine approach maintained its importance because of a concern about the rise of communism in the resurgent and belligerent Soviet Union and in a revolutionary China. While there was competition concerning military preparedness, especially with the Soviet Union, there was little doubt that the United States was the world's premier industrial nation. The United States proved that a successful country could produce "guns and butter" at the same time. Essentially, this meant that its organizations could produce military preparedness and domestic consumer goods at the same time—and that it could do both successfully.

The years following World War II were an encouraging period for the United States. Steelworkers transformed iron into steel to be used in automobiles, tanks, and skyscrapers. The management of industrial giants such as United States Steel (USS), General Motors, and Ford were the kingpins of an international (although primarily U.S.-led) marketplace. Virtually the entire world served as the market for American-made products and ideas.

Although there were fears about the Soviet Union, management in the United States knew it was on top of the world. It had helped win the war; it had developed the best workers in the world; it had developed the best soldiers in the world; it had established the best education system in the world. And, more important, it had the best businessmen to manage its organizations.

The American worker also had established views on the organization and its management. For producing cars, General Motors' workers were to be taken care of, provided for for life by management. With the assistance of labor unions, wages on the assembly lines and in the coal mines were as good as wages almost anywhere in the United States and far surpassed wages world-wide. A worker could move up the socio-economic ladder even if he lacked the formal education and skills to become a manager. The middle class was doing well. The workers were doing well. Management was doing well. Stockholders were doing well. Except for the "Red Menace," worklife in America by the early 1960s was excellent.

Pre-Automation

The first inkling that the American organization might have problems was a constant outbreak of news about a concept called "automation." While social thinkers and educators seemed to have a realistic concept of the conversion that would take place over the next thirty years, most workers believed that automation—whatever it was—would not affect them in any negative way. Indeed, many were led to believe that the thirty-hour workweek was only a short time away.

Many of the women who had been in production jobs during World War II were relegated to secretarial jobs, where they undertook clerical functions. Little did anyone know that over the next thirty years, several phenomena would take place that would revolutionize the organization.

- The "Red Menace" would be virtually eliminated as a concern and many of its leaders would adopt a capitalistic orientation to their economies.
- Robots would take over many assembly-line jobs.
- Personal computers would cause companies to reduce their clerical staffs and allow for "long-distance" staffing to occur.
- Stockholders, as a result of cutting production costs through the elimination of labor costs, would receive higher and higher dividends as their stocks rose in value to undreamed-of heights.

What do all of these factors have to do with one another? One principle not always but often true is that *everything affects everything else*. The end of the "Red Menace" meant a reduction in the Pentagon budget. A decrease in the Pentagon budget meant fewer planes and tanks would be produced. The production of fewer planes and tanks caused a decrease in steel production. Fewer workers were needed to produce steel. Because there were fewer workers needed at the steel mill and airplane factories, there were fewer people who could afford new cars.

The decrease in new car sales caused a further decrease in the need for steel. Additional jobs were eliminated at steel mills. To save money, automobile factory management decided to increase automation and more jobs were lost. The result was that former workers were paying lower taxes because they did not hold jobs. The country's tax base decreased. There was less money for public schools, prisons, libraries, and for the social safety net that many American workers had come to believe was their right, given all that they had given to their organizations. Librarians, prison guards, and teachers lost their jobs. In the "trickle up" economy, white-collar middle managers also lost their jobs. "Over the past ten years more than 3 million white-collar jobs were eliminated in the United States" alone (Rifkin, 1995, p. 9).

Thus, the security that the traditional organization once offered disappeared. Along with it went a feeling of permanence and, at the same time, the allegiance that management and individuals had to the organization was lost. The workers' (and the managers') world had "turned upside down."

In addition, the large corporations were dealt another blow. Competition from outside the United States, built upon American management, suddenly increased one hundred-fold. Americans began thinking that the Japanese were better educated and had better contacts.

In the *free enterprise system,* profit is the "name of the game." Profit is "the bottom line." To understand profit, we will use as an example a small hypothetical business, Bee Textiles.

Bee Textiles manufactures athletic shirts. As with most organizations, Bee started small. There were three people who purchased single-color sweatshirts from a wholesaler. The Bee workers then purchased logos from different local college bookstores. Initially, they sewed the logos onto the shirts and gave them to members of their own families. As the family members wore the shirts, others would ask, "Can your cousin make me one?" For a while, the seamstresses gave away their labor services and charged only for "raw materials."

More and more potential customers were created. The seamstresses found that their leisure time was being taken away from them. They began charging a modest rate for their labor, in addition to the cost of the raw materials. As the number of customers increased, the variation in requests also increased. Some customers wanted shirts of different colors. Some wanted logos of schools not readily available to the Bee seamstresses. They began ordering logos *en masse* to save money for raw materials.

FRANK AND ERNEST / Bob Thaves

Source: NEA. Used with permission of Bob Thaves.

Time became more valuable. The seamstresses found that they would have to charge more for their work, thereby limiting demand, or they would have to hire additional seamstresses. They decided to hire more workers. Early in the hiring process, the original Bee seamstresses decided to make a little profit on the labor of the workers. In a way, they thought, the original group was being paid for "mind labor" (as opposed to "physical labor") or "entrepreneurship."

The Bee group became so busy that they decided to move the business out of their homes. Such a move, however, meant that they would have to make a rather large investment—to pay for the largest expenditure (for capital) they had made to date. Because they were not charging much for the shirts, they did not have enough money to invest in buying or even renting a new building.

The original three Bee seamstresses applied for a bank loan. They learned that they would have to pay for the shirts, the logos, the labor of others, the building, the loan, and the *interest* on the loan. They had "bought" money. Because of the new investment, Bee had two choices. They could lower their prices and hope for increased demand, or they could again raise the price of the shirts. They decided to increase the price of the shirts modestly. Nevertheless, demand continued to increase. Customers wanted the shirts quicker and quicker.

The original three Bee seamstresses decided that they needed to look more closely at the business. Although the seamstresses decided they could manufacture the basic shirt, they found themselves engaged more and more in paperwork (loan information, state and federal government regulation, taxes, Social Security, warranties for equipment, and so forth). They had to hire lawyers and accountants. Demand increased, and they decided to build another factory in another state.

The new factory called for additional changes. The seamstresses wanted to ensure that the quality of the product was the same in both factories. They then needed a certain uniformity that had not concerned them when they were all under one roof. They decided to create standards for the shirts; they hired managers—inspectors to check for quality and supervisors to check for productivity. They also decided on factory policies and procedures so that workers at the two factories would be treated the same way; the managers were to ensure that the policies and procedures were carried out correctly.

Bee's workers noticed that the original three seamstresses were doing quite well, although it seemed that the owners were doing less work than previously. In fact, their work had *changed*. Several of the workers met together to demand an increase in wages. The owners felt they could hire new people for less money but feared that quality might suffer if inexperienced workers were hired. Bee raised the wages of the workers.

In our system, individual goals are to obtain and maintain the "best" jobs to secure the "best" lives for ourselves and our families. Thus, workers tend to see the job as a means for improving their lot. Profit making for the business is a motivator for the individual to achieve these individual goals. Most of the time, the goals of the organization and the individual are common goals. The success of one is dependent on the success of the other.

Bee decided to build two more factories. An issue arose, however, about where the money would come from to build these new factories. Bee could again go to a bank. But they decided instead to incorporate and sell shares of the company to shareholders, thus expanding ownership. The advantage over the loan was that the original owners would not have to pay interest on a loan. The shareholders, however, would now share in the profits and/or losses of Bee and would also have some say in the company's management through an elected board of directors. Over a period of time, dividends to shareholders became lower and lower; the stock was not selling well.

Bee's shirts had become too expensive, especially as a competitor had emerged who used labor from another country, where labor was much less expensive. The competitor, therefore, sold its products of equal quality at a lower price. Sales decreased. Shareholders felt they were losing money. The company's board of directors met and decided they would have to cut costs. The board "downsized"—fired or laid off a number of workers and lowered their prices. In such a case, organizational and individual goals are in conflict because: (a) organizations sometimes must change faster than their workers wish; and (b) profits are determined by reducing costs as well as increasing rewards.

Over time the seamstresses learned from experience with the free-enterprise system that profit could be obtained through three means: (1) decrease costs of producing goods; (2) increase prices for sale of goods; or (3) both. A fourth possibility for profit echoed their initial involvement: finding a new product or a new market. Once in the business, as more people become involved in organizational decision making, however, adaptation becomes a more difficult road to follow, while the economic choices become more obvious.

It is easy to see that as an organization grows, it also encounters new and more complex problems. Often, organizational bureaucracy increases as it seeks more and more control over product quality and production costs. Also, as the organization grows, more resources must be assigned to managing employees, to manufacturing the product, and to finding new markets.

When problems arise throughout the economy, however, the organization's problems become significantly greater. As discussed earlier, employees are also customers. When potential customers are out of work, they cannot purchase products. When the product is not purchased, workers are eliminated, and a terrible cycle begins. Traditionally held organizational beliefs are often the first casualties of such change; to survive the organization, its management and its employees must adapt or be lost in the cycle.

The complexity of the problem is related to the interactions among owners, shareholders, board members, employees, customers, government organizations, the competition, the business environment, and so forth. All of these interactions require *adaptation in communication*. Such adaptive interaction is an essential part of the New Organization.

THE NEW ORGANIZATION

Many companies today are in the same predicament as our fictional company, Bee Textiles. They cannot get people to invest in them unless the investors feel they will make a profit. In today's world, it appears that prices cannot be increased; thus, the choice remaining involves cutting costs or finding new products (with the additional cost of research and development) or new markets (with the additional cost of advertising and marketing). In any case, part-time and temporary workers are utilized to save money on benefits and wages. Remaining full-time employees often work overtime, suffering low morale and fearing that they, too, may soon lose their jobs. Management often finds itself in a situation where the workers, the shareholders, or both distrust it. On the positive side, however, new businesses start up daily, many of which are managed by those who were formerly subordinates of failed businesses. It would appear that the new employers are seeking a different type of employee—creative thinking, future-oriented "mind labor" to replace the traditional worker who mastered one job for life.

Although it is early in the New Organization, several significant principles seem to be appearing:

- *It is more profitable to invest in technology than in people* when *technology can do the same work*. Although equipment may call for a larger initial investment, there are fewer unknowns. With personnel, costs are more unpredictable; maintenance costs for technology are more predictable and less prone to increase than personnel benefits are as an employee ages.
- *The New Organization has no concept of loyalty;* evaluations are based solely on *previous* performance. Seniority, in and of itself, in fact may be a detriment to long-term security.

Fortunately, there are some exceptions to the general rules indicated above. Estrin (1996) writes in an Associated Press release: "[H]undreds of factory employees erupted in cheers as Aaron Feuerstein announced that he would continue paying salary benefits to the approximately one thousand workers left unemployed by a spectacular fire that devastated Malden Mills

---

CASE 1.1   Technology and Communication

Moving from agriculture to industry and from assembly line to automation requires a certain amount of money from the company. It also requires communication within the company. What kinds of communication actions are needed when an organization changes its technology? Why might the workers become frustrated with technological change? Is a company better off educating its workers to the new technology or hiring new workers? Why?

Industries Inc. in Methuen [Massachusetts] one month ago." Feuerstein said that he felt his employees were his most valuable asset. Thus, loyalty lives on in some places.

Recent research indicates that workers no longer have careers that last for decades. Instead, employees move about from company to company, from industry to industry, from location to location, and from career to career. Flexibility and adaptability, with communication as a base, will determine one's future in the working world.

For today's college graduate, there are important consequences for working in the New Organization. It is important to perform one's job in such a way that one not only moves up the organization but also can move to other organizations when needed. It is important that, at any given moment, the employee has assessed her own abilities, skills, and performance and realized which abilities and skills may be of importance to another company. Today's worker must have a two-pronged approach to work: (1) doing her job as well as she can, while (2) constantly looking for a better position within the company or elsewhere. Staying in one place in one company is a luxury of the past.

Such an approach requires more research to be undertaken than ever before. Every employee is an investor in his own destiny. A good investor is a good researcher. A good investor *anticipates* new situations. The good researcher should rarely be surprised by actions in her field, and should be able to separate the various images produced by organizations into a context that will enhance her career. The good communicator can work in a context where "bridges are never burned." By understanding how to undertake content research, analyze the communication of a variety of audiences, and carry on communication as a dialogue with others, the new employee may not have job security in the traditional sense, but she can have overall work security. Work security, in essence, comes from adaptation based on a working knowledge of how the New Organization operates and adaptation to change through communication.

WHERE DO WE GO FROM HERE?

The remainder of this book will focus first on the general communication skills required in the New Organization (Chapter 2). Chapter 3 will explore how we gain the knowledge we need to get ahead in the New Organization. Chapter 4 will explore how to seek a job in the New Organization, beginning with the interview experience. Chapter 5 discusses how to become socialized into the organization, how to be a member of the "team." Chapter 6 is concerned with maintaining one's individuality after socialization. Chapter 7 concerns motivation of one's self and others in the organization. Chapter 8 provides a discussion of how to work in groups, from leadership and followership perspectives. Chapter 9 considers the individual adapting to change within the changing organization. Chapter 10 develops an approach for professional conduct. Chapter 11 is a look at innovation and change from the

---

CASE 1.2   The Rhodes Company

The Rhodes Company has been highly productive for more than twenty-five years. John Rhodes and his family have owned the business of producing automobile interiors. Over the past two years, however, profits have shrunk from about 13 percent a year to less than 2 percent. The family has been proud that it employs 200 workers in its small New England town. The family is concerned that any further decrease might cause them to have to sell the company to someone else, who might move it elsewhere. John has decided to let the workers decide whether they want to take a 7 percent salary reduction "across the board," buy the company themselves, reduce the number of employees by 14 workers, or let the Rhodes family make the decision. What do you think they should do? What do you think they would do? Why?

---

viewpoint of the organization. Chapter 12 provides a discussion of women and minorities in the workplace. Terminating relationships with an organization is the focus of Chapter 13. The final chapter, Chapter 14, summarizes what we know about the New Organization, offering several communication principles to guide the employee as she moves from neophyte to senior member of the organization.

SUMMARY

This chapter has illustrated how formal organizations have worked in the United States, as well as how they will work into the next century. While the concept of "downsizing" is seen by many people as a negative organizational factor, the authors suggest that the new employee must learn a new approach to the workplace. Three factors are viewed as important in making continuous adaptations to an ever-changing business environment. They include content research, communication analysis, and communication dialogue. The remainder of the book will help explain how communication has worked in organizations, as well as how it is expected to work in the future.

QUESTIONS FOR THOUGHT

1. Do you think workers understand the free enterprise system? Why or why not?
2. In the chapter there is a discussion that assembly line workers never believed that robots would take their jobs. Do you see any similarities or differences in today's workers (college teachers, for example) who do not believe that computers will take their jobs away?

3. How can organizational communication be the focus of one's relationship to the organization? What kinds of episodes do you think occur in today's New Organization?
4. How do you think the New Organization will be replaced over the next twenty-five years?
5. What is the role of adaptation—specifically communication adaptation—in the modern organization?

REFERENCES

Boyett, J. H., & Boyett, J. T. (1995). *Beyond workplace 2000: Essential strategies for the new American corporation.* New York: Dutton.

Estrin, R. (January 12, 1996). Owner pays workers after plant burns. Associated Press.

Hammer, M., & Champy, J. (1993). *Reengineering the corporation: A manifesto for business revolution.* New York: Harper.

Harre, R., & Secord, P. (1973). *The explanation of social behavior.* Totowa, NJ: Littlefield, Adams.

Hickson, M., III (1971). A systems analysis of the communication adaptation of a community action agency. Unpublished doctoral dissertation, Southern Illinois University, Carbondale.

Hickson, M., III, & Jennings, R. W. (1993). Compatible theory and applied research: Systems theory and triangulation. In S. L. Herndon & G. L. Kreps (Eds.), *Qualitative research: Applications in organizational communication* (pp. 139–157). Creskill, NJ: Hampton.

Pearce, W. B. (1976). The coordinated management of meaning: A rules-based theory of interpersonal communication. In G. R. Miller (Ed.), *Explorations in interpersonal communication* (pp. 17–35). Beverly Hills, CA: Sage.

Peters, T. J. (1987). *Thriving on chaos: Handbook for a management revolution.* New York: Harper & Row.

Peters, T. J., & Waterman, R. H., Jr. (1982). *In search of excellence: Lessons from America's best-run companies.* New York: Warner Books.

Rifkin, J. (1995). *The end of work: The decline of the global labor force and the dawn of the post-market era.* New York: Putnam's.

2

COMMUNICATING AS INDIVIDUALS IN ORGANIZATIONS

Content Research
    Selectivity in content knowledge
    Gaining knowledge through research
    Setting a base for organizational knowledge

Types of Knowledge
    Economic knowledge
    Political knowledge
    Religious knowledge
    Aesthetic knowledge
    Social knowledge
    Intellectual knowledge
    Review

Communication Dialogue
    Dialogue as learning

Client Analysis
    Homophily
    Credibility
    Interpersonal attraction
    Messages form relationships

Objectives

By the end of this chapter you should be able to

  1. Define three key analytical factors: content research, client analysis, and dialogue.

2. Distinguish among rhetoric/persuasion, information/communication, and catharsis.
3. Define and explain six different types of knowledge and how they operate in organizational contexts.
4. Discuss the concept of "dialogue" as it relates to organizations and the individuals who make them up.
5. Explain the communication concepts of homophily, credibility, and interpersonal attraction.

All too often we think of the "organization" as a monolithic entity composed of impersonal departments interrelated by some organizational chart. In reality, all organizations are composed of individuals who work together as small groups on some assignment or task. These small groups are then combined into larger groups, each with another group responsible for overseeing their progress. This continues until we get to the very top-level management. The important thing to remember, however, is that even that top-level management is composed of individuals—but individuals who have mastered the complexities of the organization.

The process of working in a large group is as difficult a task as learning the specific skills necessary for any job situation. Most of the time we spend preparing for a position in any organization involves individual achievement. To get a job, to excel in whatever that job requires, takes an understanding of the needs of not only the job, but also those with whom we work. We must undertake a learning process most often equated with formal education—through courses offered in high school, college, and even after having a job. In some of these courses we learn a body of facts, some of which we remember and some of which we forget in relatively short order. In our formal education, we often learn some facts in one course to use in other courses. When this happens we are building a "storehouse of knowledge." Some of this knowledge lends itself to teaching us certain kinds of skills, while some of it lends itself to teaching us different ways of thinking.

There is an interesting aspect about all of what we have learned formally, while we were in school. Much of our learning involves communication—through speaking, reading, listening, and writing. Unfortunately, we often think of these learning skills as something necessary to learn, but not as integral to learning itself. Most learning skills, then, are communication skills; we learn through the process of communication. To learn the process of communication we must first explore the three key analytical elements discussed in Chapter 1: (1) content research as knowledge through communication; (2) dialogue for learning; and (3) client analysis.

CONTENT RESEARCH

By definition, content research represents knowledge. Knowledge is learned through formal education and through an informal process in interaction with others. The first point we wish to illustrate is that *knowledge* is a memory bank of perceptions.

What do we mean when we say that "knowledge is a memory bank of perceptions?" Think about what "knowledge" really is. We are battered with numerous perceptions every instant of our waking lives. Environmental stimuli provide us with information about the conditions we work in: we see ants on our desk and cockroaches on the ground; lightbulbs that are on in the room and lightbulbs that are out in the room. People around us are constantly transmitting stimuli that may shape our perceptions through their dress, their hair color, their breath, their voices, their late arrivals. Their perfume may attract us on the one hand, and their brusque voice may repulse us on the other.

Perceptions are composed of sensations and interpretations. That which stimulates a perception may be *external,* such as those listed above, or *internal.* For example, I may perceive a stimulus related to something that I did last night. I may be thinking of what I am going to do tonight. When we think about another time or another place other than the here and now, we are using the *internal perceptual field.* When we focus on something within our immediate environment, we are dealing with the *external perceptual field.* (See Figure 2.1.)

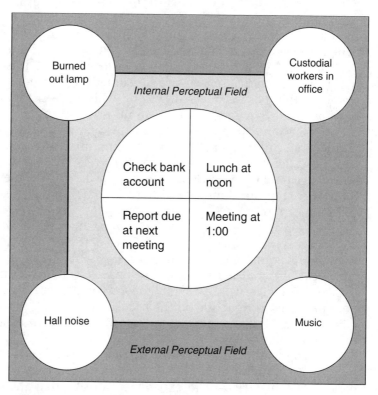

FIGURE 2.1   Perceptual Fields

To focus on what someone is saying in a meeting means that you must "zoom out" of other external perceptions and all internal perceptions. Failure to separate perceptions might yield a communication such as the one that follows:

BOSS: We had a good quarter in the second quarter of this year. This past quarter, however, showed a down turn of about 5 percent. Not that 5 percent is that much. But we can't continue such a trend. We need to investigate what the problem is. Our widget production was down. We had cuts in our sales groups as part of our downsizing. We are beginning to have an inventory problem. Juan, would you move toward downsizing more in production, or do you think this is simply a seasonal problem?

JUAN: [As he is listening to this: I've heard all of this before. I have to pick up the car after work. Did I leave that confidential paper on my desk?] I, uh, I don't know.

Perceptions, then, are part of reality; indeed, perceptions are reality for us. Essentially, we choose those sensations that we wish to interpret. Sometimes we feel that we are "forced" to choose certain sensations (or stimuli) to interpret because those stimuli draw our attention, such as Juan's concern about his car and papers. Nevertheless, we interpret only a few of the various stimuli that enter our minds. When we make an interpretation, we also decide whether to maintain that stimulus in our minds. When we decide to maintain such a perception, it becomes a part of our "memory bank of perceptions." A memory bank of perceptions is a knowledge base—it is what we know.

There are two ways to achieve a knowledge base. One is to perceive a stimulus from an external object—we see something or we hear something or we read something or we smell something. This we refer to as *intrapersonal communication*—the impetus for the stimuli is found inside the individual, who then uses it to pursue a personal dialogue or as a new stimulus for other communication. Another way is through communicating with another person—this we call *interpersonal communication* (see Figure 2.2). Thus, all of our knowledge (and our knowledge of our knowledge) is achieved through some form of communication. Everything we know we have learned through the communication process.

For each individual, knowledge is what makes him or her unique. This knowledge is used to make decisions. Some of these decisions might be whether or not to fear something, or to take a risk. Essentially, when we fear something and decide not to deal with it, we may have low motivation. When we decide to take a challenge, we are using high levels of motivation. Our knowledge base not only helps us to decide on the probability of being successful or the possibility of failure but also predisposes us toward action (motivates us to do or not to do something).

A second point is that most of our learning takes place through the process of communication. Little of what we know is learned through first-hand experience. First-hand experience is really trial-and-error. Most people

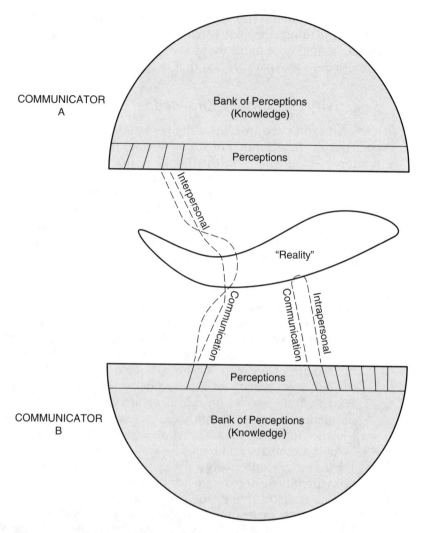

FIGURE 2.2   Knowledge Bases

Figure from *An Introduction to Communication Theory* by Don W. Stacks, Sidney R. Hill, and Mark Hickson, copyright © 1991 by Holt, Rinehart, and Winston, reproduced by permission of the publisher.

try something at least *once*. If we succeed, we tend to try it again. If we fail the first time, we either try to avoid it in the future or we devise a different way of doing it to improve the possibility of success.

Most learning is through the process of communication. We learn in formal situations, such as where individuals lecture and discuss information with us. We learn formally by reading books and magazines and newspapers and sets of directions. We also learn informally through conversations with others. We learn through watching films and television. We learn through interactions on a computer system. The successful person is always committed to the new—through reading, through listening, through asking questions, and through remembering those items that have been taught before. In the next section, we will discuss a five-part process that determines what we perceive and recall.

Selectivity in Content Knowledge

As noted earlier, we are constantly being bombarded by stimuli that form our perceptions. Take a moment to consider all the stimuli competing for your attention even as you read this book. Which are important enough to enter consciousness? Which lie just below consciousness, ready to act but still dormant as far as you are concerned? How do we deal with all these stimuli, noticing some and ignoring others? McCroskey (1992) has discussed this as a function of the selectivity process. That is through *selective exposure, selective attention, selective perception, selective retention,* and *selective recall* we manage (or are managed by) our perceptions.

The selectivity process centers on five principles (McCroskey, 1992).

1. *We cannot know everything.* Therefore, we select certain things from which we receive a stimulus. We tend to select those items that are close to us, that we are involved in, that have utility for us, and for which we are reinforced.
2. *We cannot attend to everything to which we are exposed.* We all have a certain, limited attention span. We are attracted to the novel. We are attracted to the concrete. We are attracted to items that have a minimal duration.
3. *We selectively perceive because some messages are ambiguous.* They lack redundancy, they do not provide us a schema (or organizational pattern), they do not relate to our previous experiences, or they do not fit into our own expectancies and biases.
4. *We tend to remember only a few of those items that we perceive.* Memory falters when those items were not highlighted, they were not organized, they had no realistic application for us, or they were somewhere in the middle of a message instead of at the beginning or the end.
5. *We selectively recall only a few of those items that we remember.* Thus, if we begin with a bank of, say, thirty items to pick up at the grocery store, we may return with only five or ten of them—while perhaps returning with some that were not in the original list of thirty items.

Gaining Knowledge through Research

Unfortunately, most knowledge gain is not like learning to ride a bicycle. Much effort is required to move from one place to another. Not only that, but most knowledge acquisition requires periodic re-training and re-thinking. Just because I learned how to use a typewriter thirty years ago does not necessarily mean that I know how to use a computer now—or that I will know how to use the equivalent to a computer thirty years from now. Thus, the most important thing that we can learn is to learn how to learn—how to gather and interpret the knowledge, formal or informal, we have at our disposal. And the most important facet of learning how to learn is to do research. We believe that almost every job in the twenty-first century will be a research job. We believe it so important that Chapter 3 is devoted to understanding how people conduct research both formally and informally.

This does not mean that each job a person takes occurs in a library. In fact, libraries may become virtually obsolete for doing research unless they, too, adapt to the future. It is likely that the libraries of the twenty-first century will contain few books as we know them today. Instead there will be banks of computers in what we know as libraries. The old libraries will be depositories. Access to information will be through computer-like equipment. Most people will have the same information at home. We will be able to "call up" all of the articles about job interviews, as well as all of the pages of information in former books such as the one you are reading. The computer will assist us in finding a position within an organization. And the time when all of this will happen is NOW.

The question becomes how do I find and keep a position in an organization in the meantime? In Chapter 4 we will explore the research aspect of communication as it affects preparing for the job—creating a knowledge bank of information that will help in surviving the interview process. That is, when we communicate our knowledge we are really communicating through the process of understanding not only our perceptions of the topic, but also understanding and trying to *predict* others' perceptions of that same topic.

Thus, communication involves two essential components: dialogue (internal and external) and research. We believe that the individual who can perform well in dialogue and research will have a much better opportunity of obtaining and especially of *maintaining* a position with an organization of the future.

Setting a Base for Organizational Knowledge

What, then, is the typical organization like? How will it change between now and the first few years of the new century? The most basic difference between organizations of the beginning of the twenty-first century and organizations of the beginning of the twentieth century is CHANGE. In large measure, the industrialists of the early twentieth century believed that they had learned about all there was to learn. Automobiles made transportation more efficient; communication systems made information more easily available. People had jobs. The people were dependent on the companies, and the companies were dependent on the workers because the companies were manual labor–intensive. The railroads and the automobile companies needed hands and muscles to do their work. Each worker was easily replaced as long as another person could physically do the work. Now machines are doing much of that kind of work.

Research may be considered the "content bank" of communication for "mind labor." Without research we either have nothing to say or we say something without knowing what we are talking about. We would be in trouble with the boss in either case. If we take a simple example of returning to school on Monday and someone asking us what we thought of Saturday's football game, or what was on "60 Minutes" Sunday night, we know that we had to have seen the game or the television show to carry on a *knowledgeable* conversation. Such research becomes even more important when your boss asks you on Monday morning what you thought about the proposed legislation on public utilities that you were supposed to have read over the weekend.

In all reality, you must engage in both *formal* and *informal research,* read and collect information habitually all your life. You will have to study what you read. In the next section we establish a few general types of knowledge that come from research that you may need to know wherever you decide to enter the workplace.

TYPES OF KNOWLEDGE

There are six basic types of knowledge: economic, political, social, religious, aesthetic, and intellectual. These types of knowledge are not mutually exclusive, they interact with one another. For example, let's suppose your company has a problem with noise pollution. Minimally, this is a problem of economic-political-aesthetic difficulty. It may also affect the social; if your industrial plant is near a school, it may affect intellectual; if it is near a church, it may affect religious. In this way, one problem may call for you to possess knowledge in all six areas. Let's take a look at each category in more detail.

Economic Knowledge

Economic knowledge is almost always found within all organizations. For profit-making companies—and even for most non-profits—the primary issue is "bottom line." That is, will it be profitable for us to make this decision? Such a decision may be like that when Coca-Cola decided to manufacture the "New Coke."

Traditional marketing research often provides the knowledge required to make an organizational decision. For instance, suppose we are making a decision whether to build a fast-food restaurant in a particular location. Such decisions are often predicated on economic knowledge. Questions the organization will want to answer include: Will people stop here? How many other fast-food restaurants are near this location? How well has this particular chain done in this general area? How large a restaurant should be built? How large a staff will we need? What hours should we operate? What "money" problems might we encounter? For example, is it possible that some neighbor might try to get a court order to block us out? If so, what are the chances we will win the lawsuit? How much will the suit cost us? The bottom line, is it all going to be worth it in one year? Five years? Ten years? Even though it may not make a profit, is it worth it to build even if only to block a competing fast-food business from moving in?

Economic knowledge allows the organization to effectively plan for the future. It also provides management with estimates of startup costs, expected return on investment for owners, investors, and employees. For the individual worker, economic knowledge may provide the information required when offered a competing position or, in the case of a union representative, deciding whether a strike would benefit the union's position.

Political Knowledge

Political knowledge involves a number of factors. Is the legislature likely to outlaw our product? This might be a consideration for a tobacco company or a gun manufacturer in particular. It may be pertinent for a toy manufacturer or even a software company. Political knowledge is especially pertinent for organizations moving into the international arena. What are the politics of the country? Is it likely that the country will nationalize businesses, thus causing us to lose our assets? Are political prisoners producing our products in another country?

Certainly politics is a consideration of American oil companies in other regions of the world. Is paying bribes a political modus operandi for this country? If it is, what political effects will our paying bribes have on the status of our company in the United States? Will we be fined in the United States for paying bribes in Argentina? Will criminal actions be taken against us? If we don't pay the bribes, will we be shut down in the new country? What party or parties are in power there? What would happen to our company if there were a revolution? How likely is a revolution in the country where we are placing our business?

Political knowledge is also important when looking at the organization itself. All organizations have their own political orientations (Morgan, 1997). Some organizations are run somewhat democratically, with people having input

---

CASE 2.1   The Liquor Store

Suppose that you have enough capital to build and operate a liquor store in Smallville. From the six different categories of knowledge that we are discussing, how many are pertinent to the question of where your location will be? To what extent do you have to undertake research on each of these categories? Will you use primarily formal communication or informal communication? To what extent is the use of formal or informal communication related to the category of knowledge?

into the decision-making processes. Other organizations are run like dictator-ships, with only a few "ruling" individuals making decisions and then passing those decisions down as "decrees." Still other organizations fall somewhere in between being democratic and despotic. Knowledge of the organization's political structure can be extremely beneficial; it affords strategic communica-tion and it indicates how decisions are being made and how to influence them. Political questions from the organization side might include: Who makes key decisions? How are they made? Which faction is more important? Why?

Religious Knowledge

Religious knowledge considerations also are important. Obviously, I cannot sell "Big Macs" in India. But what about "McChicken" sandwiches? What about fries? What about milk products? Will a liquor store be successful in a largely Southern Baptist county? How well will condoms sell in a Catholic commu-nity? Is "The Inferno" a good name for a bar here? How are coffee sales in Utah? Would a gambling casino be successful in Georgia?

Aesthetic Knowledge

Aesthetic knowledge involves knowing the extent to which others find something pleasing or displeasing. When the Baltimore Orioles decided to build "Camden Yards," some local neighbors were concerned that the new stadium would not "fit in" with its environment. The architects and the owners of the Orioles worked with the neighbors, discussing different styles in order to ensure that their neighbors would not try to block the building of the new stadium.

Aesthetic knowledge helps the organization create an atmosphere that pro-duces the highest quality product, whether it is a concrete product or an idea. What kind of environment would produce the best, most original advertise-ments? The television show, "Thirtysomething," demonstrated the aesthetics of a group of people in their thirties—from work, to home, to leisure. The sur-roundings reflected a certain ambiance that produced a certain perception of what would happen in many of the scenes. Consider, for example, the office of the hard-driving advertising executive (rather stark, dark, clean, business-like) and that of the creative staff (lively, messy, bright, colorful and creative).

Aesthetic perceptions provide clues as to how you should behave and communicate. Often people who are on a "power trip" establish aesthetically powerful environments. On the other hand, we have individual aesthetic con-siderations—would you invest in a bank run by tellers in Bermuda shorts and T-shirts? Are there differences, for example, in how bosses dress and how em-ployees perceive them?

Social Knowledge

Social knowledge is based on a number of factors. Will it be socially appro-priate for customers to come into my business? What are the norms here? Will a "McLean" sandwich fit into a subculture that is into dieting? What should

I name this product in another country? We must check for language/dialect differences (what is the difference between a "poor boy" sandwich and a "hoagie"?). What sub-sector of the market am I seeking? Will customers here purchase ruby red lipstick? Will people attend daytime baseball games?

Social knowledge is often the key to advancement within the organization. Who is "in" right now, who is "out"? Are there certain groups to avoid? Will affiliating with certain groups or causes enhance or detract from organizational advancement? Should an oil employee demonstrate for environmental controls? Should a political analyst register to vote Republican, Democratic, Independent, or even register to vote at all? Obviously, social knowledge interacts with political, religious, and aesthetic knowledge.

Intellectual Knowledge

Intellectual knowledge is often reflected in the creative elements of business decisions. What tack can I use to stimulate customers where they've never been stimulated before? If all the surrounding states have casinos or lotteries, might I not be more successful in legalizing gambling on college and professional sports?

Intellectual knowledge often originates from formal training. Intellectual knowledge is more than simply knowing the "facts," including how to best use those facts to your advantage. It may be the difference between making a sales pitch that is one-sided as compared to one that is two-sided. Which is most effective when? The ability to use mental reasoning is an intellectual ability that often differentiates the blue- from the white-collar worker in many organizations. How, for example, should you react (if at all) to a negative letter or memo? What would your communication do—put the issue to closure or give it more credibility than if ignored?

Review

Although many of the knowledge types are used to market something—an idea, yourself, your corporation—each category is also pertinent for other aspects of business. Should we have company parties? If so, should they be at the local park? A restaurant? At the company site? Should families be invited? How should our workers dress? Should we have a dress code? Should we support local schools? How? Should we support college sports? Which teams? Only one? In addition, these research questions are important for our dialogue with others.

COMMUNICATION DIALOGUE

Knowledge forms the substantive content of what we know and what we can communicate to others. Dialogue involves how we transmit and receive this knowledge to and from others. There are three basic types of human interaction important in any organization: (1) rhetoric/persuasion; (2) communication/information; and (3) catharsis. Each has a different outcome in mind as its goal.

Rhetoric/persuasion is concerned with trying to influence others' attitudes or behavior. As an analogy, consider a tennis match. In rhetoric, each of the players is trying to "win" the point, and subsequently the games, set, and match. One can win with "slams"; one can win with "drop shots" just over the net. In *communication/information,* the intent is to inform and to "keep the volley going." In *catharsis,* one player is simply releasing emotions; in some senses, catharsis is the result of the failure of the other two. Catharsis is like hitting the tennis ball against a wall; another player is not really needed.

As examples, rhetoric is used when we attempt to entice someone to purchase a product. We try to make the product look good; we try to make the product appear useful, even necessary. Only a few years ago, most homes included no videotape cassette recorder (VCR). Now most have more than one. Does this really mean that we "need" a VCR? Or does it mean that the marketing communication has been quite effective? When enticing an employee from another organization to join yours, your dialogue will be rhetorical, offering reasoned logic, some emotion perhaps, and your credibility as a member of the competing organization as your "proof."

An example of communication would be teaching the entire staff how to use a specially-designed piece of computer software. It would include writing directions for building the ready-to-assemble bookshelves you purchased from us. Catharsis includes those times when you simply want to "let off steam." Perhaps several workers are complaining about the increased fees for parking in the company lot. It might include when you go home and tell your spouse about what a bad day you had at the office.

There are, then, three types of social interaction: rhetoric/persuasion, communication, and catharsis. In the organization, communication is a process utilized by all who have contact with the organization, to provide positive responses to positive actions and negative responses when changes are needed in the process. Catharsis is generally a mark of failed communication and/or persuasion.

Dialogue as Learning

To this point we have explored two of the elements that make up what organizational communication is: content research and communication dialogue. In this section we will combine the two and later we will discuss client analysis in this context. We will create a model of communication that is applicable to the organization.

A model is a static representation of the ongoing communication process. Models are important because they allow us to study the different parts that constitute communication in a "steady state." That is, a model allows us to lay out in one place the parts of communication and discuss them as if they were physically before us. A limitation, of course, is that models often tend to minimize the complexity of the communication process, a process that by now should seem very complex indeed. There have been hundreds or thousands of communication models created by communication theorists. Our model has elements similar to most. These elements include (see Figure 2.3)

1. the sender
2. encoding
3. messages
4. transmitting
5. noise
6. media
7. receiving
8. decoding
9. receiver
10. intent and feedback
11. re-transmittal
12. environment

The *sender* is an individual with a body of knowledge about the topic being discussed as well as a body of knowledge about the receiver. To ensure that a message is received, the individual will try to encode a message that fits the content, the sender's purpose, and the sender's knowledge of the receiver. It is important to note, however, that each person's body of knowledge is constantly in change;

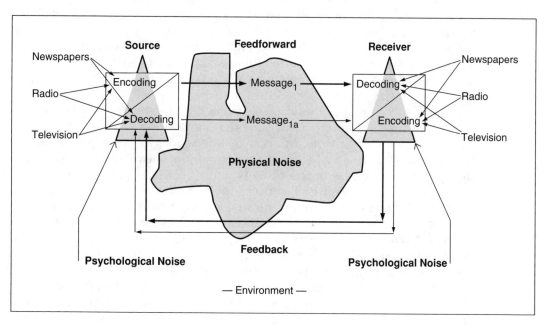

FIGURE 2.3   Communication Model

that is, we are constantly adding to our bodies of knowledge and constantly forgetting knowledge that we once knew.

Encoding of a *message* takes place through nonverbal and verbal codes. In terms of verbal codes, we can easily see that language changes over time. For example, thirty years ago no one would have said, "Burn a copy of this report and fax it to our Los Angeles office." Such a message would have been meaningless. Today most people would know to photocopy the report and transmit it over a fax machine to the California office. In addition, we use the nonverbal code to emphasize a message—to add emotion to it. For this reason, we might be much more likely to scream a message to a colleague the third or fourth time we have told him to do something that he did not do than we would have the first time we transmitted the same message. A message, then, is an idea wrapped in verbal and nonverbal coding.

Transmitting/noise/media/receiving involves the same sub-process in dialogue. We *transmit* when we place an encoded message into a medium (fax, face-to-face interaction, a public speech, a group meeting, on television, on radio, through the Internet, on electronic mail, in a brochure, in a magazine, in a newspaper, in a newsletter, on a billboard, and so forth). The *medium* is used to "ship" a message to the receiver. An idea, then, is wrapped in encoding and shipped to a receiver. *Noise* is any process that causes the "message package" not to get to the receiver. In the case of a letter, for example, the envelope may have had the incorrect zip code. Noise, however, can also be perceptual and internal to the communicators themselves; remember the communication between the Boss and Juan earlier in the chapter?

Receiving involves opening the message package. The receiver separates the nonverbal and verbal coding from the message to get to the idea. Sometimes we open a message package like a young child at a birthday party—tearing it apart as quickly as possible. At other times we carefully open it like Granddaddy does at his birthday party. Sometimes we open it even more carefully, such as when the Federal Bureau of Investigation inspects a possible mail bomb.

The *intent* of the communication process is for the receiver to discover. Regardless of the substantive content of the message, we will also evaluate its credibility at the same time. In order for the sender to "know" whether the right package was received at the right destination, the receiver is expected to sign for the package [as in the case of "return receipt requested" or "10–4"]. Such a response is positive feedback; the sender knows that the message "worked." In the case of a communicative message, the return message (called *feedback*) means "I understand." In the case of a persuasive message, it means, "Will do." When you send a present to your grandparents and you hear nothing back for days, you have neutral-negative feedback. In the case where you telephone your grandparents and they say they did *not* receive the present, you have negative feedback. We would like to receive positive feedback for all of our messages, but since the communication process is not always successful, we do not always gain the desired response. When we do not get a positive type of feedback, we must *re-transmit* the message. We may talk louder or more slowly. We may change some of the words. We may try electronic mail instead of the telephone. By changing the encoding, using another channel (medium), or refocusing the message entirely, we are trying to assure that the message at least "got there."

Further, because intent is perceptual, we have situations where intent is unclear. For instance, the sender intends a message, but the receiver does not perceive the intent (the message is ignored). Or, the sender did not intend a message, but the receiver perceived intent (the message is implied). Or, neither perceive intent to a message, but someone else perceived intent (there is no message).

The *environment* must be considered in all communication processes. If the receiver does not speak our language, there is improper verbal coding. If the receiver did not understand how important our message was, we may have had improper nonverbal coding. If the idea (the "core" message) is alien to the receiver, we must search for new ways to get our ideas across to the person. Thus, sometimes we must re-transmit a message. We may have to do this because of poor coding, alien idea, or media malfunctioning. For example, if we learn that the United Parcel Service went on strike right after we sent the message, we may have to try another medium.

There are several necessary components for a successful message transfer. The encoding (*language; nonverbal communication*) must support the substantive idea. The noise must be limited. The receiver's ability to decode must equate with the sender's encoding. All of these are substantive elements of the message. But as we have mentioned, we are also constantly undergoing a process of evaluating the message. Much of the evaluation has to do with who the other party is. We attempt to establish ourselves through what is called *impression formation*. Impression formation is composed of those factors by which others assess us and we assess them. The components are homophily, credibility, and interpersonal attraction. Impression formation allows us to decide whether to take a message seriously or not; it allows us to determine whether a message is true; it helps us determine whether a message is important. In many ways, this evaluative component of message transfers is as important as, if not more important than, the substance of a message.

CLIENT ANALYSIS

Client analysis is concerned with what has been referred to traditionally as audience analysis. In this case, a client is anyone with whom you are communicating about a topic relevant to the organization. In analyzing such clients, Powell, Hill, and Hickson (1980) found that not only do each of the previously discussed factors affect one's evaluation of a message but also that there is a pattern among the components of impression formation. Homophily (perceived similarity of a person with another person) determines whether the other has credibility (believability). The other's credibility helps us determine whether we are interpersonally attracted to the other. Each of these aspects of impression formation assists us in evaluating the message. We turn first to homophily.

Homophily

McCroskey, Richmond, and Daly (1975) have discussed the communication concept we refer to as *homophily,* defined as "perceived similarity." Generally we are attracted to other people with whom we feel homophily. Homophily can be broken into three areas: (1) demographic homophily; (2) background homophily; and (3) attitudinal homophily.

Demographic homophily includes those who are from the same geographic area as ourselves. In general, people from the southern United States seem to get along better (are more *homophilous*) with others who are from the south. Midwesterners get along better with others from the Midwest. People from rural areas get along better with one another than they do with people from cities. When we meet another person we are in the process of trying to eliminate uncertainty about her (Berger & Calabrese, 1975), and uncertainty is more easily eliminated when we know we are from the same general area.

Homophily, then, is one reason why one of our first questions of strangers is "Where are you from?". Other types of *demographic homophily* include those of the same sex, ethnic group, age group, sociological group, or economic group. Individuals of the same sex feel they "know" each other better at the outset than do individuals of the opposite sex. This is one of the reasons why one might say, "I just don't understand men [or women]." Age groups have similarities in the sense that they have grown up in the same culture. A person in her eighties understands much more what an economic depression is than a person born in the 1950s or the 1970s. The person born in the 1950s, however, probably understands what the selective service draft is better than one born in the 1970s. In Table 2.1 we have illustrated different views as a result of age.

People in the same economic group often live in the same neighborhoods, have similar values, own similar makes of automobiles, and live in similar homes. Sociological differences may involve education levels. Thus, we may find that we have more in common with someone from a different culture (of similar education) than we do with someone from our own culture who is significantly different from us in education level.

Background homophily is concerned with similarities in experience. One of the topics of conversation between strangers concerns movies. Here the interactants "test" one another to see if their tastes match. They question one another about hobbies and other issues about which they may have a common interest. Often the initial interaction between college students begins with a question such as, "Do you go to school here?" Or, "What is your major?". Both are indicative of background homophily. Perhaps this is why certain students gravitate toward the "Ivy League" schools and others toward the "Ag School." To some extent, background homophily explains why some students major in business and others in communication or mathematics.

Attitudinal homophily concerns similarity about more important issues such as politics and all of the areas of knowledge previously discussed. Are the two interactants similar in their views on religion, economics, and so forth? An evaluation of homophily will often indicate to us that we are NOT similar. As employees of a diverse corporation, we must learn to find similarities even when they do not readily appear to us. Although we may be from a different part of the country, we may agree about the importance of honesty in business. Although we may not be of the same gender, we may have similar ideas about how to make a profit. Although we may be of different ages, we can learn from one another about how a particular segment of consumers may view our product. Diversity itself can bring profit through sharing ideas.

All of these ideas about homophily are based on our stereotyping. Certainly we do not always select friends or business associates because they are similar to us. Perhaps we should not stereotype people merely to keep them away from us. What we are saying, however, is that everything else being equal, we all have a tendency to select those similar to us and not to select those who are different. But in almost every case, there will be similarities and differences, and we base our selections on both.

Credibility

Once we have perceived another as being similar to us in some way, we begin evaluating that person's *credibility*. When we evaluate an individual's credibility, we examine three aspects of that person: character, competence, and sociability. *Character* involves the extent to which we think the other person is trustworthy. Often we move through a process of "testing" another to determine whether she or he is trustworthy. We are also concerned about *competence,* especially in the workplace. Is this person a hard worker? Is this person capable of doing the job? Thirdly, we are concerned about *sociability*. How well will this person get along with others in the company? Is this person boring?

DILBERT / Scott Adams

DILBERT © United Feature Syndicate. Reprinted by Permission.

TABLE 2.1   Perceptions by Age Groups

Decade: Age in 1992:	1920s (63–72)	1930s (53–62)	1940s (43–52)	1950s (33–42)
Family	Close families the basic social/economic unit	Every member contributed to family welfare during depression	Women were 26% of work force (40) Rosie the Riveter hit 37% (42) Baby boom (46)	Members started spending more time with peers
Social Influence	Beginning of Flapper age (20) Scopes trial on evolution (25) Stock market crash (29)	Great Depression 1,300 banks closed (30) Social Security start (36) WPA enacted	Nylons replaced silk stockings (40) Nation/economy focused on war (41–45) Young girls called Bobby Soxers (42) WPA stopped (42) Religion in school violates First Amendment (45)	Juvenile delinquency problem (54) School racial segregation unconstitutional (54) Voting Rights Bill (57)
Politics	19th Amendment passed (20)	Roosevelt and the New Deal (33)	Pearl Harbor (41) War with Japan, Germany, Italy (41) U.S. Savings Bonds (41) Atomic Bomb on Japan (45)	Korean War (51–53)
Geography	First time in U.S. history that urban population surpassed rural			
Life Expectancy/ Lifestyle	U.S. life expectancy 54 (20) 60% in U.S. with income less than $2,000		U.S. life expectancy 64 (46)	Middle class more affluent Prosperity, productivity, distribution of jobs (50)

From *Effective Managerial Communication, 2e* by Rasberry and Lindsay, pp. 126–129, Copyright © 1994. By permission of South-Western College Publishing, a division of International Thomson Publishing Inc., Cincinnati, Ohio 45227.

1960s (23–32)	1970s (13-22)	1980s (10+)	1990s (less than 10)
43% of households with only 1 working spouse 48% married women work (68)	More divorces than marriages ½ eligible females work, 20% in blue-collar jobs (78) 58% of women with schoolchildren work (78) *Roe* v. *Wade* legalizes abortions (73)	Divorce hits high of 5.3 per 1,000 (81) Nuclear family (working husband, housekeeping wife, 2 children) is 7% More singles, marriage postponed, childbearing delayed to late 30s	No children in 51% of households (91) Divorce lowers to 4.7% per 1,000 (90)
Racism concern (63)/ sexism concern (69) Crime rate doubled Ecology concern (62) First U.S. astronaut (62)/moon walk (69) Public school prayer unconstitutional (63) Use of LSD/ marijuana (66) Civil rights legislation (66) Medicare for aged (66) Campus revolts (68) Hippies, liberal sex views	450 colleges/universities closed by students (70) Kent State deaths (70) 18-year-olds vote (71) Long hair worn in revolt, later became style Switch to sexism/racism concern Environment issues more important than civil rights (73)	Greed decade "Yuppies" Self-help groups (82) Status symbols: Rolex, BMW, Corona, Club Med Concern with ageism Television evangelists: Roberts, Bakker and Swaggart scandals (87–88) Space Shuttle Challenger explodes (86) Stock Market plunged 508 points (87) Hostile takeovers	Seniors' communities Junk bond king Michael Milken sentenced to 10 years (90) Reemphasis on environmentalism New spirit of "volunteerism" Demise of communist parties except in China/Cuba (91) Collapse of Soviet Union (91) European Common Market (92) New focus on Sexual Harassment Japan world leader in manufacturing (mid-90's)
Bay of Pigs (61)/Cuban missile crisis (62) Kennedy assassinated (63) Vietnam Troops increase to 475,000 (67) Martin Luther King & Robert Kennedy assassinated (68)	Environmental Protection Agency (70) Illegal corporate contributions to Nixon election campaign Watergate (72) Vietnam War ends (73) Nixon resigns (74) Bicentennial celebration (76)	Female VP candidate (84) Oliver North and Iran-Contra affair $200 billion Foreign investment in U.S. (88) $2 trillion national debt (86) Sandra O'Connor Supreme Court Justice (81)	Persian Gulf War (91) Record Federal debt of $3.6 trillion (92) Repair of savings and loan collapse Looming crisis in banks and insurance companies
Western states population boom; California had 6.9 million in 60, 16 million in 61, most populous state in 65	More in U.S. move to South and West Celebrate geographic diversity ("I love NY")	Few farms, each farmer produces for 75 people Decentralization of people from city to small towns Berlin Wall falls (89)	Shift to "globalization" era (90) Reunification of Germany (90)
Retirement villages start, first in Sun City, AZ (60) Physical fitness program started by President Kennedy (61), ¼ population exercises First heart transplant (67)	Fast food	Life expectancy 74+ Half U.S. population regularly exercising (82) More wine consumed than hard liquor (80) 500 U.S. companies directed fitness programs AIDS epidemic	Health-conscious foods/exercise "Daddy Track" considered Baby boomers turn 40

Kouzes and Posner (1993) say that credibility of leaders involves perceptions of honesty, vision, inspiration, competence, and flexibility. Credibility,
then, is not a simple concept. An individual may be socially credible (a good
party person) and very trustworthy, but incompetent at a manual job. If we
required someone who could show business partners a "confidential" good
time, we might utilize that person as a credible candidate for a social position,
but not for anything requiring manual labor (or perhaps mind labor). Most
salespeople are not only competent, they also possess high degrees of trust-
worthiness and sociability. Customers find them knowledgeable about the
product, believe them to be honest, and enjoy their company.

It is important to note that credibility is not something that resides in the
individual. As mentioned earlier in this chapter, our knowledge base is perceptual in nature. The same individual might be perceived as credible by one
person and as not credible by the next. Consider two equally qualified presidential candidates. The one who is a member of the political party to which
you belong will probably rise in your perception of credibility over the op-
posing (and member of the other party) candidate's credibility. Credibility,
then, resides in the "eyes" (mind) of the receiver.

Next, we move to the final stage in the process of client analysis. After considering an individual's perceived homophily and credibility, we become concerned about the level of attraction, more precisely, interpersonal attraction.

Interpersonal Attraction

Interpersonal attraction involves perceptions on three levels: physical, social,
and task (McCroskey & McCain, 1972). As with credibility and homophily,
the levels of attraction interact to produce a perception of an individual's personal attraction. Sometimes, however, one level will weigh in more heavily
than the others, depending on the expected outcome or requirements of the
situation or interaction.

As will be discussed later in this book, the law has somewhat "dismantled"
physical attraction as a means for making decisions about who will work with
us. There are numerous anti-discrimination laws that say that we cannot hire
someone else simply because of their physical appearance. Courts have struck
down rules about physical appearance in a number of cases. Years ago there
were strict rules about flight attendants in terms of age, sex, gender, marital status, and weight. They no longer exist. Even in cases such as a position for a nu-
tritionist in an eastern state, where an applicant was extremely overweight, the
courts have indicated that the applicant could not be turned down for the job
because the qualification as a physically fit person was not job relevant.

Nevertheless there are still discriminations made in the workplace because
an applicant looks "neat" or "sloppy." Taller applicants are usually hired over
shorter applicants (Hickson & Stacks, 1993). In addition, taller applicants receive higher starting salaries. As noted earlier, an individual's perceived physical attraction often makes them more or less homophilous or credible.

Social attraction is concerned with the extent to which one would like to be "friends" with another. In a job situation, the interviewer often considers this criterion because the interviewer is concerned with the extent to which the applicant will "get along with" the other employees. Some interviewers use the rationale that an applicant is "overqualified" to mean that they do not believe the applicant will get along with other employees because they will not have demographic homophily—they will not be socially attracted to one another.

Task attraction should be the most important element in the organizational context. Task attraction refers to "the degree to which one person perceives it to be desirable to establish a work relationship with another person" (McCroskey, 1992, p. 109). Do I feel that this person will do his/her part of the work? Is this person capable of doing this job with these people? However, high task attraction may also produce low social attraction. That is, we may wish to work with this person on the job, but not socialize with them outside of the task situation.

Messages Form Relationships

As we mentioned in Chapter 1, messages form conversations (Pearce, 1976; Davis, 1973). From what we know, using the credibility concerns for competence and sociability and/or the attraction elements of task and social attraction, we can conclude that there are at least two ways of evaluating a message's source. In the organization, the communication process involves task messages and social messages. An example of a task message may be something like, "Could you help me fix this copier?" A social message may be: "Why don't we work on this project as a team and perhaps we can come up with better ideas?" The fact is, however, that social messages are involved with tasks as well because they tell us how well the people get along with one another. For example, let's suppose that the reply to the second message is: "Thanks, but I think I'll just work on it by myself." While the results of the project may be the same, a new issue has arisen regarding the relationship between the interactants. Their conversations have become episodes; those episodes have formed their relationships. In the organization, the relationships determine the final outcomes.

You may ask why would anyone *not* want to work with another worker. As we will note in subsequent chapters, some people simply do not like to work as partners or in groups. Or it may be that they worked together previously, and while one did most of the work, the other got credit for it. But it is important to remember that every message exchange, every conversation, affects the relationship. From this perspective, we see that communication (as message exchange) is a process, it is always continuing. One message drifts into another, and while you may not have even put a conversation in your memory bank, it may have been critical to another person. One conversation may become the topic of another conversation, and so it goes. Communication is the most critical element in the ongoing of an organization; the wrong message can destroy an organization; the right one can make it an unprecedented success.

SUMMARY

In an organization, individuals must understand three key analytical factors: content research, client analysis, and dialogue. Content research involves economic, political, social, religious, aesthetic, and intellectual dimensions. Concerning client analysis and dialogue and the communication process, the individual must understand the differences among persuasion, communication, and catharsis. In analyzing others, we must take into consideration homophily (demographic, background, and attitudinal). If we perceive others as similar to us, we then consider their character, sociability, and competence as we determine how credible they are in any given situation. Finally, we must also take into account their interpersonal attraction (physical, social, and task).

We use our knowledge of the content of the message as well as our knowledge of others (homophily, credibility, attraction) to try to ensure proper communication. However, there may be problems with knowledge in either case. We must also be aware of transmittal problems with media. Thus, communication is a complex process. At its simplest level, we may have trouble when we tell a colleague that we will have lunch together "Tuesday Week" at noon. Is "Tuesday Week" this coming, next subsequent Tuesday, or the Tuesday of next week? If we are in two different time zones, noon where? Obviously communication becomes even more difficult if we are trying to transmit a change in the benefits policy of General Motors. As we progress through this text, we will find that all communicators must be extremely cognizant of each element in the process. In the next chapter, we will explore how individuals gain their knowledge both formally and informally. Then, in Chapter 4, we will see all of these principles at work in the first stage of being an organizational player—the job-seeking process—and begin our journey through the complex communication processes associated with the organization.

QUESTIONS FOR THOUGHT

1. How can you keep focused on the conversation at hand when you have all of these internal and external stimuli to encounter?
2. How can the concept of evaluating the message source at the same time you are listening to the message be both a help and a hindrance to effective communication?
3. In terms of impression formation, how would you describe your ideal boss?
4. How can you use the types of knowledge described in the chapter to aid in creating a mission statement for the company? How can they be helpful in writing a five-year plan of goals for the organization?
5. Do you believe that most messages are either persuasive, informational, or cathartic, or do you believe that they "blend" together? If you think they blend together, how do you decide the primary purpose of someone else's message?

CASE 2.2 The Boss on the Elevator

It's Monday morning. As you enter the elevator at your workplace, you discover that you—and you alone—are there with the President of the company. Although you have met only twice before, she remembers your name. As you are on your way up forty floors (and the elevator won't stop until then because she used her special key), she asks: "How are things going in your unit?" Later she asks, "How are you getting along with your supervisor?" How do you respond to these questions?

REFERENCES

Berger, C. R., & Calabrese, R. J. (1975). Some explorations in initial interaction and beyond: Toward a developmental theory of interpersonal communication. *Human Communication Research, 1,* 99–112.

Davis, M. S. (1973). *Intimate relations.* New York: Free Press.

Hickson, M. III, & Stacks, D. W. (1993). *NVC: Nonverbal Communication Studies and Applications,* 3rd ed. Dubuque: Brown & Benchmark.

Kouzes, J. M., & Posner, B. Z. (1993). *Credibility: How leaders gain and lose it, why people demand it.* San Francisco: Jossey-Bass.

McCroskey, J. C. (1992). *An introduction to communication in the classroom.* Edina, MN: Burgess.

McCroskey, J. C., & McCain, T. A. (1974). The measurement of interpersonal attraction. *Speech Monographs, 41,* 261–266.

McCroskey, J. C., Richmond, V. P., & Daly, J. A. (1975). The measurement of perceived homophily in interpersonal communication. *Human Communication Research, 1,* 323–332.

Morgan, G. (1997). *Images of Organization,* 2nd ed. Thousand Oaks, CA: Sage Publications.

Pearce, W. B. (1976). The coordinated management of meaning: A rules-based theory of interpersonal communication. In G. R. Miller (Ed.), *Explorations in interpersonal communication* (pp. 17–35). Beverly Hills, CA: Sage.

Powell, J. L., Hill, S. R., Jr., & Hickson, M. III. (1980). Path analysis of attitudinal, dispositional, and situational predictions of impression formation. *Psychological Reports, 47,* 327–333.

3

RESEARCHING IN THE NEW ORGANIZATION

Why Conduct Research?

Information Collection: Initiating Research
  Documentary evidence (reviewing the literature)
  Research questions
  Selecting a method

Formal Methods of Research: Collecting Information
  Quantitative methods
      Experimental method: Laboratory and field experiments
      Survey method
      Focus group methodology
      Content analysis
  Qualitative methods
      Participant-observation
      Historical method

Analyzing and Utilizing the Data

Informal Observation and Organizational Performance

Objectives

By the end of this chapter you should be able to

1. Discuss the role of research in organizational communication.
2. Explain how to initiate any type of research.

3. Choose the appropriate quantitative or qualitative method for the research questions you are interested in.
4. Explain the differences among experiments, surveys, focus groups, content analyses, participant-observation, and historical methods.
5. Discuss the advantages and limitations of formal and informal observation in the New Organization.

Having discussed the three elements of organizational communication, perhaps we can clarify the role of each of them. *Client analysis* is about the who, as well as the why of organizational communication. We learn who we are talking with, and we assess that person's communication and credibility to determine (a) why we should formulate a message a particular way for that individual and (b) why that person is communicating with us using the particular messages at the time. *Communication dialogue* is generally about how we communicate: how do we encode, how do we select a channel, how do we provide feedback. *Content research* constitutes the what of organizational communication. Finally, the context (when and where) provides an outline for organizational communication. This chapter focuses specifically on research, the substantive content of organizational communication, or what traditional theorists have called "invention."

One feature of the New Organization that clearly distinguishes it from the old organization is in the area of *information*. Clearly, the New Organization's worker accesses, creates, and analyzes more information than ever before and does this at a faster pace than ever before. Even compared to workers of the 1980s, for instance, today's worker deals with more information and makes decisions based on that information much faster. The question for today's worker is what to do with that accumulation of knowledge. How does he or she decide what is important and what is not? And, given today's worker's ability to store and access large amounts of information in portable (i.e., personal computer) systems, how does this affect the workplace?

This chapter focuses on how we gather the information needed to survive in the New Organization. It is a cross between understanding how information is gathered—through a process called "research"—and what limitations are placed on its use by the "type" of research employed. *Knowledge* (content research) allows us to better understand where we are, where we are going, and how to get there. Understanding our "clients" (both inside and outside the organization) is also part of the process of gaining knowledge.

The knowledge you gather ultimately will be used in establishing strategies for communication dialogue. These strategies may be externally oriented, such as those found in marketing and management plans. The strategies may be internally oriented, as in deciding which coalition in the organization you should join, who should serve as your mentor (or, later, who you should mentor), and even may be found in the initial employment interview.

The knowledge is used in adapting to new situations. How we adapt is directly influenced by our knowledge. Who would have thought, for instance, that today's new executive would find a simple piece of equipment essential to conducting business? And, that same piece of equipment thirty years ago was associated with his secretary, not the executive herself. That essential component? *The computer.* It has changed how we do business in the New Organization in the areas of storing, accessing, and processing knowledge.

We are not focusing on the computer, *per se,* but much of today's research is based in large part on an understanding that today's "personal" computers allow individuals within the New Organization access to and analysis of information that the organizational worker of the 1950s, 1960s, 1970s, and even into the mid-1980s, would have found difficult if not impossible at a moment's notice. The analysis in this chapter is more traditional in one aspect: It examines how we gather information and create knowledge. Information is not necessarily knowledge; information has no meaning until we analyze it based on some rationale, or *theory,* about how the information relates to events. We are moving beyond the traditional, however, to look at informal knowledge gathering and its effect in the New Organization.

WHY CONDUCT RESEARCH?

No organization can survive without a clear understanding of what it does, can do, and has done. This understanding comes from the gathering of "data." Organizations collect vast amounts of data. They gather data about themselves in a variety of areas: financial, productivity, image, and so forth. Traditionally, data were gathered in an empirical environment—that is, the organization counted items and related their counts to other things both within and outside the organization. Many executives were taught in colleges or schools of business that the bottom line is measured empirically and evaluated statistically. The reliability and validity of data gathered are of immense importance to the MBA-trained executive; it establishes her effectiveness in the organization.

Organizations use research in a variety of ways, to understand, to predict, and to control. First, research helps to *understand* the world. As noted in the first two chapters, we need content research to understand the organization and how it has adapted to new ideas, markets, and environments. Organizations use that understanding to predict how it should operate. In the Bee example (Chapter 1), the seamstresses' understanding of the market's needs and the requirements of successful competition allowed them to *predict* the best way to expand. In daily life we use our understanding of others to predict their behaviors. If, for instance, someone is usually late, we might predict that he would be late for some specific occasion and then inform him that the meeting is earlier than really set. When used in this way, research serves to *control* others.

Although it may sound ominous, all organizations seek to control others. On the one hand, organizations seek to control the marketplace (to make a profit), they seek to control worker productivity (to make a profit), they seek to control product quality (to make a profit), and they seek to control worker communication (to ensure a profit). On the other hand, individuals seek to control their own lives. They seek to control what others think of them, what information others have about them; they seek some control over their salaries, their way of life, and their social standing. Individuals seek control on the job. Control, however, comes at a price: *gathering information,* continually undertaking both formal and informal research.

INFORMATION COLLECTION: INITIATING RESEARCH

We are in the process of collecting information most of our waking hours. Reading and listening provide much of what we know (or think we know). We may watch the early morning news on television before we leave the house, then listen to the radio on the way to work, read the newspaper, check our electronic mail, listen to our voice mail, talk with colleagues—and we may do all of this before we even really begin our work day. We then gather more information through discussions, meetings, reading, and using the computer.

Research, however, is more than simple information collection. We may collect information about what is on television this weekend or what's on at the movies tonight. We may collect information on where to find the least expensive business suit. Research, however, is much more systematic. Research involves the process of (1) conducting a review of the literature, (2) asking specific research questions, (3) selecting a method of data collection, (4) analyzing the data, and (5) utilizing the information.

Documentary Evidence (Reviewing the Literature)

At one time, gathering information about an individual or organization was simple: You went to the library and looked up what had been written about that person or corporation. That was called a *review of the literature.* Today, however, libraries are quickly adapting to a different way of storing and accessing information. If there is one thing that differentiates today's worker and her parents and her parents' parents it is access to information. Put simply, today's workers have more access to information, can access that information faster, and have to make decisions on more information than ever before.

All this should make the worker's job easier, but it has not. A question that often arises when conducting a document search is when to stop. Given the vast resources available today, can we ever have closure? At some point we must, but deciding on when is difficult. And, given the Internet, WorldWide

Web (WWW) and Web sites, and on-line databases, the decision to stop is even more difficult (see Figure 3.1).

Most organizations have their own *libraries*—document repositories—or are connected to libraries through networks. Just ten years ago it was rare that an organizational worker would have reason to dial up a library and do a quick search of its contents. Why? First, access was limited. Second, methods of searching were primitive. Third, searching was expensive and usually done by others. And, fourth, known databases were often incomplete and updated slowly.

All of this has changed. From home or the office we can access almost any library in the country through local access sites or through the Internet. All we need to know is the library's site address on the web or the telephone number and computer modem settings to gain access. With such services as LEXIS/NEXIS we can search for information across newspapers, magazines, academic journals, and other industrial databases. FIRST SEARCH has replaced the *Readers Guide to Periodical Literature.* And we can access journals and magazines on-line, peruse their contents, and print them at home—pictures and figures as well as text. Newspapers and magazines are now "printed" on line before they are physically available through the mail or newspaper carrier.

If you wanted the text of the president's speech regarding economic indicators, it is available free of charge on-line sometimes before it is delivered. If you want to look at the annual reports of several corporations, they, too, are available on line. If you want to know what a particular company's plans for the future are, you can access their WWW site and read or download them to your personal computer. Suppose you have been tasked to establish the

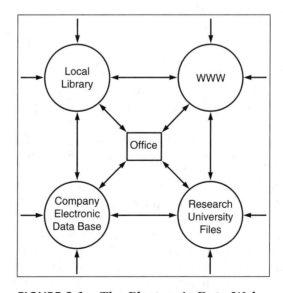

FIGURE 3.1   The Electronic Data Web

demographic analysis for a new marketing plan. A few years ago you would trudge down to the local library and look at the U.S. Census for the areas of interest. Now you can get that information on-line, or you can have your own *complete* set of U.S. Census data on-line.

The electronic library has made accessing documents very simple. Researching via the electronic library requires some sophisticated equipment (or, at least it was sophisticated five years ago).

- A computer (with lots of memory and storage)
- A modem (the faster the better)
- A printer (laser for best quality)
- The software necessary to connect to a host computer
- The knowledge to search

In other words, you can undertake research from home or from the office. And, through networking, you can share your information with others. Most organizations now subscribe to the Internet and have their own WorldWide Web (WWW) sites. Most organizations now have their own electronic libraries, as well as physical storage areas for hardcopy (printed) documents. Most have people trained to assist workers' access and store documents. However, analyzing the information is still an individual responsibility, which comes with training and experience.

We should note that research is a continuous process and certainly the collection and retention of documentary evidence is ongoing. Certain types of documentary evidence should be on the regular agenda. These include watching such television channels as CNBC and reading magazines and newspapers such as *Business Week, Forbes,* and the *Wall Street Journal,* as well as your local newspaper's business section. You should also be aware of publications, newsletters, and the like that pertain to your particular line of business. In the newspaper business, for example, one should read *The Quill* and the *Columbia Journalism Review.* In the electronic media, one should read *Broadcasting.*

Once we have read an article or book, we need to analyze and appraise its credibility. Stacks and Hocking (1992) have suggested that any document appraisal requires three types of analysis. First, the *content* is explored. How does the document relate to the question(s) you are asking? Is it central? Does it add anything new? Second, is the document from a *reputable source?* Third, does the document meet certain *critical standards?* That is, are the main points or issues clearly identified? Are the underlying assumptions and arguments clearly stated and acceptable? Is the evidence presented adequately and clearly to support its conclusions? Is there any bias, and if so, is it explained? And, how well is the document written? (McCormick, 1985)

Each document will differ according to content, source, and critical standards. However, over a period of time you can distinguish between what is appropriate and what is not. Much will come from beginning to read all you can as early as you can. After that, you can begin to critically evaluate sources that must be accessed daily and those that need only to be checked irregularly.

Documentary evidence or reviewing the literature is always the first step in research. It may save you a great deal of time if someone has already researched your topic. This evidence may be the ending point of your research if you are simply trying to verify some fact. However, the review of the documentary evidence (which certainly includes documents inside the organization) is usually the beginning point. When you are writing a five-year plan, there is no doubt that you want to look at the last five-year plan. Even when completing your annual evaluation, you want to look at last year's annual evaluation to see whether you measured up with what you had hoped. You may want to look at marketing reports over the past five years to help determine your marketing strategy for next year. The documentary evidence will help lead you to the best research questions.

Research Questions

Once you have collected enough documentary evidence, you may begin the task of developing appropriate *research questions*. Sometimes the questions are about *definitions*—writing a mission statement, for example, is really writing a statement about who the company is. Often research questions are about *values*—is it really to our advantage to terminate three workers, all of whom are competent, simply because we are not making the profits we did last year? The research question may be about *facts*—what is our least profitable subsidiary? How many other fast foods are already located in that community? Finally, research questions are about *policy*—should the company open a plant in a country run by a dictator? Should we stop selling tobacco products?

Once the general type of research question has been decided, it is important to determine the specific question. Here it is important to know why you are asking the question in the first place. What is our purpose in establishing a mission statement? Are we concerned about consistency in values? Why is this fact important to our company? How have other policy decisions been made? The specific research question will determine our focus for the remainder of the investigation. It is critical that we ensure we are asking the right question(s).

Selecting a Method

Despite the fact that the *method* may not be the most important aspect of undertaking research, method is the area that is written about the most, probably because there are so many options available. Generally, however, we can say that most research is either quantitative or qualitative. *Quantitative data* are gathered in strict accordance with methodological rules and analyzed according to how they fit some expected distribution and the error associated with both data collection and analysis. *Descriptive analysis* occurs when we simply report what we find. *Inferential analysis* is conducted when we try to generalize the data to the larger group from which we "sampled" some data. It is not our purpose to introduce statistics, but merely to note that quantitative reports tend to be number heavy and include such statistics as counts, percentages, proportions, means, medians, modes, data ranges, variance, and standard deviations.

Rather than simply counting a number of things, qualitative research explores in great detail. The qualitative empiricist is interested more in understanding an individual event, case, or communication and less in generalizing to a larger population. Most organizational books have a number of "case studies" which are qualitative in nature. They explore how one organization did this or that and hope that what they found can be applied in other areas. The problem associated with such research is that, like people, organizations are different. However, there are certain findings that transcend the individual and can be applied to others. The qualitative approach to research offers a rich interpretive analysis to the question under consideration.

Quantitative research tends to establish and evaluate facts—things that can be determined to be true or false; either they are there or they are not (Stacks & Hocking, 1992). This research often is used to establish definitively whether a concept or an idea exists. Such concepts might include credibility (and its components), homophily, interpersonal attraction, message flow, and leadership style. As such, quantitative methods may provide answers to questions of definition. (Does it exist? In what manner? Under what conditions?)

Qualitative research methods also follow rules and procedures; however, the rules are more flexible. Qualitative research can explore the questions of definition, although most qualitative research does not do so. Nor does it usually seek answers to questions of fact. Qualitative research usually explores answers to questions of value (e.g., How good was it? What value does it have? What are the ethical considerations to a product's introduction?) or policy (e.g., What *should* be done?) (Denzin & Lincoln, 1994).

In the scientific and academic communities the two methods—quantitative and qualitative—have traditionally explored different questions and issues. Organizational communication research involves *both* perspectives. Obviously, if data are gathered from both quantitative and qualitative perspectives, what we know about the problem or issue is much more than we could gain from only one perspective. Such blending of perspectives has been called *triangulation* (Webb, Campbell, Schwartz, & Sechrest, 1970). The term is based on the idea that we can find a point more easily if we approach it from several different directions. To best employ knowledge, then, we need to triangulate the findings—the knowledge—of as many different approaches as possible (see Figure 3.2).

The *communication audit* is an example of organizational research that has employed both quantitative and qualitative methods to gather information (Goldhaber, 1993, pp. 348–390). In a communication audit, the quantitative method surveys employees from all levels of the organization about their beliefs and opinions of how the organization operates; message flow analysis is conducted which tracks how messages go from level-to-level and worker-to-worker. Statistical tools are used to test for differences in perception across a variety of variables. Qualitative methods are employed in the form of participant-observation, focus groups, and in-depth interviews conducted among select organizational members, as well as intensive journal keeping and analysis. The audit then compares and contrasts the data obtained from each method to gain a better understanding of the organization and its communication patterns and problems.

The gathering of knowledge involves *observation.* When we conduct research on a particular problem, we look for previous answers to similar problems, as well as ideas as methods to test our own ideas. For purposes of research, we organize observation into two areas: formal and informal. *Formal observation takes place when we gather knowledge through quantitative and qualitative methods.* It adheres to some form of criteria and its interpretation is typically objective, either from a deductive (concept to event) or inductive (event to concept) viewpoint.

Informal observation often employs the same methodologies as does the formal, but adheres to few guidelines and its interpretation is more subjective. For example, using formal observations we might try to determine the level of satisfaction of customers with a new dishwashing liquid. Using a quantitative approach, we would select a sample, based on certain demographic

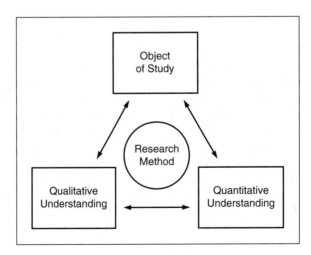

FIGURE 3.2   The Research Triangle

data; using a qualitative method we might select fewer customers, but we might interview each one more extensively and over a longer period of time. Informally, however, we might just randomly ask people in the grocery store about which liquid they use and why. It may be that the last method, although it is research, is used for quotes to use in advertising. Quantitative and qualitative (formal methods) are systematic. Informal methods are not systematic.

While most organizational decisions are based on formal observation, backed by facts, individual decisions are often based on informal observation. Survival in the organization may be a function of knowing how to collect all types of information and interpreting them into a knowledge base.

We turn now to the traditional means of gathering knowledge in the organization. The next section explores survey, focus and known group, content analysis, quantitative (experimental) methods, qualitative (participant observation), and historical methods of gathering information to establish the appropriate knowledge base.

FORMAL METHODS OF RESEARCH: COLLECTING INFORMATION

Our purpose here is not to present a research methods course. However, intelligent use of information—data—requires that you understand the advantages and limitations of how research is conducted. As Hickson and Stacks (1993) note, "our method will be consistent with what we were taught; that is our education and training will, to a degree, influence the methods we select later in our research" (p. 29). As you begin to interpret (or even conduct) research, your first questions are usually, "What are we observing?" and "How are we observing?" This, Pearce, Cronen, and Harris (1982) suggest be refined to: "What counts as data?" and "How do data count?"

What counts as data is answered by our definition of the units of analysis. If these are discrete (that is, we can see or count each individually), then they are most likely quantitative and our method will be quantitative. If they are evaluative, however, we may be better off conducting qualitative research. How do data count might be answered by looking at two factors. First, how many data "points" are we looking at? Second, what purpose do the data "points" have (e.g., what question are we answering—definition, fact, value, policy?). If we are only looking at one data "point"—the institution or the person—then qualitative methods are best. If, on the other hand, we are interested in the accumulated observations of many people, the quantitative method is best. With the latter, when we want to define or establish factual data that can be verified and projected to a larger group, then we use quantitative methods; however, when we are asking questions of value or policy, then qualitative methodology is appropriate (see Figure 3.3).

Quantitative Methods

Quantitative methods differ primarily in the amount of control we have over our results. Control is concerned with the extent to which the researcher can "filter out" some of the variables. Filtering out variables may mean ensuring that the participants in the study are in an isolated place, from which they can draw upon few ideas. Filtering out variables may include the selection of participants so that a certain number of them are drawn from certain segments of the overall group. Both types of filtering out increase one's control. At the extremes we have both the laboratory experiment and the field study. In between we have the survey or poll, the focus group, and content analysis.

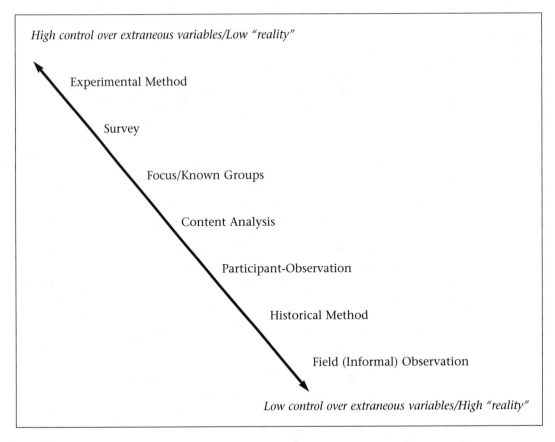

FIGURE 3.3   Levels of Research

Experimental Method: Laboratory and Field Experiments

Control means that we can safely say that one outcome was dependent on another. We establish this through the identification of a *variable*. A variable is a phenomenon that differs from one participant to another or a phenomenon that changes from time to time. Actually, there are two types of variables. The *dependent variable* is the one that is measured; it is the outcome of interest, what we are looking to find out. The *independent variable* is the one that the researcher manipulates, and one that the researcher believes will cause changes in the dependent variable.

Change reflects *causality*. When we say that success causes promotion, we are inferring that people who are successful will be promoted. However, there are a variety of other things that might cause promotion. Marriage to the boss' son might be one. The ability to invest in the organization might be another. Unless we carefully control for such extraneous effects, we really do not know if success (very precisely defined) causes promotion (again, precisely defined). Extraneous variables, then, are those that we wish to eliminate as a cause primarily because they are unrelated to what we are researching. No doubt, marrying the boss' son may cause promotion, but this is an unusual case and it is unrelated to what we are studying—success.

The *laboratory experiment* both carefully controls for causes that are not of interest and tries to establish whether a causal relationship exists between two variables. In so doing the experiment creates an artificial environment, one where all *possible* contaminants are accounted for and the probable outcome is that associated with the independent variable.

Obviously, little truly experimental research is carried out in an organization. An organization is continually changing. It would be extremely difficult to establish control conditions without disrupting day-to-day activity in the organization. However, we might use the results from laboratory studies in studying how a particular variable operates there.

Suppose, for instance, that an experimenter created two identical memos, one on white paper and the other on ivory paper. Suppose, too, that her hypothesis (prediction) was that white memos were more credible than ivory memos. In her experiment she randomly assigned workers to either the white or ivory memo condition (an experimental treatment group). She then prepared a questionnaire that asked the workers' perceptions of the importance and credibility of the memo and its author and found that white memos were more credible than ivory memos. If we informally conducted our own experiment (used white memos one week and ivory memos the next and then elicited comments on the memos and observed whether they were "posted" or "trashed"), we might find the results useful.

This hypothetical "study" is called a *field experiment*. The field experiment concedes some control but benefits from the real-world application as opposed to the artificial atmosphere of the laboratory. If the white memo is found more credible and effective, then we can infer some causal relationship. The field experiment, like its laboratory counterpart, has both dependent and independent variables and some type of condition. We are not, however, as certain of the relationship's strength in the field as in the laboratory.

Survey Method

The *survey* is used to *describe* how a large group of people feel about or react to something. While the experiment allows us to establish causality, the survey can only take a "snapshot" of whatever we are interested in at particular points in time. Because of a lack of control (we know little about the individuals providing data, the situation they are in while providing that data, or who actually is providing the data), we can only infer that one variable causes another. Many surveys, however, still refer to independent and dependent variables, only now they are used to establish differences between groups. Sex, for instance, may be used to differentiate between reaction to a "soft" versus a "hard" persuasive message in selling a product. Television viewing habits might be used to distinguish between "heavy" and "light" advertisement viewing. In each case the "conditions" of television viewing and sex are used to distinguish between responses to the dependent variable, such as advertising effectiveness.

Surveys exercise some control over the research by randomly selecting respondents from some larger population. (If you sample ALL possible respondents, then you have conducted a census.) The key is in random assignment. Random assignment means that, all things being equal, every individual who could have been surveyed has an equal opportunity to be included in the study's *sample*. The sample, if randomly selected, should mirror the responses of the larger group or *population* from which it was drawn (see Figure 3.4).

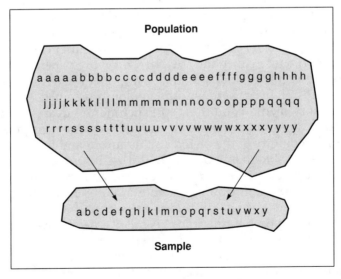

FIGURE 3.4   Populations and Samples

Thus, we can often infer from the sample to the larger population responses to questions and differences between "conditions." An effective survey, however, uses a limited population and a limited sample. For example, if we want to know how people feel about adding "call return" to their telephones, we need only use those people in the population who own telephones. Obviously you cannot add call return if you do not have a telephone. The same may be true for products that are limited to one sex. Because the opposite sex is not making buying decisions, that sex can be eliminated from the population. Mercedes does not need to survey people with very low incomes because those people cannot purchase a Mercedes anyway.

Further, based on statistical tables, we know how much *error* is present in both the sampling procedure and in respondent's truthfulness to questions. That is, what are the chances that your research is wrong? In general, if you want to be 95 percent certain that the sample represents the population, you would need 384 randomly selected participants if the population under study is infinite (or unknown) (see Table 3.1 for the sample sizes necessary for differing error tolerances).

In addition, you would know that the most a response would be in error would be 5 percent either way. That is, if we asked respondents whether they were happy with their jobs, and 58 percent said, "yes," and 42 percent said, "no," we could safely say that more people (53% to 63%) were satisfied with their jobs than not (37% to 47%). This is established by adding or subtracting

TABLE 3.1   Sampling Size and Error Rates

SURVEY RESEARCH
SAMPLE SIZE AND TOLERATED ERROR

Simple random sample size at 95 and 99 percent confidence interval with tolerated error

Error	95%	99%
1%	9,604	16,587
2%	2,401	4,147
3%	1,067	1,843
4%	600	1,037
5%	384	663
6%	267	461
7%	196	339

Random Sample Size at 5% Tolerated Error

Population Size	Sample Size
Infinity	384
500,000	384
100,000	383
50,000	381
10,000	370
5,000	357
3,000	341
2,000	322
1,000	278

Source: Backstrom, C. H., & Hursch, G. (1981). *Survey Research,* 2nd ed. New York: Macmillan.

Source: Meyer, P. (1973). *Precision Journalism.* Bloomington, IN: Indiana University Press.

5 percent in each case. To be no more than 1 percent off in responses, you would have to sample almost ten thousand people (Stacks & Hocking, 1992, p. 182). Our control comes from knowing how much error in both sampling and response we can expect.

We can survey people in at least three ways. We can conduct *telephone surveys*. These are cost effective and allow us to contact a large number of people while controlling for whom we question. However, not all people have telephones or we may not have access to their telephone numbers, so we might expect some error. A second way to survey people is to employ a *mail questionnaire*. Mail questionnaires are the most cost effective, but we are not sure who actually completed a questionnaire. Third, we can conduct an *in-person interview*. In the interview, we randomly select people and go to their homes or places of employment and conduct the survey person-to-person. This is the most difficult and expensive survey method, but it provides the most extensive data.

When we conduct telephone or in-person surveys, we typically calculate control through sampling error as noted earlier. However, when conducting a mail survey, we look at the percent of responses returned. In general, a 60 percent response rate is considered quite good, although in some areas (such as international surveys) even a 10 percent return rate is acceptable. Knowing your required response rate helps establish how many surveys should be mailed out. If your population is *all* IBM management, then you might randomly select one thousand from the IBM management directory and hope to get back between four hundred and six hundred useful (completed) responses. If you get back fewer than four hundred, then you must send out a second mailing, a third, and so forth until you get a "satisfactory" response.

Surveys are designed around a *questionnaire*. A survey is different from a *poll* in one significant way. A poll is a quick set of questions. Typically, a poll asks yes and no questions, or questions that can be answered in a word or very quickly: Are you at your desk now? Do you work hard? Are you getting paid for the level of work you produce? What is your sex? and so forth. It is used to take a quick and rather superficial snapshot of a particular group of people. A survey's questionnaire is much more complicated and asks in-depth questions regarding attitudes, beliefs, values, and behaviors. While a poll might take one minute, most surveys last between five and forty-five minutes—a few taking over an hour to complete.

Focus Group Methodology

While the survey or poll offers control via random selection, it also establishes control through the use of the questionnaire. Every respondent answers the same question. A *focus group* reduces the control placed on a study through the questionnaire. Focus groups can (and should) be randomly selected, but they differ from the survey in that participants are allowed—expected—to elaborate on their responses. Further, they are expected to pose their own questions. A focus group, then, provides more *qualitative* responses to questions, but still affords the researcher some control through group selection, environment, and the ability to record responses.

Focus groups are used to get in-depth analysis and to explore trends or new ideas. They are less expensive than surveys or polls and provide much "richer" data. Often, a focus group will be used to establish what questions should be asked on a larger survey.

The focus group is typically composed of a "facilitator," participants, and often observers. The *facilitator,* the person who asks questions, is usually a professional who has conducted a large number of focus groups. He or she is given a list of questions that are to be answered but is also given the latitude to ask more questions when the group seems to be moving in a particular manner.

Focus group results are often dependent on the facilitator's abilities. Participants are people who have volunteered to participate in the group. Typical focus groups run from five to fifteen participants. Participants respond to the facilitator and each other in discussing the questions. We attempt to randomly select participants if we hope to have some generalizability to a larger population, but most of the time those who participate are those who volunteer, thus lowering the generalizability of findings. Observers are people who listen or watch the focus groups as they occur. They help in evaluating the information received, reflecting on the statements made and the interaction between participants.

Focus group methodology requires that more than one focus group is conducted. Comparison of results from multiple groups helps to establish the reliability and validity of results. With only one group, we would never know if the participants were representative of the population or some variant.

Once the data are collected (through recordings and participant questionnaires), they must be coded and analyzed. The method used most often to analyze the data is content analysis, which we will treat as a special method shortly.

A special type of focus group used in organizational analysis is the *known group* (Gwin, 1984). While the focus group seeks to randomly select from the larger population, the known group method actively seeks participants from throughout the organization, from boardroom to the bathroom, and includes both white- and blue-collar employees. The known group is used within the organization as a sort of "mini-audit." It allows a facilitator to ask questions across the various levels of the organization and get a valid perspective of the organization's communication patterns. Because you have all levels of the organization, most known groups collect their data differently than focus groups.

The focus group communicates verbally and nonverbally through what they say and how they say it. Because in the known group you might have a vice president and a janitor and the janitor might defer to the vice president, all communication begins in writing. All responses are written down and evaluated by the facilitator (or helper) and then listed in the facilitator's handwriting on paper. These responses then serve as the catalyst for communication. Research (Gwin, 1984) suggests that once discussion begins, status differences quickly break down and communication increases. In today's world, too, the responses can be recorded on networked computers, which allow for anonymity—so that no one knows who had the "best response."

Content Analysis

Not all of the methods discussed to date refer specifically to communication or communicative messages. Content analysis provides a way to quantify typically qualitative messages; that is, it takes the message and identifies categories into which each message falls. Berelson (1952) has suggested that we can take any communication and break it into five units of analysis: word, theme, character, time/space, and item. The unit of analysis is operationally defined for the purpose of the study. An *operational definition* is one based on the needs of the moment so that everyone concerned understands the concept; it may or may not be consistent with a dictionary definition. For instance, we might conduct a content analysis of a focus group or some open-ended survey questionnaire (one that allows the respondent to respond as he or she wants and not to some forced choice, such as "yes" or "no"). Perhaps we are interested in how many times participants used "us" versus another term for the organization. The unit of analysis here is the word. "Us" may indicate solidarity and other words a lack of solidarity. We would simply count the number of times "us" was used and by whom. If we found that "us" was used rarely, we might conclude that there was a lack of solidarity in the organization—especially if the finding was replicated across groups.

Content analysis allows the researcher some control through sampling from a large population of content, as well as through following standardized procedures. For instance, when *coding* the data collected, researchers report the degree of agreement two or more coders have in coding content into categories of the units of analysis. When coder reliability is high (90 percent or higher), we have some demonstrated control over the placement of content into predefined categories.

CASE 3.1   Packaging

Your company has decided to find out whether you would sell more or less of the shampoo that you produce if you changed the color of the package from blue to red. How would you use a quantitative method to do this? How would you use a qualitative method? Would you use triangulation? Why or why not?

Content analysis can be conducted from audio and videotape, as well as from written responses to questions or even free-response journal entries. The method provides a way to objectively collect qualitative data, often in the form of communication messages. As such, content analysis bridges quantitative and qualitative methods.

Qualitative Methods

Let us, then, consider that there are three types of quantitative research: laboratory experiments, field experiments, and surveys. The focus group, the known group, and content analysis provide a bridge between quantitative and qualitative research. Formal, qualitative research includes participant-observation and historical method. There is a saying that "data have no meaning." That is, quantitative, empirical research can tell us how many, but they really *cannot* tell us how well we communicated or much about an individual communicator. Qualitative methods allow us to observe and interpret the actual communication messages of an entity, whether that entity is an organization or an individual. We will quickly look at three qualitative methods.

Participant-Observation

Participant-observation is a formal method of observing in the actual environment the communication of others (Hickson, 1992). Participant-observation, however, is not simply going out and observing. It begins with a careful analysis of what communication behaviors *should* be observed in the particular environment. From this analysis, the researcher creates a theoretical model of that behavior. The researcher then goes out and assimilates into the environment—as part of a work crew perhaps—and systematically observes and records behavior. The records are then evaluated and the empirical model (that which comes from the observation) is compared and contrasted with the theoretical model.

Participant-observation is important in establishing both communication roles and rules. Participant-observation provides us with an understanding of how communication occurs within a group by being a part of that group, thus being able to better explain the behaviors observed. Participant-observation provides a valid account of what was observed by the observer, while allowing for a subjective interpretation as to why others were communicating as they did. The major disadvantage of this type of research is that it is not *generalizable*. Reports from two different locations will likely be different. Reports from the same location will also probably be different.

Throughout the rest of this book you will read formal research about organizational communication. Some of this will become part of your content research about organizational communication. Some of it will become part of your content research about the job(s) you now hold. Some of it will allow you to better understand what you have done (correctly and incorrectly) and what is expected of you. All of it—this book, your own formal and informal research—establishes your particular knowledge base.

Formal research methods are most appropriate when engaging in client analysis. Understanding who you are working with or trying to get to do something requires that you also engage in informal research, observing how people communicate and with what effect and then contrasting that to the formal models taught both on the job and through formal education. When we have done our client analysis, our communication dialogue is more effective. And, finally, if we have an adequate knowledge base, understand with whom we are communicating, and communicate in a way that is appropriate to our goals (our predicted outcome and potential control of the interaction), we should be able to adapt to any situation we face within the organization.

Historical Method

The *historical method* explores a person, event, or organization in some detail. It is closely tied to documentary evidence and provides a basis from which we can better understand the events and conditions that surrounded a person, event, or organization over a period of time. Historical method relies upon as many *primary sources* (sources that are first-hand reports of an event) as possible. *Secondary sources* (reports of reports) must be verified and any other (tertiary) sources should be avoided. However, each source can help the researcher in finding additional materials. An example of this type of research might be on the history of the company.

ANALYZING AND UTILIZING THE DATA

Once the data have been collected using quantitative methods or qualitative methods or both, you must analyze the data. *Analyzing the data refers to the concept of making the information meaningful for the purposes you set in the beginning of the project.* It is here that the terms, validity and reliability, which we mentioned earlier, become quite important. *Reliability* refers to whether you can count on your results over a period of time or with a different group of participants. In quantitative analysis, statistics are used to measure this. In qualitative research, a number of cases might be used. A number of observers might be used. A number of time frames might be used.

Validity is a concept through which we determine that we have measured or researched what we intended to research. We may find, for example, that a worker's job satisfaction is the same as the worker's interpersonal task attraction for the supervisor. In such a case, we may find that we were not measuring two concepts at all but the same one. Validity is often determined by using our measures or observations against others, which we have defined as similar, and which were used by someone else somewhere else. For example, if we developed a test for worker creativity, we would expect that the results would be similar to those from other tests of creativity.

Having analyzed the data, it is necessary to determine how to use the data. How can the data be used to improve the bottom line? How can the data be used to precipitate innovation? How can the data be used to increase productivity? How can the data be used to increase worker job satisfaction? Research of a formal nature, then, is no small task. We should remember, though, that we also use information drawn from a variety of informal sources and less stringent methods.

INFORMAL OBSERVATION AND ORGANIZATIONAL PERFORMANCE

Knowledge of formal research methods provides you with the basics from which to informally observe. As part of an organization you are constantly in a participant-observation mode. As documents cross your desk, you are creating an informal knowledge base from which to draw on later. You may interview or informally survey others as you go about your day-to-day activities. You may quietly conduct a field experiment, manipulating a variable and observing its outcome, perhaps from something you read in a company or related document or magazine article.

Informal observation can come about through daily activity on the job and socializing with others. It may be the only form of verification you have about how others communicate or behave in a given situation. Being aware of informal observation sometimes is all that is needed to survive and prosper in the organization. Because we all engage in observation, we can use this knowledge to advance within the organization or to prepare to leave for a better position before the conditions require it. A respected source has often said "it is always better to leave a position on your own, than when your peers ask you to."

SUMMARY

This chapter has introduced the major means by which we gather and understand the information around us. We noted that much of what we know comes from several sources; some of it is held socially, some of it is intuitive, some comes from respected others, and some comes from formal methods of data gathering.

CASE 3.2   **Worker Job Satisfaction**

You are concerned that some of your workers are becoming dissatisfied working for your company. How would you use informal methods to discover whether this is the case? Do you expect that the dissatisfaction would be related to their job level? Their education level? The years of seniority in the company? Their race? Their sex? Why or why not?

The chapter then explored the formal means of gathering data and some strengths and limitations of each method. The differences between quantitative and qualitative methods were briefly explored; both formal and informal observations were examined for their use in the organization. This chapter should serve as the base upon which the following chapters are built. In many instances, experimental research will be introduced; you are now in a position to begin to understand the advantages and limitations associated with each method and to evaluate their effect on organizational communication as it relates to you.

QUESTIONS FOR THOUGHT

1. Using the questions below, determine whether they are facts (true or false) or whether it cannot be determined if they are facts or not (?). How did you find the answer?

   a. The national debt of the United States tripled between 1981 and 1988.
      True _____ False _____? _____
   b. In 1955, the United States was the most literate country in the world.
      True _____ False _____? _____
   c. Kuwait produced more barrels of oil than Iran in 1996.
      True _____ False _____? _____
   d. Ronald Reagan caused the national debt to increase between 1981 and 1988. True _____ False _____? _____
   e. The United States was the most technologically-advanced country in the world in 1965. True _____ False _____? _____

2. If you wanted to determine the readership of various articles in your employee newsletter, how would you use a quantitative method to do that?
3. If you were writing a history of your organization, explain how you would discover primary sources and secondary sources.
4. If you were going to study what share of the market you have, how would you begin your study?
5. If you own a mail-order catalog company, how can you determine customer satisfaction?

REFERENCES

Berelson, B. (1952). *Content analysis in communication research.* Glencoe, IL: Free Press.

Denzin, N. K., & Lincoln, Y. S. (Eds.) (1994). *Handbook of qualitative research.* Thousand Oaks, CA: Sage.

Goldhaber, G. M. (1993). *Organizational communication,* 6th ed. Dubuque, IA: Brown and Benchmark.

Gwin, S. (1984, April). *The known group method.* Paper presented at the annual meeting of the Southern States Communication Association, Houston, TX.

Hickson, M. III (1992). Qualitative/descriptive (participant-observation) methodology. In D. W. Stacks & J. E. Hocking, *Essentials of communication research* (pp. 147–172). New York: HarperCollins.

McCormick, M. (1985). *The New York Times guide to reference materials,* rev. ed. New York: Times Books.

Pearce, W. B., Cronen, W. V., & Harris, L. M. (1982). Methodological considerations in building human communication theory. In F. E. X. Dance (Ed.), *Human communication theory: Comparative essays* (pp. 1–41). New York: Harper and Row.

Stacks, D. W., & Hocking, J. E. (1992). *Essentials of communication research.* New York: HarperCollins.

Webb, E. J., Campbell, D. T., Schwartz, R. D., & Sechrest, L. (1970). *Unobtrusive measures: Nonreactive research in the social sciences.* Chicago: Rand McNally.

4

PREPARING FOR ORGANIZATIONAL COMMUNICATION

The Career Choice/Job Search
   Analyzing skills

Career Planning
   Content research: The corporation
   Establishing the initial contact
      The cold call method

Résumés and Cover Letters
   The cover letter
   The professional résumé
      Career objectives

The Job Interview

Objectives

By the end of this chapter you should be able to

1. Analyze your skills for organizational communication.
2. Explain how to go about researching an organization before an interview.
3. Explain how to initiate a contact with an organization.
4. Write a cover letter appropriate for any of several types of interviews.
5. Explain the differences between résumé formats and their best uses.

A major concern for college students is obtaining a job after graduation. Most desire a position with an excellent company, one where they will work throughout a career of thirty or more years. As indicated in Chapter 1, such employment rarely exists as we approach the twenty-first century. This chapter may seem "prescriptive," but there are strategies and plans that lead to a successful interview and job. There are certain "rules," written nowhere, but understood by most employers, that many first-time interviewees neither understand nor follow. In the following pages, we present a common-sense approach to successful career preparation.

Consider, for instance, the following four seniors who have signed up to interview for a manager-trainee position in a major corporation. Each comes from the same college; each has a similar academic background. Each came from a similar socioeconomic background. They will be interviewing within minutes of each other with the same interviewer. All were told to arrive at 9:45 A.M. for the interview at corporate headquarters. Unknown to them, two will be selected for a second, hiring interview.

- John, twenty-one, white, male. Communication major, management minor. Arrived and logged in at 9:40 A.M. Dressed in dark blue suit, hair freshly cut. Has a two-page résumé, printed on white bond paper, that updates the one he originally sent with his cover letter answering the job's advertisement in his college's newsletter sent to undergraduates and alumni. Spent about four hours in the library researching the corporation and visited the corporation about a week ago. As he waits, he goes over his notes. A member of a social fraternity, business honorary, and several years summer experience in differing levels of management.
- Sandra, twenty-one, white, female. Communication major, French minor. Arrived at 9:45 A.M. Dressed in a pants suit and colored blouse open at the neck, chose to wear white sandals. Has a one-page résumé printed on pastel rose-colored paper (as per the suggestion of the career guidance book she purchased). Knows only what the corporation put out in the advertisement she saw in the college newspaper calling for manager-trainees. She is still putting on her makeup.
- Nicole, twenty, white, female. Communication major, marketing minor. Arrived at 9:35 A.M., waited a few minutes, then went to the assigned office. Conservatively dressed, white blouse, tie, blue skirt and blue blazer. Has a three-page résumé printed on white paper. Has spent several hours checking out the corporation, including talking to several employees. Heard about the job through a "cold" telephone call at the suggestion of her academic advisor, was encouraged to submit a résumé and did, along with a quick cover letter covering her qualifications. She has internship experience in a similar corporation. Has several pages of notes and several questions to ask in her leather briefcase. She is reviewing the notes.
- Greg, twenty-two, white, male. Communication major, finance minor. Dressed in blue jeans, denim shirt open at the collar, and a leather sports coat. His hair is "stylish," skinned to the ears around, with a long lock of hair. Has a one-page résumé. Learned about the position through a

fraternity brother's father who works for the corporation and arranged the interview. Arrived at 9:50 A.M., only to find out the interviewer had been called into an emergency meeting. Went out and had another cigarette and has just returned when the interviewer comes out of his office. Has some idea of what the corporation does, plans to answer all questions stressing his background in finance and accounting.

Which two will be invited back for a second interview? As the interviewer, would you make any "snap" decisions as you walked out to introduce yourself and meet the candidates? Hickson and Stacks (1993) note that the decision regarding hiring or not can be made early by many interviewers; often they use the remainder of the interview to verify or contradict their first impressions. While you may be able to contradict that first impression, it is much more effective to have a good presence at the beginning of the interview. What have these four people communicated already?

Most college graduates do not understand the job-seeking process, even though landing a job is one of their primary goals. The process of gaining employment is typically a three-step process (see Figure 4.1). First, you must choose a career, something that is more difficult than most students realize. Second, after making an introduction, you must present a professional résumé,

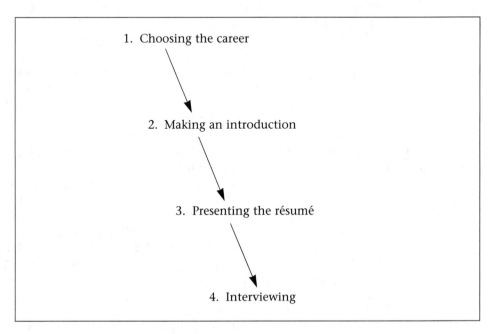

1. Choosing the career

2. Making an introduction

3. Presenting the résumé

4. Interviewing

FIGURE 4.1   The Employment Process

something that stresses your abilities, skills, and background. And, third, you must interview effectively. This chapter discusses each step as it involves the process of communication.

THE CAREER CHOICE/JOB SEARCH

Many people do not make career choices while in college, nor do they make such choices later, in mid-career change. Instead, most approach life as if its stages are separable units. That is, most college students worry about finishing a course, finishing a semester, graduating. *After* graduation they begin the process of a job search. Students fail to realize that searching for a job/career requires monumental decision making. To reach your potential, you must begin planning early. However, even with a plan, remember that career planning is a *tentative* process. As individuals exert more effort in the planning process, they increase their control over career opportunities, but the process is still tentative—unforeseeable circumstances may enter the situation. If you lose your financial aid, your graduation date may be postponed. Financial, family, and other considerations should cause us to view the career process as *goal-centered with alternative goals*. To some extent, we can plan for the unusual by having alternative and contingent planning. Thus, goals are processes; they are not fixed.

In today's world, people average three different careers and seven to ten different jobs during their lifetimes (and a student can plan on averaging three different majors over four years of college). About one-fifth of the thirty thousand different job titles today will no longer exist by the year 2000. We also know that jobs will exist in 2000 that were never imagined in 1997. Five years after graduation, more than half of the college graduates in this country will hold positions that have little or nothing to do with their college major. It may sound inconsistent, but we need both planning *and* flexibility in career decision making. The first step is to take a good look at yourself, probing your own interests and abilities. The most important factor in a long career is to do something you like.

Analyzing Skills

Even before your senior year, you need to analyze accomplishments, education, extra-curricular activities, work history, and hobbies as far back as you can remember. Did you enjoy a Boy Scout or a Girl Scout experience? If you did, you may prefer a position where you work outside, as opposed to inside an office. In each case, you need to analyze what skills you noticed that you had or what skills you improved. What you may not consider a *skill* may be important in some positions. What are some of the more important (and this list will change as we approach 2000)?

- Typing/keyboarding
- Driving, especially if you have a specialized license
- Using computer software
- Repairing equipment
- Editing others' writing
- Video technology expertise
- Personal survival techniques
- Red Cross training
- Artistic abilities (including musical)
- Time management
- Organizational skills
- Persuasive skills
- Athletic and game skills (golf, chess, bridge)

Some people do not like to discuss these skills with potential employers, fearing being required to do work that they do not prefer. However, any one of these skills may be the key to obtaining a job. You should not, however, limit your skills to psycho-motor skills. Other skills include:

- Ability to synthesize data
- Ability to read and understand directions
- Ability to present information orally
- Ability to present written information
- Ability to compare and contrast
- Ability to read and analyze graphs

By analyzing these and other skills, you discover what you do well, such as "person skills." People skills include

- People always telling you their problems
- People telling you that you are always smiling
- People telling you that you are optimistic
- Easily recalling people's names
- Finding it easy to converse with strangers

CASE 4.1   Examining Your Skills

Now that you are aware of some of the skills that you *might* have, make a list of those you *do* have. Think about how some of your hobbies may be used as a skill at work. Classify your skills in the same contexts that we have mentioned. Which of these skills do you believe might be most important for a job in the twenty-first century?

Undergoing this self-examination process helps you grasp what makes you unique; it can help you define what makes you happy. The next stage is to investigate career fields.

CAREER PLANNING

A good way to investigate career possibilities is to *observe others* in positions you would like to have. Other ways include interning in a position while in school, or participating in a cooperative education program. You may contact professionals in your field and ask to join them for a day. Or, you can interview people about their work. Professional organizations also provide important sources of information about particular careers. Most of such organizations have national, regional, state, and local affiliates. These organizations meet regularly; attending meetings is another way to discover information about a profession.

The next step is testing your alternatives through *experience*. One of the best ways of seeking primary information about a profession is working in that profession—getting "hands on" experience. As already noted, cooperative education, internships, and part-time jobs are excellent work experiences. Even if you decide not to enter that particular profession, the experience may be valuable in a related area.

The last step involves *crystallizing your plans*. The previous steps provided a sense of direction. Now you can evaluate the information you have gathered. Future decisions should be based on further improving skills necessary for a career. However, you should not focus exclusively on one particular job, but rather on a general area or areas of study.

Many college placement service professionals suggest that a college student enroll in a career planning and management course as a freshman. In so doing you identify your professional interests and skills and explore various courses of study. In the early stages of one's college career, required courses that are transferable from college to college or major to major should be taken. The sophomore should explore career opportunities related to academic areas of interest, choose an academic degree program, and consider career-related extracurricular organizations, internships, and cooperative education programs.

Juniors should continue to explore career opportunities, talk with people in fields of interest, begin evaluating post-graduate education (law school, graduate school), and verify requirements for graduation and post-graduate education. It is important, for example, to understand that a law degree requires three more years of education past the baccalaureate degree; most master's degree programs require only a year or two. In addition, most post-graduate education requires passing a standardized test of some type to qualify for admission. It is a good idea to "practice test" examinations as juniors to know what areas to study further before re-taking the examination (much like the PSAT in high school).

The senior should learn about résumé writing and interviewing, register with the university's placement service, and research employers.

In general, there are six suggested strategies for successful career planning:

1. Define what your career success means to you. What are your goals? Your long-term plans?
2. Experience self-assessment. You must know yourself before you can choose a career.
3. Research career opportunities.
4. Identify your marketable career skills, including course work, computer literacy, and work experience.
5. Network. Use contacts to spread the word that you are interested.
6. Make it happen—do not wait for it to happen! Take control over your own career decisions.

Assessing the job market is important. Geographically, where would you like to work? What jobs are you qualified to hold? Where are *your* skills needed most?

Content Research: The Corporation

The next important area of career planning is researching the corporation. This allows you to ask relevant questions during an interview without wasting time asking questions you could have answered yourself by reading corporate literature. A corporation's placement in the business world is reflective of its operations. Understand the company's relation to its competitors; know its history, reputation, ownership, and size. Often one can gain a significant amount of information by reading the last few annual reports of the company. For large companies, these are available at university libraries. Assessing the corporation's financial stability can prevent a layoff six months later. Third, you should look into the work atmosphere. A corporation's qualities are mirrored in its policies, personnel, and culture. The degree to which your personality fits into the corporate culture can determine whether you will find success. If you have friends who work there, talk with them about their work environment.

There are numerous means of gaining corporate information. Most libraries and many Internet Web sites can access corporate annual reports. While much of the information relates to finances, there is other important information to be found there. You should read the *Wall Street Journal* concerning the corporation and its competitors, as well as the business sections of newspapers in the geographical areas where you want to work. Follow its stock for about six months. How well does the corporation do when others are doing well? How does it do when others do poorly? Follow the stock on days when the market is down. How does your corporation do? The competition? Read business magazines, such as *Business Week* or *Forbes,* or specialty magazines in that industry, which may have feature stories on corporate management. You should follow anything that is said about your corporation by viewing the Consumer and Business News Channel (CNBC).

Other information may be obtained from people who work for a corporation. What are the benefits, salary, and other advantages of working for the corporation? Health benefits? Automobile? Vacation? Sick leave? Contributions to supplemental annuities? Retirement benefits? Relocation expenses? Stock shares? Parking privileges?

Establishing the Initial Contact

Once career planning and company research is complete, it is time to start making contact. The most commonly known ways to look for a job are: (1) walking-in, (2) employment agencies, (3) the company's employment office, (4) civil service, (5) friends and business associates, and (6) want ads/telephone. Walking-in, except for the service-construction trades, is the worst way to look for a job. Using the telephone will help you avoid roaming aimlessly and prevent unannounced interruptions into personnel offices. Employment agencies are only slightly better. Because they are in business to make money, and because many have bad reputations, they are often seen as a last resort. Some corporations and most governmental agencies have employment offices, which list openings on a bulletin board or have the information available through a telephone number, which has a tape recording of the latest employment listings, or have posted listings via the Internet. State employment agencies list all government jobs, as well as some private positions. Civil service jobs are available through these agencies. While they also have listings in the local newspaper, such listings are usually printed in the paper *after* they are made available through an agency.

Friends and business associates prove to be helpful connections when looking for a job. Many students do not like to use "contacts" because they feel this process is somehow unethical. However, this method is the way many people find work. You should also check with your department's alumni relations group. Want ads in the newspaper are much less effective. Such ads usually overly promote the job; many are based on commission. Advertisements for jobs in specialty newsletters and magazines, however, can be quite valuable (Wright, 1983). Finally, there is the telephone contact.

The Cold Call Method

The "cold call" method is contacting an employer who does not know you or is not expecting to hear from you. Because many jobs are never advertised, cold calling can be very effective. There are other benefits to cold calling. You can make many calls in a short amount of time. You can save yourself time and money from going around from corporation to corporation. Increasing contact also increases your chances of getting the job you want.

To make a cold call, you first want to find out who you should talk to about the job. Write down the name, job title, and telephone number. You need to research the organization to do this. You might need copies of corporate reports, company directories, and information from the Internet. Next, you need to arouse interest. Introduce yourself, describing your qualifications. Develop interest by requesting an interview. Close the conversation by making an appointment. If you are told the company is not hiring, offer a résumé and ask if you can call back in a month in case needs have changed.

Before you make the first call, there are a few things to consider. First, have a list of your skills, your master application, and your résumé in front of you. Second, call only corporations likely to hire people with your skills; third, keep a working list to avoid duplicate calls.

There are some basic job hunting errors job seekers make that potential employers never let them know about. Poor résumés reduce chances for an interview. Failing to network is another error. Friends and acquaintances often lead to a job. Limiting job sources to classified ads and employment agencies often overlook other job openings. A "canned approach" is not beneficial. Nonresponsive résumés, pre-printed cover letters, and unimaginative telephone calls lead employers to think the person may tend to take shortcuts. A short workweek will not get you far; the job search is at least a forty-hour per week process. Inadequate interview preparation reflects badly on character; responses must be timely, flexible, and company-directed.

Restricting your job search restricts chances of employment. Geographical locations, commuting time, and size and type of employer should be secondary. A negative attitude seldom brings a second interview; negative attitudes are perceived as indicative of future performance. A final error made in job hunting is poor physical appearance. Job candidates who do not exemplify self-respect by creating a positive image are usually deemed unacceptable.

Some people accept jobs only to realize later that the job is totally wrong for them. There are five prevalent reasons for this:

1. Following the advice of others rather than your own instincts.
2. Blinding yourself to what the job will be like.
3. Assuming you can live with a lower salary than that to which you are accustomed.
4. Not checking out potential problems and issues during the interview.
5. Impulsively grabbing the first job that comes along.

Career planning is not an easy task. It takes a lot of time. There are no effortless answers and no fail-safe methods for making decisions. You must be willing to take the initiative, explore, and experience. You should remember, however, that although cold calls sometimes work, they are the least effective means of getting a job.

RÉSUMÉS AND COVER LETTERS

Job markets are competitive and crowded. Employers seek applicants who are best qualified for the position at hand and for the company's overall culture. Job hunters must not only become a candidate for the job but appear as the best person for that job (Gerberg, 1984).

The next step in the process is submitting a résumé and a cover letter. Both are important because they represent your first contact with potential employers. Résumés and cover letters serve specific purposes. Each applicant has a different style, and résumés can be written using different formats. The cover letter and the résumé present what you want to relay to the person reading it. Each has guidelines that should be followed to maximize the applicant's credibility. After you have researched the company, the résumé and cover letter illustrate your knowledge of audience analysis.

The Cover Letter

The cover letter is an extremely important part of the résumé. Applicants should never send résumés without cover letters. The cover letter provides an opportunity to tailor one's qualifications to a specific position. In addition, you can indicate to the potential employer what you have to offer the company in that position. The cover letter is your chance to illustrate the qualities you possess that make you right for the job. The cover letter provides a chance to separate your application from others. This last point is especially relevant because most employers use an "elimination process" in selecting applicants for interviews. The cover letter and the résumé have the primary purpose of getting an interview.

There are a few simple guidelines for the cover letter (see Figure 4.2). First, it should be brief. It should be limited to one page—no more than four paragraphs. The letter should be typed, conforming to business correspondence standards. Whenever possible, the letter should be addressed to a particular person in the company, preferably using his or her name and title (Lewis, 1989). Concerning paragraphs, it is not imperative to have four, but four should be the maximum. The first paragraph should grab the reader's attention, it sets the tone for the remainder of the letter and should explain why you are writing to that particular person or company (Lewis, 1989).

After gaining the potential employer's attention, the next two paragraphs explain why you would be an asset to the company. Here you can highlight your personal credentials, achievements, and areas of expertise. Finally, you should close the cover letter with a short paragraph thanking the reader for his or her time and consideration. Here you may suggest that you will telephone soon to set up an interview. You should state that you are looking forward to meeting with the person you have written.

1420 Lotus Lane
Long Beach, CA 90840
(213) 555-8915

March 20, 1996

Mr. John Wilkey
General Manager
Wilkey Productions
P.O. Box 333
Atlanta, GA 30311

Dear Mr. Wilkey:

I am an intelligent, responsible, goal-oriented person seeking a challenge. I can contribute to your growing company with a wide diversity of managerial skills. Please consider this letter an application for a management position in your organization.

While researching potential employers consistent with my background and future aspirations, I was quite impressed with an article about your company in the most recent issue of *Production Management.* My skills, education, and experience fit well with your company's future.

It would be a pleasure to meet you at your convenience to discuss Wilkey Productions' employment opportunities, especially in the area of design management. You may contact me after 4:00 p.m. (7:00 p.m. Eastern) and on weekends at 213-555-8915.

I look forward to hearing from you. Thank you for your time and consideration.

Sincerely,

John L. Gonzales

John L. Gonzales

Enclosure (Résumé)

FIGURE 4.2   Example of a Cover Letter

Just as there are different kinds of jobs, there are different types of cover letters used in the job-seeking process. First, there is a *response to an advertisement* that requires studying the position requirements for the skills you have or need to have. You should communicate your strengths clearly and succinctly. Second, there is a *direct mail letter* that involves choosing several prospective employers and sending them your résumé with an individually written cover letter (form letters look and read like form letters). Third, there are *letters to employment agencies*. The purpose of these letters is to set up a conversation with the appropriate recruiter in each agency. This letter asks them to keep your résumé on file so that you can be notified of possible job openings. It is important, in this case, that you update the résumé periodically and ask to see it before it is sent to a prospective employer. This gives you a chance to update the material if you have added qualifications since you sent the résumé to the agency. Finally, there is a *letter to a colleague or friend*. This involves sending a handwritten note to someone with whom you are familiar. The letter states that you are in the process of seeking employment and would appreciate any suggestions they can offer. The cover letter actually sets the stage for the next round of the job hunt, the résumé.

The Professional Résumé

Recently, because of distance, time, and the number of applicants for a job, résumés have become essential in obtaining a job interview. The *résumé*, placed under the cover letter, serves to present a favorable image. It uses factual data, as well as work experience. Realistically, the sole purpose of the résumé is to get you an interview (Moreau, 1990). With this in mind, you need to pay attention to how the résumé is organized, what it indicates about you and your goals, and what technical aspects of the résumé are important. A résumé is relatively short; it lists your accomplishments in a one-to-two page document. A *vita*, literally, is your life history and may by the time you retire be ten to fifteen pages or longer. When looking for a job, whether your first or later, however, most employers want a concise listing of your accomplishments—your résumé.

First, your name, address, and telephone number are normally placed at the top of the résumé. It is important that you list your full name, but you should also indicate which name most people use to refer to you. For example, your résumé may say:

Charles L. (Chuck) Andersen

However, even if you usually use nicknames such as "Bubba," use a more formal name when interviewing (you can always change to "Bubba" later). Your address and telephone number is where you can *easily* be reached. You should have an answering machine or service when you are not at that number or address. You may list a business (daytime) telephone number and a home (nighttime) number if you do not object to potential employers calling you at work. Additionally, an e-mail address should be included, if you have one.

The résumé's remaining parts vary. You may want to state your educational experience first, if you do not have much work experience, or vice versa. You should have education and work experience along with school-related or work-related honors listed in the résumé. Your résumé should include a career objective, organization memberships, foreign languages spoken, computer skills (both programs and computer type—DOS or Macintosh), and military service. Although unnecessary in today's market, other personal data, such as birthdate, age, and marital status are still being provided by many.

For most people, preparing a résumé is a frustrating process. This is because you must decide on a good format, determine what you want to say, and decide how you want to say it (Wright, 1983). Remember that, like the cover letter, the first information must catch the reader's attention.

Deciding on a résumé *format* is important. Formats include the chronological, the functional, the targeted, the résumé alternative, and the creative format. Other formats may be tailored more specifically. The two most common, however, are the chronological and the functional.

The *chronological format* (see Figure 4.3) lists your job history with the most recent experience at the top descending to the first work experience at the bottom (Jackson, 1990). The chronological résumé lists your jobs exactly as they would appear on a job application form. With this format, you list the timeframe of the beginning and ending of each job (Wright, 1983). This format emphasizes career growth, highlights the names of your employers, and is fairly easy to follow. The chronological résumé is especially advantageous if you are staying in the same field as a prior job, if your job history shows growth and development, if the name of your last employer is a relevant or important consideration, or when your previous job title was important (Jackson, 1990). It can work against you if your work history has significant gaps, if you have been doing the same thing too long, if you are changing your career goal, if you have changed employers too frequently, or if you are looking for your first job.

The other most common format is the *functional format* (see Figure 4.4), which highlights major accomplishments and strengths. This format allows you to arrange items in a certain order, supporting your work objectives and job target; it places work titles and history in a more subordinate position (Jackson, 1990). The functional résumé is advantageous when trying to emphasize capabilities not based on work experience, when changing careers, when entering the job market for the first time, when your past career growth has not been good, or when you have had a variety of unrelated work experiences. The functional résumé allows you to eliminate repeating job assignments, and to be flexible in emphasizing certain items. It can work against you if you want to emphasize a management growth pattern, when trying to

John Gonzales
1001 S.E. 24th Street
Apartment 3G
Atlanta, GA 30102

SUMMARY: Seeking position within a rapidly growing, high tech company.
Concentration on internal communication/human relations.

EDUCATION: B.A., Georgia State University, 1996
Major: Communication (Corporate/Public Relations)
Minor: Sociology

EXPERIENCE: One-Way Systems Corp.   May, 1995–present
Atlanta, GA
Corporate Intern/Human Resources

Responsible for coordinating internal communications. Wrote and
copyedited internal Human Resources newsletter. Duties included
story assignment, editing, photography, layout and publication of
newsletter.

Additional responsibilities:
- wrote speeches for management on human resource issues
- created several brochures for human resource optional health
  and recreation plans
- worked on increasing employee morale as focus group facilitator

PRSSA   June, 1992–May, 1995
Georgia State University
Various offices and duties

President   1994–95
Vice President   1993–94
Special Projects   1992–93

- Responsible for planning and account management of student
  public relations agency. Created corporate public relations
  divisions, recruited clients.
- Developed a client base of over 100 non-profit "clients."

FIGURE 4.3   The Chronological Résumé

Jane Goodsell

Home: 1615 Lofton Ave   School: 121 Sales Tower
        Coral Gables, FL 33146   University of Iowa
        (305) 555-8921   Iowa City, IA 52242

OBJECTIVE: Seeking position within a rapidly growing financial institution.
                    Concentration on internal communication/human relations.

EDUCATION: B.A., University of Iowa, 1996
                    Major: Public Relations (Corporate/Public Relations)
                    Minor: Management

SUMMARY   Energetic and outgoing person who works hard to get the job
                    done. Experienced in working with others, leadership, and can
                    motivate others to do their best.

MANAGEMENT   President of Management Club
                    President of Phi Beta Phi Fraternity

LEADERSHIP: President, Panhellenic Council
                    President, PRSSA chapter
                    Omicron Delta Kappa Leadership Honorary
                    Gold Key Leadership Honorary
                    Chair of various University events

WORK
EXPERIENCE: Corporate Intern, Fiscal Services of Colorado, 1995–96
                    Corporate Intern, Bank of Iowa, 1994–95
                    Journalism Department, Student Assistant, 1994–96
                    Bennie's Grill, Iowa City, IA, Shift manager, 1993–94
                    McDonalds, Coral Springs, FL, counter worker, shift manager,
                    1990–92

REFERENCES: Available upon request

FIGURE 4.4   The Functional Résumé

enter a highly traditional field where specific employers are of interest (teaching, political), when your job duties were limited, or when your most recent employers were highly prestigious and you want to be associated with them.

The functional résumé is probably best used when trying to *change or redirect* your career. The chronological résumé is more beneficial when trying to continue in a career where you have had success. It is also most familiar to professional interviewers.

In maximizing your résumé's effect, there are certain do's and don'ts that should be considered. Presenting factual data about job experiences and life history on a résumé shows potential employers your ability to organize and communicate. There are certain criteria to follow which will demonstrate your competence even more effectively.

In general, a résumé should be *businesslike,* not "cute or chatty" (Byrne, 1986, p. 102). *Résumés should be honest and state abilities and achievements accurately.* If for no other reason, a falsified résumé may result in immediate dismissal if you are hired. You want to tell the reader about previous job responsibilities and positions (Bostwick, 1990). Another important point is that *a résumé should contain only positive information.* If negativity is displayed, you may be weeded out and not given a fair review. *Spelling and grammatical errors are unforgivable.* Many employers will dismiss an applicant solely because of such errors. They show potential employers that you lack primary skills necessary for accomplishment. In addition, you should avoid regionalisms and other informal language. If you do have a problem with grammar or spelling, the problem is even more important because errors display bad judgment, unclear thinking, and negligence and lackadaisical attitude (Bostwick, 1990). Your résumé must be proofread and critiqued; a sloppy and ill-prepared résumé does not say much for you (Byrne, 1986).

The language used is important. Field-related language is referred to as "jargon." The language of the résumé must coincide with the potential field of employment. Doctors, lawyers, scientists, and even golfers have their own specialized language. When writing a résumé, appropriate language should be used. You should not be overly technical, however, because people outside the field (those who may actually approve your hire) may not understand it. You should not use language with which you are unfamiliar (Bostwick, 1990). Other "do's" include

1. Use present tense (if presently doing the job), past tense (for previous work).
2. Use only 8½ x 11-inch paper.
3. Use only white or pastel (gray or beige) paper, preferably white.
4. Use the same color paper and type style for the résumé, cover letter, and envelope.
5. Be consistent in displaying techniques.
6. Centering and balancing the content of the page, using wide margins, and leaving plenty of white space allows you to present yourself in the best possible manner.

In contrast, there are certain "don'ts" that influence how potential employers perceive applicants. Major don'ts have to do with *race, religion, and political affiliation.* It is generally not favorable to list these because they indicate certain preferences. Even though the law forbids discrimination because of such indications, these "notifications" may change how you and your résumé are treated (Bostwick, 1990). Second, *do not include a salary history;* you are seeking new employment and hoping to improve your income. A past salary listing could restrict potential salary. It is unwise to commit to salary before the interview because you could underestimate your possibilities. Finally, *references should NOT be included.* Employers should not have interest in knowing whom you have worked for until they have decided you are a candidate. References give employers a chance to call and ask questions about you. By allowing the potential employer to do this, you lose the opportunity to present yourself first.

Before listing a person as a reference (when requested by the employer), it is important to *notify the reference that a prospective employer may call.* If there is any hesitation, do not list that person; listing your current employer as a reference can be costly (Bostwick, 1990). If your present employer is used as a reference, it could and most likely will indicate unhappiness with your job. Present employers should be the last people contacted by your prospective employer—and only when you are being seriously considered. Other résumé don'ts include

1. Don't abbreviate.
2. Don't use "I"; it shows selfishness.
3. Don't make the résumé too long or too short.
4. Don't include a photograph of yourself; the reader may not like your looks.
5. Don't handwrite anything except the signature on your cover letter.
6. Don't include anything negative.
7. Don't use slang.

Career Objectives

Résumés contain personal data, qualifications, previous responsibilities, and career objectives. *Career objectives* deal with your career goals, job targets, or reasons for the résumé. Not all résumés include a career objective; it is a personal decision whether to use one.

Stating an objective tells potential employers that you are headed in a certain direction; it informs them of your reasons for making contact. An objective serves as a focal point from which readers can review and analyze the rest of the résumé. The objective does not limit or restrict the potential employee from being considered for other positions (Nadler, 1985). It is important that the objective be clear, but not so specific that it limits career opportunities. A key to writing an objective is to know the experiences and qualifications needed for the position under consideration and to direct the résumé to describing your abilities that fulfill the requirements (Nadler, 1985).

The career objective should convey that although you have job preferences, you are not closed to other considerations (Bostwick, 1990). Writing a
clear objective does not commit you for life to a particular job or field. Most
people change jobs and careers more than once, and a well-written objective
is useful in communicating goals and qualifications to potential employers.
The objective should be concise but not rigid.

A résumé is best if it is precisely written for the position you are seeking.
Such an approach might be expensive, however. The next step, assuming your
résumé was successful, is the job interview.

THE JOB INTERVIEW

Think back to the chapter's opening example of four students getting ready
to interview for a job. What has each done correctly, that will help them get
through the most stressful part of the process? We have examined thus far the
significance of choosing the right career and preparing a proper résumé. Now
we will investigate the interview process.

The interview process has important functions on both sides of the desk.
Applicants view the interview as an opportunity to market abilities and show
the interviewer that they are suitable for a particular job. The interviewee
should also use this time for displaying informal communication skills and
demonstrating a good personality. The interviewer uses the process to learn as
much as possible about the candidate so that a good decision can be made
about whether to hire the interviewee.

The interviewer evaluates the interviewee to determine whether he or she
can fill a particular position with the corporation. "The goal [of the interview]
is to get the person to address hypothetical situations relating to the job so
you can get behind the résumé and assess likely performance" (Byrne, 1990,
p. 156). This evaluation takes place on several different levels, and can be seen
more clearly by breaking down the interviewing process into components
(Stewart & Cash, 1994). By understanding these components, a job candidate
can maximize effectiveness in the interviewing process and gain the needed
credibility to land a job. These components include personal appearance,
acute answering of questions, nonverbal communication, acute questioning
abilities, and salary negotiation.

Interestingly, nonverbal communication components are especially important in the interview. The top ten reasons for *rejection* are (Bovee & Thill, 1983)

- Poor personal appearance.
- Appearing overbearing, aggressive, conceited; showing that one has a "su-
  periority complex," seems to "know it all."
- Being unable to express oneself clearly—poor voice, diction, grammar.
- Lack of career planning.
- Lack of interest and enthusiasm.

- Lack of confidence and poise.
- Failure to participate in extracurricular activities.
- Overemphasis on money.
- Poor scholastic record.
- Lack of willingness to start at the bottom.

Interestingly, almost all of these factors are *nonverbal communication* components. Perhaps the reason that nonverbal communication is so important here is that this is the first face-to-face encounter for the interviewee and the interviewer. Remember, you should have some confidence at this point because you were called in for an interview. You're batting 1,000 at this juncture.

Personal appearance, a nonverbal component, is an important aspect of the interview (Fast, 1991). Although it is improbable that one would be hired on the basis of personal appearance alone, the first impression that an interviewee makes is through attractiveness and dress. According to Marian Faux (1985), author of *The Executive Interview,* "Even before you shake hands with an interviewer, he or she is observing how you look . . . and will see if you are acceptable or wanting. If you are found wanting, it's hard to regain lost ground during the interview" (as quoted in Green, 1991, p. 324). The interview provides an environment where your personal qualities and other qualities should stand out. Therefore, you should do as much as possible to avoid letting your appearance hinder these qualities.

John D. Drake (1991), author of *The Perfect Interview,* has several widely applicable suggestions for dressing for an interview. Drake says to dress in the same way that you expect those who interview you will be dressed. This provides homophily with the interviewer at the outset; you immediately fit in with the environment and illustrate that you comprehend the company culture. Second, do not wear anything flashy. There are many specifics including jewelry, ties, belt buckles, shoes, and other accessories. The bottom line is that you should dress conservatively. Conservative dress decreases the chances of being judged negatively. Third, you should pay attention to the finer points of your appearance. Interviewers may notice finer points such as unpolished shoes or messy hair and attribute these flaws as flaws in your character (Hickson & Stacks, 1993). Finally, just as with the résumé process, you should not wear anything that associates you with a particular religion, political group, school, or other organization (Drake, 1991, pp. 66–68; Molloy, 1988; Molloy, 1977). While dressing to trends may be important in social dress, such trends should not be obeyed in dressing for business success. You should dress just as you would for the interview when you practice your interview with a family member or friend. Finally, make certain that you are comfortable wearing your dress for the interview.

The next interview component, answering questions effectively, is a *verbal communication* component. Answering questions is the primary component in the interview for assessing the candidate's verbal communication skills. The key here is to be prepared to answer *any* question. In the past, interviewees have been able to rehearse for certain questions and then give a memorized answer in the interview. Today, interviewers create new ways to find out more about you. For example, an article in the *Harvard Business Review* analyzes the subject of an interviewer trying to find out as much as possible about an interviewee's past performance. It then suggested the following questions be asked: "Can you tell me about any project you had where you had to meet a deadline? What did you do to get the work out on time?" (Jenks, 1989, p. 39). These questions are helpful to the interviewer because answers should give some indication as to how motivated the interviewee might be. This type of questioning is representative of what interviewees should expect to hear today.

Interviewers look for more than a list of past accomplishments and future goals. They want to know about how you are going to perform, so canned answers are of little use. Interviewers who need to discover specific qualities of the candidate are using other interviewing tactics. "The scariest is the stress interview. That's where things go from some degree of cordiality to a purposeful toughness. You get asked questions designed to make you nervous, throw you off balance and measure your response" (Moreau, 1989, p. 55). *Stress interview* questions are used because the interviewer knows that the job could put you under stress. The best thing to do at this point is to remain calm, thus showing the interviewer that you have the ability to deal with the stress (Moreau, 1989).

Some interviewers stick to tried and true questions to establish rapport with the applicant. If this is the case, then you should answer questions as honestly and sincerely as possible. You should avoid rambling, let the interviewer clearly understand the answer. An answer like, "I don't know," is a perfectly legitimate answer in job interviews. The bottom line in answering interview questions is in preparing for any question and answering in a way that does not seem overly prepared. Answers that are too short or too long present a problem. In those cases where it is possible to do so, one should answer with, "I believe such-and-such because of one, two, and three." Providing a justification for your answer illustrates that you have thought about the question. Some questions, such as "What are your goals for the next five years?" should not be answered too quickly—silently count to ten—or the interviewer will suspect a memorized answer.

The next component of the interview involves other *nonverbal characteristics*. "In an interview situation, an applicant's actions can be used to verify and validate or negate what the person is saying" (Fleischmann, 1991, p. 161). By paying close attention to your nonverbal messages, interviewers learn as much from what one is doing as from what one is saying. Fleischmann (1991) points out that breathing patterns, head and face movements, eye contact, and hand and arm motions are all means of finding out about a person.

Often a heavy sigh is a sign that a person is going to be discussing something that he or she is not comfortable discussing. Avoidance of eye contact is often associated with indifference, fear, insecurity, or evasiveness.

When the hand is open, palms facing upward, you can be fairly sure the candidate is being open and honest (pp. 162–164).

It is important to understand that your nonverbal messages are being read. To make everything clear to the interviewer, make certain that what is being said with the body corresponds with the words being used.

The next interview component involves *asking questions.* At some point in the interview, you will likely be asked: "Do you have any questions you would like to ask me?" Be prepared for this. If you have content researched properly, you should demonstrate that preparation with well thought-out questions pertaining directly to the job being discussed. Richard Lynch (1985), in a *Money* article, discusses certain questions that you should ask before accepting a job. One question is: "May I talk with someone who is doing what I'll be doing?" This way you can get a more complete and accurate description of what the job entails. Another is: "How and by whom will my performance be measured?" This question can help establish what type of goals you will be expected to meet. It also offers information about whom you should try to impress (Lynch, 1985, pp. 109–114). Any interviewee should take the time to ask questions during the interview. If anything, this lets the interviewer know you are genuinely interested in the job.

The final component in the interviewing process is *negotiating a salary.* Not all interviews (initial or follow-up) are going to be the place where salary is determined, but the subject is likely to arise. Once again, preparedness and research are the keys, especially if you sense the company wants to hire you.

Paul Hellman (1986), in *Ready, Aim, You're Hired,* discusses strategies for salary negotiation. First, job offer salaries are dealt with in ranges. He points out that this range is first developed by the applicant. The low point of the range, "the applicant's reservation price," should be determined by the applicant as the absolute lowest possible offer that would be acceptable. Through research and asking questions of others in the same field, the applicant should estimate the "company's reservation price," which is the maximum the company would offer. When salary is brought up in the interview, you can get a feel for negotiating power if the interviewer "bids" first. If the interviewer bids below your expectations, then reply with a calm bid 10 percent higher than the estimated maximum offer. If the employer makes a ridiculously high bid, then you can do one of a few things. You can accept the offer. You can ask to think it over. If the interviewer is aggressive, you can ask for 10 percent more. If the employer is extremely cocky, you can ask for 20 percent more (Tedeschi & Rosenfeld, 1980).

Suppose though that the employer forces you to make the opening bid. Hellman (1986, pp. 67–80) says that you should open somewhere around 10 percent above the employer's estimated maximum offer. This negotiation may not happen in the first interview. You should, however, be prepared in case it does. You should also provide a salary range (about 5 percent). What if the interviewer does not bring up salary? The smart interviewee should find a way to ask about the salary so that it can be discussed or ask when the second interview will be held ("What is the salary range projected for this position now?" is a good opening gambit).

Landing a professional job involves hard work, determination, patience, and time. It is evident through our research that there are different methods for reaching desired employment. The career search, the résumé, and the interview are the main steps that one must carefully maneuver in order to reach the profession of choice. Consider again our four job candidates, John, Nicole, Sandra, and Greg. Although we do not know how their interviews went, we can guess which two made the "cut." We can even guess which might get the job. We can pretty much predict that both would interview well based on their preparation and knowledge of communication skills.

SUMMARY

The job search is a process of career planning, résumé preparation, and interview preparation. As we discussed, there are three major elements in each of these processes: content research (about the company, the competition), audience research (about the interviewer), and dialogic elements (interaction between the interviewer and the interviewee). Once you have successfully interviewed, you begin the work process, a much more demanding and long-lasting communication encounter, something we tackle in the following chapters.

QUESTIONS FOR THOUGHT

1. Comparing this chapter with the earlier chapters, what do you believe will be important about the relationship between you and the interviewer in finding a job?
2. Look around at the students in your class and decide, would they be able to find a job dressed as they are now? Why or why not? Does it make a difference about the kind of job? Why or why not?
3. What kinds of questions would you ask the interviewer at an interview?
4. Cover letters are fairly difficult to compose. Nevertheless, you should practice this art. Develop a cover letter for your résumé that would be appropriate for a retail sales position. Develop a cover letter for a job as a substitute teacher.
5. Go through the Yellow Pages of your local telephone directory. Find at least ten companies where you might make a cold call because the companies do what you are interested in doing.

CASE 4.2   Résumé Writing

Write a one-page résumé. The résumé should take into account all the suggestions that we have discussed in this chapter. From the result, determine your strengths and weaknesses. If you have not had a job, how could you make the résumé look better? Exchange your résumé with other students in your class. Compare and contrast your résumé with theirs. How does yours compare to theirs? How do you think it would compare and contrast with students who have no training in résumé preparation? How do you think a prospective employer would feel after reading your résumé? After comparing it against the rest of your class?

REFERENCES

Bostwick, B. E. (1990). *Résumé writing*. New York: Wiley.

Bovee, C. L., & Thill, V. (1983). *Business communication today*. New York: Random House.

Byrne, J. A. (September 17, 1990). All the right moves for interviewers. *Business Week, 156.*

Byrne, J. A. (October 6, 1986). The do's and don'ts of writing a résumé. *Business Week, 102.*

Drake, J. D. (1991). *The perfect interview: How to get the job you really want*. New York: American Management Association.

Fast, J. (1991). *Body language in the workplace*. New York: Penguin.

Faux, M. (1985). *The executive interview*. New York: St. Martin's Press.

Fleischmann, S. T. (1991). The message of body language in job interviews. *Employment Relations Today, 18,* 161–165.

Gerberg, R. J. (1984). *The professional job changing system*. Roseland, NJ: Performance Dynamics.

Green, C. M. (1991). Career strategies: Go for it! *Black Enterprise, 21,* 311–325.

Hellman, P. (1986). *Ready, aim, you're hired*. New York: American Management Association.

Hickson, M. L., & Stacks, D. W. (1993). *NVC: Nonverbal communication studies and applications*. Dubuque, IA: Brown & Benchmark.

Jackson, T. (1990). *The perfect résumé*. New York: Doubleday.

Jenks, J. M. (1989). ABCs of job interviewing. *Harvard Business Review, 67,* 38–42.

Lewis, A. (1989). How to write better résumés. *Barron's, 26,* 32–36.

Lynch, R. A. (1985). Ten questions to ask before accepting a job. *Money, 14,* 109–114.

Molloy, J. T. (1977). *The woman's dress for success book*. Chicago: Follett.

Molloy, J. T. (1988). *New dress for success*. New York: Warner.

Moreau, D. (1990). Write a résumé that works. *Changing Times, 44,* 91–95.

Moreau, D. (1989). Answers that get you hired. *Changing Times, 43,* 53–55.

Nadler, B. J. (1985). *Liberal arts power! How to sell it on your résumé*. Princeton, NJ: Peterson's.

Stewart, C. J., & Cash, W. B., Jr. (1994). *Interviewing: Principles and practices,* 7th ed. Madison, WI: Brown & Benchmark.

Tedeschi, J. T., & Rosenfeld, P. (1980). Communication in bargaining and negotiation. In M. E. Roloff (Ed.), *Persuasion: New directions in theory and practice* (pp. 227–228). Beverly Hills, CA: Sage.

Wright, D. (1983). *Hardball job hunting tactics*. New York: Facts on File.

5

SOCIALIZATION IN ORGANIZATIONAL COMMUNICATION

Anticipation
> *Formal and implied contracts*
> *Managing self-concept*
> *Organizational structure and anticipation*
>> Adapting to formal structures
>> Informal structure and the organizational "culture"
>> Informal communication networks
> *Researching the organizational structure*

Encounter
> *Analyzing the organizational encounter*
>> Work group roles
>> Linkages

Identification

Objectives

By the end of this chapter you should be able to

1. Describe the socialization process found in the organization.
2. Define and distinguish formal and implied contracts.
3. Explain the concept of organizational culture and how it relates to organizational socialization.
4. Explain how roles, rules, and routines operate in the organization and why they are important to the socialization process.
5. Explain the importance of identification in successful organizational socialization.

Surviving the interview process and being hired for a new job provides high levels of motivation. It has been suggested, however, that the new situation also confronts the neophyte worker with a number of unanticipated obstacles. These obstacles come about because new workers are concerned about doing a good job—about being successful, whatever that means based on their personal work histories (Conrad, 1994). The organization, too, unknowingly creates obstacles because it needs to maintain standards of behavior that ensure its own continuity. As Conrad (1994) notes, "Joining an organization involves a complicated process of mutual negotiation, of a newcomer and an organization finding ways to accommodate themselves to differences in their histories, perceptions, and patterns of actions" (p. 39). The organization's goal is to *socialize* the newcomer; the newcomer's role is to be *socialized* without completely eliminating a sense of self.

Take the following oversimplified example. We may have a newcomer to our organization (a bank) who likes to wear "wild neckties." The bank does not like its workers to wear "wild neckties," fearing that it sends the wrong message. In some way, the organization informs the newcomer that there has been a violation of its norms—its employee behavior expectations. At the same time, the newcomer "senses" that there are negative consequences for violating organizational norms. Unfortunately, the "wild tie" example is both a more concrete and less discrete type of violation.

This chapter explores the initial socialization process people go through when they enter an organization. It assumes that "new" and "neophyte" are synonymous, but it should be noted that every time you enter a new work environment, the processes discussed must be mastered. In socializing, the neophyte passes through a three-stage process: *anticipation, encounter,* and *identification.* The "wild tie" situation just discussed is an example of anticipation, which will lead to some form of encounter, ultimately producing some form of organizational identification.

ANTICIPATION

Anticipation may be described as expectations about how an organization works and how the individual is expected to behave and perform. All of us have had some experience with being socialized into an organization in our past. We may, for instance, have joined a swim team or a fraternity at school. Often, we were part of a group of people who joined at the same time. For example, there was a "pledge class." In many organizations, however, a newcomer is the only new member, or if others entered at the same time, they do not meet because they are isolated in different organizational departments.

Formal and Implied Contracts

Soon after hiring, most corporations or companies (if large enough) provide a new employee "orientation" session. These sessions briefly cover the company's policies and procedures, as well as a brief discussion of employee benefits. Some mention is usually made of dress codes. This session is often accompanied by copious employee benefits paperwork, information about how to obtain an identification card, a copy of the policies and procedures manual, and so forth. These sessions provide knowledge about what is expected in some general sense, but do not really help the new worker know which colleagues to believe, where to go to lunch, what topics of conversation are taboo, or who really runs the office.

Some companies' *formal communication* will be much more explicit than others, being both literal and legal.[1] Some will only provide job descriptions. The problem for newcomers, however, is not knowing whether the job description is what is *really* expected or simply another document. Some new workers typically make the mistake of complaining that their particular job task was not in the job description. Such a complaint may appear both logical and valid, but you soon discover that the job description was only perfunctory. Or you may find that such a complaint results in the boss' (early) evaluation that you are a literalist (takes things literally) and a legalist (is concerned only about the specific wording of a contract). Such evaluations this early could ruin any opportunity for success in the company.

An important consideration at this stage of your organizational career is that "contracts are flexible and always under negotiation." You see this happening in sports all the time. When a new head football coach is hired on a five-year contract and does not win after three years, the coach's contract for the two remaining years is often bought out. The written contract is important, but many workers rarely or never receive a written contract. And most written contracts have *implied provisions*. For instance, a growing number of companies are requiring that employees sign a noncompete agreement upon hiring (Barciela, 1996). Because many employees jump from company to company, often taking with them a wealth of proprietary information and clients, the noncompete agreement is designed to prevent you from calling on your old customers for a competitor or from even working in the same area for some time if you leave. Of course, the company often has it both ways: it can prevent you from divulging a confidential company list, yet divulge that same list to potential customers.

In other companies the *entire* contract is implied. One of your authors was hired as an assistant professor at a university. He had been a Ph.D. for three years; there were other faculty members who were instructors, a lower rank. When the assistant professor arrived for his first day at work, he found that he was "time-sharing" a cubicle of about sixteen square feet with one of the instructors. He shared a telephone with six instructors; he had no bookshelves and no privacy. He had anticipated a large office, like that of his dissertation advisor at another university: an office of almost two hundred square feet, his own telephone, his own part-time secretary, a wall of bookshelves and file cabinets, and plenty of privacy. No doubt what was anticipated and what was realized were two different things.

What about the anticipations of your future colleagues? These expectations vary according to the individual company. Many are based on recent history. Some positions are referred to by the "old timers" as the "revolving door slot." This means that several different people have been hired and terminated in that position over the past few years. In some organizations, there are "power plays" going on among the "old timers." Each of them may decide to recruit the newcomer to their side. This may occur despite the fact that the interviewer said that everyone got along well. *The first part of dealing with anticipation, then, is "managing inaccurate expectations."*

Managing Self-Concept

Anticipation also involves a second part: managing self-concept. According to Perinbanayagam (1985), one of the significant aspects of your self is your "generalized other." The *generalized other* is a set of motives attributed to you by others as seen through your eyes (Mead, 1934). As such, being new on the job, you might be concerned about negatives in your generalized other more so than positives. That is, it may be important NOT to appear too arrogant, enthusiastic, immature, hard-working, lazy, or ambitious. This is the generalized other developed *before* you entered the organization. Conrad (1994) argues that when you enter a new organization there are three important elements of the generalized other to consider: *competence, independence and autonomy,* and *self-respect.*

We can redefine these elements as the *homophily, credibility,* and *interpersonal attraction* needed to help us move up through the organization. In some ways, the elements are interrelated. For example, if you were hired because you claimed you could use a particular computer program, and you cannot, then you will have to ask for help. If you do this too often, it will probably influence your self-respect (and may have an impact on your homophily and interpersonal attraction—people do not like associating with others with little self-respect). It will also reflect on others' perception of your competence—your credibility to do the job.

Going back to the earlier example, where one of your authors was housed in a cubicle, several approaches might be taken to correct the situation. First, he could go to the department chair and ask for better working conditions. Second, he could assume the chair thought of him as "part-time" faculty, who really do not need to be there very much. Third, he could passively accept the situation as "typical" for one without much seniority. Or, fourth, he could solve his own problem. As it happens, he took the last alternative. Over a period of one year, he "confiscated" an office from a supply room, persuaded the chair into providing him a telephone, offered to pay the university's share for a student-worker secretary, built his own bookshelves, taught eight classes, and published several articles in professional journals. All of this was done without alienating the chair or his other colleagues. This may not always be the "best" solution, but it demonstrates how adapting to a situation requires an ability to analyze how your generalized other is seen.

The final element of anticipation is "letting go" (Conrad, 1994). As a newcomer, you must discover that you cannot hold on to old ideas from other places. Learning to adapt to the new situation is critical for success. The newcomer must learn to refrain from statements such as, "The way we did this at so-and-so was . . . " *The organization expects newcomers to adapt rather than vice versa.* One of your authors was leaving a university because he had been drafted into the Army. After the chair made the announcement in a faculty meeting, a colleague asked, "Could I have his telephone?" In other words, do not let the door hit you as you leave. The old organization is generally ready to let the person leave, but the individual has difficulty letting go of those ideas from the past, no matter how good or bad they may have been. An ability to see yourself as others see you often helps. If you leave an organization before being asked to leave, you generally leave that organization with positive generalized other perceptions, high self-respect, and credibility.

Organizational Structure and Anticipation

Anticipation involves the newcomer to any organization taking a number of actions early. To do so, you must evaluate the *formal* and *informal* aspects of the organization. The formal structure of the organization has traditionally been defined in terms of "line and staff" functions. Line functions are those job descriptions that are primarily responsible for the production component in the organization. Staff functions are those that support the *production component.* For example, in an academic institution, it may be assumed that faculty and their administrators are line people; staff people are composed of clerical workers, personnel people, student affairs administration, and the like. In other words, the staff personnel would not exist if the line personnel were not there.

Adapting to Formal Structures

The formal structure has traditionally indicated which departments or positions report to others. The extreme version of a formal organization would be one where all members of the organization strictly adhere to the structure. A military organizational structure is a good example. Such an organization is characterized by "bureaucracy" (Weber, 1947; Jablin, 1987) wherein most rules are written as policy and where there are forms—in some cases forms to order forms—that reflect the rigid structure of the organization in terms of communicating both information and responsibility.

At the opposite end is an organization based on informality. In such an organization, there are no published rules, no policies and procedures document. Many "entrepreneurial" companies begin as informal organizations (remember the Bee example in Chapter 1) but quickly establish some sort of formal organizational structure. In today's legalistic world, however, no organizations—even the military—exist at either extreme.

We might think of organizational structure in the following terms. In a young organization—simple, democratic, creative, small—a more informal structure and communication process are more likely to occur. The organizational structure fits a growing and vibrant organization, one that is trying to

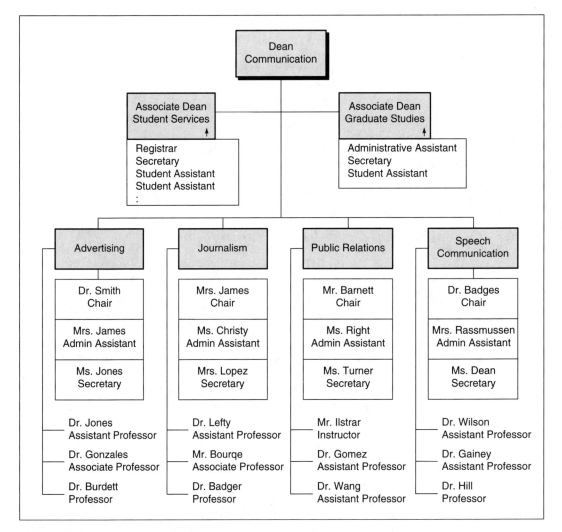

FIGURE 5.1   Line and Staff Positions

find its "niche." In the traditional larger organization—older, autocratic, rational, complex, and bureaucratic—formal structures and communication are more likely to occur as it strives to maintain the status quo and its place in a competitive market.

Informal Structure and the Organizational "Culture"
Most new workers over-anticipate, assuming that what held before is the same as today. This occurs whether you are first entering an organization or moving up the organization to a new position. To counter over-anticipation, newcomers need to become aware of *organizational norms.* In large measure, norms

are aspects of the *informal structure and communication* in the organization that yield much of what is called the organization's "culture." (Culture is the combination of formal and informal structure and the communication taking place within each structure; it is more than sum of both parts, it is "holistic.") Included in the informal communication structure are rumors, the grapevine, and informal networks (Davis, 1967; Rogers & Agarwala-Rogers, 1976).

Taken together, the formal and informal structures compose what is referred to as the *organizational climate* or *culture*. The newcomer has, then, entered a new culture (Smircich & Calas, 1987; Pace & Faules, 1989; Stohl, 1995; Pepper, 1995; Richmond & McCroskey, 1992; Morgan, 1986; Goldhaber, 1993; and Conrad, 1994). To survive in any new culture, you must (1) research the content area, (2) analyze the clients, and (3) communicate with others. We will discuss each of these aspects of the new job.

Informal Communication Networks

An *informal communication network* involves a face-to-face interaction, often about information that is not directly involved in the business of the business. Such communication is often referred to as "the grapevine." Goldhaber (1993) has outlined four important principles of the grapevine:

- The grapevine is fast.
- The grapevine is accurate.
- The grapevine carries much information.
- The grapevine travels by cluster.

There is an assumption on the part of whomever hired you that you know a certain amount of information about how to do the job. Nevertheless, very early you should begin the continual process of researching how to communicate with others in your organization. As noted in Chapter 3, observation is most important at this stage. Hickson (1992) has stated that you should be a *participant-observer*—participating in the organization as a subject, but also observing it from an objective viewpoint. One of the first observations to make is to understand the physical layout of the building where the organization is housed. On the face of it, you might think that such an analysis is relatively unimportant. However, most people primarily communicate informally with others who are physically close to them (Hickson, Roebuck, & Murty 1990; Harper, Wiens, & Matarazzo, 1978). If this is the case for your organization, you need to learn where the *communication networks* are located.

Not all communication networks occur within the physical location of the company. People who work closely together often interact with one another later. They are likely to discuss specific information about the organization and the job, as well as information that is tangential to the operations of the company but still affects the individual lives of the people who work there.

Hickson and Jennings (1993) explain a particular problem related to the informal/formal communication matrix. Casual conversation is supposed to be about casual topics such as, "How is the family? What did you think of the Redskins yesterday? Boy, this elevator is slow, isn't it?" The more a conversation moves toward the work situation, however, the greater the problems it creates. When you and the Vice President are in an elevator and the VP asks, "How's it going?" what does she *mean?* Is it time to pour out all of the complaints that you have about your new job? The answer is probably not. Nevertheless, you need to analyze all informal channels early in your tenure. You need to listen for and observe roles. You need to listen to determine such mundane things as where people go to lunch, who goes to lunch with whom, which workers keep their doors open and which keep theirs closed. In the anticipation process, you must be an observer.

Hickson (1992) also suggests that a newcomer learn to anticipate expected behavior. Over a period of weeks, you should learn to determine the general nature of the conversations that others in the office have with one another. In a sense, you are trying to analyze *roles*. For example, is there a "jokester?" Someone who appears to be the "expert?" In this early stage, in particular, it is important to avoid over-stereotyping. Most people carry out several *different* roles in an organization, and good organizational members can switch between them at a moment's notice.

Next, observe the *rules*. These rules are not stated in any organizational manual. *Rules are norms, they are expected behaviors.* Nevertheless, unstated rules should not be violated, especially by newcomers. One good example might be the office coffeepot or the water fountain. Who gets coffee first? Does anyone take coffee to anyone else? Does anyone ask a secretary for coffee? How long do conversations around the coffee pot last? Who makes the coffee? Are those who do not participate in coffee drinking alienated from others in the department?

Routines should also be observed. When participating in a conference meeting, should you try to get in your two cents' worth? Should you listen only? Listening often helps to determine the roles, rules, and routines of the other participants. Who really makes the decisions at these meetings? More importantly, are decisions really made at this meeting? Were the decisions made prior to the meeting? Is there a pattern about where each member of the group sits? When the final decision is made, to what extent can you attribute it to the discussions in the conference? Whose idea was it?

Using these concepts to gain information about informal communication is quite important. It may even be more important than reading all of the formal (written) information from the policies and procedures manual. However, understanding the formal procedures often helps analyze the informal communication that occurs, as well as predicting when a norm is both expected and what its violation may mean.

You should learn names and positions. Although it is unlikely to happen at this early stage, if the Vice President telephones you and says, "Jane, this is

Mary Gordon," you should know that she is the Vice President and behave accordingly. Understanding the corporate "who is who" provides the content research necessary to engage in substantive and credible dialogue.

These observations allow you to learn about *typicalities of behavior.* You should also be on the lookout for atypical behavior. For example, what kinds of conversations create a furor? An example is found in an instance where one general in the Pentagon was listening to a briefing on military intelligence. The briefers were using color transparencies. One of the colors used in the transparencies was red. The general blurted out, "I hate red. It's bad for my rods and cones." For years after that, even after the general was transferred, individuals in the briefing office said, "Don't use red in the overheads. The general doesn't like it." And the entire story was re-related to each newcomer as part of the socialization process for that particular sub-unit of the organization.

Mary Helen Brown (1985) discusses four phases of socializing into an organization similar to those enumerated earlier. She describes entry, encounter, role-management, and stabilization. Brown suggests that organizations as the employee knows them are composed of stories and myths. Myths, she writes, are "composites of these stories" (p. 28) and these stories allow employees to "express knowledge, understanding, and commitment to the organization" (p. 38). As people become socialized into an organization, the stories that are told seem to better "fit" the organization. Brown and Kreps (1993) suggest that organizational members become story-generating and story-interpreting creatures.

Even though stories may be part of an organization, the interpretation may be different. In general, you should take mental notes on "stories in the organization," for they often tell you much more about what is going on than the formal organizational chart. At the same time, such stories may be exaggerated, even untrue. The teller of the story, however, is trying to make a point to you, something that you must solve as it relates to the organization's cultural milieu.

CASE 5.1   Roles, Rules, and Routines

Using some organization in which you are a member, describe the roles, rules, and routines that are prevalent when you formally meet together. Are you supposed to be early? Late? On time? What do you wear? Who's in charge? Who's really in charge? How serious are the proceedings? What effects does humor have on the proceedings? Who decides on the agenda? Is the agenda flexible? What are the penalties for being absent? What different roles do individuals play in the organization? How are new members brought into the organization? How are new members socialized?

DILBERT / Scott Adams

DILBERT © United Feature Syndicate. Reprinted by Permission.

Researching the Organizational Structure

Using all the information provided thus far, you should have a good idea about how to communicate with others in your office. You should have some central cues about adapting to clients as well. It is important, however, to continue to seek out content information through research, both informal and formal. One of the central means for gaining task information informally is by observing others and taking note of each piece of paper that passes your desk. Also by now you should have read all of the policies and procedures information (formal research).

You should have read the corporate reports for the past three to five years. You should have gone through all of the files in your office left by your predecessor. As early as possible, you should try to analyze those files to determine which ones need to be updated. You should carefully observe "notes" written on files. Handwritten materials are most important. Such notes may tell you something about your predecessor's thinking; once you learn the handwriting of the various people who wrote the notes, you will have learned a great deal about them. You should retain copies of letters, both internal and external. Keeping these copies will help you avoid sending a letter formatted incorrectly. It will also help you maintain a written "memory" of what is discussed in the paperwork.

Part of content research is establishing your own files and calendars. You should develop a name and address file (possibly with sub-files) both on computer and hard copy (Gleeson, 1994). You should begin developing your calendar. One primary advantage of the calendar is finding a pattern of due dates for each year in the future. In this way, you can write in next year's calendar that such-and-such will be due on about a certain date.

In short, files and calendars allow you to *anticipate* meetings and reports. You should begin taking notes about where you gained information, including the name of the person who gave it to you. You might note that the information may come from secretaries. In this case, you should remember to

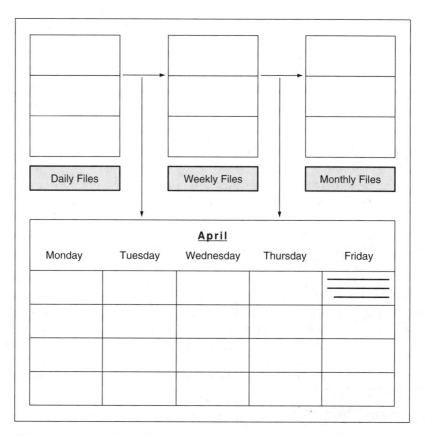

FIGURE 5.2   File and Calendar Structure

thank them—sometimes call just to thank them instead of always calling for more information. If and when you have a secretary, make sure that he or she keeps track of information resources, both organizational and personal.

At the same time, you should set aside time weekly to read information about your work. You need to keep up-to-date on technology, as well as events about your general field. Business magazines, the *Wall Street Journal,* and local newspapers' business sections are important. As you overhear office rumors, you need to verify or refute the information with that you find in publications and on television. Be aware of what your competition is doing. You need to follow the stock market not only about your area of business but also about related businesses. For example, if you find that companies that supply your company are not selling well, it may be a good time to build up your inventory because the prices will be lower.

In brief, you need to be aware of every piece of information that passes your desk or is discussed with you. You are an observer in the truest sense, much like a private detective. Your ultimate goal is to be a "Radar," the character in

M.A.S.H., who could anticipate what was expected of others, as well as what they expected of him. But one word of caution: You should not *appear* to be over-eager or an over worker. As discussed in Chapter 6, such behavior often leads others to fear you as competition, or perceive that you are incompetent, taking too long to perform tasks. Once you have learned to avoid anticipation based on previous experience, you can move on to the second socialization stage, encounter.

ENCOUNTER

The anticipation stage slowly blends into the encounter stage. The *encounter stage* is based on the notion that some of the anticipations were either met inadequately or not met at all (Conrad, 1994). Such anticipations may be about your office, your staff (or lack thereof), your hours, your relationships with colleagues, your relationship with supervisors, your relationship with clients, your available equipment, and so forth. As already mentioned, you must "let go" of your previous situation. It may be, for example, that your new position has a much higher salary, but the computer equipment is not what you are used to. Given this situation, you might think that perhaps your new employer places greater emphasis on personnel (and salaries) than on technology. You may encounter an entirely different language from that you are used to. You may find that your experiences are not what you expected. For these reasons, a systematic approach to continual analysis must be undertaken.

Analyzing the Organizational Encounter

The first step in any continual analysis is to analyze the organization's *culture*. Conrad (1994) points out that there are different kinds of structure in an organization that influence its culture. A culture is "a symbolically constructed way of interpreting reality, making choices about how to act, and making sense out of the actions and messages of others" (Conrad, 1994, p. 47; see also, Smircich, 1983). Different organizations may have cultures that are homogenous (where the organizations have similar cultures, e.g., two computer software companies), differentiated (with different but coordinated subcultures, e.g., a software company and an automobile dealership), or ambiguous (organized into anarchies, i.e., Conrad, 1994). Cultures may be formal, ritualistic, and legalistic, representing bureaucratic cultures where much communication involves "covering one's self" from error. Cultures may be informal, where most of the decisions are made through face-to-face interactions. Your analysis should begin with your own work group.

Work Group Roles

One means of investigating your work group culture is to look at small group interaction and the type of roles people take. Smith (1965, pp. 192–195) has provided a list of possible roles one may play in a small-group, decision-making interaction: the model member. He identifies seventeen different member types:

- The model member
- The eager beaver
- The talker
- The brilliant one
- The emotional one
- The bored one
- The silent one
- The conformist
- The recognition-seeker
- The playboy/playgirl
- The suspicious one
- The non-conformist
- The aggressive one
- The debunker
- The special pleader
- The politician
- The blocker

Again, although it is important to avoid stereotyping, you will find some individuals fairly consistent about the roles they play in organizational interaction. You will also find that people will adopt—adapt to—different roles depending on the situation. The *model member* makes every effort to help the group reach its goals without being concerned about who gets credit for an idea. The *eager beaver* is interested in getting things started and working as quickly as possible; this person often sees a decision as an emergency. The *talker* has a great deal to say in terms of words, but often not in terms of ideas; the talker does not know when to stop talking. The *brilliant one* knows quite a bit and functions well until frustrated with the group because some others are not as bright as they are.

The *emotional one* reacts strongly to suggestions from others in the group; ideas are "entirely off base" or "absolutely right." The *bored one* challenges everyone to say something new and interesting. The *silent one* refuses to talk. The *conformist* can go along with every suggestion, even if one contradicts another. The *recognition-seeker* is capable and ambitious, wanting to be "Mr. Big."

The *playboy/playgirl* is interested in making the meeting a social affair. The *suspicious one* does not believe that anyone can tell the truth. The *nonconformist* wants others to think that he or she is unusual. The *politician* picks fights with the leader by indicating that he has the "inside story." The *aggressive one* wants her ideas accepted no matter what.

The *debunker* has nothing to contribute and believes no one else does either—his purpose is to "knock ideas down." The *special pleader* has her own agenda, which may be based on her ideas or someone else's, but the meeting's most important factor is that the outcome be based on her agenda. Finally, the *blocker* tries to prevent something dangerous from happening at the meeting.

In addition to these roles, you will quickly learn several other *communication roles* as you socialize into the organization. Table 5.1 presents these roles in order of socialization. Before employment, for instance, all of us are interviewees and we are preparing for the workplace. Early in our employment with the organization we simultaneously occupy both formal and informal roles: We are participants in the organization at a very basic level and take on

TABLE 5.1   Communication Roles in the Workplace

Before Employment
Interviewee

Early Employment
Listener
Observer
Researcher
Writer
Presenter
Colleague
Confidant

Manager
Listener
Observer
Researcher
Writer
Presenter
Colleague
Subordinate
Superior
Confidant
Conflict Manager
(Negotiator, Arbitrator)
Leader
Evaluator
Interviewer
Spokesperson
Decision Maker

roles that will lead up to management. As such, we gather knowledge through content research, client-audience analysis, and dialogue. Note, however, that management roles include the basic communication roles learned in early employment. Additional roles are then added to those already mastered.

Linkages

In addition to the roles that members play in meetings (and at other times) it is important to recognize *linkages*. As noted earlier, organizations have both formal and informal linkages or networks. Traditionally, *formal linkages* are constructed from the top down. They represent *formal networks* and who should talk to whom within the organization. Known as a "chain of command," historically such an approach has been used by the military. At each level (from the bottom up), an organizational member communicates only with those at the same level and at the next highest level. Similarly those at the top would ordinarily communicate only with those immediately at the next lower level.

Goldhaber (1993) indicates that there are several types of communication in systems with formal linkages. For *downward communication,* we find that people tend to communicate job instructions, job rationale, procedures and practice, feedback on job performance, and indoctrination of goals. Such communication is usually sent downward through written materials (notices on bulletin boards; policy manuals). This often produces message overload—situations where the information comes faster than the human being can comprehend, store, and act upon it.

Upward communication, in the same context, is usually concerned with asking questions (feedback) and sometimes making suggestions. The idea behind this upward communication is that one person can be directly responsible for only a few others (known as the "span of control"). When a person at the bottom had a complaint, he would take it to his supervisor. When dissatisfied, he would ask if it could be taken to the next level. This pattern could hypothetically be continued all the way to the top. Allowing one to take a complaint to the next level, however, is often seen as a communication defect; the supervisor was essentially telling his boss that he could not handle his job.

Two factors have significantly changed the traditional approach (downward/upward communication) in many organizations. First, with downsizing, most organizations are also "flattening" the traditional triangle in which there were many levels between the top and the bottom. Second, the notion of the "open door" policy by upper-level management has increased the importance of informal systems, sharply reducing the space between levels. Conrad (1994) has referred to this as "open communication." The open door policy is the idea that the executive's door is always open to anyone who wishes to talk. Hypothetically, then, the new organization is one where information is open to employees and the public.

In reality, however, it would be extremely unusual for a custodian to meet with the organization's chief executive. In large measure, this is because the custodian feels that he cannot talk to the president. Additionally, most chief executives do not have time to deal with each and every problem in the organization; this, after all, is the reason that there are so many intermediaries.

Much information is transferred via *informal communication networks.* Such networks are formed in a number of ways and indicate the *patterns* of communication that exist in the organization. Just a few of the possibilities include family relationships, social relationships, and other-organization relationships.

If your brother-in-law works in another unit of the organization, you could gain information that otherwise might be inaccessible. If spouses interact at Little League games, additional information will be available that might not otherwise be. On more than one occasion, your authors have been told that an answer to an organizational question will be forthcoming when the "boss" is seen at church next Sunday. Sometimes such relationships are called "having contacts."

Within your work group are "outside" relationships, which create linkages that otherwise might not occur. Therefore, it is quite important while in the socialization process to learn and take note of such patterns of behavior. If Jill and Judy go to the same gym, if Bob and Tom play golf together, if Harvey and Jane go to the same church, if Carol and Pat both have children on the same Little League team, the results of what goes on at a meeting each has attended are likely to be influenced by such informal network linkages.

Two ways to analyze such networks were suggested by Rogers and Agarwala-Rogers (1976). First, identify *cliques* within the total system and determine how they affect communication in the organization. And, second, identify roles such as liaisons, bridges, and isolates.

For example, in terms of cliques, single people are most likely to interact with other single people in the organization; people with children are more likely to interact with others who have children; employees with things in common are more likely to interact than employees without things in common. Specific roles in these interactive patterns are sometimes more difficult to assess. However, we do know that there are three typical roles. The *isolate* is one who has few contacts with others in the organization. To some extent, you can identify this person as one with little information. A *liaison* is one who connects two or more cliques without being part of either clique. The *bridge* is one who connects two or more cliques, but is a member of at least one of them. (See Figure 5.3.)

Isolates are unlikely to dominate your work group. Generally they have little information because they do not seek a great deal of information; therefore, people do not offer them information because, according to Homans (1961), they have nothing to exchange. The liaison may well be someone outside of your organization entirely. For example, your wife is Jim's sister. She talks with each of you outside of the context of the other, yet she has some influence on both and has some information that may be beneficial to both you and Jim. Even "minor characters" may have some influence in this way. For example, the secretary for several business partners may well have information that he

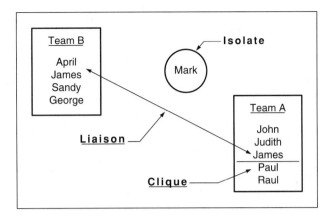

FIGURE 5.3 Cliques, Isolates, and Liaisons

can give to each of the partners that will assist them. The bridge knows information, and you have correctly identified him as a bridge—you know he knows. Because bridges are always on the lookout for information, they have information to exchange in return.

During your socialization into the organization it is important to learn who performs what linkages. In the process of socializing it is important, for example, not to divulge confidential ties as noted in the following example:

> Organization A was going through a massive re-engineering and downsizing. Peggy was employed in the media relations office. She was dating a reporter for the local newspaper. As part of Peggy's job, she took part in a discussion about selling part of the company. She inadvertently "spilled the beans" to her reporter boyfriend. The reporter followed up on the story and reported it on the front page. What Peggy did not know was that Organization A's President had not discussed this possibility with the Board of Directors. The next day Peggy was fired.

Peggy had been operating in a confidential discussion, apparently unaware of the importance of the confidential nature of the conversation. It is questionable whether she knows today why she was fired. In your early days in particular, it is important to share only information that is generally known. You will, of course, appear as one who is "not in the loop," but at the same time there are times when being out of the loop is more secure than being in it. In addition, learning information and not sharing it can increase one's credibility as a confidante. It is also important to "test" the information. Sometimes a simple question such as "How's it going?" will lead others to exchange a wide variety of information, especially if you are seen as someone who is very discreet about what you are told.

How valid is informal information in an organization? According to research by Rudolph (1973), informal information is inaccurate less than 6 percent of the time. Thus, in the encounter stage, you should be aware of the information to be obtained through informal channels. However, it is also important to have some idea what those channels are and what roles the transmitters of that information are playing.

As noted earlier, we assess others' behavior by determining the norms of the culture within which we are operating. How long do co-workers take for lunch? Is there a strict time limit? How do others look at it when colleagues arrive late at work? When they leave early? What comments are made when others must be away from work to care for their children?

In addition to these kinds of expectations, we must pay attention to organizational climate as it relates to *company morale* or job satisfaction. In the encounter stage, most newcomers go through an initial period of "I'm glad I took this job." This is often considered a "honeymoon period" with the company. After about a year and a half or less, most new workers will adopt to their "normal" level of morale and job satisfaction.

Conrad (1994) suggests that as the newcomer you must also assess your own role during the encounter period. He indicates that one may become a *custodian,* simply doing one's job; an *innovator,* generally abiding by rules but also suggesting new ideas; or a *radical,* who tends to violate all expectations of the organization. The third and final stage of socialization into the organization is identification.

IDENTIFICATION

Identification occurs when the neophyte feels a part of the organization. Kelman (1958) proposed an identification structure consisting of three phases—compliance, identification, and internalization—that are helpful in explaining what happens to the neophyte after the encounter stage. In the first phase, compliance, you act in accord with the organization's expectations to "achieve favorable reactions and to avoid censure" (Mohan, 1993, p. 61). Next you must identify with the values of the organization. Finally, during internalization, you have blended together your own values and those of the organizational culture to such an extent that they are usually inseparable.

Miller (1973) says that *functional identity* "emanates from thirdness, law, habit, shared meanings, and has no referent apart from a social process in which one individual can take the role of the other or be in the perspective of the other participant in a social act" (p. 16). Thus, in an organization, we learn to "take the role of the other." In this case, the other is the organizational culture. We learn to retain whatever ideas we have that fit into the new organization. At the same time, we slowly learn to discard those attitudes and behaviors inconsistent with organizational thinking.[2] Thus, as a neophyte you learn to empathize with the company. Such behavior occurs when people indicate that an idea would not be a good idea because "the boss will not like it." Over a period of time, new employees also begin to "mimic" the behaviors and words of others in the organization.

Identification occurs in a variety of ways. The organization presents its culture through many different communications. In-house newsletters, for example, provide general information and help its readers identify with the organization's values. Some of these newsletters are more subtle than others in so doing. The corporate "we" indicates that we are all in one big family; we all identify with one another. Corporate activities, as mundane as the yearly picnic and as exotic as employee–spouse seminars held at resort hotels, help to further establish a corporate identity. Your authors know of many corporations that pay their employees' dues at country clubs and encourage families to participate in golf, tennis, and swimming activities at the club as a way to increase identification with organizational members (thus making it also harder to leave the organization), as well as a way of opening up informal channels and increasing the productivity of the organization.

SUMMARY

After you have taken a new position with a new company, you begin the process of being socialized into the company's culture. The socialization process occurs in three stages: (1) anticipation; (2) encounter; and (3) identification. During the anticipation stage, the newcomer learns to discard former values, behaviors, and thoughts by learning new ones. The new ones are derived from observations of roles, rules, and routines in the organization. The rules are in the form of stated formal structures and policies and procedures. There are also informal rules, usually identifiable only as norms.

In the encounter stage, you learn even more. More values, behaviors, and thoughts are given second consideration. Throughout the encounter stage you are learning the informal norms—expectations—of the organization and becoming "one" with its culture. In large measure, it is at this stage that you decide whether you really want to work in this particular organization.

Through identification, you actually become part of the organization and its culture. Up to this point, you have been somewhat "marginal" (Stonequist, 1937). That is, you find yourself "in-between" your former and new life. Others in the organization treat you that way. Once you identify, however, you are an "organization man or woman" (Whyte, 1956).

CASE 5.2   Socialization

The process of socialization appears difficult for some to master. Discuss why some people have trouble with this important aspect of adapting to organizational life. As a member of the organization what can you do to assist someone in adapting to the organization? How un-socialized does a person have to be to be dismissed from the organization? Why is the socialization process so important?

QUESTIONS FOR THOUGHT

1. There is a "testing" period for beginning the socialization process. What kinds of taboos might an organization have in this initial stage?
2. To what extent do you believe the organizational chart is most important in organizations? Why is there no informal chart?
3. What communication behaviors cause one to be an isolate or a member of a clique? What kinds of problems might each of these roles cause in an organization?
4. As one moves up the organizational ladder, the number of roles appears to increase. How can the president of a company ensure that new workers receive the information that they need to begin work?
5. Socialization appears to cover a great deal of informal communication. What kinds of informal communication ("small talk") does one need to be aware of to succeed in the company? Where does one research these small talk topics?

NOTES

1.   It is important to note that structures are independent of the elements that comprise them. That is, structures are based on positions, not individual personalities. Structures are self-sufficient. Structures have common, and perhaps necessary elements, including wholeness and transformation and continuity. Certain formal structures also tend to create high or low levels of consensus and conflict. For example, in rigid, authoritarian, totalitarian, and ritualistic formal structures there is low consensus (not everyone agrees on goals or methods of getting there) yet there is low conflict because of fear imposed by the structure. It may be referred to as *rigid.* A bureaucratic formal structure creates high consensus and low conflict in large measure because the personnel believe that everyone is operating out of the same set of rules. Such a bureaucracy may be referred to as *institutionalized.* An anarchy, on the other hand, described as *segmented* or *fragmented,* is high in conflict and low in consensus. A democracy is *high* in both conflict *and* consensus. In such a system, people agree on how decisions are made, although they may disagree on outcomes or methods; this bureaucracy may be described as *flexible.*

Berger and Luckmann (1966) have indicated that formal structures create a reality (a culture) that is socially constructed, that people know it, and that it is always at a level of their subconscious. Their "social construction of reality" is not only about appearances, then, but also about the substance (content) of ideas. Such primary reality is the reality of everyday life. For example, in the mid-1990s, there are numerous statistics that indicate that the economy is doing well; however, workers "know" that there are layoffs, downsizing, and overtime commitments. From such a view, "truth" is whatever one believes to be true. Knowledge is socially distributed, and the structure of social relationships is, in part, determined by that social structure.

2.   A "newcomer" does not have to be one person hired by an organization who is just changing jobs or arriving from college. In today's world of re-engineering organizations, many employees may become "newcomers" to their own organization. In the recent "re-structuring"

of the telecommunications industry in the United States, employees of telephone companies must learn to "think" in terms of their companies going into the computer business, or

blending telephone-television-computers-cable. The "old" idea of installing telephones is just part of the "new" business, and hence the "new" culture.

REFERENCES

Barciela, S. (March 11, 1996). Signing could keep you idle. *The Miami Herald,* BM 13.

Berger, P. L., & Luckmann, T. (1966). *The social construction of reality: A treatise on the sociology of knowledge.* New York: Anchor.

Brown, M. H. (1985). That reminds me of a story: Speech action in organizational socialization. *Western Journal of Speech Communication, 49,* 27–42.

Brown, M. H., & Kreps, G. L. (1993). Narrative analysis and organizational development. In S. L. Herndon and G. L. Kreps (Eds.), *Qualitative research: Applications in organizational communication* (pp. 47–62). Creskill, NJ: Hampton.

Conrad, C. (1994). *Strategic organizational communication: Toward the twenty-first century,* 3rd ed. Fort Worth, TX: Harcourt Brace.

Davis, K. (1967). *Human relations at work: The dynamics of organizational behavior.* New York: McGraw-Hill.

Gleeson, K. (1994). *The personal efficiency program: How to get organized to do more work in less time.* New York: Wiley.

Goldhaber, G. M. (1993). *Organizational Communication.* Madison, WI: Brown and Benchmark.

Harper, R. G., Wiens, A. N., & Matarazzo, J. D. (1978). *Nonverbal communication: The state of the art.* New York: John Wiley and Sons.

Hickson, M. III. (1992). Qualitative/descriptive (participant-observation) methodology. In D. W. Stacks & J. E. Hocking. *Essentials of communication research* (pp. 147–172). New York: HarperCollins.

Hickson, M. III, & Jennings, R. W. (1993). Compatible theory and applied research: Systems theory and triangulation. In S. L. Herndon & G. L. Kreps (Eds.), *Qualitative research: Ap-*

plications in organizational communication (pp. 139–157). Creskill, NJ: Hampton.

Hickson, M., Roebuck, J. B., & Murty, K. S. (1990). Creative triangulation: Toward a methodology for studying social types. In N. K. Denzin (Ed.), *Studies in symbolic interaction: A research annual* (pp. 103–127). Greenwich, CT: JAI.

Homans, G. C. (1961). *Social behavior: Its elementary forms.* New York: Harcourt, Brace, and World.

Jablin, F. M. (1987). Formal organizational structure. In F. M. Jablin, L. L. Putnam, K. H. Roberts, & L. W. Porter (Eds.), *Handbook of organizational communication: An interdisciplinary perspective* (pp. 389–419). Newbury Park, CA: Sage.

Kelman, H. C. (1958). Compliance, identification, and internalization: Three processes of attitude change. *Journal of Conflict Resolution, 2,* 51–60.

Mead, G. H. (1934). *Mind, self and society: From the standpoint of a social behaviorist.* Chicago: University of Chicago Press.

Miller, D. L. (1973). *George Herbert Mead: Self, language, and the world.* Austin: University of Texas Press.

Mohan, M. L. (1993). *Organizational communication and cultural vision: Approaches for analysis.* Albany: State University of New York Press.

Morgan, G. (1986). *Images of organization.* Beverly Hills, CA: Sage.

Pace, R. W., & Faules, D. F. (1989). *Organizational communication,* 2nd ed. Englewood Cliffs, NJ: Prentice-Hall.

Pepper, G. L. (1995). *Communicating in organizations: A cultural approach.* New York: McGraw-Hill.

Perinbanayagam, R. S. (1985). *Signifying acts: Structure and meaning in everyday life.* Carbondale, IL: Southern Illinois University Press.

Richmond, V. P., & McCroskey, J. C. (1992). *Organizational communication for survival.* Englewood Cliffs, NJ: Prentice-Hall.

Rogers, E. M., & Agarwala-Rogers, R. (1976). *Communication in organizations.* New York: Free Press.

Rudolph, E. (1973). Informal human communication systems in a large organization. *Journal of Applied Communications Research, 1,* 7–23.

Smircich, L. (1983). Studying organizations as cultures. In Morgan, G. (Ed.), *Beyond method: Strategies for social research* (pp. 160–172). Beverly Hills, CA: Sage.

Smircich, L., & Calas, M. B. (1987). Organizational culture: A critical assessment. In F. M. Jablin, L. L. Putnam, K. H. Roberts, & L. Porter (Eds.), *Handbook of organizational communication: An interdisciplinary perspective* (pp. 228–263). Newbury Park, CA: Sage.

Smith, W. S. (1965). *Group problem-solving through discussion: A process essential to democracy.* Indianapolis: Bobbs-Merrill.

Stohl, C. (1995). *Organizational communication: Connectedness in action.* Thousand Oaks, CA: Sage.

Stonequist, E. V. (1937). *The marginal man.* New York: Scribner's.

Weber, M. (1947). *The theory of social and economic organization.* New York: Free Press.

Whyte, W. F. (1956). *The organization man.* New York: Doubleday.

6

INDIVIDUALITY IN APPRENTICING FOR LEADERSHIP

Asserting Individuality in the Organization
Individuality types and roles
Personality types
Personality orientation
Communication roles in the organization
Traits and roles

Communication Cues and Individuality
Verbal messages
Nonverbal messages
Status and power
Credibility
Review

Socialization and Mentoring
Choosing a mentor
Number of mentors
Career impact

Objectives

By the end of this chapter you should be able to

1. Explain how your personality will affect your role in the organization.
2. Distinguish among different personality types and roles.
3. Explain how communication cues—verbal and nonverbal—will impact on perceptions of your credibility, attraction, and power and status.
4. Explain the process of mentoring as part of both socializing and establishing yourself for organizational leadership.
5. Distinguish between the various mentors and how to select the most appropriate mentor(s).

Part of the socialization process discussed in Chapter 5 has to do with "fitting in." Hopefully, as a college graduate, you will not be hired as a blue-collar worker—someone who does physical or repetitive work. Instead, you are apprenticing yourself to become a *leader* within the organization. This process begins early as you begin to socialize and continues until your decision to quit or retire has been made (and then, possibly, even after). This chapter explores how to maintain individuality while still serving as a viable member of the work team. It then explores the mentoring relationships found in most contemporary organizations.

By now you know that today's organization is neither what your parent's nor their parent's organization was. The old organization was based in large part on a stable workforce, one where workers gave allegiance to the job and, in return, were rewarded by continued blue-collar employment and/or steady white-collar advancement up the organization. As we have explored in earlier chapters, the organization was differentiated by how it treated its employees and, with a little research, the employee could predict how she would be treated. In general, there was grudging support by both management and worker toward a common goal of moving the organization ahead, even if that meant negotiating through sometimes violent strikes.

Today's new organization views its workers—blue- and white-collar—differently. No longer will longevity on the job be the primary criterion for avoiding layoffs associated with downsizing, nor will it predict upward managerial mobility. If you are a gambler, then today's organization is just your cup of tea. However, the new organization still maintains much of the old. It still wants, almost expects, worker loyalty, even though it knows that competition will try to take its best and brightest. It still wants and expects to make a profit, even though it knows that overall competition has increased. Today's new organization is more bottom-line-oriented than ever; with this orientation it is very important that, as a neophyte going through the socialization process, you establish who you are while fitting the organizational mold and demonstrating an ability to manage and lead.

Before we explore this process, think about the type of employee you would hire for a position. Begin with the blue-collar worker—who ARE they? What traits would you look for? Aggressive? Industrious? Loyal? and so forth? What are you looking for in a white-collar worker—someone who might replace you after your first promotion, someone you will manage? Aggressive? Industrious? Loyal? and so forth? How will you evaluate these people? What criteria will you use? Your bosses are pondering the same questions, some of which have not changed in 50 years. What qualities in management will you look for when "raiding" the organization after you have left and created your own company?

How you answer such questions will be in part due to how you were socialized into your organization. Many of your answers will come from those who took you under their wing and taught you "the ropes." These are your mentors, both formal and informal. Some of your answers will come from the type of leader you may become—or your ability to adapt between what we will discuss in Chapter 8 as "leadership styles." And, some of your answers will come from your personal communication patterns, your verbal and nonverbal communication skills in person-to-person (interpersonal) communication, task-oriented (small group) communication, and company (organizational) communication.

We begin with an investigation of the different personalities found in the organization and how these personalities perceive and operate in the organization. We will examine the verbal and nonverbal communication patterns that project your personality. From this we explore mentoring and what it does for the neophyte.

Credibility does not totally rest with the individual; it is a function of how one is perceived by different "audiences." Audiences, in turn, may be those who are working for you, with you, and for whom you work. Learning to adapt to these various audiences is one of the most important immediate lessons neophytes learn in the organization. Who do you speak to? About what? With what effect and affect? Part of establishing yourself is to be YOU, part requires that you adapt to the organization's expectations, part requires that you seek sage counsel. Unfortunately, that seeking often occurs too late and those who may have effectively mentored your way through the organization become references for another job.

ASSERTING INDIVIDUALITY IN THE ORGANIZATION

It takes all types of individuals to run an organization. Almost by definition, working in an organization requires that you work with others. Almost always, when people work together they assert their personalities into the work-group or team. The problems arise when individuals merge with organizations and some trade-off in terms of personality must occur. Organizational and group researchers have studied the impact of the individual versus the group/team approach taken by organizations. Their research suggests that (1) there are certain personalities that emerge when individuals become "organizational people," (2) asserting individuality is both beneficial and troubling for organizational members, (3) at times people can enhance their credibility and attraction by asserting their individuality, and (4) there are subtle communication cues that people can use to enhance their individual credibility and attraction. Communication is used as a tool for adaptation by organizations and individuals.

We begin by looking at the different types of personalities in the organization. We then turn to problems associated with two different "climates" found in most organizations and how the different personalities deal with them. Finally, the various subtle verbal and nonverbal cues that enhance or detract from individuality and personal credibility and attraction in the organization are explored.

Individuality Types and Roles

Karl Weick (1969) argues that no one person can do much within the organization. The statement is probably true. However, we do know based on communication research that some people are easier to work with and more predictable than are others. The personality systems discussed below help us to better understand the communication potential and strategies of the interaction. Knowledge of who you will be engaging in a dialogue and an ability to adapt your communication to the situation or people around you should enhance your communication effectiveness.

Personality Types

What is a personality and what are organizational personalities? Personality traits are relatively constant aspects of ourselves. That is, they define how we see ourselves and others and influence our communication patterns. Sometimes we will adopt a particular communication role as part of an interaction or organizational personality. Sometimes people take on different roles to achieve different outcomes. Confusing? Welcome to the world of organizations. Let's look at some of the "personality" systems you might find in an organization.

McCroskey and Richmond (1992) note that there are 12 different personality types people encounter in the organization. They are defined in large part through their outlook on organizational life. That is, some see work as positive, others as negative, and still others as a necessary evil. The personalities and a short profile indicate much about them and how to deal with them.

- *Upwardly Mobile.* This person lives to work and likes the organizational status quo. She is the up-and-comer who wants to and will advance in the organization. She exemplifies the "organizational type." Upwardly mobiles traditionally work within organizational limits and are supportive of the organization and its policies.
- *Indifferent.* This person works to live. He accepts the status quo and focuses not on the organization but on family and personal things. Don't expect much of the indifferent.
- *Ambivalent.* This person wants change, rejects structure, and is openly critical of the system. He is uncomfortable in the system and is creative and anxious while working in the system. Ambivalents are unpredictable, often working against authority and the system.
- *Authoritarian.* Almost the opposite of the ambivalent, she is rigid and feels in control. Her approach is rule-oriented and framed within a rigid organizational hierarchy. She is predictable and respectful of authority, believes in power and status, and expects obedience.

- *Machiavellian.* Very unpredictable, except that whatever he is after he gets, anyway he can. Machiavellians are manipulators who manipulate because they enjoy it. For them, the end justifies the means employed to get to it.
- *High Achiever.* This person is the classic overachiever. She sets goals and meets them. She is the organizational workhorse. Not often upwardly mobile in her approach, she enjoys work, but because she sets high goals for herself is often left unfulfilled and self-critical.
- *Dogmatic.* This person is often perceived as difficult, although not necessarily so. He sees the world in a simplistic, concrete way. Like the authoritarian, he respects authority and power, placing great faith in what those above him say and believe. Obviously, he has a very narrow definition of problems and goals.
- *Low Verbal.* This person is quiet, almost shy. She may lack self-concept and be seen as less competent than others. She does not initiate communication, and when communicating will be brief and nonresponsive. Low verbals may be good workers, but are not seen as such within the organization.
- *High Verbal.* This person is the opposite of the low verbal. He is compelled to communicate and this overcommunication tends to reduce his effectiveness and credibility. High verbals are adept listeners who often can observe problems that others do not.
- *Argumentative.* This person can find something to take issue with. She often can argue either side of the issue, pointing out positives and negatives. She views disagreements as exciting and enjoys the debate over issues, often challenging anyone for the mere pleasure of verbal combat. People tend to range from low to high on argumentativeness (Infante & Rancer, 1982) and McCroskey and Richmond note that high and low argumentatives do not make good teammates.
- *Inadequate.* This person, like many low verbals, is low in self-esteem, often feeling that he can never live up to organizational expectations. He rejects both his work and his own worthiness.
- *Oversocial.* This person has a high need for affiliation. She sees all situations as social, hence she has difficulty focusing on the task or problem at hand. She will probably help achieve group cohesion in situations where task groups are composed of upwardly mobile, authoritarian, high achiever, argumentative, personalities. She will not do well with high or low verbals or dogmatics.

In time you will meet all twelve types. Knowing how to identify them and their communication patterns is a necessary content research requirement. It should be noted, too, that you will adopt one or more of these personality types as you work and live in the organization. At times you will do so strategically; you will adopt a personality because it is the best approach to the problem. You most likely, however, possess one personality type that best describes you; knowledge of your own personality type or role will help you in your interactions with others.

Personality Orientation

A slightly different approach to individualism comes from the work of John Holland (1973). Holland was interested in identifying personality as it related to organizational environments. He found six basic personality types. *Artistic personalities* are concerned with self-expression, creativity, individualism, and emotions. *Conventional personalities* are concerned with rules, roles, and routines and are identified with power and status. *Enterprising personalities* are individuals who enjoy verbal jousting and manipulation and aspire for status and power. *Investigative personalities* are thinkers, organizers, and theorists who prefer to work alone and are interested in mental activity. *Realistic personalities* are aggressive individuals who are interested in motor skills, strength, and coordination (physical) activities. And *social personalities* are individuals who like others and interpersonal relationships but avoid mental or physical activity.

Holland's thesis was that certain personality traits were best suited for certain positions. Figure 6.1 indicates his hexagonal model of personality relationships. Personalities that are adjacent would be complementary. For instance, if your personality orientation were artistic, you would work best with investigative and social types.

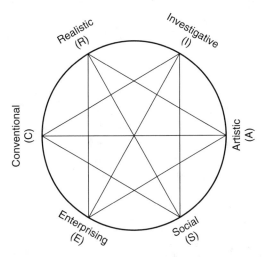

FIGURE 6.1   Holland's Personality Orientation Hexagonal Model

Source: John H. Holland et al. (1969). An empirical occupational classification derived from a theory of personality and intended for practice and research. ACT Research Report No. 29. Iowa City, IA: The American College Testing Program. Reproduced with permission.

Communication Roles in the Organization

Considering McCroskey and Richmond and Holland's personality types, it is clear that what we are dealing with are certain underlying personal traits and certain preferences or orientations toward the organization. In many instances we can identify certain predominant roles that people play in the organization. Benne and Sheets (1948) identified such organizational roles as three different, but mutually dependent, organizational activities. In some regards they are similar to those roles discussed in earlier chapters.

Self-centered roles are dysfunctional behaviors that arise from individual needs or desires. Self-centered roles include the blocker, aggressor, deserter, dominator, recognition seeker, confessor, playboy, and special pleader. These roles are not focused on the organization's needs, but rather on the individual's needs and goals.

Task roles are concerned with goal achievement and task accomplishment. Task roles include the initiator-contributor, information seeker, information giver, opinion seeker, opinion giver, elaborator-clarifier, coordinator, diagnostician, orienter-summarizer, energizer, procedure developer, secretary, evaluator-critic. These roles focus on the organization's needs and, in particular, on the accomplishment of whatever task has been assigned.

Maintenance roles are concerned with the social climate and interpersonal relationships within the organization. Maintenance roles include the supporter-encourager, harmonizer, tension reliever, compromiser, gatekeeper, feeling expresser, standard setter, and follower. These roles focus on establishing an environment that allows the task to be accomplished effectively and with as little dysfunction as possible.

Traits and Roles

As you look over the different personalities and roles found in the organization it should be quickly apparent that certain personality traits or orientations pair up with certain organizational roles. Understanding which individuals will take on what roles should maximize your communication potential. Through an understanding of what roles are expected of you at various stages of your organizational career, you can maximize your performance.

Although Weick (1969) may be correct in noting that no one person can do much within the organization, his perspective fails to appreciate what an informed individual can do to maximize his or her potential. As Wilmot (1980) has argued, we often become trapped in self-fulfilling prophecies based on expected or perceived communicative behavior. Understanding the roles and the personalities that drive us to take those roles provides a variety of communication strategies that may be applied to specific situations (audiences).

COMMUNICATION CUES AND INDIVIDUALITY

Many of the personality traits and roles identified thus far are couched in negatives. That is, except for a few traits and roles, they demonstrate credibility and attraction problems. Communication cues can enhance credibility and attraction and thus help you move up the organizational hierarchy. Such communication cues may include both verbal and nonverbal elements. Talking too much, not talking enough, talking too loudly, too many "ahs," or "and ahs," disorganized phrasing, are all detrimental communication cues. Repeating what another has said, giving credit, complimenting are positive communication cues.

The ability to communicate effectively is a plus in any situation, but more so in organizations. Because people must work with others to achieve some common task or goal, being able to (1) understand what is being asked of you (listen and decode the message) and (2) relate that message to others (encode the message's meaning and relate the message) in such a manner as to be persuasive requires an understanding of how both verbal and nonverbal messages operate. Individuals who are adaptive and socialized are rewarded and feel secure.

Verbal Messages

Organizations are characterized by their passing of messages from person to person and group to group. There are many problems inherent in verbal message processing, beginning with the symbolic nature of language itself. Quite simply, *the word is NOT the thing* (Ogden & Richards, 1923). Reacting to language is extremely dangerous. As we will see in later chapters, carefully responding to messages—especially negative or critical messages—is extremely important in establishing individual credibility. At the same time, the use of certain language can enhance or detract credibility and persuasiveness (e.g., Bowers, 1963; Miller & Burgoon, 1973).

DILBERT / Scott Adams

DILBERT © United Feature Syndicate. Reprinted by Permission.

Hickson and Hill (1975) have argued that whenever someone tells you something you need to look at three underlying things about the message. First, *why is this person telling me this?* What political or social or task considerations does the message contain? People communicate intentionally; they do so for some reason. What is that reason? Second, *how does this person know?* This may be a feature of the communication network: In formal (vertical or horizontal) situations, it is probably task-oriented and requires action; if informal, it may be social (and can be used to better understand the environment or others within that environment) or rumor-based ("grapevine"), providing claims but no supporting facts. And, third, *why is this person telling me this?* Is immediate action required or should the message be passed or delegated to someone else? Can it be done? Is it a warning? Listening to messages requires more than simply "hearing" the words, it requires active interpretation.

Messages are composed of words that may or may not enhance the message. We know from research that how you construct your message—how intense the message is—impacts its reception. Table 6.1 lists a number of words and their ability to motivate others. Notice that words such as "poor" as in "That is a poor idea," are low in motivation. Will such a message motivate you? Contrast that to "That is a bad idea" or "That is a terrible idea." The low language intensity of "poor idea" does not threaten or motivate. The "bad" message's intensity is moderate, it threatens but should not cause the recipient to become overly defensive. The "terrible" message is highly intense and may

TABLE 6.1   Language Intensity

Low Intensity[1]	Moderate Intensity	High Intensity
Poor	Very good	Like extremely
Like Moderately	Like quite a bit	Like intensely
OK	Enjoy	Excellent
Average	Highly unfavorable	Wonderful
Mildly like	Bad	Terrible
Not pleasing	Preferred	Strongly like
Fair	Good	Like very much
Acceptable	Welcome	Mighty fine
Only fair	Pleasing	Especially good
Like slightly	Like fairly well	Mighty favorable
	Like	Very bad

Source: M. Burgoon & G. R. Miller (1971). Prior attitude change and language intensity as predictors of message style and attitude change following counterattitudinal advocacy. *Journal of Personality and Social Psychology, 20*, p. 249. Copyright © 1971 by the American Psychological Association. Reprinted with permission.

[1]Higher the word or term is on the list, the higher the term is in perceived language intensity.

"boomerang" (e.g., Sherif, Sherif, & Nebergall, 1965), producing too much motivation and threat. We will explore this topic further in the next chapter.

Note that our discussion of verbal communication is rule-driven. That is, if we use language that is too abstract ("capital," "assets"), we may have problems communicating with others whose contextual dictionary defines the same terms concretely ("dollars and cents," "house," "car"). Note, too, that these rules produce expectations. Violating verbal *expectations* can be beneficial when done in a positive way, but requires an understanding of how messages are communicated in that particular organization. This is especially true with modern communications such as e-mail, which provide symbolic language (words and sentences) but very little context. Thus you might get a fairly intense message with a "happy face" (a colon and parenthesis   :)) added to it (almost nonverbal!). Shimanoff (1980) notes that verbal communication rules are prescriptive (they tell us how to interpret the communication), contextual (they apply in *similar* situations), and followable (they produce some sort of behavior).

Reacting to communication is extremely important in the modern organization. As noted in earlier chapters, the organization is a vast information-processing machine. Knowing which messages are important, understanding why a message may be sent and through which network, and how to respond (act, behave) will enhance your credibility with others and make you more attractive to those above you in the organization.

Nonverbal Messages

While verbal messages are intentional, nonverbal messages are not.[1] Nonverbal messages often function unintentionally—that is, they convey information to others that may or may not be intended as messages. Pulling on clothing during a job interview may not be intentional but often implies nervousness. Being late for an appointment may not be intentional, but it implies that you do not see the other person as important, credible, or powerful. Such messages, however, are often *intentionally* sent, but the receiver may not perceive the intentional nature of the message. Thus, nonverbal messages are important cues indicating status, power, and credibility.

Nonverbal messages have been analyzed from a number of approaches. The simplest is by *subcode*. While language itself is a verbal code, all the other things that might contribute to the message are nonverbal code. Some nonverbal subcodes have been defined as *spatial* in nature (consisting of the actual environment of a communication, a location; territory, parts of the environment that are marked off for use such as public, private, and body; personal space, elements of the territory that are used by the individual and extend from the person's body territory; and touch, the violation of body territory). One subcode (physical appearance) is *social* in nature, consisting of perceptions of individuals based on their body and the way the body is adorned. Other subcodes are either *overt* (body language and the voice) or *covert* (time perception and smell); that is, they are "seen" or "unseen" in the interaction but impact on perceptions of status, power, and credibility just the same (Hickson & Stacks, 1992).

Status and Power

Nonverbal messages conveying status and power include where your office or office space is located. Working from a permanent office as compared to a temporary space or from your auto or home conveys different status and power messages. A clean desk compared to a messy desk does the same. In a meeting, powerful people sit where they can control the interaction (at the end of a table or on the side with fewer others). Low-status people often sit behind high-status people. Closed doors versus open doors, as well as having someone to screen your visitors (secretary) are all spatial nonverbal messages of power and status. How long you can keep someone waiting is a powerful message of power and status. Whether you approach others or they approach you also indicates relative power and status. Dress and general physical appearance all are important power and status indicators; in general, powerful people dress better than nonpowerful people do. In terms of body language, powerful people establish eye contact and control the interaction; less powerful people engage in more head nodding and body leans. Higher status and powerful people initiate touch; lower status and less powerful people reciprocate touch. High-status people control conversation through pauses and establish whether the interaction is pleasant or unpleasant through conversational synchrony (I speak, you speak, I speak. . . .) or asynchrony (I speak, you speak, pause, I speak. . . .).

Credibility

Credibility is enhanced primarily through the overt and covert subcodes. Being on time enhances credibility if you are a subordinate; making a subordinate wait increases perceived superior credibility. Most research indicates that credibility is enhanced through the voice and gestures. The high credible voice is strong, resonant, and a little faster and smoother than the low credible voice. Gestures that enhance credibility include those used to emphasize points, that are spontaneous, relaxed, and unrehearsed (i.e., "natural" and show that you are in control), that clearly indicate you wish to speak or want the other to speak (establishing eye contact, breaking eye contact, self-gesture versus pointing to the other), that are away from the body, and that indicate feelings and emotion.

Credibility is reduced when the voice is weak and hesitant, perceived to be nasal or denasal (a "whiner" or someone with a cold), flat, or *too* fast. Negative gestures include poor posture, leaning away from the other (a sign of power and status), defensive and nervous gestures (to include self-touch, lip licking, hand wringing, grimacing, inappropriate smiles), body rigidity and tension, and consistent body shifts, to include leg crossing and uncrossing.

Review

How you communicate tells others a lot about what to expect from you. It allows them to predict how you will react to given situations and provides cues for message strategies designed to manipulate you. Understanding your personality and the expected role or roles you are to take in the organization is the first step in conveying messages that establish your credibility, status, and power position. Verbal messages are rule-oriented. Knowing the organization's communication "rules" and what their violations result in is an important research agenda in establishing how you are seen as an individual in that organization. Nonverbal communication is based on expectations. Knowing what those expectations are and communicating appropriately enhances your credibility and status and ultimately your power. Knowing when to violate those expectations may be even more important to career success.

Once you understand your communication potential, as seen both personally and by others, it is time to seek help from others in the organization to master the organization's many communication rules, roles, and routines. The final step in establishing who you are is to seek someone who can help you master the organization, the mentor.

SOCIALIZATION AND MENTORING

By now it should be obvious that organizational life requires you to work with a variety of people, all of whom will have an impact on how fast you advance up the organization's hierarchy. If you have done your homework—understand your personality traits and the organizational roles that you would fill as well as those small communication pluses that emphasize you and your abilities—it is time to seek out someone to help you up the organizational ladder. It is time to seek out a *mentor*.

Mentoring is not a new concept. First mention of someone advising and coaching another comes from the ancient Greeks. Homer's mentor advised Odysseus and his son, Telemachus, becoming Telemachus' guardian, teacher, and parent figure. Since then there have been many famous mentor–protégé relationships.

The modern mentoring process, however, may be traced back to the apprentice–master relationship begun when specialized occupations evolved. In those days the apprentice–master relationship was legal; you would apprentice for a number of years to gain the skills of the master. As an apprentice your relationship was almost slave-like, in fact it might be considered legalized slavery. You belonged to the master, trading your physical and mental abilities for instruction in the area of apprenticeship.

We do not find apprenticeship in today's organizations. But we still hang on to the idea that there is something to be learned by associating with someone who has already mastered the organization at a higher level. Interestingly,

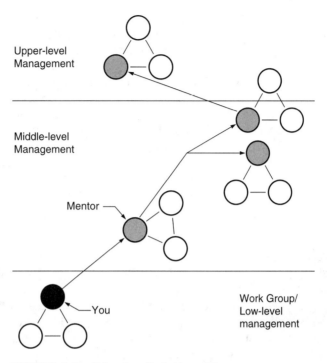

Upper-level
Management

Middle-level
Management

Mentor

You

Work Group/
Low-level
management

FIGURE 6.2   Mentor Relationships

little research has explored mentorship in the modern organization. What little research has been conducted is primarily in the form of "this person helped me through this or that stage" of socialization (e.g., Burke, 1984; Kram, 1985, 1988).

Mentorship is extremely important as you begin to socialize into an organization. In general, there are two types of mentors. One type is a formal mentor, someone you are associated with—either you picked them or they picked you—who serves as your guide and counselor throughout much of your organizational life. The other is the informal mentor, the person you observed from afar and who influenced your behavior. Over a career you will have many mentors. Some may be professional, others social, still others filling unknown roles at this time. The important thing to realize is that each mentor sets you on a certain path, influences your decisions, and may even share in your successes and/or failures.

The academic system you are now in is steeped in mentorship. Your professors each had several mentors. One brought them through the process of receiving their doctorates and served as both professional behavior and research model. In many instances knowing who your professors studied with (were mentored by) tells you much about their approach to education and research. They, in turn, often serve as mentors to their students. Unlike a graduate student, most undergraduate students cannot name a professor who served as a formal mentor. However, they can name a professor or two who set them on the right track, who spent a little more time with them and advised them about professional and personal concerns. Often these professors end up serving as reference persons.

What we know about the mentoring process indicates that it is important, especially at the earlier stages of a career, but as noted earlier, research is sketchy and focused more on the mentor impact on minorities and females. What research is available, however, seems to indicate that the mentorship process works about the same for males as females (e.g., Baugh & Scandura, 1996). Thus, there are some lessons we can draw from the limited research available. In particular you should be concerned with choosing (or being chosen by) a mentor, the number of mentors you have at any one time, and the impact a mentor may have on your career.

Choosing a Mentor

After choosing an organization, identifying and choosing a mentor may be the single most important choice you make in establishing your career and career path. It should be noted that not all successful managers and leaders have had *formal* mentors; however, research indicates that organizational success, job satisfaction, and role acceptance is associated with having one or more mentors (Baugh & Scandura, 1996).

Although most organizations do not have formal mentoring programs, almost all organizations engage in and encourage informal mentoring of employees. They understand that mentoring helps in three areas: psycho-socialization (support), role modeling, and career orientation (Baugh & Scandura, 1996; Burke, 1984; DeWine, 1994; Egan, 1994; Eisenbach, Tepper, & Brown, 1985; Kram, 1985; Noe, 1988; Scandura & Katerberg, 1988; Schockett & Haring-Higdore, 1985). Thus, a mentor may help you socialize into the organization, offer guidance into the psychological and political dramas that you will participate in, provide emotional support, and counsel you when necessary. The mentor may also serve as an organizational "coach," providing both challenges and protection, exposing you—inoculating you—to potential pitfalls as you learn the organizational ropes. A mentor may serve as a role model for organizational behavior (both positively and negatively).

Choosing the wrong mentor, especially in today's organization, can be devastating to a career. Aligning with the wrong person—the complainer, the social critic, the "lone eagle"—will reflect on your ability to make intelligent decisions. Therefore, it is imperative that you spend some time researching potential mentors, people who are two or more levels above you (it is not a good idea to have an immediate boss as a mentor, you are just too close and you may be seen as competition for the same position). To do so requires that you continue your research in the organization.

In many instances new employees will be "adopted" by their mentors. They have demonstrated certain traits or abilities that the "older" mentor sees and believes can either be of help to him or her or believes demonstrate potential for the organization. Clearly, you have no part in this choice; either you accept the mentor and are socialized as a "team player" by others observing the process or you are seen as a "loner" who seeks to make his or her own way through the organization. However, if you have done your research early on in your organizational career you may influence the process. Should you openly ask for a mentor? Research clearly is lacking regarding this most important question. However, by engaging in *content research* (who has served as mentors? in what capacity? how did they come to choose their protégés?), *client analysis* (psychologically, who are you and who are potential mentors? what are your needs and their needs?), and then adapting your *communication dialogue* to establishing rapport with potential mentors, you may well influence the mentoring process toward your long-term goals.

Katheryn Egan (1994) identified two different types of workers, one career-oriented and in control of the learning process, and the other working better within "the system."[2] She defined these styles as constructivist and proceduralist; each style can be seen as a combination of the traits and roles discussed earlier in the chapter. The *constructivist,* who combines experience and objective learning, is not afraid to work outside the system and often creates personal frames of reference for the job and organization. Egan has noted that the constructivist is "likely to succeed at whatever goal" is chosen (p. 87). The *proceduralist* conforms to expectations, works within the system, and seeks gratification by pleasing those within the system. Both personality styles are seen as "winners"—they both advance (albeit at different paces and in different directions) through the organization's hierarchy.

Egan also notes that there are potential mentors in the organization with similar personalities and that matching your personality to the mentor's is important in establishing a good working relationship. Thus, if you are a go-getter, someone who defines the situation as you see it and can frame the objectives, goals, and data in a way different than the system, your mentor should possess those same capabilities. On the other hand, if you like to work within the system and enjoy being rewarded for advancing the organization's goals as defined by the organization, then your mentor should view the job likewise.

The difference between personalities is clearly motivational. Egan points out that where organizations assign mentors to new employees, the motivation to establish a working mentor–protégé relationship may be lacking. When establishing mentoring relationships, then, the first question to answer is how that relationship is established and second, who is available to serve as mentor.

Other than personality type, what characteristics differentiate mentors? DeWine, Casbolt, and Bentley (1983) identified ten different types of mentor: Parent, White Knight, Mentor-to-Friend, Badger, Seductive Manipulator, Guilt Trip Producer, King/Queen, Self-Promoter, Cheerleader, and Groom. The labels are indicative of the type of person the mentor might be and what the mentor–protégé relationship will probably be.

CASE 6.1   Choosing a Mentor

Jane has been with the company only nine months, but wants to "learn the ropes." There are three senior workers in the same office as Jane. Barbara, age thirty-five, has been with the company fourteen years, since she graduated from A & M. She has been promoted twice. She stays at work late at night and sometimes works on weekends. Lee, forty-five, has been with the company seventeen years. He seems to get along with almost everyone in the company. He has been promoted once. He has a good sense of humor, and he likes to go out with colleagues to have a good time. He will retire in five more years. Beth, forty-six, has been with the company only five years. She has little social interaction except about business. She rarely works late, but she keeps to herself. She has been promoted twice. Which of the three should Jane select as a mentor? Why might she select one of the others? What are the advantages and disadvantages of selecting one over the other? How should Jane approach one about being her mentor?

The *parent* and *white knight mentors* are more prone to establish relationships based on "wise counsel" and "older and wiser" experience. Such mentors use their positions and achievements as motivators to their protégés. The *mentor-to-friend mentor* often begins as the protégé's sponsor and through the socialization process serves as an informal mentor once the new worker is socialized into the organization. Both constructivist and proceduralist personalities would benefit from such a mentor–protégé relationship.

Badger mentors motivate through challenges and demand excellence in their protégés. *Seductive manipulators* work behind the scenes to provide opportunities and direction to the protégé—often carefully planned and designed to promote within the system. The *guilt trip mentor* constantly focuses on negatives, on the protégé letting the system down. The relationship is more like a disappointed parent. Constructivist personalities would probably bloom under a badger mentor, likely becoming one themselves. Proceduralists would do much better under the tutelage of the seductive manipulator or the guilt trip mentor, although job satisfaction would not be enhanced by the latter relationship.

King/queen and *self-promoter mentors* are driven by a dictatorial and authoritarian personality and surround themselves with only the best and brightest. Obviously, this situation would be a proceduralist's nightmare.

Cheerleaders are mentors who see their role much like the parent, white knight, or mentor-to-friend. They observe protégé progress and offer encouragement, cheering the individual on as he or she progresses through the organization. Cheerleaders probably work within the system; therefore, the proceduralist would probably prosper under their tutelage. *Grooms,* on the other hand, are already in positions of power and can move their protégés up the organization through special assignments and access to critical information. The constructivist would probably fare better in a groom–protégé relationship, being able to create new opportunities from the information and assignments offered.

Number of Mentors

Although it may seem intuitive that having more mentors is better than fewer, research suggests that this is not always the case. If the mentor–protégé relationship is to work it must work as a partnership, almost like a marriage. Such relationships are difficult and require much maintenance, and maintenance takes time and effort. Baugh and Scandura (1996) surveyed 275 high-ranking managers about mentors and organizational assimilation. They found that male and female managers who had one or two mentors reported enhanced organizational assimilation, but those with more than two mentors were less satisfied with their assimilation. They did report, however, that those who self-reported no formal mentors were much less satisfied with their assimilation, with lower satisfaction with their jobs, career expectations, perceived employment alternatives, organizational commitment, and less successful role in the organization.

Career Impact

Almost all organizational leadership research reports that someone influenced someone else on the way to top management positions. It may be, however, that the traditional mentor–protégé relationship has changed. Just as we moved from apprenticeship to mentorship in the organization, we may have to redefine just who or what a mentor is. A different way of looking at mentors is their impact on your career at differing points in time. It is also important to look at the mentor in terms of what he or she can provide you in your advancement up the organizational ladder.

At the beginning you should find someone to mentor you. However, given the fluidity of organizations now, a formal career-orienting mentor may be neither available nor advisable. When organizations "owned" management—when management within a given organization was the rule and "jumping ship" to other organizations was the exception—mentoring was a natural process of one or two people teaching you the ropes. Now, however, a mentor may be with you today and gone tomorrow. Therefore, we need to examine mentorship at three different levels: initial socialization; team mentors; and out-of-organization mentors. Obviously, there is a timeline here; different people will mentor at different times and provide different input to advancing your career (see Figure 6.3).

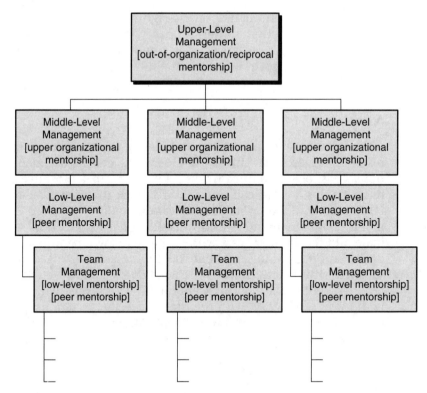

FIGURE 6.3   Types of Mentorships

When first introduced to the organization you should seek a mentor of some kind. That mentor should be at least one (and preferably two) level(s) above your current position. As such, your "formal" mentor will most likely occupy a low-level managerial position. This person should serve both a career and emotional function, teaching the ropes while serving as sounding board for problems and frustrations. This is the classic mentor–protégé relationship. However, it may be that this mentor does not have the expertise necessary to advance your career; he or she may not possess the necessary state-of-the-art skills the twenty-first century worker will need. Therefore, you will need to identify a peer who possesses those skills (other than the ones you bring to the position).

Most low-level managers have not relinquished their relationships with their initial mentors. In many instances, this is the mentor-to-friend relationship (DeWine *et al.*, 1988) described as one form of mentor. At this stage, then, peer mentorship is still important. However, at this stage we might define a second type of peer mentorship, the first outside of the organization. That peer mentor may be electronic, taking the form of an *e-mail mentor*—someone you may never see—discussing general problems and solutions with you through your computer and modem. This mentor will be up-to-date technologically and facing the same problems as you. In most instances they are at a similar organizational level.

Upon achieving middle-level management you should look for an upper-level or even a reciprocal mentor. Many people find themselves "trapped" at middle-level management. Perhaps the "Peter Principle" truly came to be; perhaps they find themselves unmotivated to fight for upper-level management; perhaps this is as far as they can go in their particular organizational system. Most likely, their mentors are equal to them, have stopped challenging them, or have moved on to other protégés. A reciprocal—an out-of-organization—mentor may be appropriate here, one that can help you by directing your career as both a potential competitor (sounds strange, but most upper-level people communicate often with rivals, sharing information and ideas) and as a possible manager in their organization.

Mentorship along this line is not exactly what it was forty years ago, but then forty years ago people entered an organization with the idea of retiring from that organization. Choosing an *appropriate* mentor for your needs may be more important than ever before. That person may or may not be in your organization. Your mentor relationships may include one or two mentors, at the same organizational level and above. Whatever your position, however, advancement will probably be easier with someone providing help from the sidelines. Research carefully potential mentors and get into dialogue with them as soon as possible.

SUMMARY

This chapter has explored how individuals operate in the organization. Although Weick (1969) argues that individuals have little influence, we note that you can use your individuality to establish yourself in the organization. We began by looking at what personality types and roles are found in the organization. Each is based in part on your personal make-up and in part on how you see yourself in that organization. Understanding and identifying personalities and roles is important research in becoming an effective organizational communicator, especially when working with or for others.

We then turned to the subtle communication skills necessary to survive. We first looked at verbal messages, noting that they are intentional and rule-oriented. Knowing who said what to whom through what channels helps you devise message and behavioral strategies. We also looked at nonverbal messages, noting they are less intentional and have significant impact on perceived credibility, status, and power. Finally, we explored the mentorship process, looking at what mentors can do for the neophyte and experienced organizational member, as well as how to select the mentor best suited for your personal organizational needs.

CASE 6.2   Dysfunctional Mentoring

Jane has now been with the company three years, and she is quite impressed with Joe, her supervisor. For the past few weeks, they have been working on a major project together. They sometimes have late dinner together after they have finished their work. Joe has asked Jane out three times, and Jane has become uncomfortable saying "no." She would like for Joe to be her mentor, but she does not want to have a romantic relationship with him. What kind of mentor might Joe be? What are the possible repercussions for Jane? For Joe? How should this situation be handled? [You might want to compare your thoughts with information in Chapter 12.]

QUESTIONS FOR THOUGHT

1. In Chapter 5, we mentioned that you have to give up some of who you are to become socialized into the organization. To what extent do you have to give up to move up the ladder of success?
2. In terms of communication, describe some of your best and worst traits in interpersonal communication. Include verbal and nonverbal aspects.
3. Assume that you are working as a writer for an advertising agency. How would you try to communicate with the artistic personalities of the art department as opposed to the engineers who work with television equipment?
4. Re-read the section on task types. Identify some specific questions or statements that you might make in a meeting to let it be known that you are a task-oriented person.
5. Using the three questions about what might underlie a message (What do you mean? How do you know? Why are you telling me this?), describe how each of those questions can be asked of another in a more tactful way.

NOTES

1. For more on intentionality, see Burgoon & Ruffner (1978); and Hickson & Stacks (1992).

2. Egan's (1994) research was conducted on females who were seeking tenure at academic institutions. However, it is clear that her definitions of "constructivist" and "proceduralist" are applicable to males also.

REFERENCES

Baugh, S. G., & Scandura, T. A. (1996). Is more really better? The effect of multiple mentors on protégé attitudes toward the work setting. Paper presented at the Academy of Management, Cincinnati, OH.

Benne, K., & Sheets, P. (1948). Functional roles of group members. *Journal of Social Issues, 41*, 19–23.

Bowers, J. W. (1963). Language intensity, social introversion, and attitude change. *Communication Monographs, 30*, 345–352.

Burgoon, M., & Ruffner, M. (1978). *Human Communication.* New York: Holt, Rinehart, and Winston.

Burke, R. J. (1984). Mentors in organizations. *Group and Organization Studies, 9*, 353–372.

DeWine, S. (1994). *The consultant's craft: Improving organizational communication.* New York: St. Martin's.

DeWine, S., Casbolt, D., & Bentley, N. (1983, May). Moving through the organization: A field assessment of the patron system. Paper presented at the International Communication Association, Dallas, TX.

Egan, K. S. (1994). Flexibility makes the difference in mentoring women for academic success. *Journal of the Association for Communication Administration, 2,* 87–94.

Eisenbach, R. J., Tepper, B. J., & Brown, S. J. (1985). Conceptual and empirical distinctions between leadership, mentorship, and mentoring functions. Paper presented at the Western Academy of Management, San Diego, CA.

Hickson, M. L., & Hill, S. R. (1975). *The progress of communication.* Starkville, MS: Communication Applications, Inc.

Hickson, M. L., & Stacks, D. W. (1992). *NVC: Nonverbal communication studies and applications,* 3rd ed. Dubuque, IA: Brown & Benchmark.

Holland, J. H. (1973). *Making vocational choices: A theory of careers.* Englewood Cliffs, NJ: Prentice-Hall.

Kram, K. E. (1985). *Mentoring at work.* Glenview, IL: Scott, Foresman.

Kram, K. E. (1988). *Mentoring at work. Developmental relationships in organizational life.* New York: University Press of America.

McCroskey, J. C., & Richmond, V. P. (1992). *Organizational communication for survival.* Englewood Cliffs, NJ: Prentice-Hall.

Miller, G. R., & Burgoon, M. (1973). *New techniques of persuasion.* New York: Harper & Row.

Noe, R. A. (1988). An investigation of the determinants of successful assigned mentoring relationships. *Personal Psychology, 41,* 457–470.

Ogden, C. K., & Richards, I. A. (1923). *The meaning of meaning: A study in the influence of language upon thought and the science of symbolism.* New York: Harcourt, Brace, and World.

Scandura, T. A., & Katerberg, C. A. (1988). Much ado about mentors and little ado about measurement: Development of an instrument. Paper presented at the Academy of Management, Anaheim, CA.

Schockett, M. R., & Haring-Higdore, M. (1985). Factor analytic support for psychosocial and vocational mentoring functions. *Psychological Reports, 57,* 627–630.

Sherif, C. W., Sherif, M., & Nebergall, R. W. (1965). *Attitude and attitude change: The social judgment-involvement approach.* Philadelphia: W. B. Saunders.

Shimanoff, S. (1980). *Communication rules: Theory and research.* Beverly Hills, CA: Sage Publications.

Weick, K. (1969). *The social psychology of organizing.* Reading, MA: Addison-Wesley.

Wilmot, W. W. (1980). *Dyadic communication,* 2nd ed. New York: Random House.

7

SUPERVISING AND MOTIVATING OTHERS

Supervision
> *What is a supervisor?*
> *The optimal supervisor*
> *Supervisory content research*

Motivation
> *Maslow's hierarchy of needs*
> *Herzberg's two-factor model*
> *Japanese or "Theory Z"*

Strategic Communication Models
> *Power*
> *Communication climates*
> *Homans' exchange theory*
> *Message-centered strategies*
>> Kelman's influence model
>> Behavioral alteration techniques

Objectives

By the end of this chapter you should be able to

1. Define supervision and discuss what it takes to become a competent supervisor.
2. Explain the role of listening in supervision.
3. Define and differentiate among different approaches to organizational motivation.

4. Discuss how knowledge of growth and deficiency needs can be used in supervising others.
5. Explain how such message-centered motivation and supervision strategies influence perceptions of power and influence on an organization's communication climate.

At some time in your organizational career you will be asked to supervise others. Before examining the processes involved in small group functioning and leadership (covered in Chapter 8), we need to further explore what is necessary to get others to work. This chapter introduces you to several approaches to motivating people within the organization. It explores the traditional approaches to internal and external organizational motivation attributed to Maslow, Herzberg, and Homans, as well as the Ouchi's Japanese ("Theory Z") model. The chapter's primary focus, however, is on communication strategies based on an analysis of individual needs.

How we approach, treat, and communicate with others in the organization influences *motivation*. Some people, regardless of how they are treated, will have problems getting motivated. As discussed in Chapter 6, there are certain personality types that find it hard to enjoy work, that do not have an internal motivation to do the job—or do it to the best of their abilities. These people make *supervision* a difficult job. The knowledge that someone is simply not motivated to do anything provides the data required to engage in motivational strategies; not knowing—failing to analyze your potential communication audience—means that you do not have the information required to successfully motivate (and therefore supervise) that person. Supervision would be easy if everyone hired were internally motivated to do the job. Supervision would be easy if all those motivated people were motivated all the time. Supervision would be easy if we understood in general what motivates people. Supervision would be easy if we knew what specific messages motivated people under what consequences. In a sense, everyone is motivated to do something because each person must use his time to do something: sleep, watch television, work. In this sense, motivation involves directing someone toward a particular task.

Unfortunately, we do know that unmotivated people are hired. We know that motivated people can quickly become unmotivated. We know some general principles of motivation, and we know that certain types of messages and message strategies tend to produce different types of motivation. Thus, supervision of others becomes a *communication* problem, a problem of finding the best strategy to produce the most motivated workers.

This chapter begins by looking at motivation and how organizations perceive their workers' motivation. A quick review of audience analysis follows, with an orientation toward predicting what motivates certain individuals. We then look at supportive climates within the organization and what role communication plays in creation of them, including the use of *power* and *conflict*.

Finally, we explore two communication approaches to motivating others: Kelman's (1961) *influence approach* and McCroskey and Richmond's (1992) *Behavioral Alteration Techniques* (BATs). We turn first, however, to the general concept of supervision.

SUPERVISION

Although most people do not differentiate between supervision and management, there *is* one major difference between the two. *Supervision* deals with the day-to-day operations of employees engaged in task-related activities. *Management,* while overseeing employee operations, deals with the planning and execution of the larger organizational picture. This is not to say that managers never supervise or *vice versa,* but it is best for the organization if their functions are considered separately.

Figure 7.1 presents several views of an organization. In 7.1(a) we see the typical *hierarchical organization* (more traditional). In 7.1(b) we see the typical *horizontal organization* (more contemporary, reflective of newer organizations, or organizations just getting started with fewer managers and more workers). They have one thing in common: they require people to oversee others. Figure 7.1(c) offers a simple rendition of the relationships among workers, supervisors, and managers. Note that the relationship is simple, and each knows what each does. When these relationships are blurred—perhaps by employee-ownership or by a manager who cannot relinquish supervision or by a supervisor with a weak manager—organizational problems occur. Your ability to move up the organizational hierarchy is often influenced by your ability to supervise others as a predictor of your leadership and managerial abilities.

What, then, is a supervisor and how can you best maximize your supervisory performance? The answer to this question lies in understanding what the supervisor does and what her employees believe she should do, as well as your manager's roles and duties.

What Is a Supervisor?

Surprisingly enough, there has been little research into what a supervisor is. As noted in Figure 7.1(c), a supervisor is someone in the middle of the planning and executing continuum. As such we might predict that supervisors are people who communicate with *both* management and workers; that is, the good supervisor must be able to "talk the talk" of both those above and below him. Supervisors must also focus more on the product or the task, ensuring that it is done on time and with minimal error. Finally, the supervisor should be worker-oriented. Most good supervisors were good workers and employees.

The supervisor must be able to "read" management's desires and worker mood. A supervisor must understand which tasks come first and which can

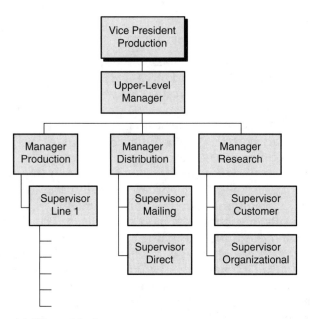

(a) Hierarchical

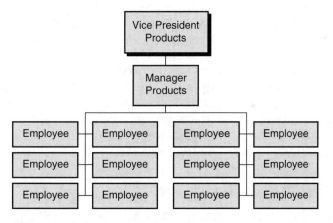

(b) Horizontal

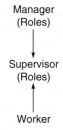

(c) Manager–Supervisor–Worker relationship

FIGURE 7.1   Organizational Hierarchies

be accomplished later. To do so, you must understand your manager and your manager's view of the workplace.

The supervisor must be a good listener. There are several levels of "active" listening that supervisors must be prepared for: phatic, cathartic, and informational (Barker & Watson, 1991). *Phatic listening* is extremely important yet little understood. Phatic listening occurs when we respond to another, by a simple nodding of the head or an "uh-huh." Listening at this level is social, it empowers the other and indicates interest in that person, even when your mind may be somewhere else. Nonverbally, the worst a person can do is ignore you, even if that other person is hard at work doing something else. The same is true of listening, or at least the perception of listening.

Cathartic listening is listening for the forces that underlie the conversation. Why are you being told this, in that manner? Perhaps an employee is just letting off steam, perhaps she is worried about her husband's upcoming physical, or perhaps there are rumors of an impending acquisition and lay-offs. Cathartic listening focuses on the "why are they telling me" type of communication. Listening for subtle nonverbal cues may yield several different messages, messages that may indicate problems with the project at hand. Learning to listen to cathartic messages can be the difference in a job coming in on time or not.

Informational listening deals with argument. This does not mean that you actively argue the conversation; instead, you must listen even more carefully, taking in all the various claims, the data that support those claims, and the conclusion being reached. Informational listening is difficult in the organization because in many cases the task being accomplished has been done so often that is has become routine—it can be accomplished without oversight. There are always better ways of accomplishing the task, however, and the good supervisor willingly listens to worker arguments for better (or safer or faster) ways of getting the job done.

The Optimal Supervisor

The best supervisors are those who are trusted by both management and worker to do the best thing for each, even when those things may be different. Richmond and McCroskey (1992) suggest that workers see at least ten *roles* supervisors fulfill, each of which is a full-time job. They suggest that the supervisory role includes being "a trouble shooter, an arbitrator, a financial wizard, a counselor, a disciplinarian, a guarantor of social justice, a job specialist, a kiss-up artist, and a scholar; they also expect the supervisor to be a public relations person" (p. 34).

Looked at another way, the supervisor is a mediator who sets both the profits and losses required to get the job done. The supervisor works best when she is supervising somewhere between five and fifteen workers (Richmond & McCroskey, 1992), works for a manager who allows her to supervise and supports her decisions, has enough credibility with workers to be in the grapevine yet enough status and power to make decisions that affect both the task and social dimensions of the job, and understands that listening is probably 90 percent of the job.

Not all good workers make good supervisors. As noted in Chapter 6, some employees work because they must, not because they enjoy what they do or have any expectations of obtaining more responsibility. In fact, many employees prefer less to more responsibility. As long as the job gets done and they are paid and looked after, they are about as happy as they will be. Sometimes, however, management will identify someone they believe has supervisory potential. Unfortunately, most chosen to supervise do not undergo specialized training. On-the-job training is their mentor and, often as not, they have problems. Hickson and Stacks (1992) note that this occurs even in academia, where people with Ph.D.s are placed in supervisory roles because administrators know they did a good job in the classroom (sort of supervisory) or in their research (all too often done as an isolated researcher).

So, what do you do when you make the supervisory level? As stated earlier, you need to (1) conduct as much research about the role expectations and duties associated with the job as possible, (2) find out as much as you can about your two primary audiences (the manager above you and the employees below you), and (3) find a way to create a dialogue with each audience.

Supervisory Content Research

As noted earlier, there is little research to help you supervise others. At this level, "management" is something more abstract than what is needed. Supervision is a concrete term, it has definite outcomes—organizational tasks are accomplished on time and within budget and the workers are content with their rewards. A lot to expect, a lot to do. It should be apparent by now that establishing a supportive communication climate and finding ways to motivate employees will be important communication activities.

MOTIVATION

While some may think that motivating others may be as simple as knowing who needs a kick in the tail and who needs a hug to get a job or task completed, it is much more complicated than that. Most bookstores have numerous publications on motivating workers, each with a special approach to getting the most out of people—from finding the "inner I" to "exciting the self" to clever slogans and sayings. Even the airline magazines are getting into the game with ads for motivational posters (nicely framed).

Motivation, regardless of how it is approached, is something that is *individualized.* It is something that we can tap into, but it remains a part of each individual's psychological composition as to what may trigger someone to do his or her job. Sometimes motivation is tied to two general external categories: (1) power and the authority of or over others; and (2) pay, advancement, work conditions, and task incentives. The first set of external motivators is what Katz and Kahn (1978) call *rule enforcement* and deals with your acceptance of the organization's rules, roles, and expectations. The second set deals with reward and *punishment*. The impact of either, however, is tied to the individual worker's *perception of self and her needs at any point in time*.

Of interest to us, then, is how to best *communicate* whatever it takes to motivate others; thus, our approach is message-centered and depends on appropriate *client analysis* and research to know what makes certain individuals behave the way they do. Our thesis is that an understanding of communication best predicts others' internal motivators. Thus, careful analysis (listening) should predict what it takes—hugs or kicks—to motivate others. It makes sense, then, that a perceived need affects one's drive, motivation to do a job, and success in that job. Thus, certain variables may be *inherent to the personality* and may be tapped to increase (or decrease) motivation on the job.

We turn to four basic approaches or theories of motivation. The first two are traditional and deal with the *perceptions of need*. The third focuses on what was labeled "Theory Z" (Ouchi, 1981) a few years back. The fourth is a communication strategy that focuses on *messages*. We begin, however, with the traditional approaches: Abraham Maslow's "hierarchy of needs" and Frederick Herzberg's motivation-hygienic theory.

Maslow's Hierarchy of Needs

Abraham Maslow (1943, 1954) posits that people are motivated based on their needs at any given point in time. He has argued that we need to satisfy needs at five different levels (see Figure 7.2), the lowest being physiological needs and the highest being self-actualization. In between he argues that we have other needs that stem from satisfying the lower need(s). For example, physiological needs and safety needs are *preponent needs;* they must be satisfied prior to our being motivated for anything beyond them (Stacks, Hickson, & Hill, 1992). Maslow (1968) noted that there are *deficiency needs* (those related to safety and health) and *growth needs* (those related to achieving growth potential, social and psychological in nature).

Obviously, people who are concerned with their health, safety, and personal security will be unmotivated toward filling tasks unrelated to these deficiency needs. A person who is starving is unlikely to buy a book on motivation. Thus, we would expect that such needs as salary, safe work conditions, and a consistent organizational environment (such as promises of continued employment) would influence internal motivation—they focus the worker not on the task at hand, but on personal (or family) self-preservation.

New workers who must undergo a training or introductory period prior to full-time permanent employment may find their motivation to do the best job counteracted by deficiency feelings. They will require added vigilance and communication to ensure that they make it though the "initiate" stage.

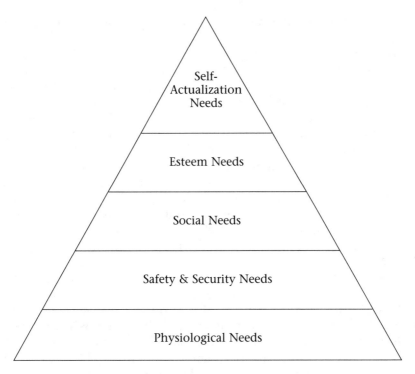

FIGURE 7.2   Maslow's Hierarchy of Needs

"Maslow's hierarchy of needs" from *Motivation and Personality*, 3rd Edition by Abraham H. Maslow, Revised by Robert Frager et al. Copyright © 1954, 1987 by Harper & Row, Publishers, Inc. Copyright © 1970 by Abraham H. Maslow. Reprinted by permission of Addison-Wesley Educational Publishers Inc.

Maslow's next two levels, *social* and *esteem*, deal primarily with psychological and sociological needs. Once the worker believes that her position is secure, her paychecks coming in, and her workplace safe (or that she has been trained to overcome any danger), she needs to fit in with her group. Organizational socialization and the identification of a mentor, as discussed in earlier chapters, play a large role in satisfying social and esteem needs. Social needs are met by acceptance into the workgroup and participation in organizational events. Esteem needs arise from social needs—now the worker needs to be praised, respected, and recognized for his accomplishments. These needs are satisfied by advancement, acknowledgment of good work, pay incentives, and the like.

Maslow's highest need level is *self-actualization*. This deals with achieving all that you can. As the U.S. Army notes, you can "be all that you can be." You have reached your highest potential (or perhaps have overcome it). Satisfying self-actualization needs has both positive and negative effects. If the worker, once she has achieved what she set out to do, has no higher goal, she may become stagnated in her position and unmotivated to continue; or, she may be "burned out" from the effort to self-actualize. On the other hand, with proper supervision, the employee should strive to master new concepts, tasks, and objectives.

At the highest level, the motivation turns even more inward. Maslow noted that there are both cognitive and aesthetic needs that stem from self-actualization. *Cognitive needs* arise from a need to understand the *processes* involved in what we do—to understand, theorize, and predict outcomes in the organization. *Aesthetic needs* are more abstract and result in needs to achieve *harmony* with the organizational environment. As noted in Chapter 6, certain personality types will never satisfy aesthetic needs, while others will spend as much time as possible on harmony and less on understanding. The ability to satisfy both—and use them as platforms for new objectives—may be an indicator of readiness to move up the organizational hierarchy to supervision and leadership.

As intuitive as Maslow's hierarchy sounds, little research has actually supported it. Only the general categories of deficiency and growth needs have been supported (Wabba & Bridwell, 1976). Empirical support for the hierarchy and impact of satisfying need levels has been inconsistent or nonexistent. This is not to say that Maslow's approach to motivation is without merit; it may not have been tested appropriately, or there may be more variables to be considered. However, a supervisor might examine which needs are most important to her subordinates at any given point in time and devise a strategy for satisfying those which appear to be of foremost concern. This would require two things: (1) an understanding of the individuals working with her (client analysis) and (2) communication strategies that reduce perceptions of deficiencies (dialogue).

We cannot make clear predictions based on Maslow's hierarchy of how groups may operate. We can, however, make predictions of how individual members of the group are motivated (or not motivated) to take on a task. We can cajole, offer rewards or punishments, or change the work environment as possible communication strategies. As noted later in the chapter, however, the use of *power* (rewards and punishments) must be approached with care.

Herzberg's Two-Factor Model

Frederick Herzberg's two-factor model (1966, 1968; Herzberg, Mausner, & Snydermann, 1959) focuses on "hygienic" and "motivator" needs. *Hygienic factors* are needs that lead to dissatisfaction and stem primarily from outside the individual and are found in the environment. Hygienic needs operate much like Maslow's preponent needs and must be satisfied before internal needs—motivator factors—are met. Such factors include work conditions, salary, personal life, supervision, and interpersonal relations. Hygienic needs include

Maslow's social level as well. *Motivator factors* are internalized and lead to satisfaction with the environment, self, and task. These include achievement, recognition, advancement, and growth potential (see Figure 7.3).

The relationship between hygienic and motivator factors is complex but predictable. When workers are not satisfied with hygienic needs, then they will become dissatisfied. Dissatisfied workers are unmotivated workers. However, merely providing for hygienic needs does not necessarily decrease dissatisfaction. Motivator needs must be met while still satisfying hygienic needs to yield worker motivation. Herzberg recommends that, once hygienic and motivator needs are met, the organization uses "job enrichment" as a way of offering intrinsic rewards.

Job enrichment can be achieved by instituting seven things into the organizational environment. First, allow individual freedom of creativity. Second, increase accountability for work produced and reward quality work. Third, do not approach work as "piecemeal," focus instead on the complete task or project and reward for completion (with quality, of course). Fourth, provide job freedom and authority, which, in turn, should increase job responsibility. Fifth, have supervisors provide direct feedback and at times have direct feedback from upper management. Sixth, to provide incentive for growth, provide new and challenging tasks. And, seventh, educate workers

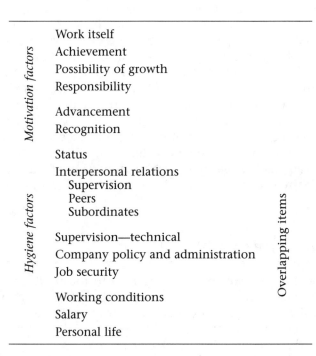

FIGURE 7.3   Herzberg's Two-Factor Model

with the goal of producing experts in specific job responsibilities and then recognize when that expertise is shown.

Like Maslow, much of what Herzberg proposed seems intuitive. However, like Maslow, research suggests that the motivational outcomes are more individual than group. That is, supervisors must constantly study and understand individual workers to find the appropriate motivational strategies. Consider, for example, a worker whose motivation is low. You have met all his needs, yet he is not motivated to do a really good job. What do you do? Making him dissatisfied with hygienic factors—giving him a poor work schedule or having him do the worst jobs—may not impact on his motivation. Providing intrinsic rewards, while in effect punishing him, similarly is doomed to failure. If he is the type of person who works because he must, neither changes in hygienic nor motivator factors will do much to motivate him. Neither the kick nor the hug will do much. There are people who are extremely hard to motivate; however, with enough knowledge and proper communication strategy, motivation is still possible.

Japanese or "Theory Z"

William Ouchi (1981) offers an approach to motivation based on a *transactional* perspective. In Ouchi's *Theory Z* approach, workers maximize their relationships with the organization through participant management techniques, such as quality circles where organizational information is shared by all organizational members, regardless of status or power. In "Theory Z" or "Total Quality Management (TQM)" (Aguayo, 1990), effectiveness of the system is dependent on employees' belief that their participation will improve both the *organization's* goals and their own. Under "TQM," employee content research becomes of paramount importance as the dialogue between supervisor and employee goes from one-way persuasion to a two-way persuasive dialogue, moving to a true dialectic of give and take on either side of an issue or task as all levels of management (now including the employee) are included in the discussion. The goal is to blend the needs of the individuals and the organization. When the best decisions are made, organizations and individuals are in a win-win situation. The company makes a profit; individuals feel secure and rewarded for their work.

STRATEGIC COMMUNICATION MODELS

While motivational approaches provide insight into the needs of employees and potential strategies to meet such needs, they do little to advance our knowledge of communication strategies. There are, however, several approaches to motivation that employ communication strategies. We begin with an analysis of power and the establishment of a *communication climate* conducive to *communication growth,* then move to Homans' *exchange theory,* which looks at the rewards and costs associated with behavior. We then explore Kelman's model of *influence.* Finally, we develop ways for engaging in communication dialogue that may alter motivation through behavior alteration.

Power

A particularly strong motivator in any organization is the use or threatened use of power. Power is really the ability to provide positive or negative sanctions. To consider this in a reverse manner, power is the ability to allow empowerment of others. *Empowerment* means that individuals have been given the time and resources to achieve their own goals, with minimal supervision. To be used effectively, however, there must be a perception by the less powerful that the powerful will use their power, when necessary. In the case of Iraq, for instance, Saddam Hussein did not believe that the West would use its military power to stop his takeover of Kuwait. Saddam continues to disbelieve that power will be used against him—even after his weapons have been destroyed. Thus, perceptions of power affect individuals's motivation to engage in proactive and counteractive behaviors.

Perhaps the best analysis of power is that of French and Raven (1968), who define power as consisting of five interrelated "bases." The first two bases can be seen as a continuum: *reward power* occurs when you control the rewards that others can receive; *coercive power* occurs when you control the punishments that others receive. These power bases reflect your ability to provide positive and negative sanctions. The next three power bases are more *social* in nature. *Legitimate power* occurs when others have given you power over them. *Expert power* occurs when you are perceived as possessing special knowledge or information that others need. And, finally, *referent power* occurs when you are viewed as attractive to the others.

CASE 7.1   Motivating in the Changing Company

Your company has had a new president now for almost two years. During those two years, the president has been a harsh taskmaster. He has downsized by three hundred workers. He has made a public statement that there will be no salary increases and that, in fact, workers should be glad that they have a job at all. Company profits are down. Workers are frustrated and disillusioned. They were fairly satisfied before. Now they have to work ten to twelve hours a day to get the job done, because many are doing work that two people used to do. You are a middle-level manager. What do you say to your workers to keep them motivated? What kind of behavior should you undertake? What rewards and punishments do you have available to you, since there will be no salary increases?

Power is an *external motivator* and must be used with care. As with most external motivators, power can be overused and its influence on motivation thus lessened ("Why do the task if I'm going to be punished?" in terms of coercive power or "I'm so sick of kind words that I could cry" for reward power). We also know from psychology that rewarding others is a more effective motivator than is punishment. However, we also know that punishment will reduce negative behaviors more so than will lack of reward (Stacks, Hickson, & Hill, 1992).

Power is a part of all organizational climates. Morgan (1997) has viewed the organization as a variety of metaphors; his perspective offers a different way of looking at power within the organization. Morgan sees power as one of the main factors in organizations that are based on politics, for instance, where power plays abound and much time and effort is spent playing office politics. Organizations that engage in unrestricted power politics create dissatisfaction and reduce employee motivation (Dunn, 1981). Thus, *when power is used to create conflict, it can be a factor in motivation,* as when you instigate a conflict knowing that you can resolve it. Your ability to resolve the conflict provides you power in future situations.

Some people seek power and use conflict to gain it. *Conflict is present any time there is the potential for movement in an organization.* In studying power and conflict Frost and Wilmot (1978) developed four primary strategies. People may actively avoid conflict, they may escalate the conflict, they may seek to reduce the conflict, or they may try to maintain the conflict. Each strategy reflects a communication goal. *Conflict avoidance* means that you will not communicate with those with whom you are in conflict; in actuality you are prolonging the conflict and legitimizing the other's power. *Conflict escalation* means that you are upping the ante and legitimizing the other person's power; communication is often intense and may lead to violence. However, there are people who seek power through escalated conflict and are thus motivated to keep the conflict at as high a level as possible.

Reducing conflict requires that you communicate with those with whom you are in conflict. This strategy seeks to maintain a state of homeostasis or balance by "talking things out." Kreps (1986) suggests that conflict reduction may not be a good strategy because conflict needs time to surface in most organizations. *Maintenance of conflict* is found in a strategy that is somewhere between escalation and reduction. Maintenance allows conflict tension to be present—not a bad thing for low-motivated individuals or groups—but controlled. As a communication strategy, you would be distributing power equally among the participants to gain some form of group symmetry or balance.

A particularly interesting model of individual perceptions of power comes from the work of Killmann and Thomas (1975). They note that individuals differ in their concern for self and their concern for others. Further, on a continuum of high to low concern, they identified five "conflict personalities" (see Figure 7.4). People who are highly assertive and low in co-operation fit a *competition* profile. People who are highly assertive and highly cooperative fit a *collaboration* profile. People who are lowly assertive and lowly cooperative fit an *avoiding* profile. People who are lowly assertive and highly cooperative fit an *accommodating* profile. And, those who are moderately assertive and cooperative fit a *compromising* profile. Thus, knowing the conflict personalities of your co-workers provides you with important information regarding how they perceive conflict, how they may react to conflict, and message strategies that might be used to either resolve or induce conflict.

Adapted and reproduced with permission of authors and publisher from: Killman, R. H., & Thomas, K. W. Interpersonal conflict-handling behavior as reflections of Jungian personality dimensions. *Psychological Reports,* 1975, 37, 971–980. © Psychological Reports 1975.

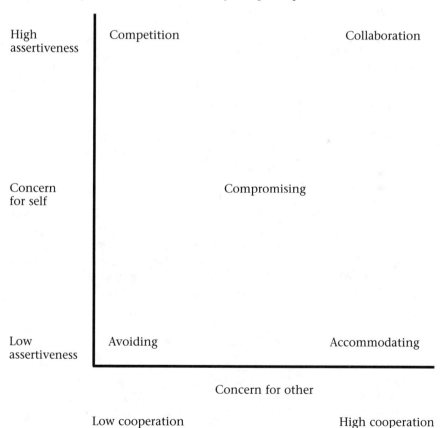

FIGURE 7.4   Killman & Thomas' Conflict Profile

Understanding what power is and how it relates to conflict helps establish communication strategies that can be used to motivate others. By careful observation of others (superiors and subordinates) within the organization you can place individuals into conflict profiles and react to different power bases. How people respond to power and conflict as motivators may be seen in the organization's *communication climate.*

Communication Climates

Most of us have worked in organizations where the climate is extremely unmotivating. In those situations, we get the job done in spite of the organization. And generally, we get the job done so that we can go home and do something more productive, perhaps while looking for a job with another organization. The communication climate of such organizations can be best described as *defensive* in nature (Gibb, 1961). Other organizations provide a climate that is *supportive* and engenders work. People in supportive organizations find that climate to be motivating, tend to spend more time on the job, and take pride in their work. Establishing a supportive climate as a way to motivate subordinates is particularly important from a supervisor's perspective.

Jack Gibb (1961) described defensive and supportive communication climates by the communication behaviors identified in each climate. A *defensive communication climate* includes the following characteristics: evaluation of others' messages; control of others' communications and behaviors; strategic communications whereby communication is used to trick and manipulate others; neutrality toward others within the organization and their positions; superiority, where communication is used to convey power in self and inadequacy in others; and certainty, whereby people are dogmatic in opinion and have a high need to win.

Supportive communication climates are characterized by: description, whereby people are nonjudgmental; a problem orientation where communication is focused on achieving common goals and cooperation; spontaneity, where communication is deception-free and honest; equal treatment of others in the organization and communication among and between peers; empathic communication, where concern is expressed and demonstrated when people identify with and share within the organization; and provisionalism, where people are flexible and adaptive and willing to experiment with relationships.

Homans' Exchange Theory

Creating a climate more conducive to communication and one that serves to reduce dissatisfiers and increase motivators can be approached from an economic metaphor. George Homans (1961) suggests, through his exchange theory, that encounters can be seen from a profit perspective. That is, out of any interaction there are rewards and costs (*Profit = Rewards – Costs*). Typically, as long as the rewards are greater than the costs, you profit. Profit can be a great motivator. It should be noted, however, that Homans has discussed the perception of "profit." That is, we feel that we are getting more out of the interaction than we are putting into it.

A communication strategy for use in the organization stemming from exchange theory deals with bargaining situations. In a typical communication exchange, each party wants something. You want a task done, done well, and completed in a particular time period. Subordinates want a reasonable wage, good work conditions, breaks, and leadership. You each have something with which to *bargain,* each of you will have certain *levels of aspiration, resistance points,* and *acceptance points.* Figure 7.5 demonstrates how the bargaining situation works. A good bargainer uses her knowledge of the organization, her reward potential, and the needs of her subordinates to create the best possible message. How she communicates, the types of messages employed, will impact on immediate and later employee motivation.

For instance, suppose that Jane needs Jim to finish a task for her. If she knows that he needs help on another project—and that one of her workers has background in that area—she might construct a message indicating that if he were to help her, she might be able to help him later. Obviously, she does not want her worker tied up completely with Jim's project, but she may be able to barter some of the employee's time. Jane's *resistance point* is the same as Jim's—the number of hours her worker will work for Jim. If Jane estimates that Jim will spend eight hours on finishing, she may offer him four hours of worker help on the other task, but may actually accept a counter of six. She may even accept a full day's loss of the worker, if the project is that important. The *bargaining range,* then, is the difference between Jane and Jim's resistance points.

Message-Centered Strategies

Thus, we know the internal and external motivators we need to tap. We also know what rewards and punishments we can employ. We know that we can

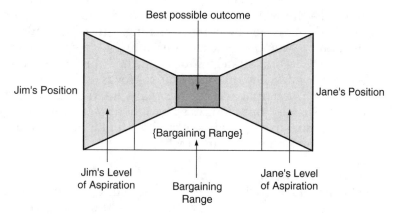

FIGURE 7.5   Bargaining Range

establish supportive communication climates. And we have an economic model that helps predict when profit (motivation) may occur. The missing part of our equation, however, involves the message strategies that help us prepare for communication dialogue. We present two. The first, Kelman's (1961) influence model, is a general approach based on three factors. The second, McCroskey and Richmond's (1992) "Behavioral Alteration Techniques," are more specific suggested message types aimed at altering behavior.

Kelman's Influence Model

To get others to change their environmental and personal perceptions, and thus their motivation, you must first understand what type of influence you are attempting. In general, subordinates can *comply* (behave, but not necessarily adopt your arguments), *identify* (accept your arguments, but only because you are someone whom subordinates respect), or *internalize* (adopt your arguments because they are intrinsically rewarding) with a request (Kelman, 1961). Kelman's model of influence requires that you, as the supervisor, understand your subordinates and that they understand you. In terms of communication outcome, in this case motivation, compliance-gaining messages will get the job done in the short term, but will do little to motivate. Compliance gaining is almost always associated with reward and punishment power; consequently, it is a poor motivator. Often compliance-gaining messages are aimed at deficit or hygienic needs (Herzberg), preponent and safety needs (Maslow), and are usually costly (Homans). In addition, they are usually associated with defensive climates. There are times, however, when compliance is required to get a task or project done. Compliance may be thought of as a message that says: "You must do this, or you will be fired."

Identity focuses more on your legitimate, expert, and referent power; messages should refer to the individual's socialization needs or establishment of group or task attraction. Message strategies are framed in identification with the organization, its goals and mission, and subordinate–supervisor relationships. Identity will produce a supportive climate as long as subordinates perceive your messages as non-threatening. An identification message may be similar to: "I would appreciate your doing this for the company and for me."

Internalization strategies focus on the things that motivate subordinates to do their job. These messages should focus on esteem, status, achievement, and growth potential and responsibility. Internalization is the most effective message strategy, but requires some subordinate motivation to begin with. A message using internalization would be: "I must get the job done. This is what I do. It is an important part of who I am."

Behavioral Alteration Techniques

Kelman's model includes content research, client analysis, and considerable dialogue. Seldom will you have the time to think through a complete message strategy and compose an effective message. How, then, can a supervisor use motivational messages to produce the best possible outcome while on the job?

McCroskey and Richmond (1992) suggest that you use one of twenty-three possible *behavioral alteration techniques* (BATs) and the message strategies associated with each.

The BATs in Table 7.1 stress the different needs the employee may have at any given time. Note that reward and punishment figures in heavily. BATs may

TABLE 7.1   Common Behavioral Alteration Techniques

Category	Sample Message
Immediate reward from behavior	You will enjoy it. It will make you happy. Because it is fun. You'll find it interesting. It's a good experience.
Deferred reward from behavior	It will help you later on in your career. It will prepare you to take a higher level position. It will count in your favor for promotion.
Reward from supervisor	I will make you "X" if you do. I will make it beneficial to you. I will count it toward your annual evaluation.
Reward from others	Others will respect you if you do. Your colleagues will like you for it. The (higher manager) will be pleased if you do it.
Internal reward: Self-esteem	You will feel good about yourself if you do. You are the best person to do it. You always do such a good job. You are good at it.
Immediate punishment from behavior	You will lose if you don't. You will be unhappy if you don't. You will be hurt if you don't. It's your loss if you don't.
Deferred punishment from behavior	It will hurt you later in your career. It will work against you for a promotion. You won't be able to qualify for a higher position.
Punishment from supervisor	I will punish you if you don't. I will make it miserable for you. I will make sure you are an outcast. I will take away "X" if you don't.
Punishment from others	No one will like you. Your colleagues will make fun of you. Your colleagues will reject you. The (higher manager) will be angry with you.
Internal punishment: Guilt	If you don't, others will be hurt. You will make others unhappy if you don't. Your colleagues will be punished if you don't.
Positive supervisor relationship	I will like it better if you do. I will respect you. I will be proud of you. It will indicate you are one of my kind of people.
Negative supervisor relationship	I will dislike you if you don't. I'll be disappointed in you. I won't be proud of you. I won't like it.
Legitimate supervisor authority	Because I told you to. You don't have a choice in this. I'm in charge, not you. I'm the person you answer to. Don't ask; just do it.

continued

TABLE 7.1 *(continued)*

Category	Sample Message
Legitimate higher authority	Do it; I'm just telling you what I was told. It is a rule; I have to do it and so do you. It's a rule; others expect you to do it.
Personal responsibility	It's your obligation. It's your turn. Everyone has to do his or her share. It's your job. Everyone has to pull his or her own weight.
Responsibility to colleagues	Your colleagues need it done. The (unit) depends on you. All your colleagues are counting on you. Don't let us down.
Normative rules	We voted and the majority rules. All your colleagues are doing it. Everyone has to do it. The rest of the (unit) is doing it.
Debt	You owe me one. Pay your debt. You promised to do it. I did it last time. You said you would do it this time.
Altruism	If you do this it will help your colleagues. Your colleagues will benefit if you do. I am not asking you to do it for yourself, do it for the good of the (unit).
Peer modeling	Your colleagues do it. Good employees do it. Peers you admire do it. Your friends in the (unit) are doing it.
Supervisor modeling	This is the way I always do it. When I first started out, that is the way I did it. Most people like me do it the way I used to do it.
Supervisor expertise	From my expertise, it is a good idea. From what I have learned, it is what you should do. This has always worked for me. Trust me; I know what I'm doing.
Supervisor feedback	Because I need to know how well you understand this. To see how well I have explained it to you. It will help you understand your problem areas.

gain compliance and possibly even identity, but the ability to truly motivate through their use will be difficult. Note that most, with the exception of internal reward (self-esteem, personal responsibility, and altruism), are aimed at establishing deficiency or social needs. And, as we know, these preponent or hygienic needs provide less, and shorter-term, motivation than do esteem and self-actualization or motivator needs.

As you read through the BATs, evaluate each and decide which may force you to engage in a power relationship. With what effect, or, as Homans' might put it, at what cost? BATs are rote message types that can be used in situations when an immediate problem comes up, or possibly with certain individuals with whom motivation has and will continue to be a problem. Again, however, an understanding of the organization and its mission, and your subordinates (and superiors and peers) is necessary for effective use. This entails content research, audience analysis, and some communication dialogue strategy.

SUMMARY

This chapter explored the superior–subordinate relationship, suggesting certain role expectations that both superiors and subordinates have of supervisors. It examined several approaches to motivation, including motivational models by Maslow and Herzberg. The chapter ended with an exploration of how supervisors might motivate subordinates: communication climate, social influence attempts, power, an economic metaphor model, and behavioral alteration techniques (BATs) or messages that could be used when time or task constraints do not allow for adequate message preparation.

The key to being a good supervisor and being able to motivate others is an understanding of (1) the organization, its structure, and its goals and mission; (2) your superiors and how they see you and your role in the organization; (3) your subordinates. Such understanding requires considerable content research, client analysis, and an understanding of human nature and communication strategies that yield motivational messages.

QUESTIONS FOR THOUGHT

1. Compare and contrast the motivation strategies of Herzberg and Maslow.
2. How does one decide how much supervision to give workers on a task?
3. Describe what one would need to do to transform a defensive climate into a supportive climate.
4. Some workers would like fewer hours, some higher pay, some a better office, some a larger office, some more assistants. How can you determine which would reinforce a particular worker better?
5. Describe the similarities and differences between supervision and management.

CASE 7.2   Motivating Successful Workers

Your company has been very successful over the past three years. Your research unit has been the most productive in the company. Each individual has been promoted to the highest level and each has the highest salary available for a non-manager. You have a successful unit. The question now becomes: Is this all there is? How do you motivate success stories? Is this easier or more difficult than motivating less successful workers? What are your worries?

REFERENCES

Aguayo, R. (1990). *Dr. Deming: The American who taught the Japanese about quality.* New York: Fireside.

Barker, L. L., & Watson, K. (1991). The role of listening in managing interpersonal and group conflict. In D. Borisoff & M. Purdy (Eds.), *Listening in everyday life* (pp. 139–162). New York: University Press of America.

Dunn, D. M. (1981). Interpersonal communication training in professional organizations. Cited in G. Kreps, *Organizational Communication.*

French, R. P., & Raven, B. (1968). The bases of social power. In D. Cartwright & A. Zander, *Group dynamics,* 3rd ed. (pp. 259–269). New York: Harper & Row.

Frost, J., & Wilmot, W. (1978). *Interpersonal conflict.* Dubuque, IA: Wm. C. Brown.

Gibb, J. (1961). Defensive communication. *Journal of Communication, 11,* 141–148.

Herzberg, F. (1968). One more time: How do you motivate employees? *Harvard Business Review, 46,* 53–62.

Herzberg, F. (1966). *Work and the nature of man.* New York: Collins.

Herzberg, F., Mausner, B., & Snydermann, D. B. (1959). *The motivation to work.* New York: Wiley.

Hickson, M. L., & Stacks, D. W. (Eds.). (1992). *Effective communication for academic chairs.* Albany, NY: State University of New York Press.

Homans, G. (1961). *Social behavior: Its elementary forms.* New York: Harcourt, Brace, and World.

Katz, D., & Kahn, R. L. (1978). *The social psychology of organizational needs,* 2nd ed. New York: John Wiley & Sons.

Kelman, H. C. (1961). The process of opinion change. *Public Opinion Quarterly, 25,* 58–78.

Killmann, R., & Thomas, K. (1975). Interpersonal conflict-handling behavior as a reflection of Jungian personality dimensions. *Psychological Reports, 37,* 971–980.

Kreps, G. (1986). *Organizational Communication.* White Plains, NY: Longman.

Maslow, A. H. (1968). *Toward a psychology of being,* 2nd ed. New York: Van Nostrand.

Maslow, A. H. (1954). *Motivation and Personality.* New York: Harper & Row.

Maslow, A. H. (1943). A theory of human motivation. *Psychology Review, 50,* 370–396.

McCroskey, J. C., & Richmond, V. P. (1992). Motivating faculty. In M. L. Hickson & D. W. Stacks, *Effective communication for academic chairs* (pp. 159–182). Albany, NY: State University of New York Press.

Morgan, G. (1997). *Images of Organization,* 2nd ed. Thousand Oaks, CA: Sage.

Ouchi, W. (1981). *Theory Z: How American business can meet the Japanese challenge.* Reading, MA: Addison-Wesley.

Richmond, V. P., & McCroskey, J. C. (1992). *Organizational communication for survival.* Englewood Cliffs, NJ: Prentice-Hall.

Stacks, D. W., Hickson, M. L., & Hill, S. (1992). *Introduction to Communication Theory.* Fort Worth, TX: Holt, Rinehart & Winston.

Wabba, M. A., & Bridwell, L. G. (1976). Maslow reconsidered: A review of research on the Need Hierarchy theory. *Organizational Behavior and Human Performance, 15,* 212–240.

8

LEADING WORK GROUPS

Small Group Communication in the Organization
> *What is a "group"?*
> *Task and social groups*
> *Group dynamics*
> *Decision making in the group*
> *Approaches to problem solving*

Leadership
> *Descriptive leadership approaches*
> *Leadership contingency*
> *Leadership adaptability*
> *Leadership through empowerment*
> *Communication strategies*

Objectives

By the end of this chapter you should be able to

1. Distinguish between managing and supervising.
2. Describe the processes through which groups operate in the organization.
3. Discuss how leadership is obtained in the organization.
4. Differentiate between various approaches to leadership and explain the advantages and disadvantages each possesses for the leader in the New Organization.
5. Explain the process of empowerment and the communication strategies that allow a leader to empower the groups she manages.

Group work—team work—is something that organizations thrive on. As noted in Chapter 7, individuals are not especially valued for their individuality in the organization; organizations are made up of individuals who have been molded into working units. These units are the workhorses of organizations. In Chapter 7 we explored the supervisor–subordinate relationship almost as an interpersonal or dyadic interaction. In this chapter we will explore how groups operate and how to effectively lead various groups on various tasks. Doing so takes you from "lower-level management" to the decision making associated with middle- and ultimately, upper-level management.

Perhaps the best way to look at organizational responsibility is to examine what you are doing at each level in the organization. As we found in earlier chapters, responsibilities change as you work your way up the organization: workers work—they perform the tasks that produce the organization's specific products; supervisors supervise—they ensure that the workers produce the specific product; administrators administrate—they do not look at specific products, but at the culmination of those products into profit; and managers manage—they take the long-term view, looking at the ideas and concepts that drive the organization. We might summarize by noting that you will be

- supervising *people;*
- administering *things;* and
- managing *ideas.*

This chapter explores the next level of organizational responsibility: *administration* and *management.* In so doing it seeks to better understand how people work in groups to administer what the organization produces (cars, information, horses, computers, ideas) and ultimately to manage large portions of the organization.

The adaptation of the individual to the small group and the processes involved in group work are essential in moving from supervision to management. The potential for leadership becomes a major focus of evaluation at this and later stages in your organizational career. You need to understand what "makes" a leader and how one "leads"; the successful manager is someone who can assert his or her individual needs, as well as the needs of the organization, in managing ideas toward particular ends. You will have to understand how groups operate in achieving their goals, especially goals that are less task- and product-oriented and more process- and idea-oriented.

The key, as we have noted before, will be an understanding of what the organization requires to meet its objectives and goals. This content research becomes paramount when you change hats, moving from supervisor to administrator to manager, and begin to demonstrate your ability to lead others. Leading a group to complete its assigned objectives requires content research about (1) the task or goal involved and (2) the dynamics of group interaction. It also requires an understanding of the individuals who comprise the work group and how those individuals operate together, whether in task- or socially-oriented labor. Finally, leading requires an understanding of when to merge into the group (lose your individuality) and when to assert yourself. We begin with an analysis of group functioning.

SMALL GROUP COMMUNICATION
IN THE ORGANIZATION

Almost by definition, *an organization is a set of groups—teams working toward a common goal.* Note that this definition does not include the individual, but focuses on "teams." A *team* is a set or group of individual workers who have a common problem to overcome or goal to meet. Much of the work of small group communication researchers is applied at the organizational level. As good as you might think you are as an individual, a group of people with similar skills will be better. When working in teams it is important to remember that

- Organizations are composed of workgroups (teams), not individuals.
- Groups may take longer to come up with a solution, but their solutions are almost always superior to individual solutions (in spite of what people say, the camel may be superior to the thoroughbred—depending upon what the original problem was).
- Advancement in the organization comes through teamwork (it may have begun with your mentor).
- Sometimes it is better to be led than to lead.
- A good leader knows when to lead and when to follow.
- And, adaptation to a group requires an ability to understand and communicate well.

What Is a "Group"?

Groups can be characterized in several ways. Although a group can be defined as a number of people working toward a common goal, groups differ in terms of their *size, channels, function,* and *communication networks.* Most people argue that a group consists of three or more people. An "optimum" group consists of five to fifteen people (e.g., Cartwright & Zander, 1973). In general, as we add people to a group, the number of potential channels increases. For example, if you are working with two other people in a workgroup, you have three communication channels: you talk to the other two and each can talk to you (see Figure 8.1). Each channel (a line in the figure) is two-way; that is, each of you

Three group members
Three communication channels

Four group members
Six communication channels

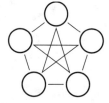

Five group members
Ten communication channels

FIGURE 8.1   Group Size and Number of Communication Channels

can send and receive messages. A four-member group has six channels. A five-member group, ten channels, and so forth. Bostrom (1970) calculated the number of interactions ((A to B), (A to C), (A to B to C), (A to B to C to D), etc.) different sized groups might have (see Table 8.1). He noted that by the time a group got to eight (8) members, there were over one thousand different interactions possible! Size, then, determines the number of communication channels available, which, in turn, influences group member satisfaction (Do they get to contribute? How so? How often?) and group task speed (as membership increases, communication increases, and the time needed to complete the task also increases).

Group size affects both function and communication channels. As noted in Figure 8.2, the greater the number of people in a group, the more communication channels there are; however, depending on how the group is networked, not all members are in communication with each other. In four of the five general types of group networking, members communicate with certain other members. In a *circle* network, you might communicate with Bill and Carol, but not with Mark and Jane. In a *chain,* you would communicate with Bill and Carol, who would then communicate with only Mark or Jane. In a *wheel* network, you would communicate with Bill, Carol, Mark, and Jane, but they would not communicate with each other. And, in the *Y,* you would communicate with Bill and Carol, who would not communicate with anyone else, but Mark would communicate to Jane, who in turn would communicate with you. In the *all star* or *concomm* network, however, all of you *could* communicate with each other.

Why the different types of networks? *Centralized networks* (wheel, chain, Y) are superior to *non-centralized networks* (circle, all star) as far as speed and information accuracy. Thus, they are best employed when a task is simple or

**TABLE 8.1   Group Size
and Potential Interaction**

Group Size	Number of Potential Interactions
2	2
3	9
4	28
5	75
6	186
7	441
8	1,056

Source: R. Bostrom (1970). Patterns of communication interaction in small groups. *Communication Monographs, 37,* 257–263. Copyright 1970 by the Speech Communication Association. Reproduced by permission of the publisher.

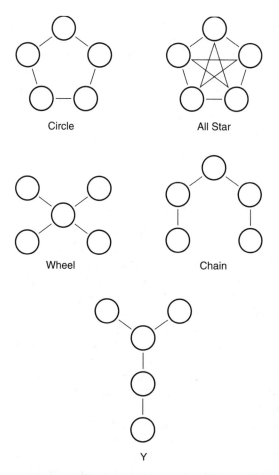

FIGURE 8.2   Group Communication Networks

when speed is of the essence. Note that centralized networks possess an individual who mediates or controls the communication with others. Often the controller is the group leader or supervisor. We might consider the supervisor the group leader, as noted in Chapter 7. As long as the task is completed in time and with the desired quality, there is little need for communication other than for instruction or motivation.

The circle and all star networks often produce higher quality products and better solutions, but take longer to come to a result. As an administrator you will find uses for both types of networks. At times you will act as the "group leader" for a number of supervisors, overseeing their combined tasks. At other times, you will be working with other administrators, seeking to find solutions to problems associated with the task. In this case, the use of a non-centralized network structure will provide better solutions but take more time. As a manager you will use centralized networks with your subordinates less and non-centralized networks more often as you seek solutions to larger problems, requiring more communication.

In general, up to a point, the greater the communication channels, the more the group is satisfied and the "better" the group outcome will be. As group membership increases, however, the potential to contribute decreases. In a three-member group, for instance, you have about a 33 percent chance of communicating at any given time. In a five-member group that percentage is at best 20 percent. Imagine trying to put together a product with twenty workers, each having his or her say on how to make that product better!

Task and Social Groups

Groups differ not only in size and communication networks, but also in why they exist. The most common group found in organizations is the task group. However, there are times when you will either be a member of or form a group to deal with problems other than the task. Sometimes a group is formed to improve or maintain social relationships. We will look at both in some detail.

Task groups, as noted earlier, almost always have a job to do (e.g., Beebe & Masterson, 1994; Cragen & Wright, 1986; DeVito, 1997). Those jobs differ, however, depending on where you are in the organization. A construction group, for instance, puts together the product, an automobile. Each member of the group has one or more specialized tasks she does to contribute to the final product. This group seldom works on its own; it is supervised and often centralized for speed.

A *problem-solving group* seeks solutions to problems. Problem-solving groups may consist of individual workers brought together for their task expertise, but most often are composed of supervisors or administrators whose years of experience provide the necessary research backgrounds to master the problem. Problem-solving groups would seek solutions to assembly line problems.

Decision-making groups also work on problem solving, but they go one step beyond finding solutions; they resolve the problem, execute the solution, and monitor and evaluate progress. Decision-making groups consist of middle- and upper-level management; they have the power and resources to enact solutions. A decision-making group might change how the assembly line is laid out to reduce redundancy of function and save money. Ideation groups are the fourth type of group.

Ideation groups consist of primarily upper-level management and, as such, are concerned about organizational problems. Ideation groups study the organization itself, looking for weaknesses and strengths in not only the product and the way it is produced, but other factors that impinge on organizational survival. An ideation group might consist of vice presidents looking at a potential hostile takeover of the engine division by a competitor. Their task is to identify potential scenarios and suggest a variety of solutions for each.

Not all groups focus on tasks. Most modern organizations understand that the best products come from motivated and satisfied workers (see Chapter 7). As such, they spend considerable time on social tasks. Social groups plan employee meetings, oversee worker councils, and even plan the yearly picnic. *Social groups* allow members to come together and discuss the conditions of work and the benefits provided by the organization. Social groups supply necessary feedback to upper-level management about the "state of the organization." As an administrator you may take the organization's pulse through focus group meetings that explore general or specific concerns. Note, however, that the social group still has a group goal—the social well-being of the organization and maintenance of hygienic conditions (see Chapter 7).

Sometimes events dictate a different social group. When the organization decides that economic conditions require lay-off or a hostile takeover is imminent or rumors of major organizational problems endanger worker morale, a *therapy group* may be formed. Often led by outside professionals, this group seeks to help individuals within the organization overcome personal problems. Therapy groups may take the form of encounter groups, where experts communicate with employees about problems and may offer a variety of solutions to the problem (such as buyouts, re-educational classes, profit-sharing).

A third social group, the *consciousness-raising group,* is also found in many organizations. The consciousness-raising group exists "to increase members' awareness of something which the members share. . . . gender, nationality, religion; a value . . . ; ways women are victims of discrimination" (Infante, Rancer, & Womack, 1993, p. 321). Consciousness-raising groups may stem from social and therapy group outcomes, or may be the result of some task group charged with social responsibility, or may be the result of legal action against the organization.

Group Dynamics

Organizational groups come and go as the organization matures. Some groups form the nucleus of the organization and, unless a major life-threatening situation occurs, will become a permanent feature of organizational life. Such groups include the management council and the CEO's board. Other groups, however, come to life, do their "thing," and die. These groups go through several phases that DeVito (1997) describes as opening, feedforward, business, feedback, and closing. Although DeVito's focus is on small group discussion, not organizational group workings, the phases operate similarly.

Each time a group is formed it takes on the unique characteristics of its members and its charge. Groups can be thought of as systems in which a change in one part of the system changes the entire system. A new group member changes the way the group operates. As noted earlier, each of us brings to our work certain roles. As these roles interact in the group, the process by which the group operates changes. Thus, although you have worked with the other members of a newly-formed group, the group's goal or task will change how it operates and that is important information that may lead you to consider different communication strategies at different phases of group development.

The *opening phase* of a group's life is *social* in nature. Although the task may be introduced, most of the time will be spent getting to know or reacquaint members. At this stage introductions are made and roles often assumed. At the *feedforward phase* the problem is discussed in general, roles and responsibilities discussed, and group routine established. The *business phase* involves the active discussion of the problem or task, the review of positions and research, and suggestion of potential solutions offered. At the *feedback phase* the group evaluates the process by which it came to potential solutions and may select which solutions or options will be forwarded to those with the power to implement the group's recommendations. At *closure* the group comes full circle, the group experience is relieved as group members take on individual characteristics, and information is stored for use in future groups with the same members.

Rarely are the five phases found in one group meeting. There may be several opening meetings where rules and roles are discussed and formalized. It may take a meeting or two to get members to agree on a common agenda or leader. The opening phase often sets the social climate for the group and may dictate whether the group climate will be supportive or defensive. Groups that have worked together in the past may not require extensive time to establish group roles and routines; other groups may take several meetings to establish such relationships. The feedforward and business phases focus on task—who will do what, when will it be reported back, in what form, and how will it be evaluated. This is the gist of the group and the reason it was created. For simple tasks, where individuals bring certain expertise together, chain or Y or wheel networking will suffice; for complex tasks, those that require novel solutions, circle or all star networking may be required. The feedback stage is often used to re-evaluate the process and members' participation, as well as to evaluate the solutions or goal achieved. Closure is often used to establish a supportive climate for the next group members may be part of. It is important to understand that, like interpersonal relationships, group relationships may produce conflict. Indeed, as you move up the organizational ladder your openness to others' ideas may be limited by your beliefs, opinions, and power.

Conflict is often a way of life in groups. Conflict is *not* disagreement, it is a perception that others' positions are antithetical to your own (McCroskey & Wheeless, 1976). Conflict occurs because of communication; it is the product of communication that is perceived as hostile, negative, and antagonistic (Richmond & McCroskey, 1992). Conflict, however, can be a motivator (see Chapter 7) or a destroyer of groups. As a motivator, conflict brings new ideas and challenges to the group. The group that can control member conflict will probably be more productive in the end. Conflict control includes the establishment of a supportive climate (Gibb, 1961) that allows members to express their ideas, concerns, and evaluations in non-personalized ways. That is, potential conflict is best resolved through communication when perceptions of conflict (hostile, antagonistic, and negative) can be changed to perceptions of disagreement about issues.

Conflict can result from group members' *hidden agendas,* agendas that are individual- rather than group-oriented. Conflict of this nature often leads to disenchantment with the group, leading to withdrawal and failure to use all members' expertise in finding the ideal or practical solution to the problem. Thus it is important to find ways of altering the nexus of the conflict to disagreements. You may agree not to agree on certain points as one option. Or, the group may agree to bring hidden agendas to the table and spend time discussing them. Sometimes it is up to the group leader to decide what is best for the group.

Decision Making in the Group

Most organizations are not democracies. They seldom allow people to decide who has authority and power and who does not. Those decisions are designated to individuals within the organization after careful scrutiny and consideration. Seldom does an organization create a task group without first appointing an individual to lead the group. We will cover leadership in some detail later; suffice it to note that leaders of groups are characterized as either appointed or emergent. *Appointed leaders* have legitimate, reward, and punishment power and authority (see Chapter 7). They may not, however, have referent or expert power. Groups with appointed leaders are often chain, Y, or wheel networked. Groups with *emergent leaders,* where leaders emerge as their expertise or ability to satisfy problem needs are required, often result in circle or all star networks.

Groups come to their final solutions in one of three ways: appointed authority makes the decision, a majority vote selects the "best" solution, or the group discusses the solutions until it comes to a consensus. Each has its advantages and limitations. In many situations the group's leader has the *appointed authority* to take the solution she believes best meets the problem. In such instances, the best group approach is to have all points of view presented with positives and negatives pointed out. If group members understand that they are to present objective solutions, little conflict over final choice should occur. However, if group members believe that they have not been afforded equal treatment or that some hidden agenda is driving the group, then conflict over the solution may occur and implementation of the solution may be difficult.

Sometimes the decision is made by *group majority vote.* If the solution or task is controversial, a group decision may deflect some of the controversy and group members may actually come to believe it advocated a position closer to the final vote than they actually were. Group voting, however, often yields cliques of members who vote based on hidden agendas or other perceived inequities. *Consensus,* on the other hand, occurs when all group members agree on a given solution. Consensus not only strengthens the group but increases the potential for implementing the solutions. With consensus, too, you have

> ### CASE 8.1   A Full Plate
>
> Karen is the Group Manager of eight researchers. She has several decisions to make, all within the next month. The decisions include hiring a secretary, who works for all eight, but mostly for Karen; writing two grant proposals for funding; purchasing a new copy machine; developing a budget for next year; and developing a new system for personnel evaluation. Of these projects, which ones should Karen do by herself? Which ones should she have a committee make recommendations for a solution, and which ones should involve all of the personnel in consensus?

fewer problems with cliques—assuming that the group's consensus is real and not one or two members agreeing to avoid conflict. Consensus, however, requires effective communication, recognition of a common goal, a supportive communication climate, and a great deal of time. Its results are typically increased group solidarity and cohesiveness and commitment to the solution. In any case, how the ultimate decision will be made should be stated to the group at the outset of its deliberations. Hardly anything is more irritating to a group of workers than for it to spend considerable time and research effort deciding on which machine to buy, for example, only to have the leader make a decision based on what some salesperson from a company suggested.

Unbridled consensus, however, can cause more problems than it solves. Janis (1971, 1972) has defined the situation where group consensus and cohesion create a dysfunctional group, one that fears disagreement and disenfranchisement from the group, as *groupthink*. Groupthink is facilitated when a group has a strong, charismatic leader, is isolated from the rest of the organization, and sees itself as failing, and fails to explore alternatives. Groupthink occurs when group members become close-minded and overestimate their own power and prestige while underestimating the power of the problem. This places considerable pressure on members to conform, to achieve a consensus not from agreement but from pressure to please the group. Groupthink almost always yields negative results. Members fail to critically evaluate information, seeking instead to find ways of bringing that information within the group's perspective; they have a biased and inadequate view of the problem. Being unable to fully understand the problem and its consequences, the group's plans are inadequate and consequently fail.

Groupthink can be countered by the establishment of a supportive group climate and by the encouragement of disagreement. Janis suggests that "mind guards" be replaced by "devil's advocates" whose job is to counterargue solutions as they are discussed. Outside experts or individuals not typically group members might be added to the group for fresh insight and an ability to counter self-appointed mind guards or group peer pressure. It is often best that superiors remove themselves from the group as a way of seeking the most open communication during discussions. Finally, one should never assume that silence means consensus; go to private votes where people are free to anonymously voice disagreement with the group (Richmond & McCroskey, 1992). Groupthink is something that can be diagnosed and combated. While most groups seek to divorce themselves from conflict, open and honest disagreement is often the best cure for both conflict and groupthink.

Approaches to Problem Solving

The *standard agenda for problem-solving groups* can be traced back to John Dewey (1910). Dewey, an educator, suggested that rational thinking evolved in six steps or phases: (1) define the problem and its scope; (2) analyze the problem for historical significance and possible cause and effect; (3) establish possible criteria and order them according to priority; (4) identify and evaluate potential solutions; (5) select the best solution(s); and (6) test the solution(s). Group problem solving has been found to operate in much the same way as Dewey's rational approach. Bales and Strodbeck (1951) found, for example, that problem solving employing this standard agenda occurred in three phases: an *orientation stage* where the group seeks information about the problem and potential criteria; an *evaluation stage* where the group discusses the information and evaluates it according to the criteria previously generated; and a *control stage* where plans for action and evaluation are discussed and implemented.

There are times, however, when conflict or extreme disagreement make following Dewey's agenda problematic. The "Delphi Technique" (Dalkey, 1969) offers an alternative problem-solving approach. *Delphi groups* do not meet, but correspond instead, reducing the potential problems associated with personalities and strong leadership that might lead to groupthink. In the Delphi Technique someone chooses the group and establishes lines of communication. The leader will define the task in writing and members respond via memo to her. Each group member's position is then paraphrased and returned for all to evaluate and respond. At some point in time the leader should *summarize* the group's decisions to date. This continues until the group reaches consensus on the problem's solution. While this technique will produce a good solution, the spontaneous nature of group discussion is reduced, and some excellent ideas may be lost due to inability to "tag" one idea upon another.

LEADERSHIP

As noted earlier, there is a difference between supervision and management. Supervision takes place in a "line" position; supervisors typically oversee people working on some production task. Although supervision requires group leadership, it is almost always task-oriented and deals with finding ways to meet deadlines and motivate employees to produce the best possible product. Management is different. Lower-level management is typically concerned with administrating *units:* people, groups of people, and products, for example. Upper-level management is typically concerned with managing *ideas or abstract concepts* that underlie the philosophical organization: capital, human resources, and physical resources, for example.

Kreps (1986) notes that to prosper, organizational management requires *multigroup communication* (see Figure 8.3). Multigroup communication is the combination of all other levels of communication, from the individual employee's personal perceptions and internal communications to small group communication. You should by now realize that the higher your organizational position, the less is your contact with "employees." Instead, your communication becomes more and more abstract (John and Mary are now "employees") and your communication to them more formal (through written channels rather than face-to-face). To prosper, then, your orientation toward communication by necessity becomes more overarching—you are no longer *supervising people,* you are *managing things and ideas.* The good manager never forgets the "people factor," although using terms such as "employee" or "human resources" sometimes tends to dehumanize your thought processes.

Management, however, is *leadership.* To this point we have referred to leadership in many ways. We know that most organizational groups have appointed leaders, people whose demonstrated abilities to get the job done put them into leadership roles. There are some organizations that allow leaders to

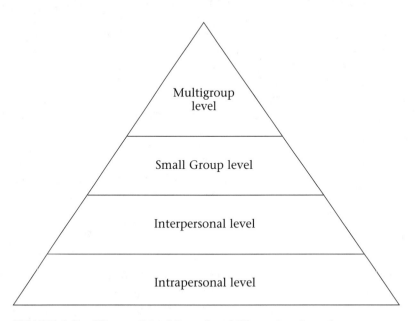

FIGURE 8.3   Hierarchical Levels of Organizational Communication

From *Organizational Communication,* 2nd Edition, by Gary L. Kreps. Copyright © 1990, 1986 by Longman. Reprinted by permission of Addison-Wesley Educational Publishers Inc.

emerge, but they are in the minority. A good manager is usually a good leader, she knows when to lead and when to let her subordinates take control. She has a variety of tools or "styles" with which to work. She will empower her co-workers and subordinates. As we will find, there are many approaches to leadership. However, the approaches are more prescriptive and descriptive than predictive of leaders and leadership.

Descriptive Leadership Approaches

How does one become a leader? Are we predestined to be a leader or a follower? Over the years there have been a number of theories of how leaders "emerge." Some suggest that certain people are genetically wired to become leaders, others suggest that leaders naturally emerge when crises occur and their talents can handle the situation. Still others argue that leadership is both an art and a science that can be learned.

Although it seems preposterous to think about *genetic leadership relationships,* consider the following. First, most leaders are taller than shorter; second, most leaders are male; third, leaders are more physically attractive than unattractive (e.g., Hickson & Stacks, 1992). Then, consider Ross Perot. He is a leader. But is he tall and attractive? What about Hillary Clinton or Eleanor Roosevelt? They certainly were not males nor tall. It may be that people who are placed in positions of leadership use their verbal and nonverbal communication better. If so, then all of us are *potential* leaders. To become a leader, then, we must understand what leaders do and how they do it.

White and Lippett (1960, 1968) suggested that leaders may emerge according to style and situation. They argue that people differ in their orientations or personal styles toward authority and control. We might visualize this approach as a continuum ranging from high to low control, as follows:

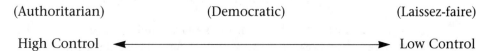

(Authoritarian)   (Democratic)   (Laissez-faire)

High Control ◄──────────────────────────────────► Low Control

Authoritarian leaders' style is best when the situation faced is clearly structured, or when the problem is poorly defined, when conflict is present, or when there are time restraints. His style would produce a quick solution. At the opposite is the *laissez-faire* leader, who eschews any control, allowing others to make decisions; the laissez-faire leader is simply an information provider. She would be effective in situations where the problem or task is unknown or highly unstructured, but not effective when conflict is present. In the middle is the *democratic* leader whose style is "participative decision-making." He provides direction and information and allows the others to participate with him in making decisions. Obviously, this approach is rather simplistic, but does allow for some degree of understanding of personal orientation toward control, leadership, and task requirements and climate.

Burgoon, Heston, and McCroskey (1974) suggested that certain behaviors are identified with leaders and leadership. They noted that leadership functions include (1) initiation of ideas and practices, (2) facilitating member participation, (3) representation to other bodies, (4) organizing or structuring the group, (5) integrating members' communication styles, (6) managing information exchange, (7) gatekeeping or filtering information within and outside the group, (8) rewarding member performance, and (9) producing a product. The *ideal leader* would integrate all nine functions into his or her communicative repertoire.

Three very popular leadership models stem from what has been labeled the "human resources school" of management. McGregor (1960), Likert (1961), and Blake and Mouton (1964) proposed leadership models that described how leaders feel about employees. McGregor's "Theory X and Theory Y" models describe two different approaches to people and communication: *X-model leaders* have little faith in their workers; they see workers as unmotivated and undirected, and they lead through demonstrations of power. *Y-model leaders* are just the opposite; they believe in their employees and support their efforts at self-direction and responsibility. *The key to Theory X/Y is concern for people and concern for task.*

Blake and Mouton have written that leadership behavior can be seen as falling into one of five categories: high concern for people and production (*team leadership*); high concern for people and low concern for production (*country club leadership*); high concern for production and low concern for people (*task leadership*); low concern for production and low concern for people (*impoverished leadership*); and moderate concern for task and people (*middle of the road leadership*).

Likert's model consists of four systems, two extremes paralleling McGregor's Theory X and Y leader and two other systems falling between the extremes. *System 1* parallels Theory X perceptions of employees—little trust and power relationships. *System 4* parallels Theory Y perceptions of employees—great trust and open relationships. *System 2* leaders place some trust in employees, but maintain a power relationship. *System 3* leaders place substantial trust in their employees and strive for open relationships.

Note that in all these descriptive leadership models two elements are central to interpretation: *concern for production* and *concern for people*. From White and Lippett's (1960, 1968) styles approach, to human resource approaches, to functional approaches, the key determiners deal with where the leader falls on some continuum or combination of continuums. Leaders, then, are identified according to their predispositions toward task or people.

Leadership Contingency

More recently Fiedler (1965, 1967) suggested that situations may determine leadership. Fiedler's *contingency model* notes that leaders' power and relationship to group members and the structure of the task all contributed to the "favorableness" of a leader's leadership. For more structured problems, a task orientation may be required. However, as the task is completed, the leadership orientation might change to less task and more social. Thus, the situation dictates contingencies that result in either task- or relationship-oriented leadership. However, organizational contingencies may be more complex. Goldhaber (1984) has identified two sets of organizational contingencies that affect leadership (see Table 8.2). Note that these contingencies are not individual/worker/employee related, but are functions of the larger organization. Thus, the contingency leadership model requires an understanding of the overall organization.

Leadership Adaptability

A more predictive approach has been advocated by Hersey and Blanchard (1977). Hersey and Blanchard see leadership as a dynamic process of adaptation to the needs of a particular situation based on leadership "style(s)" available to the leader. As such, they borrow from the descriptive leadership approaches and extend them to meet the challenges of the modern organization. Hersey and Blanchard argue that three of the more important aspects of leadership are leader style, style range, and style adaptability.

Leadership styles are consistent patterns of behavior that people exhibit, as perceived by others, while attempting to influence the activities of others. They

TABLE 8.2   Contingencies

Internal Contingencies	External Contingencies
1. Structural: degree of formality and type of structure chosen to organize the functions and relationships in the organization	1. Economic: amount of stability in current market competition and its impact on capital resources available to organization
2. Output: amount of diversity and degree of quality in the products and services of the organization	2. Technological: degree of innovation and scientific research and development and their impact on organization
3. Demographic: degree of variation among the people working for the organization in such characteristics as age, sex, education, tenure, and supervisory status	3. Legal: degree of impact of local, state, and federal regulations, guidelines, and laws affecting organizational operations
4. Spatiotemporal: degree of variation in both spatial (design, amount location, distance) and temporal (timing, timeliness) matters	4. Sociopolitical/cultural: degree of impact of social, political, and cultural considerations on the organization
5. Traditional: degree of conformity with organizational norms, history, and script	5. Environmental: degree of impact of climate, geography, population density, and availability of energy on the organization

Source: G. Goldhaber *et al.* (1984). *Information strategies: New pathways to management productivity.* Norwood, NJ: Ablex.

are developed over time and generally involve emphasis on task behavior (patterns of organization, ways of getting a job done), relationship behavior (socioemotional support, friendship, mutual trust), or some combination of the two. Style, then, is related to how the manager differentiates both task and personnel available to meet goals and objectives. *Style range* reflects the extent to which the manager can vary her leadership style. Hersey and Blanchard argue that there is no one "best" leadership style, that an ability to adapt to changing situations is more important than style type alone. A manager's effectiveness may depend on her adaptability and appropriateness of leadership style to the particular situation. A wide style range, although important, is not as crucial as the degree of *style adaptability.* The relationship between style range and style adaptability is similar to the ability of a communicator to clearly discriminate between situations (content research and client analysis), understanding that different problems require different solutions (adaptability).

Hersey and Blanchard define leadership style as the natural outgrowth of the interaction of both direction and strategy and operationalize it as falling into four mutually distinct categories (see Figure 8.4). They argue that leaders will fall into one category as a preferred style, but the importance is not so

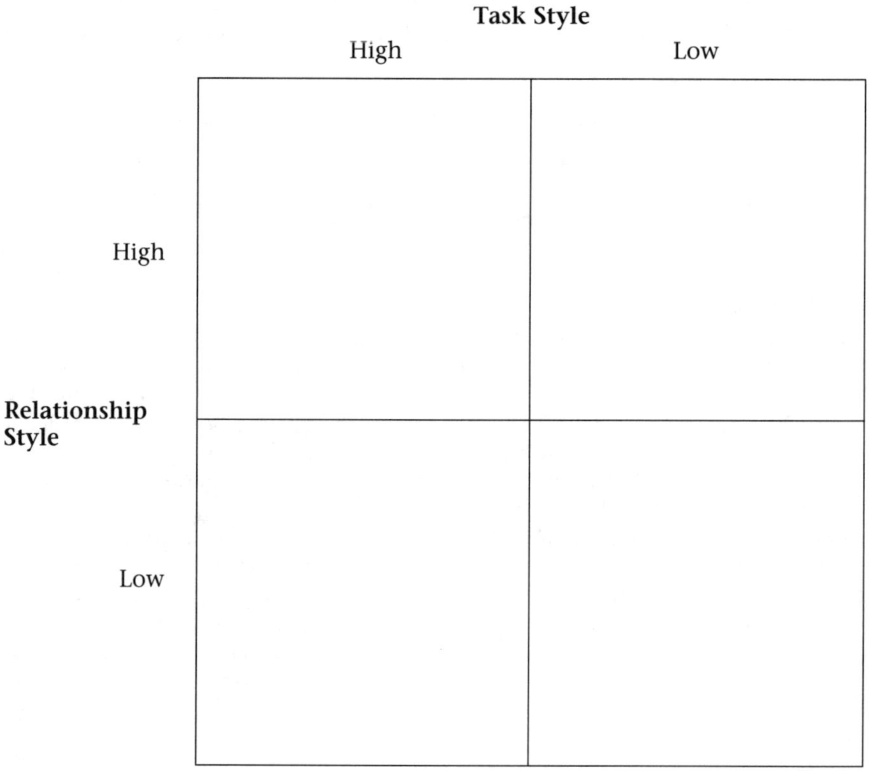

FIGURE 8.4   Leadership Styles

much the style as the total number (from 1 to 4) of categories that make up the style range. Thus an effective manager would be able to adapt to the situation by calling on any of the styles that constitute his range.

Leadership through Empowerment

In a dialogue between Warren Bennis and Robert Townsend (1995) on *Reinventing Leadership: Strategies to Empower the Organization,* Bennis notes

> The key to competitive advantage in the 1990s and beyond will be the capacity of leadership to create a social architecture capable of generating intellectual capital. The key words in that dense sentence are the last two. Intellectual capital means ideas, know-how, innovation, knowledge, and expertise. That's what's going to make the difference. Restructuring and reengineering can take you only so far; you cannot restructure or reengineer your company into prosperity. That takes ideas and reinvention. You're not going to attract or retain a work force like that under silly and obsolete forms of bureaucratic, command-and-control leadership. You can't release the brain power of any organization by using whips and chains. You get the best out of people by empowering them, by supporting them, by getting out of their way. As author Max De Pree said, you've got to abandon your ego to the talents of others (pp. 3–4).

According to Bennis and Townsend, the key to managerial leadership is *cultivating leadership by being open to the leadership potential of others.* That will require several things. First, a leader must have a strong set of convictions, a devoted constituency, and a way to gather broad support for her goals. Second, leaders must possess character, experience, intelligence, and energy. Finally, leaders must be willing to mentor—train—others to be leaders.

Bennis (1976) lists a number of *leadership characteristics* that are important to future leaders. He argues that leaders should develop vision and assertiveness; make effective and decisive decisions; look at the larger, not smaller, organizational picture; observe and interpret in the context of the organization; take calculated risks; know how to gather and interpret organizational information; be able to differentiate between organizational messages; understand and recognize the importance of the organization's unique culture; enhance organizational cooperation and loyalty; feel comfortable with themselves; and find a way to handle the stress of leadership.

Kouzes and Posner (1995) argue that "The leader who makes the difference" sees leadership as a form of self-development that is embodied in five fundamental practices. They believe that leaders

- *challenge the process,* looking for innovative ways to improve their organization;
- *inspire a shared vision* that they believe will make the difference; they not only see the future but enlist others in that vision;

- *enable* others to act by fostering collaboration and teamwork through sharing information and providing guidance;
- *model the way* by creating standards of excellence, setting the example by action, and winning the small battles; and
- *encourage the heart* by recognizing individual contributions and celebrating those accomplishments as part of their leadership strategy (p. 318).

They believe that leadership is developed on the job through on-the-job learning, observation of others, and education (see Figure 8.5). Leadership, they believe, is a matter of continuing self-development.

Communication Strategies

How does the leader *empower* her employees? The thrust of most leadership models is communication. *The good leader will utilize communication flow to her advantage.* To empower others, however, requires that communication

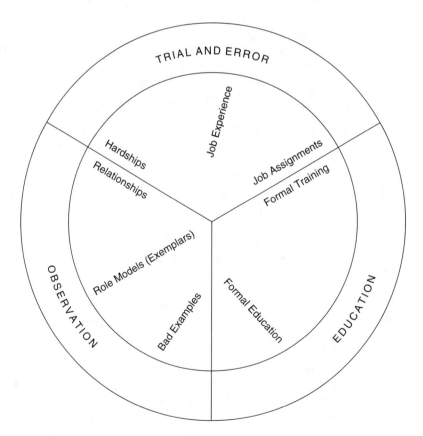

FIGURE 8.5   Opportunities for Learning to Lead

Source: J. M. Kouzes & B. Z. Posner (1995). *The leadership challenge: How to keep getting extraordinary things done in organizations.* San Francisco: Jossey-Bass Publishers.

flow go both ways: *upward and downward.* Further, communication must be actively sought and dialogue engaged in for it to have impact. The organizational culture should be such that the communication climate is supportive of communication. From the more "classical" leadership approaches, we find a Theory Y or System 4 orientation, one that encourages open communication and feedback.

Second, *the leader must establish ways of making decisions and communicating those decisions to others in such a way as to empower others to act them out.* Richmond and McCroskey (1979) linked management style and communication style, identifying what they then called "Management Communication Style" or MCS. *MCS* ranges from Theory X/System 1 style to Theory Y/System 4 style. At one extreme ("tell"), decisions are handed down from management to employees and it is expected that they will be carried out as directed. At the other extreme ("join"), the manager delegates the responsibility for decisions to the employees. Between "tell" and "join" you have "sell" and "consult" strategies. Selling involves persuading employees of the correctness or appropriateness of the decisions. Consultation involves the manager making her decision after discussing it with the employees or affected individuals. Richmond and McCroskey note that telling and selling styles are dominated by downward communication that is either non-interactive or partially interactive and consulting by upward communication that is interactive. Joining is characterized as primarily horizontal and highly interactive.

Third, *the good manager/leader should possess good communication skills.* Those skills are found in the three aspects of communication first described in Chapter 1: *content research, client analysis,* and *communication dialogue.* Understanding how to motivate (Chapter 7) is part of leadership; understanding that communication empowers employees to act on their own helps to foster a supportive communication climate, which, in turn, should foster self-development in future leaders.

SUMMARY

This chapter began with a premise offered in earlier chapters that individuals do not count in the organization. By now you should realize that this premise is wrong—individuals do count, they are in fact extremely important to the organization. Traditional approaches to management, however, see leading the organization from a rather simple "they're with us or against us" perspective. As you step up the organizational hierarchy two things change. First, you move from managing people to managing groups of people. Second, your definition of what you manage changes from the person to an abstraction. The good managerial leader never forgets that those "assets" and "resources" are human beings.

CASE 8.2   Karen in Déjà Vu

Karen has decided to allow the entire group to participate in hiring a secretary. They have interviewed twelve candidates for the job. Nine of the twelve, it was agreed by all, were unacceptable. They had a second interview with the remaining three candidates. Will is concerned that candidate one will not take the job or will not stay very long because he is overqualified. Four others liked candidate one the best. Sandra and Eduardo feel about equally about candidates two and three. Will prefers candidate three. Karen prefers candidate two. They met together again, without any of the candidates. Now Sandra, Eduardo, Will, and Karen all prefer candidate three. The four others still like candidate one. They have now met for a total of twenty hours, without resolution. Karen told them they would have to reach consensus in the beginning. What does she do now?

The chapter explored two related concepts in detail: working and leading groups. The chapter's thesis was that at some point in your organization career you will move from working with individuals to establishing a team that produces something greater than the product. We noted that at this stage you have moved from supervising to managing. Early in learning to manage you administered one or more small groups. As you mature to upper-level management your leadership goes from motivating others to do their task to communicating ideas and organizational philosophy, a much more difficult task.

The chapter then looked at what constitutes the small group, what constitutes a group, and the problems associated with group life. It also focused on identifying what a leader is, describing leadership traits and functions from a descriptive perspective. From a more predictive perspective it looked into leadership/management style and empowering leadership throughout the organization. The chapter ended with a discussion of message strategies that enhance the empowerment process.

QUESTIONS FOR THOUGHT

1. Groupthink is caused primarily by there being one strong, dominant individual in the group. Obviously if the boss is in the group, he or she is likely to function as a stimulus for groupthink. How can the boss be part of a group without triggering groupthink?
2. During a time of significant change in an organization, which is accompanied by frustration and low morale, what can a social group do to improve the situation?
3. How can we get a group with hidden agendas to disclose those agendas?
4. What are the negative repercussions of majority vote?

REFERENCES

Bales, R., & Strodbeck, F. (1951). Phases in group problem solving. *Journal of Abnormal and Social Psychology, 46,* 485–495.

Beebe, S. A., & Masterson, J. T. (1990). *Communicating in small groups: Principles and practices,* 4th ed. New York: HarperCollins.

Bennis, W. (1976). Leadership—A beleaguered species. *Organizational Dynamics, 5,* 3–16.

Bennis, W., & Townsend, R. (1995). *Reinventing leadership: Strategies to empower the organization.* New York: William Morrow and Company.

Blake, R., & Mouton, J. (1964). *The managerial grid.* Houston: Gulf Publishing.

Bostrom, R. (1970). Patterns of communication interaction in small groups. *Communication Monographs, 37,* 257–263.

Burgoon, M., Heston, J. K., & McCroskey, J. C. (1974). *Small group communication: A functional approach.* New York: Holt, Rinehart & Winston.

Cartwright, D., & Zander, A. (Eds.) (1968). *Group dynamics: Research and theory,* 3rd ed. New York: Harper & Row.

Cragen, J. F., & Wright, D. W. (1986). *Communication in small group discussions,* 2nd ed. St. Paul, MN: West Publishing Co.

Dalkey, N. C. (June, 1969). *The Delphi Method: An experimental study of group opinion.* Rand Corporation Memorandum RM 5888-PR.

DeVito, J. A. (1997). *Human communication: The basic course,* 7th ed. New York: Longman.

Dewey, J. (1910). *How we think.* New York: D. C. Heath.

Fiedler, F. (1967). *A theory of leadership effectiveness.* New York: McGraw-Hill.

Fiedler, F. (1965). Engineer the job to fit the manager. *Harvard Business Review, 43,* 115–122.

Gibb, J. R. (1961). Defensive communication. *Journal of Communication, 11,* 141–148.

Goldhaber, G., Dennis, H., Richetto, G., & Wiio, O. (1984). *Information strategies: New pathways to management productivity.* Norwood, NJ: Ablex.

Hersey, P., & Blanchard, K. H. (1977). *Management of organizational behavior: Utilizing human resources.* Englewood Cliffs, NJ: Prentice-Hall.

Hickson, M. L., & Stacks, D. W. (1992). *NVC: Nonverbal communication studies and applications,* 3rd ed. Dubuque, IA: Wm. C. Brown.

Infante, D. A., Rancer, A. S., & Womack, D. F. (1993). *Building communication theory,* 2nd ed. Prospect Heights, IL: Waveland Press.

Janis, I. L. (1972). *Victims of groupthink.* Boston: Houghton-Mifflin.

Janis, I. (November, 1971). Groupthink. *Psychology Today,* 43–46, 74–77.

Kouzes, J. M., & Posner (1995). *The leadership challenge: How to keep getting extraordinary things done in organizations.* San Fransisco: Jossey-Bass.

Kreps, G. L. (1986). *Organizational communication: Theory and practice.* White Plains, NY: Longman.

Likert, R. (1961). *New patterns of management.* New York: McGraw-Hill.

McCroskey, J. C. & Wheeless, L. R. (1976). *An introduction to human communication.* Boston: Allyn & Bacon.

McGregor, D. (1960). *The human side of enterprise.* New York: McGraw-Hill.

Richmond, V. P., & McCroskey, J. C. (1992). *Organizational communication for survival.* Englewood Cliffs, NJ: Prentice-Hall.

Richmond, V. P., & McCroskey, J. C. (1979). Management communication style, tolerance for disagreement, and innovativeness as predictors of employee satisfaction: A comparison of single-factor, two-factor, and multiple-factor approaches. In D. Nimmo (Ed.), *Communication Yearbook* (Vol. 3, pp. 359–373). New Brunswick, NJ: Transaction Books.

White, R., & Lippitt, R. (1968). Leader behavior and member reaction in three social climates. In D. Cartwright & A. Zander (Eds.), *Group dynamics: Research and theory,* 3rd ed.

White, R., & Lippitt, R. (1960). *Autocracy and democracy.* New York: Harper & Row.

9

ADAPTING TO CHANGE

Frederick Taylor's Scientific Management
  Bureaucratic machines
  Information machines
  Review

Elton Mayo's Human Relations Approach
  Review

Chester Barnard and Herbert Simon's Analytic Framework
  The small group approach
  James March and Herbert A. Simon
  Review

New Theories of Organizing
  Systems theory
  Review
  Ouchi's Theory Z (Japanese theory)
  Review
  Total Quality Management (TQM)

Objectives

By the end of this chapter you should be able to

1. Distinguish traditional and new theories of organizing as they relate to adaptation.
2. Explain scientific management as an overarching organizational theory.
3. Discuss Bernard and Simon's contributions to the study of organizations.
4. Differentiate among the "new" theories of organizing.
5. Explain how an organization's approach to organizing itself affects your communication and how you adapt in the New Organization.

As we have noted in earlier chapters, organizational life is composed of change. As an individual, the beginning of your career is affected by such change, but you have little input into the change process. When you reach middle- and particularly upper-level management, however, you begin to have a direct impact on the organization's path—how and where it grows or does not grow. You have reached the *decision-making level,* gone from being a "worker" to a "leader" and "decision maker." No longer are you supervising several people engaged in some limited production task, you now are managing *groups of people* engaged in the larger goals of the organization. As such, you have already adapted to the new role; however, your mission has changed and you must consider the entire organization, corporation, or conglomerate in your decisions. You must take an *organizational view.*

There are many different ways to analyze organizations. Sherman Krupp (1961) discussed five such approaches. Frederick Taylor's "scientific management" theory of technological efficiency has as its primary goal to produce the highest quantity at the least economic and time costs. The "human relations" studies are concerned with the feelings of individuals in the organization. Chester I. Barnard and Herbert Simon's analytic framework uses certain criteria to evaluate organizational operations, some of which include equilibrium, goal fulfillment, decision making, and interdependence. The small group approach including the works of George C. Homans, Michael Argyle, and Robert Bales, focuses on the interaction among members as the basis for analysis. The content and behavior approach of James March and Herbert Simon uses such criteria as the selection of goals and values, relations between actions and outcomes, and possible alternatives in various situations to analyze the organization.

Many of these names and concepts should be familiar by now. We have talked about them, referred to them, or described them as ways of explaining how organizations operate. However, we did not go into detail then because your exposure to the organization did not require in-depth treatment. Our purpose in this chapter is to explore the major approaches to organizations in an attempt to better understand how such approaches tint or color the way the organization adapts to change—or if it can adapt at all. As a manager you must understand the organization's approach to itself—how does it "see" itself? How does that "vision" affect communication? How does it affect performance? And, how can this knowledge help you become a better organizational communicator? We begin with one of the earliest and most basic approaches, scientific management, an approach that accounts for many an organization's approach to management (see Chapter 1).

FREDERICK TAYLOR'S SCIENTIFIC MANAGEMENT

Taylor (1911) developed *scientific management* in the early days of the twentieth century. Morgan (1997) refers to this approach metaphorically as "organizations as machines." The general idea is that workers engage in *actions.* As each action is built upon the preceding action, the result is a work outcome. For example, if you go to a restaurant, you are given a menu. As the customer, you select the items that you want to order. Morgan (1997) indicates that a checklist can be developed to indicate the preferred actions of the waiter or waitress. Each item (or action) can be viewed as a "yes" or "no" action. In greeting the customer, the waitress should smile and sincerely greet the customer, while having eye contact. The counterperson should understand the order and should have to be given the order only once (Table 9.1).

Henry Ford's notion of an assembly line becomes pertinent even for jobs in the service sector when this kind of thinking is used. The total process of any job is "broken down" into its parts. Morgan (1997) has suggested that the approach is similar to that developed by Frederick the Great of Prussia for use in the military. From 1740 to 1786, his army was composed of criminals, foreign mercenaries, paupers, and unruly conscripts—people whom we ordinarily do not consider effective soldiers. Thinking in terms of mechanized toys, Frederick was determined to transform this unruly mass into a mechanized body of fighting men. He introduced ranks and uniforms, standardized regulations, command language, standardized equipment and tasks.

The *standardization process* is essential to scientific management. Such standardization today allows you to know that ordering a Big Mac, an order of fries, and a large Coke means the same at a McDonald's in Boston, Birmingham, Atlanta, Los Angeles, Paris, and Moscow. *Decision making, then, is eliminated as a problem for the worker.*

Scientific managers use *time-and-motion studies* to determine the specific steps in the job tasks. For example, if one were ordering two hot dogs, two bags of potato chips, and two Cokes at a football game, the time-and-motion study would see a problem in the following situation. The customer makes the order. The worker goes back and brings out two hot dogs. "Mustard and ketchup?" asks the customer. The worker points the customer to the mustard and ketchup and walks back to get the potato chips and Cokes. The customer gives the worker the money, the worker goes back to get the change, the worker brings the change to the customer and says "Thank you." While all of the necessary steps were taken, the time-and-motion analyst would say that, indeed, too many steps were taken.

There should have been a cardboard tray to hold all of the items. The worker should have taken the order, told the customer the price, collected the money, and then gone to the back to make the order. Two hot dogs, two bags chips, and two Cokes should have been brought back, along with the change. The worker says "Thank you." Such a process increases the efficiency of the entire operation.

Bureaucratic Machines

The concept of scientific management has been discussed by Max Weber (1947) regarding "white-collar workers" (you, now in a managerial role) in what is referred to as *bureaucracy*. Weber suggested that such an approach includes division of labor, hierarchy, an established system of rules and regulations, and an impersonal approach, in which employment constitutes a

TABLE 9.1 Management Observation Checklist for Counter Staff in a Fast-Food Restaurant

Greeting the customer	Yes	No
1. There is a smile.		
2. It is a sincere greeting.		
3. There is eye contact.		
Other:		
Taking the order	**Yes**	**No**
1. The counterperson is thoroughly familiar with the menu ticket. (No hunting for items.)		
2. The customer has to give the order only once.		
3. Small orders (four items or less) are memorized rather than written down.		
4. There is suggestive selling.		
Other:		
Assembling the order	**Yes**	**No**
1. The order is assembled in the proper sequence.		
2. Grill slips are handed in first.		
3. Drinks are poured in the proper sequence.		
4. Proper amount of ice.		
5. Cups slanted and finger used to activate.		
6. Drinks are filled to the proper level.		
7. Drinks are capped.		
8. Clean cups.		
9. Holding times are observed on coffee.		
10. Cups are filled to the proper level on coffee.		
Other:		
Presenting the order	**Yes**	**No**
1. It is properly packaged.		
2. The bag is double folded.		
3. Plastic trays are used if eating inside.		
4. A tray liner is used.		
5. The food is handled in a proper manner.		
Other:		
Asking for & receiving payment	**Yes**	**No**
1. The amount of the order is stated clearly and loud enough to hear.		
2. The denomination received is clearly stated.		
3. The change is counted out loud.		
4. Change is counted efficiently.		
5. Large bills are laid on the till until the change is given.		
Other:		
Thanking the customer & asking for repeat business	**Yes**	**No**
1. There is always a thank you.		
2. The thank you is sincere.		
3. There is eye contact.		
4. Return business was asked for.		
Other:		

G. Morgan, *Images of Organization*, 2nd ed. p. 21, copyright © 1997 by Sage Publications, Inc. Reprinted by permission of Sage Publications, Inc.

career. For all practical purposes, the concept of "bureaucracy" can be transformed across different organizations—it does not matter what the service or product of the organization is.

According to scientific management, employees work for *money;* the atmosphere or climate under which people work is relatively unimportant. Weber's bureaucracy was characterized by specialized labor, a graded system of centralized authority, a system of central files, a set of specialized skills referred to as "office management," rigid rules, red tape, and an emphasis on *procedure.* In essence, a new worker is viewed as a "replacement part" or simply a cog in a bureaucratic "machine." The analogy of machine is appropriate. When you change your car engine's spark plugs, it does not matter which plugs you use, only that they are the plugs specified by the manufacturer; plug A can go in any of the cylinders. If plug A does not work, then you simply replace it with one that will!

One of the authors found an interesting aspect of this in a military unit. The unit was composed of military and civilian personnel. On a day when the colonel (the "boss") was on vacation, the next person in the line of authority moved into his office, and the next person below moved into the second person's office, and so forth. This reflects the feeling in a bureaucracy that people are just *replacement units.* As noted in Chapter 8, the unit is actually a person and should be treated as one; bureaucracies, however, dehumanize people—they unitize them, creating one mold yielding "soldiers" who do the same task over and over without thinking.

Thus, looking at scientific management from the blue-collar time-and-motion studies to its evolution into the white-collar world, we see several differences. For the blue-collar worker, the principle is *to use the fewest number of steps to produce items quickly with some minimal standard of quality.* Such a worker, in a textile mill for example, would want to produce as many shirts as possible, especially since many of the workers are paid by the number of units (piecework) produced rather than the number of hours worked. In addition, the bureaucrat is viewed as a *security-oriented worker*—one who wants a lifetime occupation. Because bureaucrats generally are often employed by the government, there is typically no product involved. Bureaucrats collect taxes, sell automobile license plates, operate state employment offices, file papers, and so forth.

Table 9.2 illustrates the scientific management approach. In summary, technical calculations are considered superior to human judgment. Workers

TABLE 9.2   Scientific Management

Metaphor	Machine theory
Research Method(s)	Observation (Time-and-motion studies)
Type of Organization	Industrial (Bureaucratic)
Bias	Management knows best
Organizational Communication	Written; formal; down; task
Goal	Efficiency

cannot be trusted to make decisions. Ultimately the worker receives higher wages, with fewer hours. Time-and-motion studies are used in the calculation of events. Human worth is less than a machine's worth. Rules are composed ultimately to resolve any situation and to eliminate workers' making decisions.

One can easily see, then, that scientific management is used when one orders breakfast at a fast-food restaurant at 10:30 in the morning. "We stop serving breakfast at 9:30. I'm sorry. Would you like to order something else?" Certainly, the customer is not always right. *The policy rules.* A similar kind of policy decision can be seen at many government organizations where there is a sign that reads, "Don't go past the yellow line until your name is called."

The bureaucracy is characterized by its impersonal nature. The bureaucracy is clearly defined into a hierarchy of offices. Each office is filled with a free contractual relationship so that in principle there can be free selection of persons to fill vacancies on a full- or part-time basis. Each office has a clearly defined sphere of communication. Candidates are selected on the basis of technical qualifications. Workers are paid in fixed salaries. One holds a lifetime career; promotions are based on seniority, standardized tests, and rules. The worker is subject to strict and systematic discipline and control in the conduct of her work. The official position is one's primary occupation. Table 9.3 illustrates bureaucracy.

Information Machines

While never directly associated in the past, a case can be made that "information theory" has a connection to scientific management. Traditionally, information theory has been associated with *cybernetics* (a science concerned with the comparative study of operations of electronic computer systems and the human nervous system). According to Norbert Weiner (1967), a computer operates in the following manner: Data (inputs) are introduced to obtain some effect on the outer world (output) and may involve a large number of combinations. These combinations are stored in *memory.* Data fed in which indicate mode of operation are called *taping* (now sometimes called *programming*). Control of a machine on the basis of its actual performance rather than its expected performance is referred to as *feedback.*

The overall purpose of communication in information theory is to provide *efficient message transfer.* An early pioneer in this field was Samuel F. B. Morse,

TABLE 9.3   Bureaucracy

Metaphor	Red tape
Research Method(s)	Comparison/contrast
Type of Organization	Governmental; large corporation
Bias	"Pro-formality"
Organizational Communication	Formal; written
Goal	Accountability

who devised a system whereby all messages could be transmitted by wire via a two-digit code, the dot and the dash. (Today the code for a computer is "0" and "1.") This work became more important during World War II. Claude Shannon, working for Bell Laboratories, devised a basic model of the communication process based on these premises (see Figure 9.1).

To translate this model, the source is where the data enter the system (i.e., income tax forms enter the tax office or yards of cloth enter the textile mill). Data are entered through a "coding system." The data are translated to the final product (output—that is, refund mailed or shirt completed). There are, however, sources of error, or *noise*. Of course there is the literal, physical noise that may prevent concentration. For the computer, the electricity may go out or the worker may miss a keystroke. Noise is defined as anything that may distort the message during the transmission/reception phase. Without the noise source, we would theoretically always have perfect communication. (If you work with a computer, you have probably discovered that almost always when there is an error, it was your error.)

As research continued, however, individuals found that there was something missing in this model of communication. What was missing was *feedback*. In large measure, the feedback to the scientific manager is analogous to the level of customer satisfaction. Feedback is especially important in human communication because we wish to know the progress of our communication while we are in the process of communicating. With the computer, we usually do not know whether there has been an error until we get all of the output back. In our everyday conversations with others, however, we would like to have a more efficient system—that is, we would like to detect our noise sources earlier.

For example, let's suppose that you intend to ask your boss for a raise. You have no reason to believe that she will not give it to you. The company is doing well. Your sales have been the best in the company. You go into her office. You give your planned speech about how well you have done and how well the company is doing. Finally, you come to the issue at hand. She says: "You know, you're right. I've thought about that many times. I just keep forgetting. I'll see to it right away." This is known in information theory as *negative feedback*.

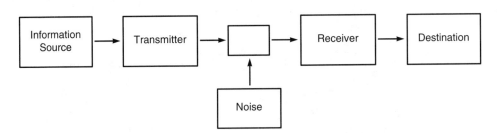

FIGURE 9.1   Shannon's Information Processing Model

The feedback is negative in the sense that you do not have to make any changes in the structuring of your message to accomplish your purpose. Negative feedback also occurs when you put a problem into your computer and the correct answer is given. Now, suppose that you have the same situation. You ask for the raise. Your boss says, "I have considered it, but I want to talk about our hiring the new secretary. Let's sit down and talk about what kind of person we want at lunch." In this situation, you have been ignored. You have received *positive feedback,* which calls for your restructuring the message (or at least repeating it).

As noted earlier, computers operate on a *binary digit system*—a bit. Each piece of information is a bit. According to a formula devised by Shannon and Weaver (1949), it should take 3.332 questions for you to guess what number a person has chosen between one and ten. Using an ordinary deck of fifty-two playing cards, with no jokers, we will attempt to illustrate this principle. Assume that the ace is considered the highest face card. A computer selects one card from the deck. By asking the fewest number of questions you can (efficiently) try to determine, asking only "yes" or "no" questions, which card the computer has selected.

Below are some possible question–answer combinations:

1. Is it a red card? *No.* (You have eliminated 50% of the cards with one question.)
2. Is it a club? *Yes.* (You have now eliminated 75%.)
3. Is it above an eight? *No.* (You have now eliminated almost 87%.)
4. Is it an even number? *Yes.* (You have now eliminated 92%.)
5. Is it above a five? *No.* (You now have eliminated all but two cards.)
6. Is it the two of clubs? *No.*

Now you know that it is the four of clubs. In a situation such as this one, you should be able to find the right answer from fifty-two options in seven or fewer binary-digit questions.

Let us look at another example, using the same questions and answers as above. What if you asked a seventh question: "Is it the four of clubs?" Information theorists call this a *redundant question.* It yields no new information. It is unnecessary. In comparison, the scientific management approach, uses a time-and-motion study to eliminate redundancy (inefficiency).

Another inefficient aspect of some people's communication, according to the information theorists, is what is known as entropy. *Entropy* may be considered the opposite of redundancy; it is the lack of information demonstrated by *ambiguity.* For example, the question, "Is it an odd or even number?" The computer will answer, "Yes." But we cannot tell whether it was odd or even.

Scientific management attempts to eliminate redundancy and entropy through time-and-motion studies. Some computer programmers are concerned about eliminating keystrokes because such elimination improves the efficiency of their operations. The waiter or waitress should be able to ask for a customer's order only once. The textile worker should not place too few buttons or too many buttons on the shirt.

Review

As an approach to organizational management, scientific management leaves much to be desired. For the simple manufacture of a rather simple product, it has its advantages: It is both efficient and economical. For more complex endeavors, however, it is extremely limited. If, for some reason, the unit you are managing is not meeting its quota or producing minimal quality products, the organization will not look at ways to motivate your unit, will not look for innovative ways to change the process, instead it will replace YOU. Your communication networks are downward—you get your orders and you then transmit them to your unit supervisors, who in turn transmit them to their workers. Transmit is a correct term here—there is little or no feedback, just instructions. Upward communication is expected to be product-oriented and positive. Your communication strategies are minimal. Knowing your workers and trying to motivate them will win you no rewards with your bosses. You produce or you are replaced.

ELTON MAYO'S HUMAN RELATIONS APPROACH

In the mid-1920s, the National Research Council's Illuminating Engineering Society decided to study the influence of lighting on workers' productivity, in a sense studying external—*noise*—factors that might influence the efficiency of an organization. Some of these studies were conducted at the Hawthorne plant of the Western Electric Company in Cicero, Illinois. At first, the researchers increased the amount of light the workers were using to produce telephones. The researchers observed that productivity increased.

Then the lighting was decreased; productivity, however, still increased. The final report's conclusion was that workers functioned differently when researchers/observers were paying special attention to them. In a sense, it could be said that the lack of "supervision" was the noise factor. Studies such as these illustrate what has become known as the *Hawthorne Effect,* wherein people behave artificially when they know they are the subjects of an experiment. In today's world, however, the employer does not have to maintain a constant vigilance to observe the workers. Computers can statistically keep track of outputs so that managers can monitor the work of their employees.

Elton Mayo, of the Harvard University Business School, and others took a particular interest in the illumination studies. They performed other experiments that produced similar outcomes. They had rediscovered the importance of *primary groups* (people working together in this case). Such groups appeared to work well together because of their informal, interpersonal relationships. According to Morgan (1997), "These studies are now famous for identifying

DILBERT / Scott Adams

DILBERT © United Feature Syndicate. Reprinted by Permission.

the importance of social needs in the workplace and the way workgroups can satisfy these needs by restricting output and engaging in all manner of unplanned activities" (p. 41).

That is to say, when people work together on a regular basis, they *share* a "workplan" together. Such a workplan may be to increase or decrease productivity. The concept of "job satisfaction" arose out of these studies and was probably at least partially responsible for the motivation work of Homans, Maslow, and Herzberg (see Chapter 7). This "human relations" school of organizations viewed workers and organizations as *organisms,* not as machines. While the scientific management manager felt that money was the only motivator, this new approach found other motivators.

The basic assumption underlying the human relations approach was that *increased job satisfaction increased productivity.* According to Locke (1976), there were three primary elements concerned with job satisfaction: (1) the physical-economic school, concerned with physical arrangements (now referred to as "ergonomics"); (2) the social, human relations school, which emphasized good working relationships; and (3) the work itself (or growth) school, which emphasized the attainment of "satisfaction through growth in skill, efficacy, and responsibility made by mentally challenging work" (p. 1300).

Network analysis (see Chapter 8) was utilized to determine much about the nature of the social groups that worked with one another. A basic concept that underlies the human relations school is that the resulting product is a group product. Morgan (1997) writes that the human relations school was about "making employees feel more useful and important by giving them meaningful jobs, and by giving as much autonomy, responsibility, and recognition as possible as a means of getting them involved in their work" (p. 42).

So far, then, we can see that jobs that call for little mental work, especially repetitive tasks, with little flexibility, might utilize a scientific management approach. The money is the reward for undertaking such boring tasks. In those jobs that call for greater flexibility, mental work, and creativity, one might prefer using a human relations approach. In these jobs, with this kind of theory, the satisfaction is in the work itself.

TABLE 9.4   Human Relations School

Metaphor	Organism theory
Research Method(s)	Sociometric; diary
Type of Organization	Manufacturing
Bias	Pro-worker
Organizational Communication	Informal; formal
Goal	Job satisfaction

The human relations approach was given even more emphasis in the work of Douglas McGregor (1960). In many ways, comparing and contrasting scientific management with the human relations school, McGregor devised what he called "Theory X" and "Theory Y." He felt that the following underlying set of assumptions distinguished the two approaches to organizations:

Theory X

1. People do not like to work. They are lazy. They avoid work except to pay for essentials.
2. Therefore, people must be forced to work. They must be supervised and controlled.
3. People do not like responsibility. They will avoid being responsible unless some manager makes them responsible.
4. Messages flow down from the top. Decision making is undertaken by a few at the top.
5. Upward communication is in the form of suggestion boxes, spy systems, and grapevines.
6. Downward communication is used for announcements, information, and orders.
7. Decision making is often undertaken with inaccurate and/or incomplete information.

Theory Y

1. Work is natural.
2. Managers are there to assist in the creativity and responsibility of the workers.
3. The average person learns to be responsible.
4. Intellectual properties of workers are never fully utilized, but managers can encourage the use of the mind.
5. Messages flow in all directions.
6. Upward feedback is encouraged.
7. Decision making is spread throughout the company.
8. There are frequent, honest interactions among the workers and between workers and management.

Review

Theory X managers differ little from their scientific management counterparts. Theory Y managers, however, are truly interested in the welfare of their workers, believing that such interest will directly influence their work and thus the organization. Theory Y managers, as noted in Chapter 8, will lead through empowerment or at least through some form of participant-management. The key, however, is communication. Communication networks will engage in upward, downward, and horizontal communication. As with complex networks, a major concern to you will be with "noise" or message distortion. Therefore, feedback becomes of utmost importance to you and a cornerstone of your communication strategies. You will be "joining" rather than "telling"; your approach may require "selling," but selling in such a manner as to understand why your messages are not being accepted. In the human relations approach you are a vital element; you will be held responsible for your worker's products. You are expected to be both coach and cheerleader, motivating workers to self-actualize when possible and kicking when necessary. As a Theory Y manager you celebrate with your workers, yet still stand apart.

CHESTER BARNARD AND HERBERT SIMON'S ANALYTIC FRAMEWORK

Chester Barnard's (1938) book, *The Functions of the Executive,* found that the "economic man" had to be replaced with the "social man." Barnard felt that the informal organization was more important than the formal organization. Instead of using scientific approaches to study the behavior of individuals, he used sociometric data and diaries. *Sociometrics* is a means by which a researcher can determine the informal lines of communication in the networks that exist at work. Such an approach has been criticized for not being quantitative by Argyris (1995), who stated: "Those of us who strive to produce usable knowledge have, I believe, a responsibility, on the one hand, to respect the taken for granted, while on the other hand, to use research methods that do not take it for granted that usable knowledge will be produced" (p. 5).

To a large extent, the work of Barnard and Herbert A. Simon, formed what would later be called the *systems approach.* They were interested in the organization achieving its goals, but they were also interested in how decisions were made. They were interested in *equilibrium,* a theory of motivation under which workers would participate in decision making and the organization would survive (March & Simon, 1958).

The Small Group Approach

Small group communication was discussed in detail in Chapter 8. It should be noted, however, that Homans (1950), Bales and Strodtbeck (1951), and Argyle and Cook (1976) were even more fascinated with those informal groups that develop in working situations. They saw informal communication net-works as central to what goes on in an organization. Their concerns were who worked with whom with what effect. As such, they were interested in what came to be labeled *interacts* (Fisher & Hawes, 1971), or connections between group members as they participate in the group process.

James March and Herbert A. Simon

March and Simon (1958) emphasized what they refer to as the *administrative man*, as opposed to economic or social man. They were concerned with the selection of goals and values in the organization, the relationship between ac-tions and outcomes, and the possible alternatives in various situations. March and Simon note that, "Most human decision making, whether individual or organizational, is concerned with the discovery and selection of satisfactory alternatives; only in exceptional cases is it concerned with the selection of op-timal alternatives" (pp. 140–141). They are concerned with the initiation of "programs"—when an alarm goes off at the fire station, or when a relief ap-plicant arrives at the social worker's desk, programs are initiated which end in a search for alternative answers. Such programs have a "performance strategy" to determine how well they have worked.

Review

As a manager working in an organization that approaches itself from a small group orientation your communication will be primarily horizontal. You are a member of a workgroup, but your relationships between those groups above you (decision makers) and below you (production teams) are of utmost im-portance. You probably are not working for an organization that is making zippers or some assembly-line product. Your organization may be service-ori-ented or one whose product is problem solving. Your task is to get your work-ers to create the best possible product, but time is still of the essence. As a member of the group, you must understand the roles and rules that determine group routine, while simultaneously enacting the role of leader in one group and follower in others (those with upper-management).

NEW THEORIES OF ORGANIZING

Thus, we have the five *traditional* approaches discussed by Krupp. The ques-tion is what has happened since the 1960s. The answer may be to look at three other theories that have tended to influence management and organizational communication over the last forty years. They are *Systems Theory, Theory Z (Japanese Theory),* and *Total Quality Management (TQM).*

Systems Theory

Warren G. Bennis (1966) has described the *open system* as "an adaptive structure actively encountering many different environments, both internal and external, in its productive efforts" (p. 45). In many ways, the systems approach incorporates elements of several other approaches that we have discussed. Katz and Kahn (1966) suggested that there are nine elements in the systems approach:

1. the importation of energy or input
2. throughput
3. output
4. the system as a cycle of events
5. negative entropy
6. information input and the coding process
7. homeostasis
8. differentiation
9. equifinality

Figure 9.2 demonstrates the system, with several subsystems, encompassed within a suprasystem, encompassed within an environment. A rather simplistic definition of a *system* is a set of objects together with relationships between the objects and between their attributes (Hall & Fagen, 1968). A *sub-system* is essentially a component of a system; a *suprasystem* is a combination of systems. The *environment* is composed of those objects *outside the system.*

To clarify these elements, let's assume that General Motors is a system. A sub-system might be an automobile assembly plant in Cadillac, Michigan. The automobile industry might be the suprasystem. The environment is composed of customers, governments, consumer protection groups, etc. The primary problem for each of these units is the concept of *boundary.* What is the boundary line between the assembly plant and the overall company? Are the workers also customers? Is the government also a customer? These boundary decisions are problems the researcher must attempt to resolve.

Using the assembly plant, we can better define specific elements of systems. First, there need to be *production inputs;* these may be in the form of labor, parts, the energy needed to assemble the parts, and so forth. The *throughput* is the transformation process through which inputs are changed into outputs. The *output* is the finished, assembled vehicle. The *cycle of events* is the continual process of exchanging inputs and outputs with the environment.

Negative entropy (*negentropy*) is the idea that systems build up a certain amount of energy to be used at another time, under another circumstance. It is a reversal of the process of "wearing down."

Information input (Hickson, 1971) is a loop in the system that may be defined as the knowledge used to adapt and maintain the system for its continued existence. *Homeostasis* is a result of continual input–output flow causing a sense of stability within the system. *Differentiation* is the replacement of diffuse

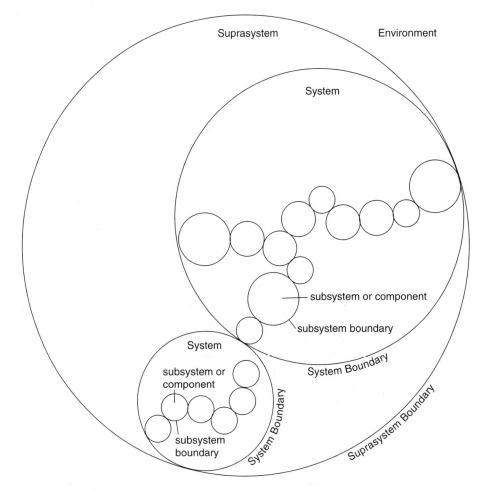

FIGURE 9.2   A Systems Approach

patterns by more specialized functions. *Equifinality* refers to the concept of reaching the same goal through different routes.

Hickson and Jennings (1993) have elaborated on the communication functions, utilizing a systems approach. Figure 9.3 demonstrates how one begins with *information input* from the environment. Such information might be a lawsuit in which a customer complains about a defect in the assembly of an automobile. Ideally, the system evaluates the input as positive, negative, or unclassifiable. This input would be considered negative, and would call for some response.

A decision, however, about a response is first based on the perceived *power* of the source. For example, do the company's lawyers believe the customer is

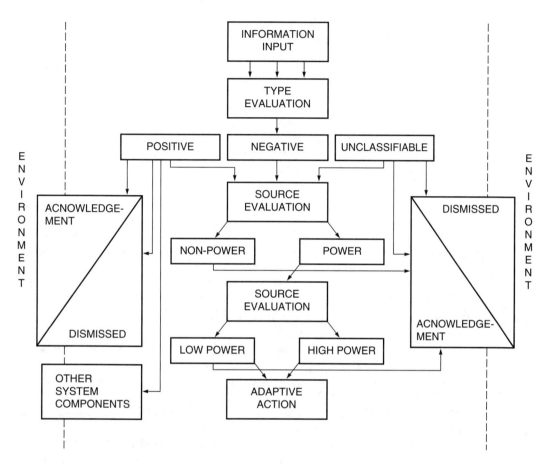

FIGURE 9.3   Adapting to Feedback

financially able to maintain the lawsuit? If at first you believe the customer may go on with the lawsuit, you have a second evaluation of the source's power. At any point, if the organization believes adaptation is unnecessary, the organization either dismisses the input or simply acknowledges it without adapting. However, if the source is perceived as high power in the second power evaluation, the organization will take adaptive action.

The general principle here is that an organization cannot adapt to every piece of information sent to it. In addition, there is the assumption that adapting is more difficult than not adapting. In this context, for example, some managers do not understand why a company decides to settle a lawsuit. The reason is that *the costs are less and the actions for adapting are minimal.* However, when there is a "class action" suit, in which there are hundreds or thousands of complaints, the company may fight the lawsuit because of the potential economic and adaptation costs.

CASE 9.1   Management Approach

Katherine has decided to open her own business. She will be doing the billing for an area hospital from her home, using a computer. Because the size of her hospital is so large, she has hired three of her friends to help. They have divided up the billing according to the first letter of the last names of patients. They have a computer network worked out so that they can also communicate with one another from their own homes. Katherine has read about all there is to read about management theory, but she does not know what kind of approach to use with this new business. What should she do?

It should be noted that the systems approach is the first to give so much credence to sources *outside* of the organization. In scientific management, human relations, and the other approaches previously discussed, the emphasis has been placed on what goes on *inside* the organization. The positive aspect of the systems approach is that it recognizes the need for change. In fact, an open system must both adapt internally *and* adapt to the environment (see Table 9.5).

Everett M. Rogers (1995) has presented a number of cases in which organizations did not adapt to their external environments. One of them is the gas refrigerator. Electric refrigerator company research and development people found that the "hum" produced by electric refrigerators was preferred by customers. Had the gas refrigerator companies emphasized that gas would still be operable even during major thunderstorms, hurricanes, and tornadoes, perhaps they would have improved their position. A similar kind of problem resulted when the makers of the "Dvorak keyboard" were unsuccessful in selling typewriters although typing would be much more efficient. Similar "marketing wars" have taken place between the Apple Macintosh computers and IBM-style computers. There have been problems in switching to the metric system in the United States because of the general resistance to change.

TABLE 9.5   Systems Theory

Metaphor	Flexibility
Research Method(s)	Network analysis
Type of Organization	Government; industry
Bias	Pro-"organization"
Organizational Communication	Crucial as interrelationship
Goal	Adaptation

Review

Working in a systems theory organization requires an understanding of the environments the organization works in. It also requires an understanding of the various boundaries that exist within the organization and its suborganizations. Communication networks in organizations that take a systems approach are vertical and horizontal. Indeed, the assumption you must make is that any message, positive or negative or neutral, will influence the organization somehow. Most systems move to their own death (Stacks, Hickson, & Hill, 1992). As such, you must be aware of entropy and negative entropy—establishing communication strategies that encourage growth while simultaneously maintaining a healthy work environment. Motivation and leadership style are extremely important in systems organizations. Because the system is affected by any change, you are constantly being impacted and impacting on the organization.

Ouchi's Theory Z (Japanese Theory)

By the late 1970s, many American managers were beginning to see the rise of productivity in other countries, especially Japan. Ouchi (1981) writes: "The most important characteristic of the Japanese organization is lifetime employment: Lifetime employment, more than being a single policy, is the rubric under which many facets of Japanese life and work are integrated" (p. 15). Whereas many Americans attempt to separate their worklife from the remainder of their lives, most Japanese consider lifetime employment as integral to the rest of their lives. It is important to note, however, that Theory Z accounts only for major Japanese *corporations* who account for only the top of the corporate hierarchy. Many Japanese work for smaller companies whose approach is more scientific management-oriented.

Theory Z includes *slow* evaluation and promotion, non-specialized career paths, implicit control mechanisms, collective responsibility, collective decision making, and a holistic concern for the organization (Ouchi, 1981). It is significant to note that the concept of *non-specialization* has been part of the Japanese system. In contrast, the past fifty years have brought about an extremely specialized system in the American corporate structure.

The 1990s, however, are indicative of the New Organization. In the New Organization, workers must be able to visualize the big picture; workers must understand how each part of the corporation fits into a plan. Workers must understand the concept of the "bottom line" (the accountant's view of the company). Only those workers who can move from job to job, from pencil and paper to computer, from lower-level positions to upper-level positions and back to lower-level positions, will make it in the New Organization. It is the Theory Z characteristic, non-specialization, which has probably been accepted by the American corporation more so than any other.

Another area of difference is between short-term and long-term thinking. The concept of "planned obsolescence" has been a primary ingredient of the traditional product in American business. That is, a light bulb only lasts so long. An automobile lasts only 50,000–60,000 miles. But, because of competition from Europe and especially Japan, American automobiles now last almost as long as their competitors' models. To produce these higher-quality products, more money and emphasis must be placed in research and development. The *long-term thinking* must involve workers thinking about customers; that is, workers taking the role of customer.

Rasberry and Lindsay (1994) have listed other Theory Z characteristics. All levels share information about the organization, which has a common and understood set of goals in Theory Z. Information is shared based on competence and knowledge, not hierarchy. Status barriers are not present. Communication is upward, downward, and horizontal. And, communication is "open, direct, and accurate" (p. 48). To an extent, the Theory Z organization is virtually "flat." Theory Z, however, has fallen out of favor, replaced instead by the Total Quality Management approach, an adaptation of Theory Z.

Review

What if you were to find yourself in a Theory Z organization? What communication strategies would you employ? Much like those utilized by systems theory managers, you must be open and responsive to the environment. You must see the organization from both internal and external perspectives. You must phrase your questions and answers from both upper- and lower-level management perspectives, seeking in many instances a middle ground. Your relationships will be dictated not so much by corporate but by cultural perspectives. For instance, although status is not a barrier in Theory Z organizations, you will not find many top-level female managers—a cultural bias found in many Asian organizations.

Total Quality Management (TQM)

Total Quality Management (TQM) was developed in the late 1980s by W. Edwards Deming (Aguayo, 1990). One of Deming's basic principles was that organizations are productive when they have loyal customers, not just satisfied customers. "Planned obsolescence" became obsolete. Automobile companies, for example, Deming said, should be concerned that the customer will come back to buy another Ford or Oldsmobile or Chevrolet. In addition, the company wants the customer so dedicated that she will recommend that brand to her friends. Unlike most other approaches, Deming advocated that the first thing an organization needed to do was establish what the barriers were to doing the best job possible. Deming favored seeing to it that the appropriate resources were present to accomplish the most.

Such an approach differs from other contemporary approaches that are still based on merit. Each year workers are asked to do more and more with less and less. In addition to damaging company morale or climate, products are likely to be of lower quality. Over a period of time, because of returns and lack of customer loyalty, lower quality (cheaper) products cost the company more than quality products. Unlike the scientific management approach, for example, where doing something is significant, Deming suggests that *doing it right is more important than doing it quickly.*

Thus, worker input into the product, the production line, and research and development is encouraged. *Quality circles* of management and workers oversee the process and help chart the organization's adaptation to market and environmental conditions that may affect it. Communication is placed at the fore and leadership is at a premium. As a TQM manager you must be the total communicator: open to others, encouraging them to find new and better ways, and then leading them to implement these new solutions. Motivation is important, as is the establishment of open communication climates.

SUMMARY

One factor with which almost all theories of organization agree is that the managerial approach to an organization determines its ability to change. It is important for the new manager to understand the philosophical perspective of the organization. Traditionally, the oldest of such managerial philosophies is scientific management. Such an approach, which considers employees simply as tools, may work in a limited number of organizations. However, most of the organizations where this approach works will be limited in the twenty-first century. Similarly, bureaucracy establishes an accountability approach, which limits creativity and innovation because of its emphasis on paperwork and keeping track of one's own work. Bureaucracies are seldom customer- and new product-oriented.

Elton Mayo's human relations approach goes in the opposite direction. Such a primary concern with the workers' job satisfaction could create a different type of non-innovative worker. Job security replaces high levels of motivation and produces low quality productivity.

More recently, the systems approach takes into account various interactions between and among different segments of the organization, as well as different segments of the organization's environment. The goal of such an approach is, perhaps, admirable, but the implementation is left to the individual organization. Ouchi's Theory Z and Deming's Total Quality Management provide a form of implementation based on customer loyalty.

Of importance to the middle- and upper-level manager is an understanding of the advantages and disadvantages of each approach. It would be too simplistic to think that organizations take one perspective over another. Organizations survive because they can adapt to different "organizational styles." Thus, at a particular point in time you might have to take a scientific management approach, yet at another point in time take a TQM approach. Your ability to adapt to changes in the organization—especially those which come from an external source that you have foreseen—may be the best predictor of your ability to thrive and work yourself up the organization.

CASE 9.2   Consolidation

Peter has been president of a small bank for fifteen years. All of the employees know one another. Peter has tried to work with his employees on an individual basis. No one has been fired in his time as president. The employees know most of the customers and call them by name when they come to the bank. The bank is known as "The Friendly Bank." Now a large city bank has bought Peter's bank, but they are going to allow him to remain as president, although he won't have the clout that he did. What kind of approach was Peter using? Will he have to change it? Why or why not?

QUESTIONS FOR THOUGHT

1. Despite the fact that most organizational theorists have determined that the scientific management approach is virtually unworkable, why do so many institutions still use it?
2. What are the dangers of using a human relations approach with unmotivated workers?
3. What kind of metaphor would you use to create a new theory of management?
4. Establish some policies for work attendance, tardiness, and leave. Write a policy based on scientific management. Write a policy based on the human relations school.
5. Assuming your employees are all educated people, with graduate degrees, what kind of management approach would you use? Why? Does it make any difference what their jobs are? Why or why not?

REFERENCES

Aguayo, R. (1990). *Dr. Deming: The American who taught the Japanese about quality.* New York: Fireside.

Argyle, M., & Cook, M. (1976). *Gaze and mutual gaze.* Cambridge, MA: Cambridge University Press.

Argyris, C. (1995). Knowledge when used in practice tests theory: The case of applied communication research. In K. N. Cissna (Ed.), *Applied communication in the twentieth century.* Mahwah, NJ: Lawrence Erlbaum.

Bales, R. F. (1970). *Personality and interpersonal behavior.* New York: Holt, Rinehart, and Winston.

Bales, R. F., Strodbeck, F. L., Mills, T. M., & Roseborough, M. E. (1951). Channels of communication in small groups. *American Sociological Review, 16,* 461–468.

Barnard, C. I. (1938). *The functions of the executive.* Cambridge, MA: Harvard University Press.

Bennis, W. G. (1966). *Changing organizations.* New York: McGraw-Hill.

Fisher, B. A., & Hawes, L. (1971). An interact system model: Generating a grounded theory of small groups. *Quarterly Journal of Speech, 57,* 444–453.

Hall, A. D., & Fagen, R. E. (1968). Definition of system. In W. Buckley (Ed.), *Modern systems research for the behavioral scientist.* Chicago: Aldine.

Hickson, M. L. III. (1971). A systems analysis of the communication adaptation of a community action agency. Unpublished Ph.D. dissertation, Southern Illinois University.

Hickson, M. III, & Jennings, R. W. (1993). Compatible theory and applied research: Systems theory and triangulation. In S. L. Herndon and G. L. Kreps (Eds.), *Qualitative research: Applications in organizational communication* (pp. 139–157). Cresskill, NJ: Hampton.

Homans, G. (1950). *The human group.* New York: Harcourt, Brace.

Katz, D., & Kahn, R. L. (1966). *The social psychology of organizations.* New York: John Wiley and Sons.

Krupp, S. (1961). *Patterns of organizational analysis: A critical examination.* Philadelphia: Chilton.

Locke, E. A. (1976). Nature and causes of job satisfaction. In M. D. Dunnette (Ed.), *Handbook of industrial and organizational psychology* (pp. 1297–1349). Chicago: Rand-McNally.

March, J. G., & Simon, H. A. (1958). *Organizations.* New York: Wiley.

McGregor, D. (1960). *The human side of enterprise.* New York: McGraw-Hill.

Morgan, G. (1997). *Images of organization,* 2nd ed. Beverly Hills, CA: Sage.

Ouchi, W. G. (1981). *Theory Z: American businessmen can meet the Japanese challenge.* New York: Avon.

Rasberry, R. W., & Lindsay, L. L. (1994). *Effective managerial communication,* 2nd ed. Belmont, CA: Wadsworth.

Rogers, E. M. (1995). *Diffusion of innovations,* 4th ed. New York: Free Press.

Shannon, C., & Weaver, W. (1949). *The mathematical theory of communication.* Urbana: University of Illinois Press.

Stacks, D. W., Hickson, M., & Hill, S. J. (1992). *An introduction to communication theory.* Fort Worth, TX: Harcourt, Brace.

Taylor, F. (1911). *Principles of scientific management.* New York: Harper and Row.

Weber, M. (1947). *The theory of social and economic organization.* London: Oxford University Press.

Weiner, N. (1967). *The human use of human beings: Cybernetics and society.* Boston: Avon.

10

ORGANIZATIONAL COMMUNICATION AND PROFESSIONAL CONDUCT

Professional Competence
  Hiring
  Employee evaluations
  Firing
  Review

Daily Legal Concerns
  Alcohol and drug addiction
  Workplace safety and product quality
  Confidential information
  Marketing and advertising issues
  Financial accounting
  Computer-based information systems
  General legal issues

Ethical Conduct

Professional Etiquette

Objectives

By the end of this chapter you should be able to

1. Explain what professional competence is and why it is important to consider in the New Organization.
2. Demonstrate how to hire, evaluate, and terminate an employee.
3. Define and discuss daily legal concerns you may face in the organization.
4. Explain what organizational policies should be in place regarding general legal issues.
5. Discuss the importance of ethical conduct and professional etiquette in the New Organization.

At what point in your organizational career are you taught right from wrong? Theoretically at least you went through a socialization period which taught you the "do's" and "don'ts" of organizational communication. Theoretically, too, you had a mentor who taught you the ropes, and that included how to communicate with your peers, superiors, and subordinates. In practice, however, we know that the socialization process—as well as the mentoring process—seldom really prepares you for day-to-day interaction. Most organizational communication textbooks do not cover "professional conduct." Organizational handbooks pay lip service to "professional conduct." However, it is up to you to understand what "professional conduct" is and practice it.

Simple, you say. But in real life nothing is that simple. Consider the following example:

Jim just joined Situational Software as manager of its distribution branch. Prior to this, Jim was distribution manager for Small Tractors, Inc., a farm implement company. At Small Tractors for ten years, Jim had worked his way from sales to management. He had become fast friends with his mentor and boss, Bubba Jones. Bubba built the company from a small repair service to one of the largest tractor builders in the region. Jim's new CEO, Dean, reminds him very much of Bubba, a hard-working, salt-of-the-Earth type.

While at Small Tractor Jim's subordinates were primarily male. His only female employee served as both a clerk for him and Bubba's secretary. A part-time receptionist helped out, but didn't stay long after meeting Bubba, who liked to treat them as "daughters."

Situational Software has ten females working, accounting for about forty percent of the workforce. No females, however, are on the management team; most are in distribution, although two are software programmers. Jim's socialization period was short; Situational needed to get its distribution network reworked and on-line fast. Both Jim and Dean unconsciously chose each other as mentor and protégé; Jim particularly enjoyed the after hours socialization at the bar, where he and Dean talked about business, social relationships in the company, and appraised the abilities of the "fair sex."

After only three weeks on the job, Jim has had to fire five workers, three male and two female (one of whom was a part-time receptionist), and is actively seeking to hire their replacements. Dean has already indicated that two of the programmers are complaining about Jim's casual comments to them. Although Jim doesn't know whether they are male or female, he suspects the latter.

What has gone wrong? Given Jim's socialization experiences and mentors his concept of *professional conduct* is probably different than we would expect of a manager of his capabilities and experience. Or is it?

This chapter explores problems that middle- and upper-level managers encounter daily: firings, hirings, employee evaluations, and establishing competent superior–subordinate relationships. It also explores the legal aspects of daily interaction. Twenty years ago these concerns could be passed on through on-the-job training. Today and into the next century, however, being prepared to be forewarned is the first step in establishing a competent organizational communication strategy.

As a basic tenet, we can say: Organizations have cultures (values, needs) which circumscribe appropriate and inappropriate behaviors. *Appropriate* and *inappropriate behaviors* are limited by laws, ethics, etiquette, and socialization processes. *Laws* are created by legislative bodies and are interpreted by the courts. Both are important for understanding organizational culture. *Ethics* are values generally agreed upon by society at large. "Do unto others" and similar maxims are part of our culture. *Etiquette* is merely an extension of ethics. In many ways, etiquette is the "how" of the ethical "what." The *socialization process* is the method used by organizations to teach its members about culture through laws, ethics, and etiquette. The socialization process does not end. It is a constant from the interview to the last day on the job. There are communication processes at each stage.

We begin by looking at your credibility. After that, we turn to the hiring and firing process, something that most managers would prefer others handle. We then look at legal concerns and finish the chapter with a discussion of ethics and organizational etiquette. Once again, however, these are all topics that should have been covered during the socialization and mentor stages of organizational assimilation. Our experience in academia—reinforced by discussions with professionals and our readings of organizational behavior— is that they are rarely covered formally in any detail, if at all.

PROFESSIONAL COMPETENCE

Professional competence is concerned with your effectiveness in undertaking the variety of tasks imposed on you in an organization (Willis & Dubin, 1990). As discussed in other chapters, a professional's credibility is essential for effective action. According to Kouzes and Posner (1995), the four top characteristics of admired leaders are that they are honest, forward-looking, inspiring, and competent. We will discuss these characteristics in reverse order, as one tends to lead to the next.

Competence includes intelligence, formal education, experience, judgment, and wisdom. It is important for all employees to be competent in the New Organization. As we have mentioned, the competent professional adapts to changing situations. The competent professional does her homework. She knows answers to questions. And, she knows what questions to ask and when to ask them.

How do you prepare for such competence? First, you should read as much information as possible about the company, about related companies, about organizational change, about the general economy, and about the future of society. Second, the competent professional *retains* the information to be used later. Third, the competent professional *shares* her information with others in the organization. And, finally, the competent professional remembers that she is a member of a team and that decisions should be based on the good of all or most.

The professional takes on those roles that have been mentioned in discussing motivation (see Chapter 7). Instead of dwelling on the past or the present, the inspired professional constantly looks toward the future. What factors might change the costs of our raw materials? What characteristic of a potential employee might be needed five years in the future that we do not necessarily need today? What new products might replace our products? In addition to researching these questions, the inspiring manager also serves as an example. If employees feel that you are not doing your part, they are unlikely to do theirs. The inspiring leader also provides the resources for current employees to be inspired—and empowers them to make decisions based on inspiration (see Chapter 8). The inspiring leader is not negative in her first response to an idea. Although there may be barriers to achieving success with the idea, such barriers can be presented later. The inspiring leader encourages visionary thinking.

The inspiring professional is directly associated with the forward-looking leader. Such a leader must himself have a vision of what the company will look like in five years, in ten years, in twenty years. Such a vision is created with the assistance of the others in the organization. That is, the organization must have a "common vision." All of the employees should understand where the company is intending to go. Various formal and informal means of communication can be used to facilitate such a vision. Some organizations use videotaped presentations, others use brochures and newsletters to do so, and still others use small group interactions to ensure that the entire organization is "on the same page" about where the company is going. As an effective manager, part of your ongoing research may be to conduct formal and informal focus groups that explore where others think the organization is going, where it is effective, and where it needs work (see Chapter 3).

Honesty involves not being shortsighted about ethical concerns. The honest professional makes decisions that are in the long-term, best interests of the organization. The long-term best interests involve not only honesty itself but also the perception of honesty.

Willis and Dubin (1990) have suggested that *professionalism* is based on personality traits, attitudes, values, motivation, and intellectual ability. The personality traits are associated with communication patterns. The professional should know all of the names of those with whom he is associated. Colleagues should be addressed by their names, not by "buddy," "friend," "honey," or other terms of endearment which indicate that you simply do not know the names of colleagues.

Additionally, you should show an interest in the families of the organizational members, at least those with whom you have daily contact. It may be a good idea to develop a file for this purpose. Such a file might contain the names of spouses and children, as well as the ages and birthdates of children and even important event dates, such as hirings, promotions, or even anniversaries. At appropriate times, you should engage in some communication to demonstrate your concern with what is going on in employees' private lives. Such conversations should not invade their privacy, but should illustrate that there is an ongoing concern about the employee as a person.

According to March and Simon (1958), professionalism involves a number of variables, including independence of individual rewards, the amount of competition (both within and outside the company), the number of individual needs to be satisfied within the group, the extent to which goals are considered to be shared, and the amount of interaction. In the context of a leadership position within an organization, several specific concerns must be set forth.

For example, how is responsibility defined? How is loyalty defined? What is trust? What is honesty? What is privacy? Many of these factors must be considered in several different contexts: (1) the law; (2) ethics; (3) etiquette. In Chapter 12, "Women and Minorities in the Workplace," we will consider the concerns specifically as they involve minority groups and women. Our concern here will be a more general overview. We begin with personnel concerns: hiring, firing, and evaluation.

Hiring

Hiring may be one of the most important things that you do as a manager. As we noted in Chapter 7, managing would be simple if we could knowingly hire nothing but motivated people as employees. Hiring used to be a fairly simple process. Today's organization, however, is overburdened and tied up in governmental red tape. You must, for instance, keep all files for a position for years, certain forms must be completed, and often you may be required to report to governmental agencies the number of people you tried to hire according to a quota system. There is no end in sight to governmental oversight of the hiring process.

In general, the law on hiring limits the kinds of questions that may be asked of a prospective employee. However, the hiring process begins much earlier, with the placement of advertisements for a particular position (see Figure 10.1). Where, when, and for how long advertisements must be placed is an important legal and governmental concern. Must you advertise nationally? Must the job really be available? Have you already filled the position and are now just advertising it? Do you have a particular person in mind and have tailored the advertisement to that person? These are both legal and ethical concerns that must be considered before the process actually begins. Knowing your potential applicant pool certainly helps, but it may also open you to claims of bias against hiring others who may be "different" or "more qualified" or older, younger, political, and so forth.

COMMERCIAL PROPERTY MANAGER

Exp. Comm. Prop. Mgr. Needed with leading mgmt. firm in Co. Sprgs., CO. Mixed office/medical/retail portfolio. Must have minimum 7 yrs. Exp. With strong operation, financial, communication and computer skills. CPM required. Send resume w/salary requirements to:
Griffis/Blessing
102 N. Cascade, 5th Floor,
Colorado Springs, CO 80903
FAX 719-520-1204

Marketing

Medical Capital Corporation, a fast growing nationwide provider of financial services for healthcare providers has the following opening:

Director of Marketing

Experience in marketing/sales to healthcare providers. Financial service experience desired. Please fax resume with salary history to:
W. Johnson
(714) 282-6184

MANAGEMENT TRAINEE - INTERNATIONAL

CPA, 2 years "Big 6", train in finance & operations in divisions throughout the world. Foreign language skills a big plus. Top interpersonal and communication skills. High visibility with top management. Free to relocate & travel as required. **Resume** to **Boyd Search Firm**, 15445 Ventura Blvd. #165, Sherman Oaks, CA 91403 or Fax 818-981-6505.

VP - Director Sales & Marketing

Richards Industries Valve Group completed another record year. This growth has created the need for a VP-Director of Sales & Marketing based at our Cincinnati plant (150 people) where we manufacture the Jordan Valve, Hex Valve, and Bestobell Steam Trap product lines. We seek an executive who can lead us to new higher levels of performance.
Please reply in confidence to:
President Box 43270,
Cincinnati, Ohio 45243. Fax:
(513) 533-2583 or Email:
rihr@one.net. EOE.

BRAND STRATEGY SENIOR CONSULTANTS

We are a small team of highly qualified consultants specializing in the areas of brand strategy, brand valuation and management training.
We are seeking senior consultants to join us in developing effective solutions for our domestic and international clients. Significant prior project experience is required. The successful candidates will have initiative, drive and a willingness to work in a fast-growing speciality consultancy. We offer a good working environment with significant opportunity for personal growth. Equity participation will be considered. Please send your resume in strict confidence to:
Box TZ350, The Wall Street Journal
1233 Regal Row, Dallas, Tx 75247

CEO "World Class"
and CFO for IT Staffing/PEO/Payroll company. Must have run $100 Million+ company profitably & have consolidation & Merger & Acquisition experience. Call H. Bell (610)718-8810.

SALES DIRECTOR

Beverly Hills, Ca. healthcare software apps. company.
Sal/bonus to $125k.
John Gilbert Co.
281/363-3310, 298-5152 fax

Job Opening

International Biotech company seeking in-house Accountant/bookkeeper/ finance professional. Salary/DOE. Send resume & background with salary expectations to:
Biotech Service Consultants,
12345 Lake City Way NE,
Suite 310, Seattle, WA 98125.

TIME FOR A CAREER CHANGE?

...Retired or bored? Need a part time income? Want to be your own master? Sold your business & would like a new challenge? We are seeking qualified affiliates F/P time to benefit from your own experience & our 40 year background as a BUSINESS MEDIATION CONSULTANT. Exceptional training & technical support can provide a substantial income & personal satisfaction (Suppliers, bank loans, insurance, R.E. Mortgages, business transfers, etc.) $12,000 required. Call for free brochure & video.
800-998-9843
VALCOR ARBITRATION SERVICES, LTD.

COMMERCIAL LOAN UNDERWRITER

A leading national apartment lender has an opening for an **Apartment Loan Underwriter.** Three years experience underwriting or appraising commercial income properties req'd. Must have strong writing, analysis, credit and computer skills. Knowledge of real estate finance and appraisal methodology a must. Salary DOE + benefits. Send resume to:
EF&A Funding, 4746 11th Ave NE, Suite 102, Seattle, WA 98105. Fax 206-522-7033
or email:
jmarsh@efafunding.com.

Accounting/Controller

Dynamic Nat'l Real Estate inv./dev. co. seeks exp'd CPA for key mgmt position. Send resume to Panattoni, Catlin, 826 17th St., #16, Sacramento, CA 95814

Accounting
AUDITOR III

Perform full scope audits that encompass financial, operational, compliance, economy, efficiency, and effectiveness in accordance with professional auditing standards. Requires a theoretical background in related area, a thorough understanding of auditing theories and principles, accounting, and general administration; a working knowledge of university/healthcare concepts, principles and policies, and excellent interpersonal/leadership skills. Prefers an MBA, CPA, CISA, CIA. Salary commensurate with qualifications and experience. For immediate consideration, apply by 10/1/97, referencing Job #113200-Y, to: UCSD Human Resources, La Jolla, CA 92093-0967. AA/EOE. Web Site: http://www.hr.ucsd.edu
UNIVERSITY OF CALIFORNIA, SAN DIEGO

Management Consulting
Senior Business Development Professional

An entrepreneurial marketing strategy, consulting and research firm seeks an outstanding professional with a demonstrated track record of new business development. 7-10 years of relevant experience with a recognized management consulting firm a must.

We want to grow our practice in the areas of:

● Strategic Marketing Research
● Business/Marketing Strategy Consulting

in the following sectors:

● Health Care/Pharmaceuticals
● Hi-Tech/Telecommunications
● Financial Services

If you would like to be a part of our team, please send resume with salary history and expectations to:
Recruiting, G. Bhalla & Associates, 8605 Westwood Center Drive, Suite 207, Vienna, VA 22182 or fax to: (703) 556-8653.

DIRECTOR OF PATIENT BUSINESS SERVICES

Childrens Hospital of L.A. Responsible for Admitting, Billing, Credit Collection, Cashiering & Utilization. HBOC experience preferred, Bachelors required.
Contact: L. Robinow
Health Search (714) 955-1991
Fax (714) 955-1023

FIGURE 10.1   Sample Hiring Advertisements

When applications for the advertised position have been received, you—employer or interviewer—begin the process of *selection*. In reality, the process is a process of elimination. Because there are often so many applications for a position, you should be concerned about limiting the application "pool." Such applications may be composed of formal written forms, resumes, and letters (see Chapter 4). In some cases, letters of recommendation are included. Probably the most common approach is to first eliminate all of those applicants who do not meet the minimal qualifications. In most organizations, the personnel or human relations office will automatically eliminate those who do not qualify for non-professional jobs, but they may not have that power for professional positions.

Deciding what factors are important greatly reduces the elimination process. Does the applicant lack the academic degree needed for the position? Does the applicant lack the necessary experience for the position? These are the two most important considerations. In many cases, eliminating those who do not qualify cuts the pool by 50 percent. Thus, if you started with fifty applications, you may actually really consider only twenty-five. If hiring is a committee decision, all of the information should be shared with all committee members. As an ethical dimension, this part of the process should be considered *confidential*. People outside of the selection group should know nothing about the hiring process until it has been completed or reached the formal interview stage.

A second phase involves eliminating those who are not specifically qualified for the particular position that has been advertised. It should be noted that by this phase, however, *all* applicants should receive some message that the company received the application. While a personal letter is most appropriate, with the number of applications in today's market, most applicants are simply pleased to know that someone read their application letter. Letters should be checked and double-checked so that the appropriate letter is included in the appropriate envelope. The letters should be mailed no later than one week after the application deadline. If possible, you should notify the applicants when interviews will begin and when a decision will be made.

At this point, the applicant pool is probably less than twenty. You next look for gaps in one's employment history, especially if the applicant does not explain such gaps. The files of applicants are usually numbered so that the committee members are discussing "applicant seventeen" instead of personalizing the list at this point. In most cases, however, you may not wish to interview all twenty applicants, and you probably will not have the time. Those applicants with gaps should be placed in a separate file.

Remaining applicants should be evaluated based on their job experience and other qualifications. You should seek out those who appear to have moved up during their careers. Although the selection committee should agree on the procedures for making decisions, a typical approach is to divide the final candidates into three sub-groups. You may want to classify them as "outstanding," "excellent," and "good." As noted earlier, certain limitations are placed on the hiring process. By now you should know not to eliminate candidates because of race, color, age, sex, religion, handicap, or country of origin (Manley & Shrode, 1990).

Once you or your hiring committee has progressed this far, it is important to understand the nature of the remainder of the selection process. If you chair a hiring committee, you should notify all members how the process will proceed. Often such committees wish to make only one recommendation. The committee should know whether it is making one recommendation, several recommendations, or a selection. It should also know whether its work is actually to hire someone or to recommend that someone be hired. Many times the committee is frustrated when someone else is hired; often this is the result of poor management communication as to what the committee's *real* task was.

The interviewing process should involve as much open and honest communication as possible. Both the positive and negative components of the job should be explained to candidates. While "tricky" questions might be utilized, interviewers should not intentionally try to "trip up" or embarrass candidates.

In verifying the facts in a candidate's job application or résumé, you should notify the candidate that references will be checked. Often candidates do not want current employers called. As the potential employer, you should notify the candidate that his current employer will have to be called, but that you will do so only if the candidate is a finalist.

In addition, candidates should be notified early in the process as to what, if any, other checks will be made. Will the candidate be tested for drugs? Will the candidate be fingerprinted? Will the candidate have to take personality or intelligence tests? Other tests? If so, the processes should be undertaken early in the process, though not necessarily in the beginning. If all applicants took all such tests, the costs to the employer could be overwhelming. In instances where a candidate is in a different location, you need to make clear how expenses will be handled for the interviewing process.

Layne (1989) strongly recommends that a policy be established about all of the items we have discussed for legal purposes. You cannot be selective about drug tests, for example. Background checks must be reasonable. Such processes should be legal, based on federal and local law. And, all processes should also be ethical. That is, *all* candidates should be treated the same way. When you or your committee members obtain candidate references by telephone, there should be a pattern to the questions being asked—again to eliminate potential discrimination. While there is a strong temptation to carry on a conversation on an individual basis, such a process could cause severe problems for the organization, resulting in loss of prestige or a perception of unfairness due to a hiring lawsuit.

Finally, it is important to use proper etiquette in dealing with candidates. Unnecessary waiting, disorganized itineraries, an overbooked interview process, and the like are improper and send the wrong impression to potential employees. In addition, engaging in gossip about members of one's organization or the competition's organization is improper (Baldridge, 1993). Just because you do not hire a particular candidate now does not mean that you will never offer her a job in the future or that she will not talk to other, potential candidates about your treatment of her.

The best rule of thumb?—the "Golden Rule": Hire as you, yourself would like to be hired. Treat all candidates as you, yourself would like to be treated. By now you have been interviewed at least once (you got YOUR job!) and know what was good and bad about the process. As a leader and manager, it is your responsibility to make the process as positive as possible. As a good manager you will even have those not hired wanting to apply again.

Employee Evaluations

Although most organizations have a procedure for evaluating employees on an annual or semi-annual basis, employee appraisal should be approached as a continuous process. Knowing where she is at any given time helps an employee assess her own potential as an employee and also helps maintain and motivate the worker. Appraisals should not always be conducted in your office, but in the employee's office or work area also. This reduces the tension associated with being called in to "see the boss." The formal employee evaluation, however, almost always takes place in the superior's office. Remember

TABLE 10.1   The Hiring Process

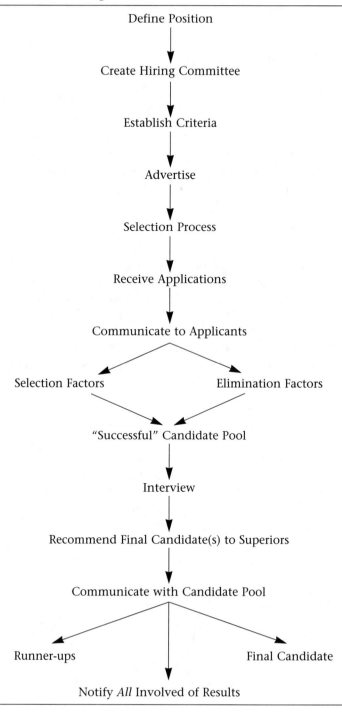

DILBERT / Scott Adams

DILBERT © United Feature Syndicate. Reprinted by Permission.

how you feel when you are being evaluated by your superior and conduct your evaluations as you would like your own evaluation to be conducted.

When you engage in any employee evaluation, you must be concerned that all legal matters are followed. In general, the important aspect of such a process is that it should be systematic. Stano (1992) provides ten criteria for effective employee evaluation:

1. The appraisal should be fair.
2. The appraisal should occur in the proper environment.
3. The appraisal should be properly scheduled.
4. The appraisal should not include both past performance and future expectations in the same meeting.
5. Appropriate goals for future performance should be set.
6. The employee should be allowed to participate in the appraisal process.
7. Appropriate praise and criticism should be given.
8. The proper communication climate should be established.
9. Appraisal discussions should not be limited to the formal appraisal period.
10. The discussion should be summarized.

Most of these suggestions speak for themselves, but we will elaborate on some of them here. The typical problem with being fair is that bosses often emphasize a particular event, either positive or negative, rather than focusing on the entire year. In addition, you are more likely to recall those events of the previous few months than those earlier in the year. As noted previously, you should remember that the *process covers the entire year.* If possible, an appropriate setting for the formal evaluation is a neutral site, such as a boardroom, rather than your "home territory." The interview should be scheduled so that there is enough time; arrangements should be made to ensure that there will be no interruptions. The interview should be neither too long nor too short;

although experience will help you dictate evaluation length, negative evaluations will generally last longer than positive ones.

Stano (1992) recommends that there be two evaluations during the year: one for *planning;* and the other to cover *past performance.* The first interview should not be associated with salary or other merit considerations. Goals for future performance should be clear and as precise as possible; when possible, they should be stated in quantitative terms, such as "I would like for you to increase your sales by $500,000." There should be a discussion of the goals. The employee should indicate whether she believes the goals are reasonable and obtainable. You should also ask employees to tell you what kinds of assistance are needed. For example, with the goal above, the employee might say, "I believe I can increase sales if I can be less bogged down with paperwork. Is it possible that I could get some additional secretarial and accounting help?" There should be no more than two or three goals for the upcoming year. Finally, the goals should be adapted to the talents of the individual. For example, some salespersons might be better at gaining new clients; others might be better at increasing the sales to current clients. Thus, for the former, a goal might be to open accounts with ten new clients rather than to increase sales per se.

All goals should initially be set by you. Then the employee should be asked for input. The process should always be considered a deliberative action, not a set of demands. You and he should combine your knowledge. The amount of praise and criticism should depend on the individual employee. The interview should begin with praise; there should be some sort of evidence to back up the praise or criticism. For example, "The manner in which you handled the Jacobs' problem was especially effective," or "You are ninth on the salesforce this year, perhaps we should think in terms of your moving up to seventh or sixth next year." Obviously this means that you should have done your homework (research) prior to the interview. You should generally have a positive and enthusiastic attitude. The evaluator should carry out evaluations on a regular basis. That is, there should be praise and criticism all year long. Finally, the entire discussion should be summarized *orally;* later the same summary should be made in writing, to be signed by both parties.

Just as the hiring process should be held in confidence, so, too, should the evaluation process. It may well be that employees will share comments with one another. However, as the evaluator, the entire written file and oral discussion should be considered a matter of privacy. At the end of the next year, the evaluation process should include a look at the goals from last year. If the goals have been met, appropriate praise should follow. If goals have not been met, the employee should provide details of why they were not met. Using this procedure, you can easily establish goals for the next year.

Firing

Layne (l989) has written that "[f]iring is a chore most people would prefer to pass to someone else" (p. 51). Further, that "[i]t is difficult, if not impossible, to terminate employment and leave the unfortunate person with feelings of goodwill toward the employer" (p. 51). Your goal should be to leave the employee with as much self-respect as is possible given the circumstances. The fired employee minimally should feel that he has been treated fairly. For this to happen, it is important that there *exist a fair and comprehensive policy on termination.* If your company has an employee handbook, such information should be provided regarding termination. If there is no handbook, the policy should be communicated in some fashion. All rules should be followed by the company. Prior to firing, you should counsel about any behavior that might lead to termination and these counseling sessions should be documented. Finally, your decision to terminate an employee should be based on a fair analysis of all available facts in the case.

Communication skills are especially important during the firing process. You should make an effort to ensure that the employee is of a demeanor that discourages any violent behavior. You should let the employee know that things may, in fact, be better. One particularly effective method is to discuss "the fit" between the organization and the individual being fired. Here you might suggest that the employee may "fit" better with another organization.

The *location* of all termination discussions should be private and away from other members of the organization. If possible, you should ensure that two employers are present, to prevent confrontations and to assure professionalism. Direct supervisors, who may have had confrontations with the terminated employee, should not be present. As Layne (1989) notes, "All matters should be discussed unemotionally, fairly, and professionally" (p. 52). In many cases, the employee will ask for "one more chance." However, once you have made the decision to terminate, there should be no turning back. The terminated employee has a right, however, to know why he was fired, whether he violated any company policy, as well as how pay, benefits, and equipment turn-ins will be handled (Layne, 1989, p. 52).

In a diplomatic way, you should suggest when the terminated employee might want to turn in keys, take away personal possessions, and the like. At the same time, the employee should be notified not to return after the keys have been turned in. In other words, there should be no encouragement to "Come back and see us sometime."

Suggestions for types of assistance, job training, and the like should be made at this time, along with any indication that the company will assist in these areas. Certainly there are differences between a layoff/downsizing situation and firing. Volunteering to write references when firing someone is not a good idea, whereas it may be with a layoff or downsizing. Whether an individual decides to do so depends on the nature of the firing offense.

Legally, recent wrongful terminations have involved "violations of public policy, implied contracts in employee handbooks, and torts of outrageous emotional distress" (Koys, Briggs, & Grening, 1987, p. 565). The *violation of public policy* is probably the most outstanding of these issues. The courts have been unwilling to allow an employer to fire an employee because she refused to commit an illegal act. They have also sided with employees when they were dismissed for missing work while serving on a jury and the like. Finally, the courts have taken the side of the fired employee for exercising a legal right. Another possible issue has recently arisen on whether an employee should be fired for "whistle blowing." Such a case arises when an employee takes a case to the government, for example, that may be a violation of the law by the company (Baucus & Dworkin, 1994).

An obvious prerequisite to firing is some type of *counseling interview* (Stewart & Cash, 1994, pp. 204–208). Specifically, the type of interview being discussed here is the *disciplinary interview*. Monroe, Barzi, and DiSalvo (1989) discuss four general types of conflict situations that may occur in disciplinary interviews:

1. apparent compliance;
2. relational leverage;
3. alibis;
4. avoidance.

Apparent compliance occurs when there is overpoliteness, apologies, promises, and the like. *Relational leverage* refers to an employee indicating that he or she knows more than you do about the event or things that have led to the discussion. *Alibis* include being sick, tired, overworked. *Avoidance* involves failure to respond to phone calls, memoranda, and the like. The rules for such conferences should be applied to all employees equally; the employee should know that a record is being kept of the conference. If allowed in your organization, the interviewers (two) and the employee should sign the record of the disciplinary interview. Again, privacy is extremely important, otherwise the employee may decide to sue the company for defamation (Bies & Tripp, 1993). A record of disciplinary action is an important component for a later firing that will withstand legal perusal.

What, however, if rather than terminating a subordinate, you are the terminated person? Baldridge (1993) writes about how to be fired (because of downsizing) in a "classy" manner. She suggests that you tell your office friends yourself, in private. You should try to assist your secretary, if possible. You should write a note to your employer (CEO) stating how you feel about the company. You should also write notes to those who have helped you during your stint with the company (pp. 104–107). All parties should remember to maintain an ethical stance as well as a legal stance.

Review

Many lawsuits are filed not because of the firing itself but because of the way in which the firing was handled. Hiring, evaluation interviews, and firing are among the more difficult aspects of maintaining a professional stance in an organization. How you communicate during these situations may impact on your own career. Perhaps the "Golden Rule" mentioned earlier is your best personal guide—treat others the way you would like to be treated yourself.

TABLE 10.2   Terminating Employees

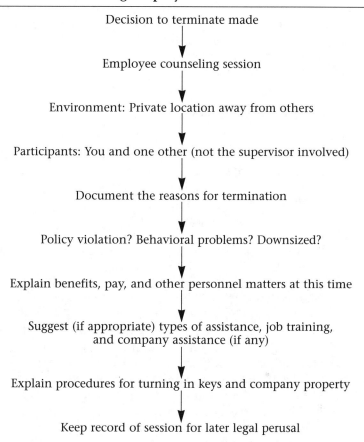

Decision to terminate made

↓

Employee counseling session

↓

Environment: Private location away from others

↓

Participants: You and one other (not the supervisor involved)

↓

Document the reasons for termination

↓

Policy violation? Behavioral problems? Downsized?

↓

Explain benefits, pay, and other personnel matters at this time

↓

Suggest (if appropriate) types of assistance, job training,
and company assistance (if any)

↓

Explain procedures for turning in keys and company property

↓

Keep record of session for later legal perusal

There are a significant number of other issues that promulgate the daily work of leaders. We will briefly discuss some of the legal, ethical, and etiquette concerns faced by managers in their daily activities that affect their perceived professionalism. These may seem mundane, but as we noted in earlier chapters, much of what a manager does is defined by seemingly mundane things that really make a difference.

DAILY LEGAL CONCERNS

No doubt your company has a legal office that can account for almost any issue that arises in the legal realm. Nevertheless, a good manager does not need to or want to call the legal office every day. There are times, however, when you will require the assistance of corporate counsel. The kinds of things that might require such assistance typically involve alcoholism and drug addiction, sexual and nonsexual harassment, equal opportunity (see Chapter 11), workplace safety and product quality, confidential information, marketing and advertising issues, financial accounting and reporting issues, computer-based information systems, contracts, security laws, fair trade practices, and international relationships.

Alcohol and Drug Addiction

According to Manley and Shrode (1990) "11.9% of the 3.9 million American private-sector employees who were tested for drugs tested positively" in 1989 (p. 53). Drug problems are a significant money problem for companies; *each should have a specific drug and alcohol policy.* Many now have screening programs that increase productivity, assist in employer liability, increase work safety, and increase company security. Manley and Shrode (1990) recommend blood tests if your company is going to use tests. The legal problems that might arise from such tests, however, include privacy, defamation, wrongful discharge, and emotional distress. Generally speaking, rehabilitative programs, as opposed to punitive programs, are preferable.

Obviously certain problems arise when drinking alcohol is "part of the job." In those occupations where taking clients out to lunch or dinner often involves drinking, the employee should take care to limit drinking alcoholic beverages significantly or to restrain from drinking altogether. Early detection of potential problems might be avoided by testing new employees (Manley & Shrode, 1990). Random testing of current employees should be utilized only for jobs that are dangerous or affect public safety. Of course, when any driving is involved, almost every job involves public safety. Your company should have an employee assistance program; the effective manager should be aware of such programs and how and when she may make a referral.

CASE 10.1   The Competent Alcoholic

Six months ago, you hired Charles from a competing company. Charles' job has been to sell paper to companies in other countries. The sales in each case were over two million dollars. Part of his job is to "wine and dine" the potential customers. Most of the rest of his time is spent in travel. You have noticed that Charles has been late on some of his reports lately, but his sales for six months have been more than $10 million. He has done better than any other salesperson on your force. Yesterday he had a violent argument with his superior, but he apologized about an hour later. Your secretary has told you that Charles sometimes has alcohol on his breath after lunch and on one occasion had alcohol on his breath early in the morning. As a professional, what do you do?

Sexual harassment and other harassment, as well as equal opportunity, will be discussed in particular in Chapter 11. Suffice it to say, your company should have policies and procedures in place for dealing with any form of harassment and to ensure that all people are afforded the opportunity to work for you and that work conditions are pleasant and safe. Chapter 7 explored the motivational factors associated with "hygienic" environments, environments that were free of harassment and yielded safe working conditions.

Workplace Safety and Product Quality

The Occupational Safety and Health Act of 1970 established the basic elements of what any organization needs to know about *work safety.* That act requires you to maintain records of work injuries and illnesses (Manley & Shrode, 1990). While such records are legally required, they may also be of benefit to the organization in other ways. Professionals should anticipate work-related injuries as a result of workplace inadequacies in buildings, equipment, and the like. An inventory of machinery should be kept, as well as a maintenance record of that equipment so that breakdowns can be anticipated. If all organizations maintained such records in a fashion similar to the better airlines, many companies could avoid needless accidents caused by faulty equipment. In a sense, you should take the following view on safety: "If the worse thing could happen, it will."

Care should also be taken to see that *toxic substances in the workplace* are properly disposed of. The Environmental Protection Agency (EPA) administers this program. The problem is that organizations do not always think of substances as being toxic, though they may be toxic at least in the long run. Such long-term thinking is critical to a professional organization. An example may be a darkroom used for developing photographs in a number of organizations. Is the darkroom properly ventilated? Are the chemicals properly disposed of?

Consumer protection and *product quality* are also important factors. While some organizations utilize a "bottom-line" approach to such problems, such an approach is unprofessional and probably detrimental in the long run. Therefore, it is useful to notify consumers if there are flaws in products, and to warn them of improper or dangerous uses of your products. In essence, the questions that should arise from any product's creation should be: "What will be the effects on the consumer?" "What are side effects?" Especially when the products are used by children or the elderly, you should take into account that many children cannot read and the elderly may not be able to make quick responses to remove themselves from danger.

Confidential Information

"In 1982 as a result of a sting operation involving FBI agents posing as IBM employees and accepting bribes, IBM filed suit against Hitachi, other Japanese and American firms, and two former IBM employees, alleging theft of trade secrets and confidential information" (Manley & Shrode, 1990, 153). Many lawsuits in today's highly competitive market involve millions of dollars. In addition to being concerned about in-house problems of security of information, companies must police the marketplace to determine whether any ideas or patented products have been copied illegally. Employee contracts should guard against former employees sharing trade secrets of their former employer (Manley & Shrode, 1990).

Marketing and Advertising Issues

In 1989, firms spent over $128 billion marketing and advertising their products (Manley & Shrode, 1990). Today that figure probably is more than $200 billion; tomorrow it will be much higher. Because of the inability to raise prices in an international market, today's companies must focus more on new, larger, and different markets to sell their products and services. Especially in the United States where so many companies are merging and splitting off from one another to save on costs, marketing is a most significant factor in a company's success. The marketing of a product is probably the most publicly visible aspect of any organization.

You must take care to ensure that the image being presented is the image your company desires. As a professional, you must take into account the competition, society-at-large, and consumers as well as the company itself.

Beer and tobacco companies often argue that they are advertising to gain a larger share of consumers that already use their products. However, criticism is directed toward them because consumer advocates claim that they are trying to create new, young drinkers and smokers. "Old Joe" Camel has been the target of such groups for several years. Consumer advocates argue that the Camel cigarette advertisements are directed toward young, non-smokers (Rasberry & Lindsay, 1994). Thus, marketing and advertising campaigns should try to avoid any kind of deception in the campaigns.

The public relations personnel in the organization can be especially helpful in assisting the company in avoiding potential problems in advertising, especially because they are often the people who must answer the questions after the fact. The *Harvard Business Review* (Greyser & Reece, 1971) has made four suggestions about improving advertising:

1. Eliminate untruthful/misleading ads.
2. Establish/enforce a code of ethics.
3. Upgrade intellectual level.
4. Increase information content.

Those companies who assume the best in their customers are the ones who appear to be the most successful in the long run. Using long-lasting companies' marketing and advertising as examples or cases to work from may be in the best interests of your company.

Financial Accounting

The business/financial office is usually responsible for accounting. Nevertheless you must be aware of problems that may be created in this area. The Securities and Exchange Commission (SEC) regulates financial reporting. Generally speaking, though, you should realize that "insider trading"—where your financial interest or your company's is enhanced by knowledge you have based on information not made available to others—is illegal. As well, you should be aware of the importance of contracts in every kind of transaction and should be aware of the possibility of a tort (wrongdoing) action that might be brought against the company, as well as certain individuals in the company. In addition, many organizations now have an "ethics board" which oversees actions of its employees.

Computer-Based Information Systems

Throughout this text, we have focused on the importance of research and information. From an external viewpoint, it is important for the organization to maintain security of all of its computer information in today's world. From the internal viewpoint, it is important for individuals to realize that information in a company's computer belongs to the company. *Computer-based information systems* (CBIS) are becoming commonplace in businesses today. It is important to realize how much or how little privacy one has when operating such computers.

Consider, for instance, the problems the information system giant LEXIS/NEXIS faced after announcing that they had in their "P-Trak" data base the addresses of people whether they were listed in the phone book or not. Within hours they were inundated by irate people accusing them of giving out highly sensitive information. The same is true when an organization provides its employee lists to organizations that produce mass mailings or to political parties. The new organization will probably face new regulations regarding not only the privacy of employee and other data but also safeguards that will be enforced to maintain that privacy.

General Legal Issues

The most important general legal issues are *that you and your organization should provide full, fair, complete, absolute, total, redundant disclosure with those with whom they feel they have a fiduciary (trust) relationship. Privacy* must be secured and maintained regarding competitors and other outsiders who may interfere with the general success of the organization. Re (1987) argues for fifteen maxims of *equity,* of which six have special applications to the business organization.

1. *He who seeks equity must do equity.* Examples of this principle are when a person feels another has broken his contract; therefore, the first person breaks his part of the contract. Generally, one should fulfill her obligations if she expects the other to do so. Even after the other has violated the contract, the first party should continue doing what she promised. Courts of law will force the second party to abide IF the first has abided.
2. *He who comes into equity must come in with clean hands.* That is, the first party must have undertaken every part of the agreement legally in the first place. For example, a party cannot get another to legally pay off a debt on a bet in a state where such gambling is illegal.
3. *Equity aids the vigilant, not those who slumber on their rights.* One should not delay in bringing her legal rights to bear in a case.
4. *Equity follows the law.* The law will be the basis for actions in court. (There is an exception to this when binding arbitration takes place, but it is generally true.)
5. *Equity delights to do justice and not by halves.* In other words, compromise is NOT the basic principle of equity. The idea is that the one will win who has operated most responsibly and legally. Fairness may not and usually does not mean that we split by half what is asked. For example, if someone has allegedly been illegally dismissed from a job and the former employee asks for a million dollars and the company thinks only $30,000 should be paid, equity does NOT say pay $515,000. Fairness might say the former employee gets little or nothing. Fairness might say the former employee gets more than one million dollars.
6. *Equity regards substance rather than form.* If one says he tried to pay and submitted a "bad check," generally this will not be good enough.

There are nine more of these, which might be valuable information for the manager to know and understand (Re, 1987, pp. 42–44). With the open disclosure to fiduciaries, privacy from non-fiduciaries, and the maxims of equity, you should be in excellent legal condition. But as we have indicated, communication prevents litigation. Open communication will often prevent legal issues from arising; thus, it is critical that ethical conduct and professional etiquette form the bases of everyday worklife.

ETHICAL CONDUCT

Much of this text has been concerned with institutional *bottom-line* thinking and functioning. There is nothing wrong with considering the bottom line because without the bottom line neither the organization nor any of its inhabitants will continue to exist. However, considering the bottom line means more than simplistic, short-term economics. Deetz (1985) asked: "If we innovate in this way, if we manage in this way, if we create this kind of product, what kind of people will we become?" (p. 257).

Conrad (1994) discussed the ambiguous nature of ethical decisions. In large measure, they would not be ethical decisions unless they were ambiguous. Recently the Federal Aviation Administration (FAA) confronted an important issue when a Valujet exploded, killing all on board. The Administration immediately came to protect the airline saying that its safety record was good and that passengers should feel safe if flying Valujet. Just a few days later, the FAA reversed itself. Several news commentators asked why the reversal? A few days later, the FAA went before Congress asking that its ambiguous duties be simplified so that they could exclusively deal with safety.

In other words, the consumer public had essentially been misled by the FAA because the administration had duties to protect the consumer but also to protect the airlines. If this were not a government organization, one might call it a conflict of interest.

Some companies also disregard notices to have a recall on their products, hoping that settling lawsuits (filed from people who can ill afford them) will affect the "bottom line" less than recalling the product. In other words, the short-term economic impact is the ONLY consideration.

In the past, the sales approach of most organizations was to try for "repeat customers." Today the emphasis should be on "loyal customers," who not only will return to the company again and again but who will also recommend the company to others. Not recalling products and making hasty decisions and public statements, while not illegal, demonstrate to the customers how little the organization cares about them. With today's mass media market, even in the short haul, such unethical behavior may also damage the bottom line. While most would like for us to present a list of ethical decisions, the ambiguous nature of professional ethics makes such a list impossible. However, we will discuss some considerations.

1. *Try to avoid making hasty decisions.* Sometimes this is impossible, but it should be followed whenever possible. A quick decision often creates a situation where complete research does not occur until later.
2. *Consider all parties involved.* How does the product affect the environment? How does the product affect workers?
3. *Consider privacy and secrecy.* Obviously these are not the same. They are both pertinent both inside the organization and outside the organization. What should an airline do if it knows the pilot of a crashed plane has a history of alcoholism?
4. *Take the high ground.* If the decision affects you and perhaps even your job, take whatever responsibility has been yours.

5. *Think about the law.* Having conversations with disgruntled employees and disgruntled customers can keep you from having more serious problems.
6. *Go overboard to correct a wrong.* It may be valuable to ask a customer or an employee how that person feels the wrong can be corrected. Sometimes it takes as little as an apology.

PROFESSIONAL ETIQUETTE

Baldridge (1993) has provided advice for the "new kid on the block." Much of that advice is applicable as you move up the line of the chain of command. She first suggests that you should listen and learn rather than do all or even most of the talking. It is probably especially important that the newcomer to the company or to the new position try to avoid telling people how things were done in the other company or the other department. Second, she suggests that you should be nice to all parties. Because we never know what position we will have nor what position someone else may have, even as a practical matter it is important to be nice. Third, she suggests that you should not make hasty judgments about people. Having an open mind and considering varieties of motives in attributing why someone behaves as he does on a certain day can be beneficial. Fourth, Baldridge suggests that you periodically ask a peer out to lunch. Finally, she recommends that you not ask prying questions about others (Baldridge, 1993, p. 9).

As you run through your organizational career there are four sets of words that can be especially beneficial. They are: "please," "thank you," "I'm sorry," and "congratulations." The first two are particularly important when dealing with clerical people. One of the reasons they are important is that so many people do not use them. Secretaries are more likely to provide more efficient service and to respond beyond the call of duty to bosses who show respect for them. "Please" and "thank you" go a long way in showing such respect. "I'm sorry" and "congratulations" should be used with anyone who deserves hearing them.

When the matters are important, you should go to the trouble of *handwriting* a short note of "thank you, "I am sorry," or "congratulations." Such handwritten notes are taken to be more important than formal, typed letters on a letterhead.

While *political correctness* may bring with it a number of controversies, *professional etiquette* will always be acceptable. Referring to the people in the office as "my girls," "my guys," "gals," and the like is unacceptable. Terms of endearment are also unacceptable. "Honey," "sweetheart," and "dear" are good examples of words that should not be used. You should not discuss your sexual behavior or anyone else's in the office. Racial and ethnic slurs are to be avoided at all costs.

Maintaining a *professional look* is also important in the office. While Molloy (1977, 1988) has provided guidelines for appropriate dress at the office, those statements should be used only as general guidelines (e.g., Hickson &

Stacks, 1993). Many contemporary researchers disagree with much of what Molloy has to say. Probably the best way to learn how to dress at the level in which you are working is to observe others at your level, in your company, in your occupation, in your geographic area.

Baldridge (1993) has also provided guidelines for how to talk on the telephone, how to give a speech, how to have an artful conversation. However, it is important that you can be reached within a reasonable amount of time. Not returning telephone calls is rude. It is also troublesome if you suspect that the call is going to be negative. One reason is that avoiding issues may lead to legal problems. While a number of current electronic devices are useful, they are often trouble for others who do not use them. Thus, you may use e-mail, the WorldWide Web, faxes, and beepers, but traditional methods such as person-to-person conversation, telephones, and letters should be handled promptly because these other people may not have other methods available.

SUMMARY

The professional communicator takes into account all aspects of her position and the company's position. In this context, one needs to consider etiquette, ethics, and the law. Although the legal repercussions may have the greatest economic impact, one should also behave in such a way that is ethical and socially appropriate.

By now you should realize that Situational Software's Jim has a lot of professionalism to learn—and fast. The socialization process alone cannot teach you everything you need to know about professional conduct. Neither can even the best of mentors. Much of what we have discussed in this chapter you will learn by having to do it: hire, evaluate, and terminate; work with daily potential legal problems; and establish an environment that is ethical and proper. Jim's lessons will probably be hard, as were probably those of Dean and Bubba. Learning from your mistakes early will make your organizational career both rewarding and long-lived.

CASE 10.2 Perplexing Hiring Problem

You have known Juan personally for about eight years. You know that he has been in his own business of computer maintenance consulting for the last three of those years. In fact, your company has hired him as a consultant from time to time. You desperately need a full-time person to handle all of the computer problems you now have. You make him an offer and he accepts. However, after the offer has been made and accepted, the human resources (personnel) office gives you a call to tell you that they discovered Juan had been found guilty of a felony theft charge when he was in high school. To hire Juan, you must sign a waiver. What do you do?

QUESTIONS FOR THOUGHT

1. What would make you change the method you use to provide annual personnel reviews? How do you tell someone that he is not doing a good job?
2. What communication techniques could you use to get a worker to quit so that you do not have to fire her?
3. If you have a company that uses heavy machinery, what kinds of tests might you give individuals before they are hired?
4. Discuss the similarities and differences between privacy and secrecy.
5. On a regular basis, what kinds of personal notes should you send people in your company as a matter of appropriate etiquette? What is the value in doing this?

REFERENCES

Baldridge, L. (1993). *New complete guide to executive manners.* New York: Rawson.

Baucus, M. S., & Dworkin, T. M. (1994). Wrongful firing in violation of public policy: Who gets fired and why. *Employee Responsibilities and Rights Journal, 7,* 191–206.

Bies, R. J., & Tripp, T. M. (1993). Employee-initiated defamation lawsuits: Organizational responses and dilemmas. *Employee Responsibilities and Rights Journal, 6,* 313–324.

Conrad, C. (1994). *Strategic organizational communication: Toward the twenty-first century,* 3rd ed. Fort Worth: Harcourt, Brace.

Deetz, S. (1985). Ethical considerations in cultural research in organizations. In P. J. Frost, L. F. Moore, M. R. Louis, C. C. Lundberg, & J. Martin (Eds.), *Organizational Culture.* Beverly Hills, CA: Sage.

Greyser, S. A., & Reece, B. B. (1971). Businessmen look hard at advertising, *Harvard Business Review, Advertising: Better Planning, Better Results,* pp. 141–153.

Hickson, M. L. III, & Stacks, D. W. (1993). *NVC: Nonverbal communication: Studies and applications,* 3rd ed. Dubuque: Brown & Benchmark.

Kouzes, J. M., & Posner, B. Z. (1995). *The leadership challenge.* San Francisco: Jossey-Bass.

Koys, D. J., Briggs, S., & Grening, J. (1987). State court disparity on employment-at-will. *Personnel Psychology, 40,* 565–577.

Layne, S. P. (1989, June). A closer look at hiring and firing. *Security Management,* 49–52.

Manley, W. W., II, & Shrode, W. A. (1990). *Critical issues in business conduct: Legal, ethical, and social challenges for the 1990s.* New York: Quorum.

March, J. G., & Simon, H. A. (1958). *Organizations.* Chicago: Follett.

Molloy, J. T. (1988). *The new dress for success.* New York: Warner.

Molloy, J. T. (1977). *The woman's dress for success book.* Chicago: Follett.

Monroe, C., Barzi, M. G., & DiSalvo, V. S. (1989). Conflict behaviors of difficult employees. *Southern Communication Journal, 54,* 311–329.

Re, E. D. (1987). *Cases and materials on remedies.* Mineola, NY: Foundation.

Stano, M. (1992). The performance interview: Guidelines for academic program chairs. In M. Hickson, III, & D. W. Stacks, (Eds.). *Effective communication for academic chairs.* Albany: State University of New York Press.

Stewart, C. J., & Cash, W. B. Jr. (1994). *Interviewing: Principles and practices,* 7th ed. Madison, WI: Brown & Benchmark.

Willis, S. L., & Dubin, S. (1990). *Maintaining professional competence.* San Francisco: Jossey-Bass.

11

ORGANIZATIONAL CHANGE AND INNOVATION

Types of Organizational Change
  External change
  Technological change
  Information/knowledge change
  Economic change
  Political change
  Cultural change
  Demographic change
  Social change
  Task change
  Personnel changes
    The bean-counting syndrome
    The warm fuzzy syndrome
    The pragmatic syndrome
    Decision making
  Structural change: Formality, complexity, and size
Implementing Organizational Change
Assessing Organizational Change

Objectives

By the end of this chapter you should be able to

1. List and discuss the types of change found in organizations.
2. Differentiate among the various types of change.
3. Explain how task and structural change influence the adaptation process.
4. Explain how to implement organizational change.
5. Discuss how to assess organizational change.

We have discussed how individuals working in the New Organization need to learn to adapt to change as situations require. For these individuals, such changes may arise when the organization expands or reduces its size, thus changing the individual roles, rules, and routines. When individuals are promoted, demoted, given raises, and praised, they change. Sometimes these changes are for the betterment of both the organization and the individual, sometimes they are not. Whether individual changes are effective is largely dependent upon the person's willingness and ability to adapt to the new conditions. Even changes in employees' personal lives will affect how they work. With all of these changes going on in the individual lives of organizational members, it is important to note, too, that *organizations as a whole change, and successful ones adapt so that the changes bring benefits.*

Rogers and Agarwala-Rogers (1976) have written: "There are several ways to bring about change in an organization, in addition to innovation. One way is to terminate or destroy the organization" (p. 153). Most *self-initiated change* is intended to avoid the negative and uncontrollable changes that result in termination or destruction. In earlier chapters we have discussed changes that have taken place as a result of *technological change.* Consider, for example, the changes made in organizations as a result of the invention of electricity or the automobile. Changes in *theories of management* also have occurred, often dependent on management's view of the potential labor force and the need for workers to use first manual labor and later mind labor. We have also discussed change as a result of *economic modifications.* The internationalization of the economy and "bottom line" thinking have created an entire new vocabulary (downsizing, rightsizing, reengineering) Other types of *external environmental change* also influence how an organization might undergo change. These are found in the areas of political (and legal) change, social change, knowledge change, demographic change, and cultural change. It is important to note that change and adaptation are not new to organizational communication.

Despite the considerable changes that took place in the nineteenth century, those changes found in the twentieth century have been more dramatic. And, in all probability, the changes in the twenty-first century will be even more significant. Horton (1983), for instance, has written that "corporate histories reveal that organizations that fail have often continued to operate in the same old way, even after successful competitors demonstrated how to do things better" (p. 3).

For example, if you review the *Fortune 500* list of top corporations, only seven of the "Top 20" were on the top of the list in both 1963 and 1993. General Motors, Ford, Chrysler, Mobil, Chevron, Texaco, and Shell continue to make the "Top 20" list. Why? *Technology* is definitely a factor. More and more people needed to utilize the combustion engine automobile for driving to and from the workplace (a change that each of these corporations benefited from). However, because of the social and political impact of committed environmentalists, and the fear of changing political situations in the Middle East, a number of corporations have been looking at the possibility of producing an electric automobile. What kind of changes would this make for these seven corporations? It would appear that such a change would have a major impact on the oil companies, unless they *adapt* in some way such as building more efficient batteries for electricity or, through some legal change, were allowed to purchase shares of various electric power companies.

What about automobile corporations? Since the mid-1970s, the "Big Three" (Ford, General Motors, Chrysler) have already been forced to undergo a major change from the large, gas-guzzling Cadillac El Dorados, Chrysler Imperials, and Lincoln Continentals to smaller, more efficient cars. That change resulted from the impact of Japanese and European automobiles, which had already been adapted to the new ecological and economic realities of the price of oil, which has historically been much higher in countries other than the United States. To a large extent, those changes were made first in Europe and Japan, as a result of necessity. The city streets were smaller in those countries, parking spaces were smaller, and gasoline prices were higher. However, a change to electric autos would call for an even more dramatic change on the part of the "Big Three."

The American consumer—as well as the international automobile consumer—seeks smaller, more efficient, and safer cars. Add the environmental problems that continue to occur, even with pollution devices on combustion engines, and one can easily see the need for the electric car. In the beginning, such a car will need to have its battery recharged about every seventy-five to one hundred miles. Less oil and gasoline will be needed in the marketplace. However, one's power bills will increase if drivers decide to recharge their autos at home. How much more electricity will we need? Will nuclear power plants resurface as a means to fuel American autos through electricity?

What about service station operators? Will drivers continue to stop at service stations to get their batteries recharged? The answer, of course, is "It depends." How will all of the segments that are concerned with automobile technology adapt? Will someone research producing more efficient electricity? Perhaps electricity will be sold at fast-food restaurants, where drivers can have their automobile batteries recharged while eating and drinking or while driving through. The time element will become a more significant aspect for when and where we decide to have our automobile batteries recharged; that is, how long will it take to recharge the engine? In any case, technological change is a major factor for businesses to consider when adapting to society.

TYPES OF ORGANIZATIONAL CHANGE

Organizational change and innovation is probably one of the most discussed topics involving the corporate communication process. It is also one of the most complex. For this reason, we will try to explain change in the following manner. First, we will discuss *types of change*. While most of the changes that occur are *within* the organization, many are created by the external environment.

Such changes include technological change, knowledge/information change, economic change, political change, cultural change, and demographic change. We will also discuss social change as it occurs within the organization, including task change, personnel change, size and complexity change, and formality/informality change. Second, we will discuss *how to bring about change* both in terms of process and initiator. Third, we will discuss *how to evaluate the effectiveness of change.*

External Change

A model of change incorporates the principles of adapting to the negative information inputs from the outside as well as changes within the organization. Negative input may be any feedback that calls for adaptation. The first such external change we will discuss is that of *technology*. Technological change occurs because of the need for a company's products, as well as the need for a company to incorporate changes that have been made in the marketplace.

Technological Change

Probably the most significant change in technology over the past twenty years has been the personal computer (Rogers, 1995). If we consider information processing alone, we have moved from the 1950s, when manual typewriters and carbon paper were used to complete forms and produce copies, to the 1960s, when electric typewriters and Thermofax copies with special paper replaced them. For massive copies, Ditto machines and mimeograph machines often made up to one hundred copies. By the 1970s low-grade computers and massive photocopiers replaced 1960s technology. Today, those copiers can produce full-color brochures. With the advent of even smaller and more powerful personal computers, fax machines, the Internet, and the like, information processing has become a task that can be performed anywhere by virtually anyone with the appropriate equipment and technology. Information, once something that took time to find, process, and interpret, is available immediately.

TABLE 11.1   Change

External to Organization	Internal to Organization
technological	*social*
knowledge	task
information	personnel
economic	size and complexity
political	formality/informality
cultural	
demographic	

Of course, personal computers have been used extensively over the past 15 years for more than information processing. In a sense, the personal computer has not only replaced the massive mainframe computers in many organizations but has also replaced various accounting records, statistical records, personnel records, and the like, many of which were previously handled by hand. The flexibility and portability (Kerlinger, 1986; Stacks & Hocking, in press) of such machines has made it possible for managers to "think" with the computer at virtually any time and in any place. Projections can be made. "What if" statements can be asked in terms of questions like, "What if we chose the other vendor?" "What if we downsized by ten people?"

As previously mentioned, changes in technology require *social changes,* as well as task changes in the organization. Socially, the personal computer creates a situation where you do not have to be in an office to accomplish tasks. This "relative isolation" creates fewer interactions and less face-to-face feedback. Task changes create situations where clerical workers are terminated because managers begin doing their own information processing and information collection. Files, which at one time were part of the *human* system, are now part of the *computer* system.

Information/Knowledge Change

Virtually every type of change is preceded by a change in the *information/ knowledge base* of society. For many years, physicians were certain that stomach ulcers were caused by stress and diet. Recently, however, stomach ulcers have been found to be caused by a bacterium. This knowledge changes the manner in which physicians deal with ulcer patients, if those physicians are *aware* of the research—the information and knowledge found in their professional research journals. Successful businesses are knowledge receivers and are on the cutting edge of developments as soon as they happen. The research-oriented blacksmith of the late nineteenth century would have known that he needed to adapt to the new technological knowledge base of the automobile. Instead of creating more horseshoes, he probably began finding out how to purchase oil and change the automobile's tires.

In today's world, while some crime has actually decreased in the past few years, we know that *perceptions* of crime are that it is worse than ever. Such knowledge allows us to look into home security systems, bulletproof glass for companies and homes and automobiles. The research-oriented manager knows that she needs to be aware of how research-oriented her suppliers are. With the electric auto now a reality, which suppliers are undertaking the most advanced research on batteries? What innovations are consumers willing to accept and which ones will they reject? The information/knowledge base requires that managers consider technological changes, the consumer responses to such changes, and those economic, political, cultural, and demographic changes that may affect them.

Economic Change

Most economists view the economy as *cyclical*. The economy has its ups, and the economy has its downs. Is it a good time to enter the real estate business? That depends not only on the costs of materials and labor, but also on the costs of money. What is the lending rate? What are the demographics of people who own homes and those who do not? Do non-owners have enough money to make down payments? Are there regional influences? Is a new highway going to be built near the property? Will the government take action to increase or decrease the probability of more homeowners? For example, if the tax deduction for paying interest on your home is eliminated via some "flat tax" proposal, what effect will that have on potential homeowners? Depending on your answer to the question, the *research-oriented* real estate person might consider building homes or building apartments. What kinds of products are seasonal? How does advertising affect consumer feelings about a particular product? Do beer commercials simply cause beer drinkers to change brands, or do they create new beer drinkers?

R. J. Reynolds has received negative public reaction to its "Joe Camel" advertising. Critics claim that such commercials generate new cigarette smokers, specifically youngsters. That critical response has caused significant damage to R. J. Reynolds and to the tobacco industry in general. Do the short-term economic pluses account for the long-term economic losses? Congress and the law courts appear to be much more open to legislating and hearing cases against cigarette companies today than they were even five years ago (Rasberry & Lindsay, 1994, pp. 212–215).

Understanding economic change requires that the organization perceive not only the economic elements of change, but also the *psychological and social elements*. This requires continual research by management—both in terms of content research found in the research and legal journals and an ongoing analysis of its clients and customers. Economic change is often misinterpreted; therefore, for adaptation to occur, management must maintain a constant dialogue with all concerned.

Political Change

The political change generated by "Joe Camel" is a good example of how political change affects other changes in the business world. "Flat tax" proposals are another. While President Clinton's first term proposed changes in the health-care industry were not implemented, there was still an underlying atmosphere that they might result in other changes in the future. As a result, many hospitals began making changes by purchasing or selling some of their resources. Health maintenance organizations (HMOs) began buying and selling and merging as well as making changes to try to adapt so that legislation would not force them to make unwanted changes. Drug companies may also be impacted by virtue of Congress' concern that they appear to be overcharging American consumers for research and development.

Politically, what difference does it make whether the Democrats or the Republicans are in charge? While the Republicans felt that their 1994 "Contract with America" meant that most voters agreed with their views on budget issues, when they attempted to make changes by reducing the increases in some federal programs, they were met with a great deal of resistance, in part because of the lobbying efforts of the American Association of Retired Persons (AARP). And, if the electric automobile becomes a popular reality, will Congress attempt to create more federal regulations on electric suppliers? How will Congress attempt to assist auto companies and oil companies? Will electric car owners receive a tax break because they are producing less pollution?

Political change is more *problematic* than technological or economic change. While an observant manager can chart where technology may be headed, or where the economy is currently and where it should be in a given time period, charting political change is difficult. As in the 1994 "Contract with America," the public most distressed by proposed changes was the same public who brought many Republicans to power, the AARP. Further, political change occurs approximately every four years, with each presidential election. Perhaps the best advice for dealing with political change is the saying, "the more things change, the more they stay the same."

Cultural Change

As mentioned, most large corporations are international or are in the process of becoming international. How does this affect change? More and more, companies are seeking employees who speak more than one language. They are training employees to understand how people from other cultures *function* (see Chapter 12). Some of these issues also overlap with our system of ethics. For example, in many countries, what we call "bribes" are an essential part of doing business. In the United States, such behavior is considered unethical and illegal. As the international environment becomes more competitive, is it likely that politicians (and political change) will allow American companies more flexibility in regard to what we consider bribes?

The public relations impact of what some consider unethical behavior has been indicated in the case of Kathy Lee Gifford. Ms. Gifford had a line of fashions for a major retailer in the United States. A journalist determined that illegal aliens in the United States and child labor in other countries were used to produce products she promoted as "her line." Understanding that child labor is not illegal in some other countries—or that at least the laws are not enforced—what should the retail manager do? One of the reasons for the large media play was the impact of the information on Americans who had been losing jobs in the textile industry for some years. Congress even held hearings on the issue, providing an even larger media frenzy.

Looking back, little was actually accomplished in the Gifford case, but the competent manager might want to consider several things. First, what are the long-range economic, political, and cultural effects of this information? Second, how will the ethics of doing business be influenced by the international marketplace? Third, what will be the ultimate result of deporting jobs to other (usually third-world) countries? And, fourth, what impact will the North American Free Trade Agreement (NAFTA) have on all of these changes in general and in your company in particular? Change—whether it be economic, political, or technological—can be understood, predicted, and to a degree controlled through

1. a continued research of both the marketplace and clients,
2. a continued dialogue with all factions (technological, political, economic) involved in any potential cultural change,
3. a knowledge of the public's perceptions.

Demographic Change

A major demographic change occurring in the United States is that there are larger numbers of persons considered now to belong to minority groups. The Spanish-speaking population, for instance, is increasing. Today, in certain urban areas—as well as in states like California, Florida, and Texas—knowledge of Spanish is almost essential for small business owners. Over the next decade, many of these Spanish-speaking workers (and customers) will move into other states such as Georgia, Alabama, New Mexico, Oklahoma, Arizona, Nevada, and Louisiana. Airports, bus stations, and railroads need to become bilingual. Restaurants, service industries, and government agencies need to utilize the Spanish language. Most mailed packages have directions written in two, three, or four languages. What will be the effect of a company's creating products specifically for a minority population? Will it be greeted with "thank you" for considering this group? Or, will it be considered racist? Does it make a difference who the stockholders are?

While cultural change influences how business is done in the United States, it also influences how business is done with other countries. How does the concept of time involved in creating a contract differ from place to place? As early as the late 1960s and early 1970s Garfinkel (1967) and Hall (1977) discussed cultural differences as *taken-for-granted behavior.* When we are part of a culture—a demographic—we *assume* that we can operate a certain way everywhere with everyone; this simply is not the case.

Another type of demographic change can be found in the percentage of females who attend college. Even in the 1960s, the vast majority of college students were male. Women are now the majority on many college campuses. How does such a demographic change influence the college environment? Dormitories have been built. Student affairs personnel have increased. Sexual harassment laws have a greater impact. And more women have been hired as professors. How will organizations adapt to this changing demographic?

A third demographic change variable for business in the United States deals with age. "Baby boomers" (children born between 1945 and 1960) are quickly approaching fifty years of age. In a very short time (ten to fifteen years), a significant part of the workforce will be retiring. How is society going to provide? In addition to the problems associated with social security funding are health care problems. Nursing homes should be in a growth phase; people are living longer. What happens when a significant portion of the population is in its 90s, which could occur as early as 2035? And, now that there is no limit on the age of retirement, what happens when employees decide that they wish to continue working after age 75, 85, 95? What impact will it have on productivity? On decision making? On the workforce now graduating from college?

The competent manager must be prepared for external change in technology, knowledge/information, economics, politics, culture, and demography as factors that influence the operations of organizations. The question becomes one of how will the businesses adapt? There are several internal changes that organizations typically undertake in adapting to external change. They include task changes, personnel changes, formality of structure, and size and complexity of structure. However, all of these changes are *social* adaptations to external change.

Social Change

The coffee pot or the water fountain may have been the central place for interaction before the advent of the personal computer, but today the Internet, the WorldWide Web, and e-mail have created new types of "interpersonal" and "group" interaction. Although face-to-face communication has been enhanced by the technology of interactive television systems, and managers in Seattle and New York can now interact face-to-face without leaving their offices, its communication impact has yet to be fully explored. A significant communication question arises from whether interactive television or e-mail is as effective as *personal* conversation.

In essence the question becomes one of how important is personal interaction? Even in most large board meetings, separate, individual conversations occur during breaks. Such conversations often play a major role in the ultimate politics of the decision making. Some more apprehensive members of the organization may feel freer to interact or make suggestions on a one-to-one basis than in the meeting itself. While they may have good ideas, they may be less willing to express them over interactive television. Any organization needs to be aware of such changes, and whether the decisions are more or less effective.

Another social change problem that is created with increased technology is that of psychological and physical *stress*. Increased technology often creates information overload. Increased technology also increases production expectations. Workers are expected to undertake many more actions because of their newfound technological capabilities. The human-oriented manager must be concerned with how these two factors affect the overall productivity as well as the job satisfaction of workers, especially as highly qualified mind labor becomes more difficult to find. Three means of resolving these problems within the organization are task change, personnel change, and structural change.

Task Change

While most managers did not need to know how to type (or use a keyboard) in the past, most must master some form of data entry today. In many instances, today's manager undertakes numerous tasks that were once the province of clerical personnel. Because time is finite, the question becomes one of what, if any, previous functions does the manager no longer have? Dictation and repeated proofreading are two of them. However, there are fewer inputs, increasing the possibility of error.

For example, while most computers now have spell checks, such systems do not find when a word such as "not" is omitted from a sentence. Thus, quality checks must be taken with much more intricacy than in the past. Further, some managers trust too much in technology to catch their errors. Not only do spell checkers *not* find certain words, they may change the meaning of the message when automatically changing what they believe are misspellings. While technology has advanced our ability to do several tasks simultaneously, that technology is only as smart as we let it be. The competent manager carefully reviews output, especially at middle and upper levels, where the output is not a product or service, but some abstraction of that product or service.

Personnel Changes

Personnel changes are a fact of life in companies large or small. Individuals are hired, fired, and they retire or resign. Individuals are transferred. Probably the most significant of these changes for most of us involves dealing with a new boss. In "You Can't Change Your Boss, So Change Yourself" (1995), it is recommended that the individual subordinate consider first of all what the differences are between the "old" boss and the "new" one. For example, you may need to use humor less, or you may need to increase your use of statistics. It is impossible to describe all of the possible personality differences, but it is important to know and understand that new bosses try to put their imprint on the job. This understanding comes from knowing how others (especially bosses) think.

There are a number of different ways in which people think, how they approach their position as manager. These approaches are not typically found under leadership or supervision, but instead deal with an orientation toward *the job*. We will discuss only three stereotypical types. You should understand, however, that no one specifically falls into these categories. Nevertheless, stereotypes of personalities do assist us in understanding.

The Bean-Counting Syndrome

Sometimes this approach is referred to as the "accountant's syndrome." The accountant is concerned about the bottom line—the profit-making of the company. Earlier in this text we discussed the notion that technology is generally considered less expensive than people are in the long run. Many organizations implement new technologies to save money, only to discover that business is lost because of the innovation. For example, one recent innovation is the use of telephone-answering machines and menus. With many organizations, a caller will never talk to a person, or the caller may receive a message something like this: "Hello, you have reached the X Company. If you are ordering, press one. If you are requesting a catalog, press two. If you are returning an item, press three. If you are trying to reach a specific person, press four." You press four. Now you get a message, "If you know the extension of the person you are calling, enter that number followed by the pound sign. If you do not know their extension, enter their name, beginning with the last name." You enter H-I-C-K-S-O-N. Then you receive another message. "Mr. Hickson is not in right now. If you would like to leave a voice mail message, enter one now. If you would prefer to talk with someone else, hold." You hold. You hear some music that plays on all of these systems, often with intervening "specials" for potential customers.

Now let's suppose that the public relations person in your office indicates that this menu system is causing the company to lose business. How do you and the public relations person talk the boss into hiring operators instead of using this new technology? If the boss's approach is as a bean counter she is going to want to know, how *much* business? Thus, you must undertake research prior to making such a request. You must also be able to "prove" that the cost of hiring operators will be considerably less than the amount by which business will be enhanced. (You should remember to include the benefits the company provides to the operators in your figures.) One way of knowing that a boss is likely to be a bean counter is where she came from. For example, an accountant, an engineer, and many people with a scientific orientation will have such an approach.

The Warm Fuzzy Syndrome

If your boss comes from the human relations field, counseling, or was a liberal arts major, it is probable that you would *not* want to use the same line of argument that you used with the bean counter in resolving the problem indicated above. People who are oriented toward a "warm and fuzzy" approach are people persons. They are as interested in how their customers or clients perceive the organization, its product, and its personnel as the "bottom line." (They often argue that the people approach produces better products and thus a larger bottom line by promoting a more healthy and supportive climate than a climate based on a chart of profits and losses.)

Instead, your argument would center on the message that customers and others are complaining about feeling alienated and impersonal toward the company because of the telephone system. The "human touch" is the basic argument here. Clearly, by hiring one or two operators to handle those who are either alienated by the answering system or who have problems that take a "real person" to fix, profits will go up through a reduction of negative perceptions about a company not interested in its clients or customers.

The Pragmatic Syndrome

While many bean counters feel that they are pragmatic, often they are not. The pragmatist is concerned with the long run. While the telephone system may save money and raise profits in the short haul, we may find that some people become frustrated with the system, especially if there is no shortcut to getting to the person they want to speak with. In some sense, by blending the warm and fuzzy with the bean counter, the boss can be convinced that an increased cost for operators brings with it more loyal customers. Maintaining loyal customers is a significant long-term effect of such a pragmatic approach (Bhote, 1996).

Decision Making

There is little doubt that all bosses hold on to a little of each of these approaches to the job, but the important feature is that each boss has a way of making decisions. Most bosses do not change the way in which they make decisions impulsively. Some may function with numbers, others with metaphors and analogies, others with charts, and still others through some type of internal "gut-feeling." Most new bosses require some kind of change on the part of their subordinates, and the successful subordinate adapts.

The boss may change not only his nameplate on the door, he may change the company logo. He may change the titles of others' jobs. He may change their job descriptions. These relatively minor changes may be readily accepted by subordinates with little conflict.

More dramatically, however, the new boss may wish to change *tasks* (as mentioned above). He may change the organization's goals, placing less focus

DILBERT / Scott Adams

DILBERT © United Feature Syndicate. Reprinted by Permission.

on domestic sales and increasing international sales. He may try to micro-manage everything about the organization. Good new bosses will generate change moderately with the speed at which it needs to be made. Others, how-ever, will take the "ax" approach, often selecting those to ax who disagree with the changes. It is important to understand that the subordinate cannot and should not try to change the boss. The key word is "adaptation." More likely than not, the subordinate can survive, because ax-bosses are often short-lived. In addition, it is quite possible that some or many of the new boss's ideas are good ideas, especially in relatively non-productive organizations. The smart subordinate can separate negative personalities from negative decisions.

Structural Change: Formality, Complexity, and Size

There are a variety of ways in which an organization might decide to make structural changes. These include the simple matter of changing personnel (through hiring, firing, promotions, demotions, transfers, and the like), leveling or flattening the organization by reducing the number of levels of decision mak-ing, downsizing (or "rightsizing") as well as expanding, or totally reorganizing.

A goal of many organizations is to narrow the gaps between the top of the organization and the bottom. The intention is to reduce complexity and formality. When such changes are made, they often occur quickly, at what might be considered by some "super speeds." In a sense, such a change cre-ates an "open door" policy where there previously was none. Often the in-tention is to simplify while reducing. This, however, often does not happen. The increase in horizontal communication at such breakneck speed is often viewed by workers as vertical communication, and many workers cannot decide who is a boss and who is not. Obviously, this creates a situation of employee stress and a chaotic vacuum whereby "power brokers" may at-tempt to use change for their own benefit. The opposite effect is produced when organizations expand the *vertical organizational chart*. Decisions often become more bureaucratic, new forms are created, and most employees try to "cover" their actions. Often more time is spent keeping track of what you have done than in doing something. Increasing vertical communication slows the decision-making process.

Structural changes in the organizational chart are often accompanied by reductions or increases in the number of personnel. Rasberry and Lindsay (1994) have suggested that such a process involves a process of unfreezing, moving, and refreezing (p. 554). It is often difficult for many to understand that organizations sometimes undergo downsizing simply to begin rehiring people in less than a year. Estes (1996) has indicated that bad change deci-sions are made because not all factors are considered in the bottom line. He argues that stockholders are the only sub-group considered by many decision makers. According to Estes (1996, p. 29), employees, customers, stockhold-ers, suppliers, lenders, neighboring communities, and society as a whole should be taken into account. Gordon (1996) also emphasizes that effective *relationships* between the top management and workers create improved long-term changes. He indicates that management should emphasize the carrot, not the stick (Downs, 1995).

At the same time, it should be emphasized that some personnel changes are the result of a need for not necessarily fewer personnel, but *different* personnel. For example, telephone companies hired significant numbers of personnel after World War II to the middle 1960s. Many of those personnel were not well educated. Their technical expertise may have involved dialing numbers and providing information for long-distance customers (operators) and installing telephones and replacing poles and lines (linesmen and repairmen). Many of them were well paid, when taking into consideration their education and expertise. Today, though, those same companies are expanding into cable television and computer systems. Most new homes are already "fitted" for telephones. Many lines, especially fiber optic lines, are more stable and need replacing and repairing less often. In addition, if one looks into the future, television, computers, and cable television are likely to be wireless.

Decreasing the number of personnel, however, does create a need for significant organizational change. New workers must learn to be more flexible and able to perform more than one particular task. Downsized companies almost always find an increase in employee stress levels, and the stress is not only from being potentially laid-off, but also from the knowledge that they may have to learn a new skill. Some employees may be asked to switch to sales. Others may be asked to create new products, to enhance products, to suggest means of reducing production costs. Most of these employees will have never thought about these ideas before because their jobs were more focused and they performed fewer tasks.

Strangely, increasing personnel also meets resistance from employees who are already on the job or have survived a downsizing. Unless new job descriptions are strictly enforced, veteran employees will continue to try to do all of the work that was previously assigned to them. New personnel may have problems determining how to do their jobs without having a negative impact on their relationships with others. It is important that all veterans are on the same "page" about how the new employees are to be utilized for the most effective operations of the company.

External changes, then, especially technological change, knowledge/ information change, economic change, political change, cultural change, and

---

CASE 11.1   Preparing for Change

Assume that you work for one of the regional "Bells," the former telephone companies. You now know that you can also move into the cable television business. What kinds of changes internally will you need to make? How will you prepare your personnel for these dramatic changes in what you do?

demographic change affect how an organization operates. Companies usually adapt to these changes by changing tasks of their employees, changing personnel, and influencing the formality, complexity, and size of their structure. It is important to note that most changes will meet resistance in the organization. The question the competent manager must keep asking is: How can the organization most effectively implement change?

IMPLEMENTING ORGANIZATIONAL CHANGE

To implement organizational change, you must first determine what the organization's goals are. An effective organization must be stable and integrated and it needs to motivate and provide incentives for motivation. *The effective organization achieves its goals.* While the organization must utilize both competition and cooperation in achieving several of its goals, it is generally agreed that when change occurs, cooperation among elements within the organization are most important. From the organization's viewpoint, change occurs because there is a *problem.*

The concept of *problem solving* is found in reflective thinking (Dewey, 1933), small group communication (Smith, 1963), and decision making (Rasberry & Lindsay, 1994), and is utilized in a number of different contexts including the health care industry (Rogers & Agarwala-Rogers, 1976). While the terminology is somewhat different among these various sources, they all essentially use the same process, involving five or six steps (see Table 11.2).

The first step in the process is to *define the problem*. For many organizational members, the problem is likely to be stated "Profits are down" or "Sales are down." The concept of a problem, however, must be defined in a more specific manner. Smith (1963) has suggested that problems are best stated as

TABLE 11.2   The Problem-Solving Process

I. Define the Problem	B. Eliminate Impossible Solutions
A. Goals	V. Selecting Best Solution(s)
B. Barriers	A. Short-term Implications
II. Analyze the Problem	B. Long-term Implications
A. Worth of Goal	VI. Implement the Solution
B. Barriers to Meeting Goal	A. Putting Solution into Action
C. Research	B. Communicating Solution
D. Evaluate Previous Attempts	C. Maintaining Consensus
E. Brainstorm	VII. Evaluating the Solution
III. Suggest Possible Solutions	A. Did it Work?
IV. Evaluate Potential Solutions	B. Short-term Implications
A. Eliminate Impractical Solutions	C. Long-term Implications

"How can we best increase the sales of product X?" Smith defines a problem as "any situation in which an individual or individuals seek a practical means by which to overcome barriers to a worthwhile goal(s)" (p. 23). To define the problem, then, it is necessary for the group to define their worthwhile goals and the barriers.

Smith is clear in pointing out that a problem and a task are different. Problems require decision making. In the process of defining the problem, it is important that status differentials be eliminated as much as possible. It is also important that the final wording of the problem be reached through *consensus.* That is, all of the people involved in the decision-making process must agree with the problem. One example, taken from one of our classes, involved a group who had decided to tackle the problem: "How can we best ensure that the state prison system rehabilitates prisoners?" The wording of the problem was sufficient. However, there was no consensus about what was the actual problem. As the discussion went on, some of the members appeared to be more concerned with *punishing* prisoners than with *rehabilitating* them. Perhaps the problem should have been stated: "How can we best ensure that our state prison system will reduce its recidivism rate?" Such a problem may have generated a more complex discussion, but it certainly would have drawn consensus whereas the previous problem did not.

While many might think there is no need to research the definition of the problem, Rogers and Agarwala-Rogers (1976) have suggested otherwise. Qualitative analyses, especially observations and literature reviews (see Chapter 3), are needed to define the problem (p. 152). One way of approaching such an analysis is to consider this type of research as "counting to one" (Van Maanen, Manning, & Miller, 1986, p. 5).

In the business organization, consensus is important in talking about change. As such, consensus is constituted by thinking in terms of a *common goal.* If it were possible for several college students to work toward obtaining one degree, then they would have a common goal. When students are each working toward their own individual degrees, we have the same goal, but not a common goal. Individual and sub-unit interests must be discounted to develop a common goal and a definition of the problem.

The second step in the process is to *analyze the problem.* It is important in all of these early stages that group members resist the temptation to state solutions. Smith (1963) notes that analyzing the problem involves exploring the worth of the goal. The group should also explore the nature of the barriers to the goal. Third, the group should research what has been done in the past to overcome the barriers. Fourth, the group should evaluate the effectiveness of previous attempts to overcome the barriers. Finally, the group should consider what the repercussions might be if nothing is done (p. 34). Various members of the group should be able to bring in different information, all of which can be used to analyze the problem.

The third step is to suggest all possible solutions. One of the most useful tools for suggesting solutions is that of *brainstorming.* The idea is that the group should first present as many ideas as they can think of to resolve the problem. These ideas are presented openly and quickly. Someone must record all of these suggestions. Rasberry and Lindsay (1994) have developed rules for brainstorming:

1. Criticism is ruled out.
2. Freewheeling is welcome.
3. Quantity is desired.
4. Combination and improvement are sought (p. 441).

Because this is a creative process, it is important to eliminate (or at least suspend) criticism during the suggestion phase. No matter how ridiculous a suggestion may be, both verbal and nonverbal critiques should be avoided. *Freewheeling* means being wild and crazy. Often some ridiculous idea will generate someone else's thinking of a similar notion that is not so ridiculous. This is known as *piggybacking,* where one person takes off on an idea generated by someone else. The basic idea is that the more suggestions there are, the better will be the final solution. The combinations (piggybacking, or hitchhiking) also improve the possible best solution.

Once all of the solutions have been recorded, it is time to move to the fourth step: *evaluate the ideas.* Often this involves the process of elimination of impossible or impractical solutions. However, sometimes the group sees a light bulb, and all may agree at once.

In any case, we are now at step five: *selecting the best solution or solutions.* What are the short-term and long-term implications of implementing this solution? Has this been tried by us before? How is our situation different NOW? Has this been tried by others? What were the results? How will the solution affect various sub-groups within the organization? How will it affect the company's public relations? How will it affect suppliers?

Finally, the group should suggest ways of *implementing the solution.* How long will it take? How much will it cost? When should we begin? How will we notify the different segments of our organization? How will we notify the public? It is important at this stage, and at all others, to ensure that consensus is being maintained. Questions like: "Does everyone agree?" "Bob, what do you think?" are important for maintaining consensus. What does one member's silence mean? What can you tell about the nonverbal communication of the members of the group?

After the solution has been implemented you must *evaluate its effectiveness.* Of all the problems associated with problem solving, evaluation seems the most problematic. It often seems that once the problem has been "solved" it no longer exists. It is sort of like "out of sight, out of mind." A competent manager will, after ensuring consensus among the task group that the solution has been implemented, keep track of the original problem and see that it does not recur. Problem solving is a systematic process, one that suspects that the problem is never really solved, but that it may come back in one of many different forms.

This problem-solving process can be invaluable to any organization going through change. For it to work, however, the final decision must come from the group, not from the CEO or CFO. All members must agree to the problem and its solution; all members must be *committed* to it. Therefore, the idea is to prevent some members from leaving the meeting or meetings saying, "Well, I don't agree, but that's what they decided to do." This is particularly important where downsizing is involved. Of course, it is also important who is involved in the group.

Total Quality Management (TQM) is often used to create inter-departmental, decision-making groups, referred to as *quality control circles*. The idea is that members of a number of groups take part in the innovation of change (Aguayo, 1990). While the term, "quality circles" has somewhat lost its popularity, the idea behind the concept remains important. Listening, openness, and understanding are the important ingredients in making these groups work (Rasberry & Lindsay, 1994, p. 566). The question then becomes one of who selects the members from each group. Top management should *not* select all of the members and department heads should *not* be the only members. An important aspect of quality circles is that *all* groups involved should have a voice, and if all members are managers, you are unlikely to achieve the best solutions.

While in a quality circle, it must be re-emphasized that status should be a relatively unimportant factor. Once all the solutions have been offered in the brainstorming process, it is probably best to have members write down their individual best solutions in an anonymous way so that the group is not talking about "Bob's solution" or "Jan's solution." The known group research method discussed in Chapter 3 might serve as the initial model for putting together a quality circle. In addition, there are electronic brainstorming computer programs available that create anonymous potential solutions. However, even in interpersonal situations, after the circle has met several times—and participants truly understand how and why the circle operates—status differences quickly disappear and an open and positive communication climate is obtained. Once open communication occurs, reticent members begin to open up and participate; once participation is across the circle, consensus is possible.

ASSESSING ORGANIZATIONAL CHANGE

At some point, probably in the implementation stage, the group should decide how long it would take to determine how well the solution (the change) has worked (step seven of the problem-solving process). It may be better to establish a new quality control circle to implement the assessment process. The concept of consensus is important here, too, at least in its early stages. Obviously, facts and figures will be part of the assessment process. That is, many of the aspects of the process will be quantitative and empirical. However, the process should also involve a description of members' *perceptions* of the organization, as well as perceptions of members of all segments that have been or will be affected. As such, evaluations must be qualitative as well as quantitative (Patton,

1980). For example, if there has been an increase in profits and downsizing, how do these combined effects influence the work and behavior of the remaining employees? Has the process increased tensions? Do employees have a greater sense of insecurity? Of course, one means of preventing or at least reducing stress and insecurity is to inform all employees of the changes in advance of the change. It is also important not only to notify them of the change but also to explain how the decisions about the changes were made.

Evaluation is a continual managerial job. Chapter 3 introduced a variety of methods that help to gather data. When you are faced with change that may be controversial or require major readjustments of the organization and its workforce, focus groups and a continued form of participant-observation are extremely important. Actually surveying affected personnel—either through a formal survey passed out by management or through questionnaires inserted in the company newsletter or with paychecks—may be the first step in gauging the proposed change's effect on the organization. However, no survey can replace face-to-face conversations, either interpersonally or in groups, about changes, fears, and potentials due to change. The competent manager is always looking for information with which to evaluate attitudes toward the company and herself. Remembering that innovation by definition requires change should temper any decision about altering the organization.

SUMMARY

Organizational change and innovation, then, is a difficult process. Such changes are often initiated because of changes in society: technological, informational, economic, political, cultural, and demographic. Once the organization becomes aware of these changes, internal changes are made in tasks, personnel, and structure. The means by which the organization accomplishes these changes is through some group, often a quality control circle, which undertakes a seven-step process of defining the problem, analyzing the problem, suggesting all possible solutions, evaluating the ideas, developing the best solution, and implementing the solution. Finally, that group or another group assesses the changes at a date decided upon by the previous group in its implementation stage.

CASE 11.2   Implementing Innovation

The research and development people at your oil company have determined that the number of electric automobiles will increase from less than 1 percent to more than 10 percent by 2005. They also anticipate that the change will increase to 33 percent by 2010. Currently your company's stations make about 80 percent of their profits on gasoline and oil. What kind of changes do you need to make during the next five years? Ten years?

QUESTIONS FOR THOUGHT

1. Given case 11.2 (above), assuming that you will begin charging people for buying electricity, how would you determine how to charge them?
2. What kinds of innovations can you anticipate might be made in the retail grocery business over the next fifteen years?
3. What kinds of companies are likely to see a decline in their profits over the next fifteen years, if they are not innovative?
4. Discuss the pharmaceutical industry in terms of tapping new international markets over the next fifteen years.
5. What kinds of content research does a manager need to undertake innovations in her field?

REFERENCES

Aguayo, R. (1990). *Dr. Deming: The American who taught the Japanese about quality.* New York: Fireside.

Bhote, K. R. (1996). *Beyond customer satisfaction to customer loyalty.* New York: American Management Association.

Dewey, J. (1933). *How we think: A restatement of the relation of reflective thinking to the education process.* Boston: Heath.

Downs, A. (1995). *Corporate executions: The ugly truth about layoffs—how corporate greed is shattering lives, companies, and communities.* New York: American Management Association.

Estes, R. (1996). *Tyranny of the bottom line: Why corporations make good people do bad things.* San Francisco: Berrett-Koehler.

Garfinkel, H. (1967). *Studies in ethnomethodology.* Englewood Cliffs, NJ: Prentice-Hall.

Gordon, D. M. (1996). *Fat and mean: The corporate squeeze of working Americans and the myth of managerial "downsizing."* New York: Kessler.

Hall, E. T. (1977). *Beyond culture.* Garden City, NY: Anchor.

Horton, T. (1983, October). Building through change. *Management Review, 3.*

Kerlinger, F. N. (1986). *Foundations of behavioral research,* 3rd ed. New York: Holt, Rinehart, and Winston.

Patton, M. Q. (1980). *Qualitative evaluation methods.* Beverly Hills, CA: Sage.

Rasberry, R. W., & Lindsay, L. L. (1994). *Effective managerial communication,* 2d ed. Belmont, CA: Wadsworth.

Rogers, E. M. (1995). *Diffusion of innovations,* 4th ed. New York: Free Press.

Rogers, E. M., & Agarwala-Rogers, R. (1976). *Communication in organizations.* New York: Free Press.

Smith, W. S. (1963). *Group problem-solving through discussion: A process essential to democracy.* Rev. ed. Indianapolis: Bobbs-Merrill.

Stacks, D. W., & Hocking, J. E. (in press). *Communication research,* 2nd ed. New York: HarperCollins.

Van Maanen, J., Manning, P. K., & Miller, M. L. (Eds.). (1986). *Sage qualitative research methods series.* Vols. 1–4. Beverly Hills, CA: Sage.

You can't change the boss, so change yourself. (1995, October). *Executive Strategies,* 1–2.

12

WOMEN AND MINORITIES IN THE WORKPLACE

Discrimination

The New Culture
   A comparison
   Moving ahead

Sexual Harassment

Racial Harassment

Non-Discriminatory Language

Other Human Factors in the Workplace
   Employees with disabilities
   Religion in the workplace
   Internationalism in the workplace
   Age discrimination

Objectives

By the end of this chapter you should be able to

1. Define discrimination and explain how it occurs in the workplace.
2. Distinguish among racial, sexual, and non-discriminatory language forms of harassment.
3. Explain how to combat discrimination in the workplace.
4. Discuss the special discriminatory problems faced by women and minorities in the New Organization.
5. Differentiate between human factors that influence discrimination in the workplace.

The place of women and minorities in the workplace has changed significantly over the past fifty years. The Second World War created a situation in which women and minorities were needed in the workforce for building aircraft and other government materials because so many men were enlisted into combat. Women learned to become an essential part of the workforce, not only in previously gendered professions such as clerical workers and nurses, but also as production workers and managers. Minority representation in the workforce increased for the same reasons. Yet "equality" has yet to reach most organizations in the United States. The problems involving differences between men and women in the workplace are historical. Generally they fall into two categories: (1) discrimination and (2) harassment. Similar problems are found for people associated with various minorities because of their culture, age, health, race, and religion, to name but a few.

DISCRIMINATION

Discrimination involves the hiring and firing of personnel, their compensation, and the terms, conditions, and privilege of employment based on a person's gender or race or other legally protected categories. On the positive side, then, we are talking about hiring, promotion, and compensation. On the negative side, however, we are talking about layoffs, downsizing, rightsizing, and any other term which means that some employees are retained while others are dismissed from the organization. The important point about all of these actions is that to avoid discrimination the actions must be *systematic* and they must be based on *work-related behavior,* not country of national origin, gender, race, age, or physical handicap.

Probably the most significant issue involving discrimination has been that of *equal pay for equal work.* Schwartz (1996) has reported that women are improving their lot regarding salaries, but there remains a gap. She indicates that in some fields, such as computer analysis, gains have been made. However, bank tellers, brokers, and financial analysts lost ground between 1994 and 1996. Generally, females earn about eighty-five to ninety-five cents for every dollar compared with men. These changes in earnings, however, represent an improvement of sorts. Pepper (1995) reported that women received about sixty-five cents to the male's dollar in 1987. More changes in favor of women and minorities can be expected in the workplace of the twenty-first century, when an even higher percentage of the organization will be composed of these groups. As their numbers increase, more fairness is likely simply because of the numbers involved and because of more class-action lawsuits. For those working in the New Organization, the changes will have significant positive consequences for women and minorities.

In looking at your own organization to determine whether there has been discrimination in compensation and/or promotion in regard to gender, it may be valuable to establish a chart such as the one found in Table 12.1. By using such a chart, you can begin to ask some significant questions. In this case, all four employees have the same position, senior salesperson. All have been promoted within two years of one another; there is more than a $1,500 difference in their last salary increases. There is more than a $100,000 difference in the amount of sales over the preceding year. Elizabeth has the second highest amount of sales but the lowest salary.

You, as manager, need to look at why this is the case. If productivity is the bottom line, perhaps Elizabeth's next increase should be closer to the one at the top. Of course, if increases are made solely on sales or if commissions are the entire basis for salary, there should be no problem, but in most organizations it is not that simple. Only by making such comparisons can you determine whether you are making a rational, non-prejudiced decision about the next increase and not one based on some unconscious bias.

There may be other reasons for different salaries. For example, let's suppose that Will has supervisory responsibilities that Jane and Elizabeth do not. A question may arise as to why the male has supervisory responsibilities and the women do not. Or perhaps Bob and Will have seniority in terms of total years with the company. Whatever the variables may be, all of them should be included in the chart.

A typical reason given for providing a higher raise for one person over another is something that a boss might refer to as *poor attitude.* To avoid legal problems, as well as to be fair, the boss needs to better define "poor attitude." In fact, the concept of attitude probably needs to be dismissed entirely. The question is: What kind of behavior does the employee engage in which enhances or harms the organization? *The behavior of being rude to customers or potential customers,* for example, is a much more specific condemnation than is "poor attitude." Being *tardy for work, absenteeism,* or *number of errors in the account,* are better than "irresponsible." Thus, when decisions are made about hiring, firing, and compensation, those decisions should be based on categories of *specific behavior.* Part of the responsibility here is in the form(s) used for evaluation, probably developed by the human resources office in your organization. However, if you just have "bad feelings" about an employee, you need to determine what you mean by that—how you would defend your evaluation.

TABLE 12.1   Salaries and Discrimination

Name	Salary	Last Promotion	Last Increase	Dollars of Sales	Protected
Bob	$55,750	1994	$4,250	$375,600	No
Will	53,000	1993	3,250	300,500	No
Jane	45,800	1992	2,800	275,000	Yes
Elizabeth	43,000	1992	2,700	311,800	Yes

The concept of discrimination as a significant problem resulted from Title VII of the Civil Rights Act of 1964. In a sense, discrimination is something involving a major decision about an employee. However, the truth of the matter is that the employee may discover that the initial problem is in the culture of the organization itself.

THE NEW CULTURE

The culture of the New Organization in the twenty-first century will be different from that of the previous four decades. Many clerical jobs, previously assigned almost exclusively to females, will be non-existent. With the advent of the computer, some traditional roles have been switched. Instead of the office worker typing a letter for the boss to approve and proofread, the boss may type the letter for the office worker to proof. Many office worker jobs will become "information processing" jobs—and they will be held by both males and females. As well, corporate management will be comprised of both sexes. Finally, corporate boards will contain a proportionate percentage of female directors (Bradshaw, 1996). From the bottom to the top, the organizational culture will include both sexes. Such a culture calls for significant changes in the work environment.

But the culture of the New Organization is being changed by other factors of importance also. The number of minority workers has increased and is expected to continue to do so. Some companies, such as Texaco in 1996, have found that it is not only the external appearance of gender and ethnic equality that is important, it is also a matter of how the people *in* the organization adapt to it. Texaco settled a lawsuit filed by minorities because of audiotapes of executives expressing their deep-seated racial biases. Gender and racial discrimination and harassment are not just words for which the organization must formulate a policy—they are *real,* with real consequences to the organization.

While the first Civil Rights Act was passed in the United States in 1866, just after the Civil War, it was not until the Civil Rights Act of 1964 that the concept of equal protection in work became a reality. In today's world, and certainly in tomorrow's world, an organization's culture must not only represent a *knowledge* of equal treatment and equal opportunity both within the organization and to the public, it must be *demonstrated.* Public trust in companies is now vested with a twenty-first century understanding of humane treatment—to workers, to customers, to vendors, to the media, and to the public.

The question may be: What does all of this mean to the individual organization? Indeed, what does it mean for the individual worker? As a starting point, let us view some of the work–family issues for workplace 2001. The human resources division of most companies now attempts to make the workplace "family friendly." What does this mean?

For one, the companies make resource referrals for their workers. This could be along the lines of alcohol or drug problems, potential divorces, child custody problems, financial difficulties, and the like. They provide child and elder care workshops, they have created child care credits, some provide direct financial assistance; there is more long-term health care, emergency child care, job sharing, voluntary reduced time or part-time employment, flextime, and working from the home (Boyett, 1995, pp. 94–99).

A Comparison

While many of these initiatives were developed for female workers, they have now become essential for *male* workers, too. In the past, it was assumed that the male (husband) would come to work all day and that the female (wife) would take care of the children and whatever other personal and family issues were involved. The husband would work in the office from 8:00 A.M. to 5:00 P.M. and whatever other times were necessary to get the job done. He would not receive "troublesome" telephone calls from home during work and generally would have lunch with colleagues for a period of thirty minutes to one hour each day.

The family was not expected to be present in the workplace. The wife was to be seen only at organizational social gatherings and the children only at certain parties, usually around Christmas time. The wife was to keep the social calendar and act as a hostess for the husband's company whenever necessary (at no compensation, of course). In certain situations, the wife was to take the new executive's wife to "the club" and introduce her or perhaps show her where "the better homes" were to be found in the community. In other words, the husband's job was task-oriented and the wife's job was socially-oriented. The women who worked in the organization were to perform the social tasks (organizing the Christmas party), but they were not to bring the family into the organization either. Bringing sick children to work was forbidden. A female secretary could stay home with a sick child on occasion, if she took sick leave, or more likely, vacation time. In many ways, there was a total separation of one's personal life and worklife.

For a number of reasons, this old-fashioned, patriarchal mode of work has changed. For one thing, in many families both parents have full-time jobs. The raising of children is considered an equal partnership. Fathers take their children to the doctor. Fathers have to check up on their own parents in nursing homes. For another, state and federal governments have changed how they view the family's problems. The Family and Medical Leave Act of 1993 provides time for females *and/or* males to work out their family problems caused from long-term illness, childbirth, and the like (Gowan & Zimmerman, 1996). In essence, it allows you to take unpaid leave of up to twelve weeks a year for such crises without losing your job (Boyett, 1995, pp. 103–106).

In addition, in 1996, President Clinton signed a bill that allows workers to transfer their medical health insurance from one job to another without penalty. Finally, the "baby boomers" (those born between 1945 and 1960) find themselves in a double-bind of trouble because of having to hold two jobs, take care of children (sometimes grandchildren), and often their own parents. In part, however, we should realize that so many of these added benefits, non-existent in the 1960s, are what cost the companies so much that they must downsize. For most workers, their companies provide an additional 25–35 percent of their salaries in additional benefits; a $25,000 a year salary adds up to a cost for the company of something between $31,000 and $42,000.

Moving Ahead

The number of factors that enter into the differences in cultures between the sexes or among various races appears to be virtually infinite. To discuss only a few of the differences, we will provide a comparison and contrast between an organizational culture invented by and controlled by white males for several centuries with an organizational culture that is essentially raceless and genderless. In this context, we will again discuss the concepts of *roles, rules,* and *routines.*

The traditional organizational culture was developed around a white male thinking pattern. Because of when the culture was established, it was primarily a linear culture. And lines were drawn between the units within the culture. The concept of hierarchy was important. Thus, most organizations had a large number of workers "at the bottom," a lesser number of middle persons, and few at the top. The roles in the hierarchy were essentially tasks and reporting roles.

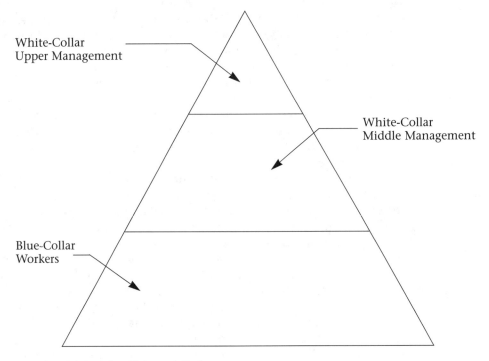

FIGURE 12.1   Traditional Culture

Take the organization of a catalog company as an example, although such organizations are relatively new. In such an organization, many "telemarketing" salespersons answer a 1-800 phone number. They request the customer's name, address, some number at the back of the catalog, the items the customer wants to buy, and the credit card account number. At the end of the conversation, the telemarketer attempts to "sell" the customer a "special" for the day. The telemarketer places all of the information into a computer for transfer to a warehouse. There, a large number of people "take the orders" and mail them out. Others are responsible for billing—if a computer does not do this automatically. Such telemarketers have a role: they are to be friendly, but not so friendly as to waste time. (Some may be paid a commission on the number or amount of sales.) There is a task involved. Computers with voice recognition probably could replace the telemarketers with *minimal* artificial intelligence programmed into them, and they probably will. *There are no decisions to be made.* Many cannot answer questions, except whether the item is "in stock" or the cost of the item, shipping, and tax, information readily available in their computers. There can be many of these workers. They "report" to the warehouse automatically through the computer; their billings are automatically recorded (as an accountant or bookkeeper might do). There are fewer warehouse personnel and fewer "accountants," who report to management, where there are fewer still. The roles are essentially that of "friendly automatons," voices for computers. Their routines are outlined just as they would be in a computer program. Their rules are to abide by the structure.

The beauty of all of this is that there is a running account of inventory—a running account of the popularity of the product or service. Those at the top, then, make decisions about which products and/or services to sell, often based on a combination of data and intuition. They also make decisions about which workers to keep, how many to keep, whether to keep particular ones, etc. (The computer can also generate error data.) Another fascinating aspect of this approach is that the managers never have to see or meet the workers, as long as everything is going along well. In the future, most of these telemarketing positions will be terminated because the customer can simply order the items through the Internet to the computer itself. In today's world, even retail stores and production companies can keep track of inventory so as to not produce too much of a product, to know when to stop trying to sell a product, to increase productivity, and the like. When the item is taken off the shelf, the computer "feeds" the information to a central computer through the identification number on the product. The company "knows" that it has one less. The company can even raise or lower the price through the computer without having to change anything on the physical product. It can be programmed to order fifty more of product X when the inventory is reduced to less than twenty or whatever number is selected. The process is, in essence, technology-efficient scientific management.

Because of "down time," however, these workers have conversations with one another. It is in this social role that the culture is changing. Formerly workers could talk about just anything they wanted to; they could and did make sexist jokes or racial slurs without receiving much criticism; it often came with the territory and they were socialized into acceptance of such behavior. Most managers rarely knew anything about what was said or done, other than productivity. Traditional male occupations, such as automobile mechanics, could have Playboy foldouts hanging in the garage or racist cartoons posted on the bulletin boards. Women rarely entered the garage; minority males, who worked there, seemed to take the racism without much outcry for fear of losing their jobs.

Today, men and women work together in the garages. Blacks and whites work together, as do Hispanics and Asians. The point is that in today's work world such discriminatory and harassing behavior is unacceptable by law (as it has been for quite some time) and it is NOW unacceptable by culture. This is not to say that all of this does not occur in some places, but more and more such behavior is becoming extinct. There is a simple rule of thumb about all of this: *Each person is to be treated as an equal human being.* There are many issues involved in the creation and maintenance of a gender-free and race-free culture. The first one that we will discuss is harassment. Harassment is about the tone of the work environment. The most extreme cases have been those involving sexual harassment.

SEXUAL HARASSMENT

Sexual harassment legislation is found in Title VII of the Civil Rights Act of 1964, which prohibits discrimination on the basis of gender. The Equal Employment Opportunity Commission (EEOC, 1980), charged with investigating sexual harassment complaints filed by employees, has guidelines which define sexual harassment in its simplest form as *unwelcome behavior.* Verbal or physical acts of a sexual nature that denigrate or create an uncomfortable work environment are included. There are two types of specific behavior that are not permitted:

1. when a direct *offer* is linked to employment, promotion, or pay increase (*quid pro quo* harassment)
2. when a direct *threat* of job loss or demotion significantly interferes with an individual's work performances by creating an intimidating or offensive working environment (a hostile work environment).

Quid pro quo simply means something for something: a person in authority uses that position to demand sexual favors in exchange for pay raises or promotion. A single incident or isolated incidents of offensive sexual conduct or remarks generally will not create a hostile work environment unless the conduct is quite severe. The more severe the incident, however, the less need to demonstrate a repetitive series of incidents; this is especially the case when the act is physical.

In *Meritor Savings Bank* v. *Vinson,* a 1986 case, the Supreme Court held that the bank was liable for the actions of a supervisor despite the fact that the bank had not known about the sexual harassment. In a 1988 case, *Hall* v. *Gus Construction Company,* the Court found that hostility toward women can be considered harassment even though there are no explicit sexual advances. In *Harris* v. *Forklift Systems, Inc.* (1993), "hostile environment" was defined more explicitly. The EEOC has provided a list of factors to consider:

1. Whether the conduct was verbal, physical, or both.
2. How frequently the actions were repeated.
3. Whether the harasser was a co-worker or supervisor.
4. Whether the conduct was hostile or patently offensive.
5. Whether others joined in perpetuating the harassment.
6. Whether the harassment was directed at more than one individual. (Gallagher, 1994, p. 19).

Those are the legal suggestions. It is important to note, however, that there are at least four different personal perspectives on what constitutes sexual harassment. Gutek (1993) has provided a list of these perspectives (see Table 12.2). They are *historical* and, in a sense, they are also *autobiographical.* The autobiography of each individual worker, to some extent, determines how he or she feels about sexual harassment. When considering harassment from a historical perspective, the age of the worker must be considered; most males who started working in the 1950s and 1960s, for example, see nothing wrong in asking an employee out on a date. Many see nothing wrong with "mild" sexual joking. They certainly see nothing wrong with asking a female subordinate to bring them a cup of coffee or to arrange social events. And there probably is not much wrong with the latter two if male subordinates are given similar responsibilities, but these problems involve a *gender stereotype.* That is, bringing coffee can be seen as a household duty, with females being responsible for household duties. Even a somewhat positive gesture like a male's opening a door or helping move a heavy package could fall within the same stereotype.

Such perceptions are certainly not mutually exclusive. In fact, with the exception of the older managerial view, they are quite similar except in their attribution of motives. Gutek (1993) has also indicated that the *environment* in which one works makes a significant difference in how much sexual harassment is likely to occur. She states that it more often occurs in "sexualized environments" where people commonly use sexual comments, jokes, and innuendoes and often dress in a sexually attractive or seductive way (p. 335). A complaint, even if not brought formally, should provide the manager with a clue of perceptions of *potential* harassment in the work environment. Mentally at least, as a manager you should take note, especially if two or more women (men) complain about the same man (woman). However, typically, if a woman complains about two or more men, she will be thought of by the

TABLE 12.2   Perspectives on Sexual Harassment

Feminist Perspective
- Reflects a power relationship, men over women
- Constitutes economic coercion
- Threatens women's economic livelihood
- Reflects the status of women in society
- Asserts a woman's sex role over her work role
- Parallels rape

Legal Perspective
- Reflects unequal power that is exploitative
- Involves both implicit and explicit terms of employment
- Is used as a basis for employment decisions
- Produces consequences from submission to, or refusal of, advances
- Promotes an intimidating, hostile, or offensive work environment

Managerial Perspective: Older View
- Reflects personal proclivities
- Consists of misperception or misunderstandings of a person's intentions
- Is a result of "a love affair gone sour"
- Can hurt the reputation of the accused

Managerial Perspective: Newer View
- Is improper use of power to extort sexual gratification
- Treats women as sex objects, asserts sex role over work role
- Is coercive, exploitative, improper, unprofessional
- Is aberrant behavior

Source: B. A. Gutek, (1993). Sexual harassment: Rights and responsibilities. *Employee Responsibilities and Rights Journal, 6,* p. 330, Plenum Publishing Corp.

boss as a troublemaker; if a man complains about two or more women, his complaint will be dismissed as "sour grapes." The most "sensible" action (compromising) for a manager historically has been to transfer the employee. Such an action, however, is not acceptable in today's organization. Today's manager has a responsibility to take all complaints seriously and to "talk them out" with those involved. Should a formal complaint occur, the manager should follow the rules in the policies and procedures manual of the company. If needed, punishments to perpetrators should be undertaken. It is easy to see, however, that individuals have different perceptions, and something seen as no sexual harassment in one situation may be considered mild sexual harassment in another, and even flagrant harassment in a third situation.

Most employees have different views on harassing behavior. Blakely, Blakely, and Moorman (1995) surveyed 352 workers to get their views. The following, in order of importance, is a list of items that the group considered sexual harassment:

1. A male supervisor touching or patting a private part of a female subordinate's body
2. A male supervisor requiring sexual favors from a female subordinate in exchange for organizational rewards.
3. Male supervisor repeatedly asking out female subordinate who is not interested.
4. Male supervisor making sexually suggestive remarks or gestures to a female subordinate.
5. A male supervisor displaying sexually suggestive visuals.
6. A male supervisor telling sexually oriented jokes to a female subordinate.
7. A male supervisor asking a female subordinate to run a personal errand (such as picking up his laundry).
8. Male supervisor telling sexually oriented jokes in the presence of a female subordinate.
9. Male supervisor touching or patting a female subordinate on nonsexual parts of her body.
10. Male supervisor asking a female subordinate for a date.
11. Male supervisor paying for a female subordinate's meal.
12. Male supervisor helping female subordinate with physically demanding work (p. 269).

The first three were considered severe; the middle four were considered ambiguous; and the last five were considered innocuous. The severe and innocuous items were rated the same by male and female workers. The sexes disagreed about those ambiguous items, with women rating them as more harassing.

Although the list is couched from the female's perspective, the victim of harassment can be male or female. Most of the cases, however, involve a male harassing a female. Part of the reason for such different perceptions stems from the fact that males have rarely been the *reported* victims of such harassment. Given the male stereotype of being the stronger of the two sexes, it may be that there is more sexual harassment of males in the workforce than is actually reported. The New Organization will certainly see more male complaints of sexual harassment as females occupy more managerial positions.

The issue of supervision is also changing. A co-worker can be the harasser. Nevertheless, from a legal standpoint, sexual harassment is primarily a control issue. If a supervisor condones such behavior, even though not specifically engaging in it, a problem exists. Harassment can even be same-sex harassment. Cases have been won by plaintiffs who have been males, by same-sex harassers, and the like.

Economic damages, in sexual harassment cases, have been relatively small, but some have been as much as several million dollars. The basic rule of thumb is that *you cannot use someone's sex against them in the workplace.*

As for comments that might be considered harassing, consider whether the *same* comment or comments would be made to a worker of the other sex.

In addition to the potential economic impact on the company, the real costs of sexual harassment are also found in the anger, emotion, hostility, and hurt feelings that accompany the case. An entire company can be torn apart by such allegations—the mere perception that sexual harassment might be occurring is almost as damaging as the actual harassment itself. *False* allegations often damage the reputations of reliable workers.

Hickson, Grierson, and Linder (1991) recommend several actions for today's work world. First, the company should have a sexual harassment policy stated clearly and prominently for all to read. Second, workshops should be provided to all employees. These workshops should include several different examples for the employees to consider. Third, written records of complaints should be excised (removed from personnel files) in those cases where an employee has been found innocent of the charges. Fourth, everyone should know the grievance policy. Fifth, the policy should be revisited periodically, based on legal cases and changes in legislation.

Peterson (1994) has several suggestions concerning the creation of a grievance policy for *all* employee complaints. Such a policy should be timely; assistance should be made available through the human resources office (if non-union); and there should be a peer process of investigation and review. That is, managers cannot always be fair when making decisions about grievances from subordinates. After all, that is how the problem often became a grievance in the first place. Grievance groups should be composed of different people at different levels. Finally, the employee charged in the grievance should be given access to relevant information, but the names of complainants should be kept confidential, at least until it is necessary to make such information public.

Hickson, Grierson, and Linder (1991) have also indicated that there are measures to be taken *before* such behaviors get out of hand. Most harassers have a habit of such behavior. Many of the harassers are *older and married*. Sexist behavior is, at best, out of date. In today's work environment, such

---

CASE 12.1   Sexual Harassment Policy

Frank Blumfield is the human resources director for Smith and Caulfield. Because the company has been sued so many times recently in sexual harassment cases, he has two proposals which he intends to take to the Board. One of them is that any personnel who date one another will be fired immediately. The second is that the company takes no responsibility for personal actions of its employees. He wants one or the other accepted so he doesn't have to spend so much time and so the company does not have to spend so much money on the issue. Will either of these policies work? Is there a better solution? What would you do?

behavior is more likely found in places where males traditionally held most of the jobs, but it can and does happen everywhere.

If your company is just beginning to be sexually integrated, it is probably worthwhile to have workshops not only on sexual harassment but also on sexism, per se. There is little question that males and females behave differently. Even organizations that have never had problems should engage in educational projects to avoid future difficulty. Tannen (1994) has indicated some of male and female differences in her book, *Gender and Discourse.* Basing a workshop on books such as this one allows all members of the organization to understand how people tend to stereotype one another, as well as having a greater understanding of the socialization process which brought them where they are. Workshops like these can be valuable to the women in the workplace who sincerely do not understand some of the male "business behavior" that differs from their own communication style. Such education allows for communication to precede legal interference. The organization should consider any grievance that ends up in a lawsuit to be a failure.

A general overview of gender differences in communication tells us that males talk more in public, while females talk more in private. Therefore, getting input from top females employees may call for less formal occasions with fewer people involved. At the same time, the amount of male talk in public may be a result of some cathartic effect of just wanting to say something rather than truly contributing to the conversation. In addition, females are able to "read" the nonverbal communication of most participants better than most males (Hickson & Stacks, 1993). Females engage primarily in inquiring and communicative behavior; males engage primarily in persuasion. While many traditionalists have suggested that some female employees need to have assertiveness training, the opposite may also be the case—some males may need courses in listening and sensitivity. The purposes of communication also vary by gender: women tend to negotiate and men tend to control. Finally, males and females may differ in the structure of their organization. Male organization is typically more linear, while female organization may be more holistic. Understanding all of these differences and more is necessary if you are to have a productive, healthy, and supportive organization. Training and identifying gender differences in communication style can be beneficial to everyone in the organization.

Gender differences exist and will always exist as long as males and females work together. Part of the differences is historical and social; part, however, is physical and hormonal. Education can change the way people respond to physical and hormonal stimuli and channel responses appropriately. The competent manager works hard to educate his employees not only about actual communication differences caused by gender but also about the perceptions that people hold about members of the opposite sex. Where it is not possible to discuss these openly and frankly (such as with teenage or young, physically mature employees), workshops should become a standard managerial tool. Contact with employees—informal "rap" sessions around a water cooler, as well as more formal educational discussions—will certainly let them know your view on the topic and you will better understand their responses to your educational programming.

RACIAL HARASSMENT

Just as the socialization process includes adapting to the needs of women in the workplace, we must also learn to adapt to the codes, language, behavior, and values of members of other cultures. During the past few decades, the number of non-white, non-Anglo-Saxon individuals in the workplace has been on the rise. Of course, America has always been a "melting pot," but today we have a significant number of people from places other than western Europe in our workplace. Hispanics and African Americans are a large part of the population and a large part of the organization. With the rise in numbers, there has also been an increase in the reports of racial harassment and intimidation. The complaints involve racial threats, slurs, and jokes, as well as displaying harassing symbols and drawings.

Harrick and Sullivan (1995) investigated 131 cases of racial harassment that took place between 1971 and 1987. Sixty-three percent (63%) of the complaints were filed by African Americans. Most of the complaints involved people in jobs with little formal education: laborers, production workers, city workers, retail sales personnel, and food service workers. Of the employers, 76 percent were in the private sector. The kinds of complaints were: verbal or written comments (45%), offensive symbols (14%), racial jokes/slurs (9%), physical abuse (8%), and unspecified (24%). Most of the cases (91%) involved a discrimination case involving employment as well as harassment. Virtually half of those complaints involved firings.

As with sexual harassment, the courts must decide what motivated the harassment. As we all know, some bosses simply behave in a harassing way to all workers. While such behavior may be uncomfortable for the employee, it is not a legal issue. Leap and Smeltzer (1984) discussed a case in which there was a "hazing" process to see if a particular black worker, among other workers, could stand up under stress and uncertainty. His co-workers seized him, stripped him, and covered his genitals with grease. He was referred to as "nigger," "coon," and "black boy." But the complainant was not one of those hazed. He simply thought of the experience as humiliating and resigned. The court, however, found that the hazing was applied to everyone and was not racially motivated. Similar results have occurred in other cases, where the employee was not an ideal worker. Such behavior, even if not illegal, should be considered inappropriate in the work environment. Harrick and Sullivan (1995) indicated that an employer cannot allow an employee to be humiliated by co-workers. And while a single racial epithet or "good-natured" play between workers is acceptable in the eyes of the law, they are ethically inappropriate and rude.

As a manager you must be open and ready to discuss what constitutes racial harassment among your workers. There may be a fine line between humor and harassment, but if you have taken the time to get to know those working for you, you will have a better understanding of what the connotative (psychological) reaction of the behavior will be. The competent manager lets others know what she believes is harassing behavior and works hard to educate her workers about what is appropriate communicative behavior.

NON-DISCRIMINATORY LANGUAGE

A third form of harassment comes from discriminatory language. Frost (1987) has indicated the importance of language in the workplace as a statement of power:

> As meaning, communication is an important part of the ongoing development and exercise of power in organizations. Actors attribute meaning to the material, active and passive verbal symbols that exist in organizational settings. In part, the meaning derives from the interpretive schemes actors bring to organizations. In part, this meaning derives from the surface distribution and exercise of power (p. 508).

In this sense, what is referred to as "politically correct" or PC language is simply a language where all employees are spoken to in a way that is not humiliating or degrading. Comments about one's age, sex, race, physical size, and so forth in a negative way are simply means for one person to demonstrate some kind of superiority over another.

While several court cases have determined that politically correct language, as an institutional requirement in an organization, is illegal because of the First Amendment to the U.S. Constitution, certainly no organization would want to have language condoning such behavior. The tradition has been to substitute other language for language which "sounds" less biased and discriminatory. However, perhaps the better way to talk to a person or about a person is as an individual. Pat is Pat whether white or black, Hispanic or Italian, tall or short, male or female. The language is an important part of any culture. In many ways, the language determines the culture. McCarthy (1991) has indicated that the organizational culture should be one where "employees [feel] appreciated and valued" (p. 6).

In this context, however, the competent manager will remember that cultures are composed of human beings. In a sense, the culture of an organization is determined by its lowest common denominator. It is important that you, as a manager, ensure that *all* workers understand that language which lessens the quality and productivity of the organization is unacceptable and counterproductive to the organization's mission.

OTHER HUMAN FACTORS IN THE WORKPLACE

Certainly the vast majority of information about the workplace, regarding discrimination and harassment, has been concerned with gender and sex. Nevertheless, there are other factors that must be considered in the New Organization. In general, the Civil Rights Act of 1964 protects one from discrimination because of sex, race, color, religion, or national origin (Manley & Shrode, 1990, p. 95). Other factors include ancestry, marital status, age, disability, or veteran status. In suggesting that *all* types of harassment in the workplace should be prevented, Manley and Shrode (1990) write:

> Nonsexual harassment in the workplace can be as demeaning, insidious, and destructive as sexual harassment. It inhibits productivity and morale growth and should never be tolerated. Examples of such harassment are: the use of profane, abusive, or demeaning language; disorderly conduct such as fighting; causing physical harm to another; intimidation; any activity or speech that disrupts other employees; slurs or jokes in bad taste; and any activity or speech that discriminates against any employee on the basis of race, color, ancestry, marital status, age, disability, or veteran status (pp. 85–86).

Employees with Disabilities

Probably the most recent emphasis has been upon disabilities. McAdams, Moussavi, and Klassen (1992) have provided information about the relationship of an employee's physical appearance and the Americans with Disabilities Act (ADA). They define *disabled* as "a person [who] is (a) one who has a physical or mental impairment that substantially limits one or more major life activities, (b) has a record of such an impairment, or (c) is regarded as having such an impairment" (p. 328). Employers are not required to hire individuals who cannot do the "essential work," but they are required to "reasonably accommodate" the needs of the disabled employee.

What does all of this mean? Cancer, blindness, mental retardation, AIDS, alcoholism, and drug abuse all are covered by the Act. However, employers are not required to hire someone who currently is abusing drugs or alcohol. Those with cosmetic disfigurement, anatomical loss, and scars are also under the Act. Tobacco smokers are not covered by the ADA (Warner, 1994). Some questions regarding obesity and height are yet to be litigated in a manner for us to make explicit decisions about whether they are covered by the Act. However, it would appear that eventually almost everyone could be covered under the Act. Nevertheless, many companies have not adapted to the ADA. As with other laws about discrimination, change is quite slow.

The manager in the twenty-first century, however, should be aware of the law and its ramifications on both the organization and its workers. Measures such as ADA are as political in nature as they are social, thus their introduction often arises from social events that should be predictable. The competent manager should identify potential problems and be prepared for change mandated by federal, state, or even international government; even though they may not have much legal power for change, they will possess a degree of social power (see Chapter 11).

Religion in the Workplace

While many of the other variables regarding discrimination and harassment are easy to see at first sight, most of us forget that religion is an aspect of the workplace. A Wal-Mart employee sued the retailer, claiming that he was forced to work on Sunday (Ettorree, 1996, p. 16). Wal-Mart agreed to allow the employee more flexibility in his working hours. In Massachusetts, the legislature enacted a law allowing individuals not to work on holy days. The courts struck that law down as unconstitutional. With all of the changes in other aspects of diversity in the workplace, there is no doubt that religion will take a more dominant position. Ettorree (1996) recommends that companies accommodate employees' religious beliefs. A matter of whether employees may wear certain religious symbols at work should be dealt with on a case-by-case basis. Even the U.S. armed forces, not the most liberal of organizations, allow for specialized headgear or facial hair, as long as such attributes do not interfere with the force's mission.

The twenty-first century manager will have to deal with differing religious perceptions, especially when working for an international corporation. She should consider training about religious beliefs and rights. Although her twentieth century counterpart's workers were from the immediate neighborhood—most were of a similar religious background—the new manager will have to deal with a complex mix of religious beliefs in the workplace. In today's world of transfers and diversity, more organizational flexibility is required in both religious perceptions and practices.

Internationalism in the Workplace

As mentioned in Chapter 11, significant changes are taking place in today's workplace because most businesses are becoming *internationalized*. Such a viewpoint is obvious in that businesses are making products in other countries and customers from other countries are necessary for the well-being of the organization. Rasberry and Lindsay (1994) have noted that by 2000, 88 percent of our workforce will be composed of women, African Americans, Hispanics, and Asians (p. 174). Companies need to learn to adapt to the verbal and nonverbal aspects of the interpersonal communication of such employees. Many companies will have to produce policies and procedures manuals in more than one language. Company memoranda and newsletters may have to be printed in Spanish, Chinese, Japanese, German, and other languages in addition to English.

The avoidance of ethnic or racial terms is a necessity. No longer can jokes be made in the workplace about a particular ethnic group. No longer can stereotypes be maintained or fostered. Even statements about food can be considered inappropriate if the assumption is that one group eats that food and others do not. Educating workers that such behavior is not condoned is essential to having a well-educated, professional workforce. Even regional stereotypes about westerners as "cowboys" or southerners as "rednecks" or people being on the "mommy track" can have significant negative repercussions.

In addition to having these problems with stereotypes within the country, managers need to be concerned about vendors, about customers, about other clients, and about the competition. Having a realization that nonverbal components are different is also important. There is nothing magical about the American, frantic concept of time. In many other countries, patience is a value. We must learn to have an appreciation for the dress, customs, food, and values of those from other countries. Refusing to eat sushi at a dinner may result in losing a multi-million dollar account. Crossing one's legs (showing the bottom of one's shoes) could lose an account in the Middle East. Not taking off one's shoes in parts of Asia could do the same. Anyone doing business with one from another culture should make a study before beginning any negotiations.

Age Discrimination

Finally, the area likely to create the most problems for management over the next ten years is age discrimination and harassment. As we have mentioned, many organizations utilize the downsizing, rightsizing, re-engineering of the corporation as a means to increase profits. A tactic utilized by a number of companies is that of eliminating older employees who have large salaries and replacing them with younger workers at a much lower salary. This is patently illegal. Most courts have ruled that "as a rule of thumb" if someone is dismissed who is over fifty years old and is replaced by someone at least ten years younger, age discrimination has taken place. Dealing with employees who are older is a very sensitive business. In today's world there is no mandatory retirement age. Sometimes this creates other problems for an organization in addition to the high salary. Older workers may be utilizing more extensive health care, increasing the costs of health insurance. Some become mentally less adept. Others' memories are just not what they were in their earlier ages. The effective manager must learn to check the facts (do the research). The manager must have a relationship with the older worker to determine what his goals may be and how his goals fit in with the future of the organization. Perhaps some suggestions for part-time work (with full-time benefits) can be utilized in a sensitive context. Such a manager should realize that these are hard times for the older worker, whether she is fifty or ninety. Retirement is seen by many as their death in work. We will discuss these concepts in more detail in the next chapter.

SUMMARY

This chapter describes some of the problems associated with mistreatment of others—whether that mistreatment is by superiors or by co-workers. Both discrimination and harassment were explored. Legal definitions and examples were provided to make you as the twenty-first century manager aware of the problems and pitfalls associated with a changing workforce and increased internationalization of organizational communication. Technology, changing markets, and the drive for profits all fit in with harassment and discrimination charges filed against organizations and their members. As a manager in the New Organization, you must be prepared to define, educate, and discuss potential discrimination and harassment in your workplace. A closing note: Discrimination and harassment is as old as the first organized effort to produce some product; it will always be with us, but through awareness and education its impact can be reduced. A large part of management in the New Organization will be identifying and eliminating such behaviors before they impact on the organization's mission and product.

QUESTIONS FOR THOUGHT

1. Explain how you would review the physical plant of your company to determine whether there are problems meeting the ADA.
2. Develop a complaint procedure for sexual harassment complaints. What should you do with information that never becomes a formal complaint?
3. What should you do when a superior tells you a racist joke?
4. What steps should you take to ensure against discrimination in hiring practices?
5. To what extent do you feel companies are obligated to have bilingual signage in their facilities?

CASE STUDY 12.2   Developing Training

You have just been hired as a cultural sensitivity trainer for the company. As you are developing an outline for what you are going to cover you begin your content research. What kinds of items will be included in your outline?

REFERENCES

Blakely, G. L., Blakely, E. H., & Moorman, R. H. (1995). The relationship between gender, personal experience, and perceptions of sexual harassment in the workplace. *Employee Responsibilities and Rights Journal, 8,* 263–274.

Boyett, J. H., & Boyett, J. T. (1995). *Beyond workplace 2000: Essential strategies for the new American corporation.* New York: Dutton.

Bradshaw, P. (1996). Women as constituent directors: Re-reading current texts using a feminist-postmodernist approach. In D. M. Boje, R. P. Gephart, Jr., & T. J. Thatchenkery, (Eds.), *Postmodern management and organizational theory.* Thousand Oaks, CA: Sage.

Ettorre, B. (1996, December). Religion in the workplace: Implications for managers. *Management Review,* 15–18.

Frost, P. J. (1987). Power, politics, and influence. In F. M. Jablin, L. L. Putnam, K. H. Roberts, & L. W. Porter (Eds.), *Handbook of organizational communication: An interdisciplinary perspective* (pp. 501–548). Newbury Park, CA: Sage.

Gowan, M. A., & Zimmerman, R. A. (1996). The Family and Medical Leave Act of 1993: Employee rights and responsibilities, employer rights and responsibilities. *Employee Responsibilities and Rights Journal, 9,* 57–71.

Gutek, B. A. (1993). Sexual harassment: Rights and responsibilities. *Employee Responsibilities and Rights Journal, 6,* 325–340.

Harrick, E. J., & Sullivan, G. M. (1995). Racial harassment: Case characteristics and employer responsibilities. *Employee Responsibilities and Rights Journal, 8,* 81–96.

Hickson, M., III, Grierson, R. D., & Linder, B. C. (1991). A communication perspective on sexual harassment: Affiliative nonverbal behaviors in asynchronous relationships. *Communication Quarterly, 39,* 111–118.

Hickson, M., III, & Stacks, D. W. (1993). *NVC: Nonverbal communication studies and applications,* 3rd ed. Madison, WI: Brown and Benchmark.

Leap, T. L., & Smeltzer, L. R. (1984). Racial remarks in the workplace: Humor or harassment. *Harvard Business Review, 62,* 74–75, 78.

Manley, W. W. II, & Schrode, W. A. (1990). *Critical issues in business conduct: Legal, ethical, and social challenges for the 1990s.* New York: Quorum.

McAdams, T., Moussavi, F., & Klassen, M. (1992). Employee appearance and the Americans with Disabilities Act: An emerging issue? *Employee Responsibilities and Rights Journal, 5,* 323–338.

McCarthy, J. (1991, September). Company culture—it makes a difference. *CBI, 6.*

Pepper, G. L. (1995). *Communicating in organizations: A cultural approach.* New York: McGraw-Hill.

Peterson, R. B. (1994). Organizational governance and the grievance process: In need of a new model for resolving workplace differences. *Employee Responsibilities and Rights Journal, 7,* 9–21.

Rasberry, R. W., & Lindsay, L. L. (1994). *Effective managerial communication,* 2nd ed. Belmont, CA: Wadsworth.

Schwartz, K. (1996, January 16). Women closing in on still wide gender gap in pay, survey finds. *Birmingham News,* B1, B5.

Tannen, D. (1994). *Gender and discourse.* New York: Oxford University Press.

Warner, D. M. (1994) "We do not hire smokers": May employers discriminate against smokers? *Employee Responsibilities and Rights Journal, 7,* 129–140.

13

SEPARATION FROM THE ORGANIZATION

The Psychological Pattern of Separation

Types of Organizational Separation

Involuntary Termination
    Firing
    Downsizing

The Early Retirement: Involuntary and Voluntary
    Involuntary retirement: The buyout as downsizing
        Considerations
    Voluntary separation

Starting a Business or Changing Careers

Avoiding the Inevitable

Objectives

By the end of this chapter you should be able to

1. Identify and define various ways that people separate themselves or are separated from the organization.
2. Discuss the psychological reactions people have when they have been voluntarily or involuntarily separated from an organization.
3. Differentiate among "layoffs," "firings," "downsizing," and "rightsizing."
4. Discuss the advantages and disadvantages of voluntary and involuntary separation.
5. Design a communication strategy to deal with any of the various types of separation you might face in the New Organization.

People, of course, always lost their jobs. In the nineteenth and early twentieth centuries, it didn't take much; job security was not yet an American concept. Indeed, the nature of work was changing drastically a hundred years ago, just as it has been today. Tens of millions of Americans migrated from farms and rural communities to the new work growing up around urban centers. Millions of new jobs materialized, for example, in the auto industry, in highway construction, in the expanding network of railroads and commuter lines and, above all, in the shift from cumbersome steam-powered equipment to sophisticated factory machinery powered by electricity. That shift ushered in mass production. The giant department store and the big retail chain also appeared in this era, elbowing out smaller enterprises. The advertising industry was born and office jobs mushroomed. (Uchitelle & Kleinfield, 1996, pp. 14–15)

We can see, then, that jobs have always been lost and jobs have always been gained. However, there are no urban areas where jobs are seeking employees today. A retrospective view of what we have discussed in this book tells us that today's college students will enter a work environment far different from that of their parents and certainly of their grandparents. Our great-grandparents might tell us that things at work have certainly been worse. "Well, let me tell you about the Great Depression," they may begin. The problem, however, is that—in today's world—it is not just the world economy that has changed. As discussed in previous chapters, we have a *new world of people in the work environment*. Governmental regulations about work have changed. Corporate boards have different expectations than they did fifty, twenty-five, or even ten years ago. There are more educated people available for work today than there have ever been in the past. The workforce is composed of people diverse in age, race, ethnic group, religion, and gender. In short, social change has caught up with technological change.

The New Organization has created an entirely new process of transitions in our lives. As we mentioned in the beginning of the book, your lifespan was formerly considered as a time for education, followed by a lengthy career (usually with *one* employer) in the same geographic location, followed by retirement, either in the same location or in one of those retirement communities in sunny Florida or Arizona.

Today we must expect the unexpected. As Downs (1995) has noted,

The preferred solution to this industrial dilemma has been to cut operating expenses. Cut, gouge, rip, and layoff until the numbers look right. It has been a very bitter pill, but one that was prescribed with the best of intentions. Unfortunately, the side effects of this pseudo-cure have turned out to be more disastrous than the disease. (p. 1)

Such *layoffs* (downsizing, rightsizing) in previous times were precipitated by hard times for all in a particular industry and usually involved non-managerial, often uneducated workers. But in 1994, the American Management

Association found that two-thirds of all people "laid off" were college-educated, salaried employees (Downs, 1995, p. 3). As noted, many of these layoffs occur in organizations that are having their largest profits ever. The fear of *involuntary separation* from the workplace has become significant in the late twentieth century (Gordon, 1996, p. 69). We have discussed the process of laying off co-workers in a previous chapter. In addition, we mentioned the possibility that you, too, may become a victim of such a process. The impact of such downsizing on society and on corporations has been noted by a number of authors (Estes, 1996; Downs, 1995; Hall, 1996; Gordon, 1996; and Boyett & Boyett, 1995). The workplace has often become "unnerving" (Kleinfield, 1996), personal dignity has been lost (Bragg, 1996), communities have been frayed (Rimer, 1996), and, perhaps most importantly, downsizing has been relatively ineffective for the companies that have downsized (Boyett & Boyett, 1995). But what happens to the former employees who have suffered such a transition in their lives? Rifkin (1995) has written: "Americans, perhaps more than any people in the world, define themselves in relationship to their work. In their minds, productive work is so strongly correlated with being alive that when employment is cut out from under them, they manifest all of the classic signs of dying." (p. 195)

Camille Stogner (1995) has recounted the experience:

> The words and flat tone of her voice are forever imprinted in my memory: "I need you to bring your company car, keys, and anything else that belongs to Crawford and Company to my office as soon as possible." My immediate reaction was shocked silence. Then, with a voice I could not identify as my own, I choked, "Can you tell me what is going on?" The jagged edges of the next few words assaulted my ears and tore my gut: "I am laying you off, effective immediately. I have ordered your final paycheck, and I need you to come get your personal things from your office." (p. 109)

The fact of the matter is that each one of us will have to be separated from the organization at some point in time. As Phillips and Metzger (1976) have indicated, relationships go through a variety of processes from beginning to ending. In the early chapters, we discussed how to gain entry into an organization through the research and interview process. Then we discussed socializing into the organization, a process that takes place over months and even years. The socialization process may occur again and again even within an organization because of changing work groups, changes in location, or changes in ownership. In many ways, the analogy to human personal relationships is appropriate here. As we learn more about the other people, we proceed through a process of *uncertainty reduction* (Berger & Calabrese, 1975). Nevertheless, the separation process is more difficult than the initiation process because the uncertainty that you thought you had reduced is back in the forefront moreso than ever before.

But each human relationship must end at some time. Either married couples divorce or leave one another or one of them dies. The same is true with

---

CASE 13.1   Old Friends

Susan was your mentor when you first came to the company fifteen years ago. Now she is sixty-two. The company has not been doing well. Susan has been a fantastic employee. For the past five years, you have been her boss. Her salary, however, is triple what you are paying new employees. Although she is still valuable to the company, changes must be made. You know that if she retired, you could replace her for much less money. How do you approach the notion of an early retirement package without making Susan resentful? Are there other solutions?

---

our relationships with organizations. These relationships always end. As Conrad (1994) has noted, new relationships go through the processes of *anticipation, encounter,* and *identification.* Arriving at a process model of separation is not as easy to determine, but perhaps we can look at the literature in two different areas of personal relationships. In many ways, separation from an organization is similar to one of these. Kubler-Ross (1993) has discussed the stages that terminally ill patients go through in accepting their own deaths. These include: (1) denial and isolation; (2) anger; (3) bargaining; (4) depression; and (5) acceptance. Belli and Krantzler (1988) have discussed the "seven deadly emotions" of divorce: (1) fear; (2) guilt; (3) self-pity; (4) failure; (5) anger; (6) self-flagellation; and (7) hatred. It is important to know that most people go through relationship terminations of some type, and it is important to note that responses to termination follow a systematic pattern.

THE PSYCHOLOGICAL PATTERN OF SEPARATION

First, as we have mentioned, termination is another phase in a relationship—it is a transition. However, when you are going through it, you can hardly think of it that way. The first stage is that of *denial* and *isolation.* You really cannot believe this has happened to you. Perhaps you know that the company has been downsizing, yet like those who smoke cigarettes and who do not wear seatbelts, the "it can't happen to me" syndrome appears to be dominant. In reviewing the firing in your own mind, you think of it as a movie or a nightmare. This is accompanied almost immediately by isolation. You will no longer go to work at 8:00 A.M., you will not interact with the same people, you will not be able to see them. You begin to fear whether you will be able to work somewhere else. You fear the economic repercussions to yourself and your family.

The second stage is *anger.* In this stage you blame others for your plight. Who was it in the organization that wanted to get rid of you? You feel that you did nothing wrong on the job. There were others who did much worse. You become angry at external forces that may have been factors, such as the company that "bought out" your company. You may even blame your family for taking away so much time you could have put into work.

The third stage is *negotiation*. While this stage may not always be acted upon, it is certainly in the "back of the mind" of the one who has been downsized. "Just give me another month to find another job," is a typical response. "Give me one more chance." Some actually ask the boss for these favors at the moment they have been fired. Others may come back a day or a week later. And still others never ask, but do consider.

The fourth stage is *depression*. At this stage the laid-off employee feels guilt, that perhaps everything was his fault. He has self-pity, believing that he never should have trusted those people over the years that he was there. He feels that it was not their distrust so much as it was his naiveté. He feels that he has been a failure. Because the job is a relationship for many of us, there was perhaps something that we should have done. Now there are no solutions.

The fifth stage is *acceptance*. By this time, the individual has decided that he must go on, and he seeks out other work or decides to retire from work entirely.

TYPES OF ORGANIZATIONAL SEPARATION

There are obviously a number of different ways in which such relationships end. As we have been discussing, the "other" party, in this case the organization itself, can dissolve the relationship. Such dissolutions occur through lay-offs or downsizing or rightsizing. The concept of a *lay-off*, however, has traditionally implied a re-"laying on," if you will. That is, the expectation of a lay-off is that it is temporary; when you are laid off you will be called back. When *downsizing* occurs, however, there is no such expectation. Additionally, you can be *fired*. This involves a breakup of the relationship by the company precipitated by *your own* actions.

Of course there are separations you may institute yourself. You may leave simply because you have found a better situation with another organization. You may leave for personal reasons. For example, your spouse may have found a better position with a company in a different location. You may leave because you have become dissatisfied with your company. You may leave because you anticipate that you are going to be laid off in the near future. Finally, you may leave because you are retiring, the implication being that you are no longer going to be an active participant in your career field.

Obviously there are many types of repercussions to any separation from an organization. We have discussed the emotional aspects—gratitude, anger, frustration, elation. In large measure, what type or types of emotional responses you have to such a separation will be dependent on two things: (1) what your wishes are; and (2) how you handle the situation. In the next few pages, we will discuss several of the possible reasons for separation and how the communication process relates to each one of them.

INVOLUNTARY TERMINATION

Involuntary termination occurs when the company wants to rid itself of workers. You can be involuntarily terminated in two ways: *firing* and *downsizing.* While your short-term repercussions are about the same either way—you are either without a job or soon will be—there are different paths available to you, depending on why you were terminated. Of course, downsizing means that there are others leaving at the same time you are.

Involuntary termination almost always carries with it the stigma of failure, of not meeting the job requirements, regardless of whether your termination was due to your own negligence (to include not meeting goal expectations) or the company's inability to fend for itself in the marketplace. Usually, if you have been fired, you are aware of the exact reasons for being fired; *part of the termination process requires that you be told of the reasons for dismissal.*

An employee may be fired for many reasons including, but not limited to, the following. First, you can be fired because you engaged in some *illegal action involving the company.* Obviously if you steal from the company you can be fired. If you provide information in violation of the rules of the Securities and Exchange Commission, you can be fired. Second, you may be fired for *illegal actions that you have taken,* even if they do not involve the company. For example, if you received a DUI (driving under the influence) citation while in a company car, you may be fired. If your credibility is important to the company, virtually any felony will leave you jobless. Some companies wait for a conviction; for others, the accusation may be enough. Third, you may be fired for *ethical violations.* For example, if you claim the work of another employee to be your own (in a sense, plagiarism), you can be fired. If you make "side deals" with customers, you can be fired. Fourth, especially after extended problems, you can be fired for *alcohol or drug abuse.* Fifth, you can be fired because you *have not met the standards of the job.* For example, if you must pass a bar examination to be an attorney and you fail it, you can be fired. The same may be true for finishing a degree within certain time limitations. Sixth, if you *lack the skills to do the job,* even though they were not required when you first started working, you can be fired. Seventh, if you are *incompetent or unproductive* you can be fired (although some warnings would probably have to be issued). Eighth, if you engage in behavior that may be considered *mentally incompetent,* you can be fired.

In most of these cases, the employers will work with you. However, most do not want to invest in educating, improving skills, or paying for drug and alcohol rehabilitation or mental illness on a regular basis for someone in whom they lack confidence. It is important to note that all of the above reasons would appear to be controlled by the employee.

Firing

If you are fired, it is important to make a "clean break" from the organization; you will probably want to notify those who had helped you along the way; in all probability, you will not want to return to the organization nor have lunch with your former bosses. One important aspect of leaving, however, is asking carefully selected colleagues to write *letters of recommendation,* given directly to you. Before you ask, however, it is important that you know whether the letters will be positive or negative. Research becomes a factor here too. You need to know whether individuals have written letters for fired employees before and the success rate those individuals had in finding another position. To some extent, your leaving after being fired will relate to why you were fired. For example, if you have misappropriated funds, colleagues will be unlikely to write a letter, and you should not expect them to do so. However, if you were fired for an alcohol abuse or drug abuse problem, your previous employers may be willing to be helpful after you have proven that you have solved your health problems. The same may be true with mental problems, such as temper tantrums; in all reality they may be unlikely to provide a letter in the near future, but may do so at a later time, especially if you can demonstrate that you have overcome your problems.

Downsizing

Involuntary termination due to downsizing is a significantly different matter. In most cases, you have not been dismissed because of any particular action that you took or did not take. Generally, if you are part of a downsizing process, you will be able to obtain positive letters of recommendation. Where possible, obtain copies of your recommendation letters. How you approach being downsized is important. If you have done your homework and made contacts with others, you should act as if the layoff is temporary, something that you will have to live with, but something that can be overcome. The perception you want to portray is that you are "doing business as usual" and that, for reasons beyond your control, a temporary change in employment status has occurred. That is, you should not "burn any bridges" behind you through claims of being victimized. Instead, try to maintain positive contacts with those with whom you have worked at the company.

In many ways, the concept of *not burning bridges* is a communication concept. That is, you should not say or do anything in anger. You should avoid making *negative comments* about any individual in the organization or about the organization itself. Another important consideration is that you should attempt to "tie up all the loose ends," if you are given time to do so. That is, to the extent possible, you should attempt to complete the projects you have been working on; if you cannot complete them because of time constraints, you should leave the materials concerning those projects in such a way that another worker can more easily complete those projects. Such behavior will be beneficial in getting those letters of recommendation. Although this may take considerable self-restraint (being dismissed for any reason tends to produce an emotional response), by completing or leaving with all project materials ready for someone else you show that you are a "professional" and able—even if seething inside—to conduct yourself in a manner above and beyond the organization's current problems.

No doubt you should begin immediately trying to find another position, but you should also remember that you want to maintain your credibility with the previous organization. Of course, maintaining that credibility involves being thought of as *trustworthy and competent.* It may well be that the organization will have other openings in the future for which you will be qualified. In fact, if you think along those lines, you may also wish to continue your education process by taking courses that would qualify you for the positions that you believe will be opening at a later date.

Involuntary separation is quite difficult to take. Your early reaction may be to be angry and not to care whether those in the previous organization know that you are angry. However, such an attitude will not work out in the long run. Even potential new employers are not appreciative of such behavior. Others— even those you are acquainted with outside the organization—will note your reactions to dismissal within the organization. Although a firing is more difficult to overcome, it can be done through a *professional* approach to the situation. (If the firing is associated with illegal activities, of course, you will have to go through a period of rehabilitation—possibly including jail time—from which you can still move to another position.) Being downsized or rightsized may actually offer you new opportunities; often letters of recommendation will point out to prospective employers what you are capable of but could not do in the previous position.

THE EARLY RETIREMENT: INVOLUNTARY AND VOLUNTARY

According to federal law, there is no specific age at which you *must* retire. In most organizations, retirement is based on either the number of years of service or one's age or some combination of the two. Generally, one can retire after twenty years of service or at age sixty-two, at the earliest. Many organizations, when faced with financial problems, will offer "buyouts" in lieu of dismissal or lay-offs. A *buyout* is a separation from the organization, but one that clearly indicates that the organization is looking to downsize and you have been placed in that group which will have to go. A buyout, then, is a form of involuntary retirement.

Involuntary Retirement: The Buyout as Downsizing

According to Downs (1995), many organizations are using early retirement as a means for downsizing. "By loosening the requirements for retirement and easing the financial penalties on the employee, payroll expense can be reduced with few up front costs" (Downs, 1995, p. 167). Take, for example, du Pont as a case in point:

> Consider what would have happened to a fifty-year-old, $50,000-a-year employee with twenty-five years of service at du Pont when it offered early

retirement in 1992. Normally, if this employee retired early, he or she would receive only $7,512 a year. But since du Pont waived the actuarial reduction for those who would leave early, the pension jumped to $18,756 a year—more than twice what it would have been and a very attractive offer to the sixty-five hundred du Pont employees who accepted it (Downs, 1995, p. 167).

Dallas (1996) has indicated that we need to take time to consider many factors involving early retirement. According to one person who took retirement from the Air Force at age thirty-eight, "People fear retirement because they don't know what they're going to do. They hem and haw. They say 'Things are going good, so why mess with them?' You should retire when you get bored with what you're doing" (Dallas, 1996, p. 47). Of course, many people believe they want to retire before age sixty-two; however, once they consider the financial repercussions, their minds may change. Richards (1995) provides five "hard truths" about early retirement:

1. You will have less time to save for retirement.
2. Your retirement money will need to last longer.
3. You might get less help from Social Security.
4. You may get a smaller pension.
5. Your medical benefits will be slashed (pp. 11–12).

In part, many of these factors are based on the fact that many things have changed about retirement since the concept was initiated. For one, people are living longer, and it is important to recognize that more money will be needed for retirement than was needed in the 1950s and 1960s. It is obvious that you will have less time to save if you retire early. Virtually everyone expects there to be changes in the Social Security system over the next ten years. In some way, there are likely to be fewer benefits upon retirement and there will likely be increased costs to contributors. Another aspect of downsizing, or another way for companies to save money, is to decrease their participation in pension plans. Because Medicare does not kick in until age sixty-five, the earlier that you retire the longer you will be responsible for your *own* medical care.

Nevertheless, Dallas (1996) reports that, in 1995, 52 percent of those eligible for Social Security benefits signed up at age sixty-two, as opposed to just 36 percent in 1981 (p. 47). Barrett (1995) has reported, then, that there are two segments of those who are offered early retirement packages. The first group "jumps" at the possibility of a slower lifestyle and the other group is pushed by the organization.

Considerations

When an organization offers what is referred to as a "buyout package," there are a number of serious things you must consider. For example, Kollath (1995) reports that one man was offered the following package: (1) eighteen weeks severance pay ($19,000); (2) five weeks' vacation pay of $5,000; (3) a pension of $21,000 a year; and (4) a health insurance subsidy that provided full coverage at a personal cost of $47 month. His current salary was $53,000; however, you must remember that was his gross salary. Once everything was taken out, including Social Security, he actually netted closer to $32,000.

Another element of the financial discussion has to do with the *taxes* one must pay for such a buyout. Rowland (1996) has reported that several individuals who have received buyouts recently have claimed that their buyout was part of an age discrimination legal settlement, a problem discussed in Chapter 12. The most recent cases brought to the Internal Revenue Service indicate that such cases are taxable and that "voluntary settlements" are subject to these taxes. Depending on how much you get, this could be a considerable loss. Regardless, such buyouts and early retirements indicate that you are willing to make considerably less money in retirement than you did while working, unless you have planned far, far in advance for retirement—probably when you began working. Such early retirements and other, similar, economic packages, of course, will change between 1998 and 2040, when many current college students retire.

Although the financial aspects may change, in all likelihood the emotional factors will remain pretty much the same. Barrett (1995) writes: "Your new status can also push your insecurity button. You want to stay in the game, so you had better stay busy" (p. 35). For him, as a former correspondent for *Time,* turning down any assignment appeared to be the wrong thing to do. In many ways, he found that he was working just as hard as he was before. Barrett writes: "Making the leap is difficult for even the most willing volunteers, because it involves risk" (p. 35). He says that "emotionally, people in this situation either can adopt a victim mentality, which often forces them back to familiar turf, or take the view that, regardless of minor reversals, they still enjoy a great opportunity" (p. 35). *Acceptance of a buyout offer, however, may carry with it a requirement that you not enter a similar field or take a position with a competitor for a specified period of time.*

To some extent, the negative view places retirement and death in the same group. One retiree said, "I realized I was playing cards seven days a week with the same guys. When I died, I didn't want the main thing people remembered about me to be that I played gin rummy" (Dallas, 1996, p. 48). While that gentleman decided to undertake volunteer work, six out of ten people expect to work in another job somewhere even after they retire (Dallas, 1996, p. 48). Robert Lewis (1996) has indicated that this approach can be a very successful one: "Andrew Betz goes from running a bank's trust department to dealing blackjack. Mimi Kaplysh gives up acting for psychotherapy. One-time sales manager Joe Johnson becomes a flight attendant. And former school teacher Mary Andes flies a commercial airplane" (p. 1). These individuals not only changed jobs, but they also changed careers. Johnson, for example, began his new career ten days after his sixty-second birthday.

The primary reluctance about entering a new job or career after retiring is that people feel they will lose their Social Security benefits. However, Hey (1996) has reported that the amount of money that you can make after retirement, without Social Security problems, is on the rise. In 1996, the allowable earnings were $12,500. The amount will increase incrementally to $17,000 in 2000 and up to $30,000 in the year 2002. These changes apply only to people who are now between sixty-five and sixty-nine years old. It is anticipated, however, that this kind of change may continue as the baby boomers (those born between 1945 and 1960) reach retirement age, beginning in 2007.

Voluntary Separation

Along with many of the early retirees, others also decide to leave the organization voluntarily. As we have mentioned, there are several reasons for making such a choice. One of them may be that your spouse is taking a better job at another geographic location. Because today's families must consider the total income of both partners, more and more families are moving to new locations, sometimes when only one has a position prior to relocation. Especially when one of the members has more flexibility by being self-employed, this is a reasonable decision to increase the overall income. A second reason to leave your current organization is that you are retiring. A third reason is to gain a better position for yourself, and a fourth reason is that your job has become overly stressful.

With downsizing, the employees who remain in the organization often find that their work has increased tremendously. Carpi (1996) suggests several methods for reducing stress on the job, including biofeedback, meditation, relaxing posture, imagery, and passive stretches. Such methods may be effective. Of course, in the New Organization much of the stress is caused by what is going on in the organization. Because of the downsizing, the remaining members are concerned about whether they, too, will be downsized. For many, especially those in managerial positions, the number of hours worked per week has increased. And the fact of the matter is that one may be "at the office" more during periods of downsizing simply to stay abreast of what is going on as well as to present an image of working harder.

Even if you happen to be in an organization that has not been downsized, the threat is always there, lurking. And even organizations that have not downsized have changed significantly over the past few years. As noted in earlier chapters, changes can occur because of technology as well as economics. When organizations move from "paper" management to "computer" management, each individual in the organization must learn to change.

For example, the means by which we formerly found out what was going on was through official memos from the top and through our grapevine communication networks. Now we must daily check our *e-mail*. Today's messages are often more succinct, and they appear to be more directive than before. They provide data. They are less personal. In addition, most budget and accounting information is also maintained on the computer, rather than in books kept by hand. In a sense, the *information seems more temporary*. Of course, information has always been temporary, but the new technology drives this point home.

Because of space requirements, messages may be automatically deleted after being in the system for a certain amount of time. Therefore, computers have caused a situation where you have to place your reception of messages in line with what the system says. You must respond more quickly. You must have greater accessibility and you do have greater accountability. All of these changes may be too much for individuals who have been in an organization for twenty or thirty years. In addition, as we have indicated, the non-technological systems, too, are in the process of change. Thus, each one of us is learning how to work, on the job, each and every day. This massive influx of change is more than many people want to cope with, so they decide to "get out." But often those formerly in management are driven to do something, to create and to manage. Perhaps the biggest negative to retirement is deciding what to do after "work." After all, you can paint or fish or travel only so long.

STARTING A BUSINESS OR CHANGING CAREERS

One of the most common decisions upon retirement is to decide to "start one's own business." O'Brien and Bergstrom (1995) write: "Out in the job market, it would be easy to assume that age and experience are no longer assets. However, a growing number of fledgling entrepreneurs are shattering this myth by hiring . . . themselves" (p. 58).

As noted, many retirees "love their work, often make a profit and still have the leisure time they have looked forward to" (O'Brien & Bergstrom, 1995, p. 58). There are numerous suggestions, enough for another book, for saving on costs associated with beginning a new business. The about-to-retire might consider using their home as their office, not hiring outside employees, avoiding loans, purchasing the least amount of equipment, and putting profits back into the business (O'Brien & Bergstrom, 1995, p. 60).

For many, then, retirement means operating one's own business minus many of the hassles of working for someone else. Harris (1996) has written that there are a number of occupations for which retired persons can find access, even in today's job market:

> Staying put is the easy solution. In this era, however, the easy solution may not be the safe one. Experienced workers who find themselves trapped in a dead-end job or shunted out the door in a corporate reorganization will often be much happier and better off in the long run if they switch to a completely different career in a growing industry. (p. 59)

She has developed a list of ten jobs for those over fifty who are seeking work, if they are willing to learn a new skill. Those jobs and prospects are listed in Table 13.1.

TABLE 13.1 Jobs by 2005

Job title	New jobs by 2005	Salary range	Requirements
Computer systems analyst	445,000	$25–59K	Bachelor's degree in computer science
Construction and building inspector	14,000	$19–58K	Background in area; preference two years college in engineering or architecture
Cosmetologist	110,000	$9–27K	State license
Loan officer	50,000	$27–76K	Bachelor's degree in business or economics
Medical assistant	121,000	$15–27K	Usually certification
Physician assistant	13,000	$38–57K	Two-year program at medical schools
Occupational therapist	39,000	$34–49K	License
Private detective	24,000	$15–55K	No formal training required; states vary about license requirements
Property manager	37,000	$10–53K	Business degree helps; nothing formal usually; on-the-job
Teacher	634,000 (elementary) 206,000 (Special education) 167,000 (Adult education)	$19–60K	B.A. in education and state certification

Source: M. Harris, (March, 1996). The best new careers for over-50s. *New Choices,* 59–62.

The point that Harris is attempting to make is that there will be many new jobs by the year 2005. Having this knowledge may be beneficial to you, the college student who may be seeking the first job around this time. The second point about the New Organization and the other changes that are taking place in our society is that *the job market is always changing.* Brimelow (1996) has presented a more historical view of this problem. His view, too, though, is optimistic. He has provided an analysis of occupations in the years 1900, 1960, and 1995, to illustrate how jobs change (see Table 13.2).

Interestingly, none of the top three jobs in 1900 required higher education. By 1995, more and more have required higher education. Teaching, for example, has increased substantially, more than doubling between 1960 and 1995. But other jobs in the top 30 in 1995 also require some education beyond high school. These include nursing, engineering, financial sales, health technicians, accountants and auditors, wholesale commodities brokers, computer programmers, lawyers and judges, and professors. Even the kinds of skills

TABLE 13.2   Changes in Jobs 1900–1995

Top Five Jobs	% All Jobs
1900	
1. Farming	10.1%
2. General labor	2.6%
3. Household work	1.6%
4. Retail sales	1.4%
5. Secretarial	0.6%
1960	
1. Retail sales	4.4%
2. Farming	3.8%
3. Teaching	1.7%
4. Truck driving	1.7%
5. Secretarial	1.5%
1995	
1. Retail sales	6.6%
2. Teaching	4.5%
3. Secretarial	3.4%
4. Truck driving	2.9%
5. Farming	2.3%

Reprinted by permission of *Forbes* magazine © Forbes Inc., 1996.

required in secretarial work today are far different than they were in 1900 or even 1960.

While Lewis (1996) believes there will be more jobs available in the twenty-first century, he is more pessimistic about the nature of the jobs. He agrees that there will be jobs in retail sales (which have jumped from 1.4% in 1900 to 6.6% in 1995), computing careers, and education and childcare, but also notes that many of the jobs will be menial (janitors and housekeepers) and others will require additional education, often of a substantial nature. For jobs in health care, education, and computing, for instance, the question becomes whether a fifty-something-year-old wants to go to college or go back to work in order to pursue a new career. Of course, all of the new job situations that we have discussed here involve going back to work for someone else. In today's world it is doubtful that any one will create less stress than any other will. However, many people fifty or older (and sometimes younger) have decided to stay at home and work for themselves.

AVOIDING THE INEVITABLE

Louis (1996) has indicated that most of us want a "safe haven" at work. Many of us do not want to be terminated, even voluntarily. To avoid most of these forms of separation, she writes, there are several factors that all of us need to consider. The first is the need for *new skills*. We need to learn to plan, develop, and manage our own careers. It is obvious by now that we cannot take a job out of college and expect the company to take care of us for forty or more years. We also need to learn *entrepreneurial skills*. We need to "keep track" of how productive we are. We need to maintain a list of our skills. We need to search for new skills that may be beneficial in the current job or in the next job. She recommends that we take the time to reflect. In this reflection, we should ask questions such as: "Am I patient and genuinely present in my dealings with others?" "Do I invite others to do the same with me?" "Do I create opportunities for others to share?" "Do I speak the truth, even in the face of pressure?" "Do I support the efforts of others to improve my effectiveness and their own?" (pp. 231–232).

Downs (1995, p. 141) has provided a list of issues for a safe haven by way of avoiding trouble. If you take a "promote me or lose me" stance, have not received pay raises or bonuses the last couple of years, another company is bidding for your company, your performance review is past due, your boss is taking away job responsibilities, and the like, your job is in danger. Downs recommends that you (1) cross-train; (2) do not play politics; (3) mind your corporate manners; and (4) manage your own career. By taking these suggestions, you may be able to make your own decision about when you separate from your organization.

SUMMARY

Sooner or later you will have to make a decision about separating yourself from your company. This decision may come after many years with that same company, but that looks less and less like an option you will have with the New Organization. More than likely you will be one of the thousands who will be projected to have changed *occupations* (not just jobs, but actual occupations) at least twice before finally retiring. It has been estimated that the typical college student now changes majors four and one half times in his or her academic career; perhaps that portends even more change in the New Organization.

Your options regarding separation depend on whether that separation is voluntary or involuntary. If you are leaving on your own, then you have a number of options open to you, including starting a new business or changing a career path. For some reason a lot of "retired" people have entered the teaching profession as a second career. Perhaps they want some "people" time; others have taken positions that will afford them some additional money, but not so much as to cause them pension problems.

If you have to separate, your options change. Being downsized or right-sized may actually play to your advantage, if approached with the same research and client analysis used in management to establish a dialogue with other potential companies. Burning bridges is not a recommended communication strategy, regardless of how good it might feel to criticize or ridicule the decision to let you go. The competent organizational communicator will take a communication lesson from each experience she has in the organization, and this will not change with the New Organization.

We will end our study of organizational communication by reviewing what we have said about your communication role in organizations, listing a number of communication principles that seem to apply to the twenty-first century.

In any event, our study of the Old to the New Organization has now come to an end. It has not been a full circle and there are probably more questions raised than answered. That is good; understanding that the best answer to most questions may be "it depends" indicates that the key to success in the New Organization will depend on your ability to conduct content research, analyze potential clients, establish a communication dialogue, and—of course—adapt, adapt, adapt.

QUESTIONS FOR THOUGHT

1. How should a human resource department be set up to deal with the problems of individuals who are terminated?
2. How should you always be prepared for losing a job? What kinds of things should you do on a regular basis to be prepared for this possibility?
3. What communication problems will you likely encounter if you are fired from a job?
4. What would you tell a future employer about your being dismissed from your last job?
5. What are some of the positive consequences of changing jobs?

CASE 13.2   Downsizing Policy

Some companies have policies about downsizing. Most do not. If you were in a position to do so, to what extent would you allow the employees to have input into a downsizing policy? What kinds of problems might such input create?

REFERENCES

Barrett, L. I. (1995, January). Early retirement? You're in for some surprises. *New Choices,* 32–35.

Belli, M., & Krantzler, M. (1988). *Divorcing.* New York: St. Martin's.

Berger, C. R., & Calabrese, R. J. (1975). Some explanations in initial interaction and beyond: Toward a developmental theory of interpersonal communication, *Human Communication Research, 1,* 99–112.

Boyett, J. H., & Boyett, J. T. (1995). *Beyond workplace 2000.* New York: Dutton.

Bragg, R. (1996). Where dignity used to be. In *The downsizing of America* (pp. 77–110). New York: Random House.

Brimelow, P. (May 6, 1996). What happened to all those blacksmiths? *Forbes,* 46–47.

Carpi, J. (1996, January/February). Stress: It's worse than you think. *Psychology Today, 29,* 34–41, 74, 76.

Conrad, C. (1994). *Strategic organizational communication: Toward the twenty-first century.* Fort Worth: Harcourt Brace.

Dallas, S. (January, 1996). Early retirement: Making it work for you. *New Choices,* 47–49.

Downs, A. (1995). *Corporate executions: The ugly truth about layoffs—how corporate greed is shattering lives, companies, and communities.* New York: American Management Association.

Estes, R. (1996). *Tyranny of the bottom line: Why corporations make good people do bad things.* San Francisco: Berrett-Koehler.

Gordon, D. M. (1996). *Fat and mean: The corporate squeeze of working Americans and the myth of managerial "downsizing."* New York: Free Press.

Hall, D. T. (1996). *The career is dead—long live the career: A relational approach to careers.* San Francisco: Jossey-Bass.

Harris, M. (March, 1996). The best new careers for over-50s. *New Choices,* 59–62.

Hey, R. P. (May, 1996). Retirees may earn more benefits before losing Social Security benefits. *AARP Bulletin,* 2.

Kleinfield, N. R. (1996). A new and unnerving workplace. In *The downsizing of America* (pp. 37–76). New York: Random House.

Kollath, M. L. (November, 1995). How to decide whether to take a buyout package. *New Choices,* 88.

Kubler-Ross, E. (1993). *On death and dying.* New York: Collier.

Lewis, R. (January, 1996). Jobs 2000. *AARP Bulletin, 1,* 6–9.

Lewis, R. (May, 1996). Up and away: Second careers taking off. *AARP Bulletin, 1,* 8–10.

Louis, M. R. (1996). Creating safe havens at work. In Douglas T. Hall, (Ed.), *The career is dead—long live the career* (pp. 223–245). San Francisco: Jossey-Bass.

O'Brien, T., & Bergstrom, R. (September, 1995). How to succeed in (your own) business . . . for less than $5000. *New Choices,* 58–60.

Phillips, G. M., & Metzger, N. J. (1976). *Intimate communication.* Boston: Allyn and Bacon.

Richards, P. (1995, Fall). Here's what you must know to stop working before age 65. *Stages,* 11–13.

Rifkin, J. (1995). *The end of work.* New York: Putnam.

Rimer, S. (1996). The fraying of community. In *The downsizing of America* (pp. 111–138). New York: Random House.

Rowland, M. (1996, August). Are buyouts taxable? *Modern Maturity,* 62.

Stogner, C. (1995). Have a great vacation. In A. Downs, *Corporate executions: The ugly truth about layoffs—how corporate greed is battering lives, companies, and communitees* (pp. 107–116). New York: American Management Association.

Uchitelle, L., & Kleinfield, N. R. (1996). The price of jobs lost. In *The downsizing of America* (pp. 3–36). New York: Random House.

14

SUMMARY AND CONCLUSIONS

Goal Orientation in the Workplace

Social Interaction in the Workplace

The Process of Organizational Communication

The Future of Organizational Communication

Social Aspects of the New Organization

Objectives

By the end of this chapter you should be able to

1. Summarize how the New Organization operates.
2. Explain twenty principles of organizational communication.
3. Discuss the communication processes found in the New Organization.
4. Explain how adaptability and communication management will influence the future of communication in the New Organization.
5. Discuss from a communication perspective the social aspects of the New Organization.

Unlike many other organizational communication textbook authors, we have discussed the roles of individual communicators in organizations as both the individuals and the organizations grow through various stages of their relationship with one another. To discuss the individual without the organization would be ludicrous, but to discuss the organization without some focus on individual goals would appear to be just as ridiculous. Therefore, we have discussed organizational communication as an interface between the individual and the organization, which involves cooperation for success but which also involves conflicts between individual goals and expectations and organizational goals and expectations.

GOAL ORIENTATION IN THE WORKPLACE

In this goal-centered environment, there are several principles that appear to cover individuals and organizations in the workplace:

1. **In a free enterprise system, such as ours, the goals of the organization are to**
   a. **Make a profit; and**
   b. **Continue to exist.**

2. **In our system, individual goals are to obtain and maintain the "best" jobs to secure the "best" lives for ourselves and our families.**

3. **Most of the time, the goals of the organization and the individual are common goals. The success of one is dependent on the success of the other.**

4. **However, the individual and organizational goals are sometimes in conflict because**
   a. **Organizations must make rapid decisions in personnel.**
   b. **Organizations often must change faster than some individuals are willing or able to change.**
   c. **Profits are determined by reducing costs as well as by increasing rewards.**

The free enterprise system begins with an innovative idea, which grows in complexity as it grows in size. Recalling our discussion of the Bee Textile Company, we noted that what was first viewed as a hobby became a complex of managers and workers utilizing various land, labor, and capital resources to produce a product which the consuming public wanted to buy. With each change in the organization, other changes became necessary. Different kinds of expertise were needed at different stages in the growth of the organization. Once the complex organization has been created, there is no return to the old ways. There are now people in the organization who are dependent on the continued existence of the company for their livelihoods and their families' well-being.

We discussed the fact that organizations seek out various types of employees to succeed in their *goals*. The United States was initially primarily a farm-driven economy. There were thousands of small family farms throughout the

United States. The goal was self-sufficiency. People grew and raised products for their own consumption. Those products they had to buy were purchased by selling excess food to others who were not on farms.

The industrial economy of the late nineteenth and early twentieth century was created to make work less strenuous. But the nature of the work was still primarily manual labor. People who could lift heavy objects, who could undertake a great deal of manual labor in one day, could survive better than most others who could not. In the second phase of the industrial economy, workers were chosen because of their abilities to repeat the same actions over and over again.

In the last half of the twentieth century, however, work and organizations have changed substantially. Menial labor (not to necessarily be confused with manual labor) was replaced by machinery. Therefore, although humans were needed to produce robotics machines that could undertake repetitious actions much more efficiently than human bodies, fewer humans were needed. The robotics machines were more efficient, more effective, and longer lasting than human labor. In the past quarter of a century, clerical work (typing, filing) has also been partially replaced by an information robot, the computer. Thus, technological changes have not taken over *all* jobs, but they have taken over many of the lower paying jobs of the past. In addition, these technological changes have resulted in the need for fewer supervisors and managers. The supervisor or manager in the past had as one of her roles "overseeing" the workers. As the number of workers decreased, the need for overseers also decreased. In addition, in the last quarter of a century, global competition has increased. Much of the work that cannot be done by robots or computers can be done by cheaper labor from other countries throughout the world.

Individuals have learned that they must adapt to the economy and the needs of organizations. On a regular basis, workers attempt to meet the needs of their companies. As technology improves at a higher rate, the speed of change in organizations also increases. Individuals must be able to understand not only how things were done in the past and how they are done now; they must also understand how they will be done in the future.

As a result of these changes, organizations often find themselves with the *inappropriate* personnel. Just as a manual laborer who could not place tires on automobiles quickly and efficiently had to seek different employment, so, too, does today's worker who was hired to do repetitive tasks that are now completed by robots or computers. Individuals, then, must have the quality of adaptability to survive in a sea of change. In addition to having the skill of adaptability, the individual must know how to research everything about work. He must know about his company. He must know about the competition. He must know about technology. He must know about the new skills that will be required tomorrow. That is, he must have strong "mind labor."

In addition, he must know how to deal with others—to negotiate, to listen, to empathize, to present, to evaluate, and to sell. He must be able to identify audiences (or clients) both within and outside the organization. For mind labor, then, the worker in the New Organization must know how to do *content research* (about his business), he must know how to *analyze clients,* and he must be *adaptable.*

If the new worker does not have these capabilities, conflicts are likely to occur between the worker and the organization. Because of the time constraints, the worker and the organization. will make rapid personnel changes. Less capable employees will be out of work. Workers who cannot adapt quickly will be gone. Finally, it is important that the worker understand that the organization may change its focus entirely in a relatively short time span.

   5. Thus, goals are processes; they are not fixed.

We believe that the skills required will obviously call for a more intelligent worker than was needed one hundred or even twenty-five years ago. We also believe, however, that communication is the key to all of the skills we have described. With that in mind, there are principles concerned with the uses and roles of social interaction.

SOCIAL INTERACTION IN THE WORKPLACE

   6. There are three types of social interaction: communication, persuasion, and catharsis.

We have described communication as the process of exchanging messages using symbols to enhance elucidation and build relationships. *Feedback* is a primary component of the successful communication process. The goal in this process should be to create, transmit, interpret, recreate, and evaluate ethical messages for the long-term improvement of the persons involved as well as the organization itself.

   7. In the organization, communication is a process utilized by all who have contact with the organization, to provide positive responses to positive actions and negative responses when changes are needed in the process.
   8. In today's world, change is a constant.
   9. Communication is used as a tool for adaptation by organizations and individuals.

Adaptability again plays an important role here. An individual in the organization should realize that, considering that most other employees are also seeking the best for themselves and the organization, *knowledge is based on perceptions.* Obviously some perceptions are better than others, but in many cases there are simply differences of opinion, all based on adequate information. But all of these perceptions are based on the individual's *selective exposure, attention, perception, retention, and recall.* When perceptions are based on information, that information is fluid and it must be assessed for its authoritativeness. The perceptions of others, too, must be evaluated. We assess their opinions based on their *credibility, interpersonal attraction, and homophily,* and we should be aware of our own and their biases in regard to these factors.

Organizations, too, utilize communication as an adaptive tool. Public relations people must adapt to the situation. Employees must be notified of changes in benefits. New work policies must be transmitted to the workers. Organizational goals must be shared. Above all, communication is a tool for *sharing.*

10. The communication process involves task messages and social messages.

Task messages are interactions directed toward production within the organization. These are messages specifically about work. They may include directives, requests, suggestions, and complaints. These messages are often supported by *social affiliation messages,* which are messages about the relationships of the interactants. Grapevine (informal communication) falls within this category. It should be noted, however, that even task messages are accompanied by social messages. This can be reflected in the intensity of the language used. For example, "This is very important." Or, "We must do this today." Or "Let's work on this." Or "This is an emergency." Nonverbal, the social aspect is always present, whether the messages are task or social or a combination. The amount of eye contact, the distance between interactants, the loudness of voice, and other nonverbal factors indicate similarities and differences between interactants in terms of whether they like each other and whether one has status over the other.

Another type of social interaction is *persuasion.* Persuasion is also used with social and task messages.

11. Persuasion is used as a tool to decide tasks within the organization.
12. Persuasion is used to convince another that an idea is appropriate for the situation.
13. Persuasion involves a competition among ideas.

If there is no conflict between ideas, there is no need for persuasion. It is important for those in organizations to realize, however, that the *competition is between or among ideas, not between people.* Persuasion utilizes all of those self-presentation concerns that we have previously discussed (credibility, interpersonal attraction, and homophily). In addition, persuasion uses knowledge and logic. In most situations, the best task decisions are based highly on *content research.* And persuasion is based on the use of emotions. Understanding and being sensitive to the emotions of the other interactant(s) is an important aspect of the successful communicator. Persuasion involves *dialogue,* not monologue. Like communication, persuasion is an ongoing process. Feedback is an important characteristic of this process. By listening and understanding the other person, the persuader is better able to select the most effective messages for achieving the persuasive purpose. Finally, *adaptation* is needed for effective persuasion. Timing is important. Understanding the need to present information at a specific time can mean the difference between effective and ineffective interaction. Adaptation also means that the same message may not be effective with all clients or in all situations. Therefore, continual *client analysis* and defining of the situation is fundamental.

14. **When the best decisions are made, organizations and individuals are in a win-win situation. The company makes a profit; individuals feel secure and rewarded for their work.**
15. **Catharsis is the failure of communication and persuasion.**

Catharsis is the outpouring of words and feelings. In the organizational context, these words and feelings are most often expressed to the inappropriate person. Catharsis allows the individual temporary satisfaction with no positive long-term results for either the person or the organization. Maximum levels of catharsis by a significant number of employees are indicative of ineffective management. No doubt, *catharsis is a necessary aspect of life.* We may get frustrated when we cannot drive through the bank window quickly enough or when the fast food restaurant will not serve us breakfast after 9:30 A.M. Such frustrations, however, should not be part of the office situation.

THE PROCESS OF ORGANIZATIONAL COMMUNICATION

16. **Organizations have cultures (values, needs) which circumscribe appropriate and inappropriate behaviors.**
17. **Organizations' cultures are limited by laws, ethics, etiquette, and the socialization process.**

    a. **Laws are created by legislative bodies and interpreted by the courts. Both are important for understanding organizational culture.**

It should be noted that *sexual harassment* was not a term in the vocabulary of any organizational culture fifty, or even twenty years ago. *Equal opportunity, politically correct language,* and *age discrimination* are all relatively *new* ideas that have re-invented organizational culture.

    b. **Ethics are values generally agreed upon by society at large.**

"Do unto others" and other similar maxims are part of the culture. While certainly there are unethical people and unethical companies in the world, such behavior should be contradictory to the culture of the organization, if for no other reason than it creates *chaos*. Chaos disallows for systematic operations. Treating different people differently, for example, causes members of the organization to become suspicious, frustrated, and angry. Ultimately, chaos creates additional unethical behavior.

   c. **Etiquette is merely an extension of the notion of ethics.**

Ethics sets out what kind of behavior should be expected. *Etiquette* designs how this kind of behavior should be implemented.

   d. **The socialization process is the method used by organizations to "teach" its members about its culture.**

The process certainly involves sets of policies, procedures, rules, and guidelines, but it also includes *norms of behavior.* In the ideal organization, all workers will be taught effectively about the organizational culture. In essence, when the process does not work it is indicative of a failure of the organization. After all, the organization hired the failure in the first place.

18. **For the individual, the socialization process is constant, from the job interview to the last day on the job. There are communication processes at each stage.**
19. **Organizations that contain adaptive, socialized workers are effective and profitable.**
20. **Individuals who are adaptive and socialized are rewarded and feel secure.**

THE FUTURE OF ORGANIZATIONAL COMMUNICATION

In this book, we have attempted to provide an analysis of how organizations work and how we expect them to work over the next few years. Because of technology and changes in the social aspects of the work world, we anticipate that the New Organization will become less centralized but more "connected" than its twentieth century counterpart. The New Organization will probably not reside in one major building, where its entire workforce operates. Instead, the workers will be all over the world. Transporting workers from one location to another will become less and less necessary. There will continue to be plants where physical products are produced, but these will be satellite plants, away from central headquarters. Headquarters may be more of a centralized computer network than a centralized building with parking spaces, security guards, and workers coming in at 9:00 to drink coffee and begin their daily work. The need for office space will be reduced significantly.

This type of loose-knit organization will produce a variety of communication problems for the New Manager. The loss of interpersonal contact will reduce the daily exchange of information about research (as well as about "good movies" and what's going on in the political world). Although she may visit through cyberspace, what the new manager sees and hears will be different from her twentieth century counterpart, who could use information from the "real world" to help her understand problems and solutions.

Management, supervision, and leadership will change. Much of the information (if not most) will be received through technology, not the physical senses. Long-distance conferencing will be commonplace. Interactive television conferencing will be available on the home computer so that the manager will not even have to go anywhere to participate in these meetings. In addition to those "old" methods of obtaining information: newspapers, television, the Internet, fax, and e-mail, new methods will evolve, probably turning one entire room of one's home into a communication center. More and more confidence will be given to electronic files. Paper copies will become outdated. Because of the mere speed of electronic transfers of information, the prices of products on shelves will change constantly, perhaps even several times a day. Consumers who have greater access to information will make better choices. Groceries will be bought over the computer and delivered by services similar to UPS and Federal Express.

It is even possible that job interviews, as discussed earlier in the book, will no longer be person-to-person. Interviews may be held over the Internet. Tests for various jobs can be given over the Internet. In many cases, the organization's liability for its workers will decrease. The workers will be in their own homes. Problems with drug and alcohol abuse will be moot because the work will be done on the computer and the computer will analyze the effectiveness of one's job performance. The manager can take those data and place them in another computer program, which will decide whether the individual deserves a salary increase.

For organizations in the United States, the shift from producing goods to producing services and information will continue. Costs associated with doing business will continue to drive goods-oriented business from the United States.

As part of personal information management, we have *message management.* The electronic message has not replaced the paper message. Most people still make paper copies of anything they think is really important. A problem with electronic messages is that they have a propensity to disappear with a keystroke or with a damaged disk. The "paperless" office is a misnomer. The same individuals who cannot find a file in their file drawer, because they cannot remember what they filed under, will not be able to find the file in the computer.

Another problem area is that of assigning importance to incoming messages. If you have a computer and are on the Internet, now you have the problem of bringing up e-mail and having ten to fifteen messages waiting. While you are reading one of them, several more may arrive, each demanding a reading and a potential response. The fact that you can create a distribution list, and with several keystrokes distribute your message to a very large number of people, creates more problems. However, it is possible that a "status system" could evolve on the computer. Even so, priority and information overload are problems that will simply be enhanced in the coming years.

Security and *privacy* will be additional problems. Most e-mail users discover sooner or later that there is no such thing as privacy on a networked computer system. Almost every e-mail message you receive is stored somewhere, and the network administrator has the ability to read and monitor your messages without your knowledge. Network administrators and "hackers," who daily gain entry to even the most secure computerized systems, easily break even encrypted messages.

While security is an organizational problem, privacy is a personal problem. What would happen if your personal information manager (PIM), left on your desk, were read by someone—and it contained notes for an upcoming employee evaluation? Although electronic communication systems are as confidential as their paper counterparts, PIMs and computers are often left accessible to others. Even disks, which may have very compromising data on them, are stolen from major corporations. If they are found, it is virtually impossible to determine whether copies have been made.

SOCIAL ASPECTS OF THE NEW ORGANIZATION

The increased internationalization of the New Organization will yield new and diverse socialization processes. Problems associated with discrimination and harassment will continue; new problems may even arise because people from other cultures are not aware of American legal and ethical bases in these areas. Even among American workers, there will be a greater need for adaptability.

Supervising and motivating workers will continue to be a major challenge. Because many of the workers will be operating from their own homes, more independence will result. Flextime is likely to be a built-in factor. Many companies will not care whether work is done between 9:00 A.M. and 5:00 P.M. or between midnight and 6:00 A.M.

In the 1960s, it was argued that technological advancements would significantly increase our personal, free time. Common wisdom had it that we would be working about thirty-two hours a week instead of forty. By the mid-1990s, however, it became apparent that the combination of technology and corporate downsizing was significantly reducing free time. Many workers must put in more hours today than they did ten years ago.

Work that was once completed at the office is now taken home. Little free times, such as commuting to and from work, are now work times thanks to cellular telephones and other in-car devices. We get more done in less time; however, we are working harder and socializing less. While less time may be spent on those tasks associated with the job (such as commuting), more time will be spent in research, reading, analyzing, and thinking.

DILBERT / Scott Adams

DILBERT © United Feature Syndicate. Reprinted by Permission.

SUMMARY

The twenty principles outlined above should provide the New Manager in the New Organization some valuable advice. The manager will have more access to more information than ever before. Understanding and processing the information quickly will be the role of the New Manager. A major task will be finding and analyzing the credibility of it. Finally, change will take place at a faster and faster pace. In light of all of this rapid-rate sea of information and technology, the New Manager needs to remember to take time to reflect, because careful reflection is the key to adaptation.

INDEX

AARP. *See* American Association of Retired Persons (AARP)

Abilities, 12

Absenteeism, 235

Abstract concepts, 158, 222

Academic journals, 42

Acceptance, 257

Accommodating profile, 139

Accountability, 135, 173, 264

"Accountant's syndrome," 223

Achievement needs, 135, 142

Actions, 169

Active listening, 130

ADA. *See* Americans with Disabilities Act (ADA)

Adams, Scott, 31, 92, 112, 177, 199, 224, 279

Adaptation, 4, 10, 12, 40, 168–189
  to boss, 225
  communication and, 12, 149, 273
  communication climate and, 140
  communication cues and, 112
  credibility and, 107
  to formal structures, 87–88
  to groups, 148, 149
  by individuals, 272, 273
  internationalism and, 249, 278
  knowledge and, 40
  knowledge base and, 56
  leadership and, 161–163
  New Organizations and, 4, 10, 214
  new/neophyte employees and, 87, 107
  persuasion and, 275
  reflection and, 279
  socialization and, 246, 276
  systems theory and, 181, 183, 184
  technology and, 272
  work security and, 12

Administration, 135, 148

"Administrative man," 180

Advancement
  motivation and, 131
  social knowledge as key to, 25
  teamwork and, 149

Advancement needs, 135

Advertising, 11, 206–207
  for job applicants, 194–195

Aesthetic knowledge, 24, 25

Aesthetic needs, 134

African Americans, 246, 249.
    See also Blacks

Agarwala-Rogers, R., 89, 98, 104, 214, 227, 228, 232

Age
  demographic changes regarding, 221
  homophily and, 30, 31
  perceptions and, 32–33

Age discrimination, 234, 250–251, 275

Aguayo, R., 136, 146, 186, 230, 232

AIDS, 248

Airlines, 209

Alcohol, 204, 236, 248, 277
  involuntary termination and, 258, 259

Alibis, 202

Alien idea, 29

All star network, 150, 151
Alternatives, 180
Ambiguity, 175
Ambivalent personality, 108
American Association of Retired Persons
     (AARP), 219
Americans with Disabilities Act (ADA),
     248–249
Analysis, 44–45
  approaches to, 169
  audience, 4, 29
  Barnard and Simon's framework for,
     179–180
  client. *See* Client analysis
  communication audit and, 46
  content. *See* Content analysis
  data, 45, 56–57
  descriptive, 45
  inferential, 45
  problem, 228
  data, 56–57
  focus groups and, 53
  in-depth, 53
  inferential, 45
  qualitative/quantitative. *See* Qualitative
     research/analysis; Quantitative
     research/analysis
  units of, 47, 54
Anger, 256–257, 260, 276
Anticipation phase, 84–94, 256
Apology, 210
Apparent compliance, 202
Applicant pool, 195–196
Apprenticeship, 116
Arbitration, binding, 208
Argumentative personality, 109
Argyle, Michael, 169, 179, 188
Argyris, C., 179, 188
Artistic personalities, 110
Asians, 240
Assembly line, 6, 7
  groups and, 152
  scientific management, 170
  as system, 181
Assertiveness, 139, 245
  leadership and, 148, 163
Assessing organizational change, 230–231
Assimilation, mentors and, 121
Attention, 20, 274

Attitude, 52, 68
Attitudinal homophily, 30, 31
Attraction, 29, 30, 34–35, 86
  communication cues and, 112
Audience analysis, 4, 29. *See also* Client
     analysis
Audiences, 111, 272
  credibility with different, 107
  motivation and, 127
  supervision and, 131
Audiotapes, content analysis and, 55
Authoritarian leadership, 159
Authoritarian personality, 108
Authority, 135
  behavioral alteration techniques (BATs) and,
     143, 144
  leadership and, 155
  motivation and, 131
Automation, 7–10
Automobiles, 7, 21, 186
  change and, 214–215, 219
  electric, 215, 219, 231
Autonomy, 86, 177
Avoidance, 202
Avoiding profile, 139

"Baby boomers," 221, 237–238, 263
Background homophily, 30–31
Backstrom, C. H., 51
Badger mentors, 120
Baldridge, L., 197, 210, 211, 212
Bales, Robert, 157, 167, 169, 179
Baltimore Orioles, 24
Barciela, S., 85, 103
Bargaining, 141
Barker, L. L., 146
Barnard, Chester I., 169, 179, 188
Barrett, L. I., 261, 262, 269
Barzi, M. G., 202, 212
BATs. *See* Behavioral alteration techniques
     (BATs)
Baucus, M. S., 212
Baugh, S. G., 118, 121, 124
"Bean-counting" syndrome, 223, 224
Beebe, S. A., 152, 167
Beepers, etiquette and, 211
Beer companies, 206
Behavioral alteration techniques (BATs), 128,
     142–145

Behaviors, 84, 275, 276
  anticipation of, 90
  discrimination and, 235
  exchange theory and, 137, 140–141
  leadership and, 160, 162
  male vs. female, 245
  norms and, 100. *See also* Norms
  participant-observation of, 55
  professional conduct and, 192
  questionnaires and, 52
  reward vs. punishment of, 138
  role models for, 118
  rules and, 90
  typicalities of, 91
  unwelcome, 240
  work-related, 234
Beliefs, questionnaires and, 52
Bell Laboratories, 174
Belli, M., 256, 269
Benefits
  downsizing and, 238
  new/neophyte employees and, 85
  part-time and temporary workers
    and, 117
Benne, K., 111, 124
Bennis, Warren, 163, 163, 181, 188
Bentley, N., 119, 125
Berelson, B., 54, 59
Berger, C. R., 30, 37, 255, 269
Bergstrom, R., 264, 269
Beyond Workplace 2000, 2
Bhote, K. R., 224, 232
Bias, 235, 274
Bies, R. J., 212
"Big Three," 215
Biofeedback, 263
Blacks, 240. *See also* African Americans
Blake, R., 160, 167
Blakely, E. H., 242, 252
Blakely, G. L., 242, 252
Blanchard, K. H., 161, 162, 167
Blue-collar employees, 106, 172
  in new vs. old culture, 238–240
Body language, 115
Books, content research and, 19
Boss, 222–225
Bostrom, R., 150, 167
Bostwick, B. E., 75, 76, 77, 82
Bottom line, 22, 23, 40

consumer protection and, 205
  ethics and, 208–209
  leadership and, 106
  product quality and, 205
  structural change and, 225
  "warm and fuzzy" syndrome
    and, 223
Bovee, C. L., 77, 82
Bowers, J. W., 112
Boyett, J. H., 2, 14, 255, 269
Boyett, J. T., 2, 14, 255, 269
Bradshaw, P., 236, 252
Bragg, R., 255, 269
Brainstorming, 228–229, 230
  electronic, 230
Bribery, 23, 219
Bridges, 98, 99
Bridwell, L. G., 134, 146
Briggs, S., 201, 212
Brimelow, P., 265, 269
Broadcasting, 43
Brown, Mary Helen, 91, 103
Brown, S. J., 118, 125
Bureaucracy, 10, 87, 88, 94, 163
  scientific management and, 170,
    172–173
  structural change and, 225
Burgoon, M., 112, 113, 125, 160, 167
Burke, R. J., 117, 118, 124
"Burned out," 134
Business, starting own, 264–266
Business phase, 154
Business Week, 43, 66
Buyouts, 153, 260–262
Byrne, J. A., 75, 82

Calabrese, R. J., 30, 37, 255, 269
Calas, M. B., 89, 104
Calendars, 92–93
Campbell, D. T., 45, 59
Careers, 12
  choosing, 62, 63–65
  leadership and, 148
  lifetime, 173
  mentors and, 117, 118, 121–123, 118
  planning, 63, 65–68
  preparation for, 61
Carpi, J., 263, 269
Cartwright, D., 149, 167

Casbolt, D., 119, 125
Case studies, 45
Cash, W. B., Jr., 77, 82, 202
Catalog companies, 239
Catharsis, 25, 26, 245, 275
Cathartic listening, 130
Causality, 49
Cellular telephones, 4
Certainty, 140
Chain network, 150, 151
Chain of command, 97
Champy, J., 2, 14
Change, 213–232, 273. *See also*
        Organizational change
    adaptation to, 168–189
    causality and, 49
    downsizing and, 263
    external vs. internal, 216
    in future, 279
    goals and, 271
    knowledge and, 21
    motivation and, 137
    personnel, 222–225
    preparing for, 226
    quality circles and, 230
    retirement and, 264
    self-initiated, 214
    structural, 225–227
    systems theory and, 184, 185
Chaos, 4, 276
Character, 31, 78, 163
Cheerleaders, 120, 179
Chevron, 214
Child care, 237
China, 6
Chrysler, 214, 215
Circle network, 150, 151
Civil Rights Act of 1866, 236
Civil Rights Act of 1964, 236, 240, 248
Client analysis, 3, 4, 29–35, 39, 273
    communication roles and, 97
    formal research and, 56
    leadership and, 165
    mentors and, 119
    motivation and, 132, 142, 145
    organizational culture and, 89
    persuasion and, 275
Clients, 220, 272

Climate
    communication. *See* Communication
        climate
    organizational, 89, 100. *See also* Culture (of
        organization)
Clinton, Bill, 218, 237
Clinton, Hillary, 159
Cliques, 98, 156
Closure, group, 154
CNBC. *See* Consumer and Business News
        Channel (CNBC)
"Coach," 118, 179
Coal mines, 7
Coalitions, 39
Coca-Cola, 22
Coding, 174
    content analysis and, 54
    verbal vs. nonverbal, 28, 29. *See also* Non-
        verbal codes; Verbal codes
Coercive power, 137, 138
Cognitive needs, 134
Collaboration, 139, 164
Collectives, 2
Columbia Journalism Review, 43
Commitment
    consensus and, 156
    and implementing change, 230
    mentors and, 121
Communication. *See also* Messages; Organiza-
        tional communication
    adaptation and, 12, 149, 273
    consensus and, 156
    downward vs. upward, 97, 165. *See also*
        Downward communication; Upward
        communication
    face-to-face, 221, 231
    formal vs. informal, 23. *See also* Formal com-
        munication; Informal communication
    horizontal. *See* Horizontal communication
    information theory and, 173
    interactive, 165
    internationalism and, 249
    interpersonal, 18, 107, 249
    intrapersonal, 18
    motivation and, 127
    multigroup, 158
    open, 97, 208, 230
    organizational culture and, 89

perceptions and, 21
process of, 4, 273, 275–276
social change and, 221–222
technological change and, 221–222
technology and, 11
TQM and, 187
verbal vs. nonverbal, 53–54. *See also* Nonverbal communication; Verbal communication
vertical, 225. *See also* Downward communication; Upward communication
vision and, 169
Communication audit, 46
Communication channels, 149–150, 152
Communication climate, 136–137, 140
defensive vs. supportive, 140, 142. *See also* Defensive climate; Supportive climate
power and, 138
Communication dialogue. *See* Dialogue
Communication growth, 137
Communication knowledge, 3–5, 18–22
Communication models, 26–29, 136–145, 174
Communication networks. *See* Networking/networks
Communication roles. *See* Roles
Communication skills, 15–37, 273
firing and, 201
leadership and, 107, 165
learning of, 16
Communication strategies, 164–165
"Communication/information," 25, 26
Communication/message flow, 46, 164–165, 178
Community, downsizing and, 255
Compensation, discrimination and, 234. *See also* Pay; Salary; Wages
Competence, 192–203
credibility and, 31, 34, 35
involuntary termination and, 258, 260
new/neophyte employees and, 86
task changes and, 222
Competition, 8
content research and, 93
European, 215
among ideas, 274
Japanese, 215
professionalism and, 194
short- vs. long-term thinking and, 185–186

Competition profile, 139
Competitive advantage, leadership and, 163
Completion, 135
Compliance, 100, 142
behavioral alteration techniques (BATs) and, 144
disciplinary interviews and, 202
Compromise, equity vs., 208
Compromising profile, 139
Computer networks, 4. *See also* Networking/networks
focus groups and, 54
research and, 42, 43
Computers, 226. *See also* Personal computers; Technological change
binary digit system of, 174, 175
change and, 216, 217, 263
content research and, 20, 21, 40–43
human labor vs., 272
information theory and, 173–176
knowledge and, 40
"marketing wars" and, 184
messages and, 264
monitoring of workers by, 176
new vs. old culture and, 239
security and, 207, 278
spell check on, 222
Concern, 139, 140
leadership and, 160
professional conduct and, 194
Concomm network, 150, 151
Confidential information, 99, 205–206
Conflict, 127
disciplinary interviews and, 202
group, 154–155, 156, 157
motivation and, 138, 140, 154
power and, 138, 140
Conrad, C., 84, 86, 89, 94, 97, 100, 103, 209, 212, 256, 269
Consciousness-raising group, 153
Consensus, 155–156
in assessing organizational change, 230
Delphi groups and, 157
and implementing change, 228, 229
quality circles and, 230
Consolidation, 188
Constructivists, 119, 120, 121

"Consult" strategy, 165
Consumer and Business News Channel
    (CNBC), 43, 67
Consumer protection, 205
Consumers, in future, 277
Content analysis, 4, 48, 54–55
   focus groups and, 53
Content research, 3, 4, 16–22, 39, 273
   careers/job seeking and, 66–67
   communication roles and, 97
   leadership and, 148, 165
   learning and, 21
   mentors and, 119
   motivation and, 136, 142, 145
   organizational culture and, 89
   organizational structure and, 92
   participant-observation and, 56
   reason for, 40
   selectivity in, 20
   supervisory, 131
Context, 39
   leadership and, 163
   messages and, 114
Contingency model, 160–161
Continuous basis/continuity, 2, 84
"Contract With America," 219
Contracts, 207, 208
   employment, 85–86, 206
   in different cultures, 220
Control, 40, 41, 56
   bureaucracy and, 173
   change and, 220
   defensive communication and, 140
   groups and, 151
   leadership and, 159–160
   male vs. female behavior and, 245
   problem solving and, 157
   span of, 77
Conventional personalities, 110
Conversation, 3, 35
   e-mail, 221
   formal vs. informal communication matrix
     and, 90
   by interactive television, 221
   learning through, 18
   new vs. old culture and, 239–240
   synchrony vs. asynchrony in, 115
Cook, M., 179, 188

Cooperation, 139
   communication climate and, 140
   and implementing change, 227
   leadership and, 163
Corporate activities, 101. *See also*
     Social group
Corporations. *See also* Organizations
   bureaucracy for large, 173
   researching, 66–67
Costs, 11
   behavioral alteration techniques (BATs)
     and, 144
   exchange theory and, 137, 140–141
Counseling interviews, 202
Country club leadership, 160
Cragen, J. F., 152, 167
Creativity, 135
   "human relations" theory and, 177, 178
   intellectual knowledge and, 25
Credibility, 5, 29, 31, 34, 35, 274
   communication cues and, 112, 114,
     115, 116
   of documents, 43
   of information, 279
   involuntary termination and, 258, 260
   linkages and, 99
   new/neophyte employees and, 86, 107
   supervision and, 130–131
Crime, 23, 217. *See also* Illegal actions
Critical messages, 112
Cronen, W. V., 47, 59
Culture (of organization), 94, 100, 275. *See*
    also Organizational climate
   careers/job seeking and, 66
   discrimination and, 236
   formal vs. informal, 94
   identification and, 100, 101
   informal, 88–89
   language and, 247
   leadership and, 163
   new, 236–240
   professional conduct and, 192
Culture (of people), 250
   Asian, 186
   change and, 214, 219–220, 221
   homophily and, 30
   racial harassment and, 246
Custodian (role), 100

Customers, 223–224
  credibility and, 34
  employees as, 10
  internationalism and, 249
  loyalty of, 209, 224
Cybernetics, 173

Dalkey, N. C., 157, 167
Dallas, S., 261, 262, 269
Daly, J. A., 30, 37
Data
  "points" of, 47
  quantitative, 44–45. *See also* Quantitative
    research/analysis
  utilizing, 57
Data analysis, 45, 56–57
Data collection, 40, 45, 47
Databases, research and, 4, 42
Davis, K., 89, 103
Davis, M. S., 35, 37
De Pree, Max, 163
Decision makers, 169
Decision making, 10
  alternatives and, 180
  change and, 224–225
  groups and, 152, 155–157
  hasty, 209
  "human relations" theory and, 178
  and implementing change, 227
  intellectual knowledge and, 25
  knowledge and, 18
  leadership and, 163, 165
  observation and, 47
  organizational culture and, 94
  organizational politics and, 23
  participative, 159, 179. *See also* Participant
    management
  problem definition and, 228
  scientific management and, 170
  structural change and, 225
  systems approach to, 179
Decision-making group, 152
Decoding, 29, 112
Deetz, S., 212
Defamation, 202, 204
Defensive climate, 140, 142
Deficiency needs, 132, 134, 142
Definition, problem, 227–228

Definitions, as research questions, 44, 47, 54
Delphi Technique, 157
Deming, W. Edwards, 186, 186–187
Democratic leadership, 159
Demographic homophily, 30, 35
Demographics
  change and, 214, 218, 220–221
  perceptions and, 32–33
Denial, 256
Denzin, N. K., 59
Dependent variables, 49–50
Depression, 257
Description, 140
Descriptive analysis, 45
DeVito, J. A., 152, 153, 167
Dewey, John, 157, 167, 227, 232
DeWine, S., 118, 119, 122, 125
Dialogue, 3, 4, 21, 25–29, 39
  change and, 220
  client analysis and, 56
  communication roles and, 97
  internally vs. externally oriented, 39
  leadership and, 165
  mentors and, 119, 123
  motivation and, 134, 136, 142, 145
  persuasion and, 274
  strategies for, 39
  supervision and, 131
Differentiation, 181–182
Dignity, 255
Disabilities, 248–249. *See also* Handicap
DiSalvo, V. S., 202, 212
Disciplinary interviews, 202
Discipline, 173
Disclosure, 207–208
Discrimination, 234–236, 240, 248
  ADA and, 248–249
  age, 250–251
  consciousness-raising groups and, 153
  internationalism and, 278
  language and, 247
  New Organizations and, 234, 251
  physical attraction and, 34
  religion and, 249
Distribution, 45
Diversity, 254
  homophily and, 31
  religion and, 249

Documentary evidence, 42–44, 56
Documents, credibility of, 43
Dogmatic personality, 109
Downs, A., 226, 232, 254, 260, 267, 269
Downsizing, 10, 97, 106, 225, 255,
        259–260
    age discrimination and, 250
    benefits and, 238
    discrimination and, 234
    early retirement and, 260–261
    firing and, 201, 257
    and implementing change, 230
    layoffs and, 257
    motivation and, 137
    professional conduct and, 201
    rehiring after, 225, 226
    stress and, 226, 263
Downward communication, 97
    "human relations" theory and, 178, 179
    leadership and, 165
    scientific management and, 172, 176
Drake, John D., 78, 82
Dress, 24
    for employment interview, 78
    power and, 115
    professional look in, 210–211
    status and, 115
Drug companies, 218
Drugs, 204, 236, 248, 277
    involuntary termination and, 258, 259
Du Pont, 260–261
Dubin, S., 192, 193, 212
Dunn, D. M., 138, 146
"Dvorak keyboard," 184
Dworkin, T. M., 212

E-mail, 4, 263
    context and, 114
    etiquette and, 211
    problems with, 277–278
    social changes and, 221
E-mail mentor, 122
Economic knowledge, 22–23
"Economic man," 179, 180
Economics. *See also* Physical-economic
        school
    change and, 214, 218, 219
    homophily and, 30, 31

Economy, cycles of, 218
Education, 16, 265, 266
    content research and, 16
    homophily and, 30
    male vs. female behavior and, 245
    motivation and, 135
EEOC. *See* Equal Employment Opportunity
        Commission (EEOC)
Efficiency, 170, 172, 175
Egan, K. S., 118, 119, 125
Eisenbach, R. J., 118, 125
Elder care, 237
Electronic brainstorming, 230
Emotional distress, 204
Emotions
    communication dialogue and, 28
    persuasion and, 274
Empathic communication, 140, 272
Employee assistance program, 204
Employees. *See also* Workers
    adaptability of, 12
    as customers, 10
    economic knowledge and, 23, 23
    flexibility of, 12
    investing in technology vs., 11
    neophyte and new, 84. *See also* New/neo-
        phyte employees
    new vs. traditional type of, 11
    orientation for new, 84–85
Employment agencies, 67, 68, 71
Employment contracts
    formal vs. implied, 85–86
    trade secrets and, 206
Employment interviews, 61–63, 66, 77–81
    asking interviewer questions during,
        66, 80
    communication dialogue and, 39
    in future, 277
    professional conduct in, 196–197
    salary negotiation during, 80–81
    stress interview as, 79
Employment process, 62
Empowerment, 137
    "human relations" theory and, 179
    leadership through, 163–165
    professional competence and, 193
Encoding, 28, 29, 112
Encounter phase, 94–100, 256

Encouragement, 164
Encrypted messages, 278
Enterprising personalities, 110
Entrepreneurial companies, 87
Entrepreneurial skills, 267
Entropy, 175, 181, 185
Environment
    change and external, 214, 215–216
    hostile work, 240, 241
    of message, 29
    of system, 181, 182, 184, 185
Environment (protection of), 209, 215
Environmental Protection Agency
        (EPA), 205
EPA. *See* Environmental Protection
        Agency (EPA)
Episodes, 3
Equal Employment Opportunity Commission
        (EEOC), 240, 241
Equal opportunity, 205, 275
Equal pay for equal work, 234–235
Equal protection, 236
Equal treatment, 140
Equifinality, 182
Equilibrium, 179
Equity, 208
Ergonomics, 177
Error, 174, 235
    task changes and, 222
Esteem needs, 133, 142, 144
Estes, R., 225, 232, 255, 269
Estrin, R., 11, 14
Ethics, 192, 193, 208–210, 246,
        275, 276
    in advertising, 206
    cultural change and, 219
    in firing, 202
    in hiring, 194, 195, 197
    in international business, 219, 220
    internationalism and, 278
    involuntary termination and, 258
"Ethics board," 207
Ethnic groups, 236, 250
    homophily and, 30
Etiquette, 192, 197, 208, 210–211,
        275, 276
Ettorre, B., 249, 252
European automobiles, 215

Evaluation, 272
    of credibility, 31
    of employees, 197, 199–200
    of ideas/solutions, 229
    of job applicants, 196
    of message, 29, 35, 140
    of organizational change, 231
    of performance, 11, 197, 199–200, 235
    problem solving and, 157
Exchange theory, 137, 140–141
Executive Interview, The, 78
Expansion, 225
Expectations
    production, 221–222
    verbal, 114
Experience
    careers/job seeking and, 65
    homophily and, 30–31
    knowlege and, 18
    leadership and, 163
Experimental method, 48, 49–50
Expert power, 137, 142
Expertise, 136
    groups and, 152
    leadership and, 163
    in old organization, 5
Eye contact, 115, 274

FAA. *See* Federal Aviation Administration
        (FAA)
Face-to-face communication, 89, 94,
        221, 231
Facilitators, 53, 54
Facts, 45
    observation and, 47
    research questions and, 44, 47, 52
Fagen, R. E., 188
Fairness, 208, 234
Family
    corporate activities involving, 101
    perceptions and, 32–33
    professional conduct and, 193–194
    work and, 236, 237
Family and Medical Leave Act, 237
Fast, J., 78, 82
Faules, D. F., 89, 103
Faux, Marian, 78, 82
Fax transmission, 4, 211, 216

Federal Aviation Administration (FAA), 209
Feedback, 28, 135, 174, 273
    adapting to, 183
    behavioral alteration techniques
        (BATs), 144
    computers and, 173
    group, 154
    "human relations" theory and, 178, 179
    persuasion and, 274
    scientific management and, 176
    social group and, 153
    systems theory and, 183
    technological change and, 217
    upward communication and, 97
Feedforward phase, 154
Feminist perspective, 242
Feuerstein, Aaron, 11–12
Fiber optic lines, 226
Fiduciary relationships, 207–208
Fiedler, F., 160–161, 167
Field experiments, 48, 49–50, 55
    informal, 57
Files, 277
    organizational structure and, 92–93
    technological change and, 217
Films, content research and, 19
Financial accounting, 207
Firing, 200–202, 203, 258–259
    discrimination and, 234
    downsizing and, 201, 257
    layoffs and, 201, 257
First Amendment, 247
First impressions, 62
FIRST SEARCH, 42
Fisher, B. A., 180, 188
"Flat" organization, 97, 186, 225
Fleischmann, S. T., 79, 82
Flexibility
    communication climate and, 140
    credibility and, 34
    of employees, 12
    "human relations" theory and, 177
    religion and, 249
    structural change and, 226
    technological change and, 217
Flextime, 237, 278
Focus groups, 46, 48, 52–54, 55
    organizational change and, 231
    professional competence and, 193

Forbes, 43, 66
Ford, Henry, 6, 170
Ford Motor Co., 6, 214, 215
Formal communication, 23
    bureaucracy and, 173
    conversation and, 90
    "human relations" theory and, 178
    new/neophyte employees and, 85
    professional competence and, 193
    scientific management and, 172
Formal contracts, 85–86
Formal cultures, 94
Formal linkages, 97
Formal mentors, 117, 118, 121, 122
Formal networks, 97
Formal observation, 46–47, 57
Formal organizations/structure, 87–91,
    179, 225
Formal research, 47–56
    client analysis and, 56
    informal vs., 4, 22, 56
    organizational structure and, 92
Fortune 500, 214
Free enterprise system, 8, 10, 271
Freedom (job), 135
Freewheeling, 229
Freezing/unfreezing, 225
French, R. P., 137, 146
Frost, J., 138, 146
Frost, P. J., 247, 252
Functional identity, 100
Functions of the Executive, The, 179

Garfinkel, H., 220, 232
Gender, 153, 236
    discrimination and, 234
    new vs. old culture and, 240
Gender and Discourse, 245
Gender/sex, homophily and, 30, 31
General Motors, 6, 214, 215
Generalizability, 55
Generalized other, 86–87
Genetic leadership relationship, 159
Gerberg, R. J., 69, 82
Gestures, 115
Gibb, J. R., 140, 146, 154, 167
Gifford, Kathy Lee, 219
Gleeson, K., 92, 103
Goal orientation, 271–273

Goals, 169, 180. *See also* Objectives
  change and, 224–225, 271
  common, 10, 228, 271
  consensus and, 156
  cooperation and, 140
  downsizing and, 10
  employee performance, 200
  groups and, 149–150
  and implementing change, 227
  individual and organizational, 9–10, 271
  leadership and, 148
  motivation and, 136
  orientations of, 148
  as processes, 273
  professionalism and, 194
  systems approach to, 179
"Golden Rule," 197, 202
Goldhaber, G. M., 46, 59, 89, 97, 103,
    161, 167
Gordon, D. M., 225, 232, 255, 269
Government regulations, 254
Governmental organizations, 2
  bureaucracy and, 173
  systems theory and, 184
Gowan, M. A., 237, 252
Grapevine, 89, 113, 178, 274
Green, C. M., 78, 82
Grening, J., 201, 212
Greyser, S. A., 206, 212
Grierson, R. D., 244, 252
Grievance policy, 244, 245
"Grooms," 120–121
Group cohesiveness, 156
Group majority vote, 155
Group solidarity, 156
Groups, 147–157, 221. *See also* Multigroup
    communication; Small groups; Team-
    work; Teams; Work groups
  brainstorming by, 228–229, 230
  conflict in, 154–155, 156, 157
  defined, 149
  Delphi, 157
  dislike for working in, 35
  dynamics of, 153–155
  dysfunctional, 156
  "human relations" theory and, 177
  informal, 179–180
  known, 48, 53, 55, 230
  leadership and, 151, 147–148, 157–165

  management of, 169
  messages and, 112
  motivation and, 142
  primary, 176–177
  problem analysis by, 228
  problem definition by, 228
  roles in, 94–97
  size of, 16, 149–152
  social, 153
Groupthink, 156–157
Growth needs, 132, 134, 142
Guilt trip mentors, 120
Gutek, B. A., 241, 242, 252
Gwin, S., 54, 59

Hackers, 278
Hall, A. D., 188
Hall, D. T., 255
Hall, E. T., 220, 232
Hall v. Gus Construction Company, 241
Hammer, M., 2, 14
Handicap, 234. *See also* Disabilities
Harassment, 205, 234, 236
  age, 250
  internationalism and, 278
  language and, 247
  New Organizations and, 251
  nonsexual vs. sexual, 248
  racial, 236, 246–247
  sexual, 240–246, 275
Haring-Higdore, M., 118, 125
Harmony, 134
Harper, R. G., 89, 103
Harre, R., 3, 14
Harrick, E. J., 246, 252
Harris, L. M., 47, 59
Harris, M., 264, 265, 269
Harris v. Forklift Systems, Inc., 241
Hawes, L., 180, 188
Hawthorne Effect, 176
"Hazing," 246
Health care industry, 227
Health insurance, 250
Health maintenance organizations
    (HMOs), 218
Hellman, Paul, 80, 82
Hersey, P., 161, 162, 167
Herzberg, Frederick, 127, 132, 134–136, 142,
    146, 177

Heston, J. K., 160, 167
Hey, R. P., 262, 269
Hickson, M. III, 1, 2, 14, 19, 29, 37, 47,
    55, 59, 62, 78, 82, 89, 90, 103, 113,
    125, 131, 132, 138, 145, 146, 159,
    167, 181, 182, 185, 188, 189, 210,
    244, 245, 252
Hidden agendas, 155
Hierarchical organizations, 128, 129
Hierarchy
  in bureaucracy, 173
  roles in, 238
Hierarchy of needs, 132–134
High-achiever personality, 109
High-verbal personality, 109
Hill, S. R., Jr., 19, 29, 37, 113, 125, 139, 146,
    185, 189
Hiring, 194–197, 198, 211
  advertising and, 194–195
  discrimination and, 234
Hispanics, 240, 246, 249. *See also* Spanish-
    speaking workers
Historical method, 48, 55, 56
Hitachi, 205
HMOs. *See* Health maintenance
    organizations (HMOs)
Hocking, J. E., 43, 45, 59, 217
Holland, John H., 110, 125
Homans, George C., 98, 127, 137, 140–141,
    142, 144, 146, 169, 177, 179, 188
Home
  researching from, 43
  working from, 237, 266
    in future, 277, 278
Homeostasis, 181
Homophily, 29, 30–31, 34, 35, 274
  new/neophyte employees and, 86
Honesty, 140
  credibility and, 34
  in hiring, 196
  homophily and, 31
  "human relations" theory and, 178
  professional competence and, 193
"Honeymoon period," 100
Horizontal communication, 165, 179, 180
  "human relations" theory and, 179
  structural change and, 225
Horizontal organizations, 128, 129
Horton, T., 214, 232

Hostile takeovers, 152, 153
Hostile work environment, 240, 241
"Human relations" approach, 169, 176–179
  systems theory vs., 184
Hursch, G., 51
Hygienic factors, 134–136, 142, 144

IBM, 205
Ideas
  brainstorming and, 229
  goals and, 148
  leadership and, 157, 163
  persuasion and, 274
  trade secrets and, 206
Ideation group, 152
Identification, 100–101, 142, 144, 256
Illegal actions, 258, 260
Imagery, 263
Implementing change, 227–230
Impoverished leadership, 160
Impression formation, 29–35
In Search of Excellence, 4
In-depth analysis, 53
In-depth interviews, 46
In-depth questions, 52
Inadequate personality, 109
Incentives, 135, 132, 227
Independent variables, 49–50
Indifferent personality, 108
Individuality, 105–125
  communication cues and, 112–116
  group work and, 147
  leadership and, 148
Individuals, 2, 270–279. *See also* Personality
  change and, 214
  communicating as, 15–37
  communication knowledge and, 4
  group work and, 147
  groups vs., 149
  power and, 138–140
  professionalism and, 194
Industrial organizations
  scientific management and, 172
  systems theory and, 184
Industrial Revolution, 5–6
Industrial workers, 6
Infante, D. A., 153, 167
Inferential analysis, 45
Influence approach, 128, 137, 142

Informal communication, 23, 89–91, 98–100.
   See also Grapevine
   conversation and, 90
   "human relations" theory and, 178
   professional competence and, 193
   small groups and, 180
Informal contracts, 85–86
Informal cultures, 94
Informal groups, 179–180
Informal interviews, 57
Informal knowledge base, 57
Informal mentors, 117
Informal observation, 46–47, 57
Informal organizations, 179
Informal research, 4, 22, 92
Informal structure, 87–91
Informal surveys, 57
Information, 93. *See also* Knowledge; Research
   change and, 217
   communication dialogue and, 25, 26
   confidential, 205–206
   in future, 277, 279
   gathering of, 40, 41, 163
   interpretation of, 163
   knowledge vs., 40
   new vs. old organizations in regard to, 39
   scientific management and, 173–176
   security of, 207, 278. *See also* Trade secrets
   temporary, 263–264
Information input, 181, 182, 183
Information overload, 221, 278. *See also* Message overload
Information processing, 174, 236
   change and, 216–217
   in future, 279
Information theory, 173–176
Informational listening, 130
Innovation, 217, 231. *See also* Change
   implementing, 231
   leadership and, 163
Innovator (role), 100
Insider trading, 207
Inspiration, 34
Intellectual capital, 163
Intellectual knowledge, 25
Intent, 28, 29
Interactions, 273–275
   adaptation and, 10, 56
   communication dialogue and, 25–29

content research and, 16, 19–20
   face-to-face, 89, 94
   "human relations" theory and, 178
   informal communication and, 89, 94
   professional conduct and, 191, 192, 194
   small group, 94–95
   social change and, 221
   technological change and, 217, 221
Interactive communication, 165, 221
Interactive television, 221, 277
"Interacts," 180
Internalization, 100, 142
International business, 23–25, 206
   bribery and, 23, 219
   ethics and, 219, 220
   in future, 277
Internationalism, 249–250, 278
Internet, 41–42, 43, 216
   careers/job seeking and, 66, 67
   in future, 277
   new vs. old culture and, 239
   social changes and, 221
Interpersonal attraction, 29, 30, 34–35, 274
   new/neophyte employees and, 86
Interpersonal communication, 18
   internationalism and, 249
   leadership and, 107
Interpersonal relations, 135
Interrelationship communication, 184
Interviews
   communication audit and, 46
   content research and, 4
   counseling, 202
   disciplinary, 202
   employment. *See* Employment interviews
   in-depth, 46
   in-person, 52
   informal, 57
   survey, 52
Intrapersonal communication, 18
"Invention," 39
Inventory, computers and, 239
Investigative personalities, 110
Investors, 23
Involuntary retirement, 260–262
Involuntary separation, 255
Involuntary termination, 258–260
Isolates, 98, 99
Isolation, 256

Jablin, F. M., 87, 103
Jackson, T., 72, 82
Janis, I., 156, 167
Japanese corporations, 8, 215
Japanese model (Theory Z), 127, 136, 185–186
Jenks, J. M., 79, 82
Jennings, R. W., 1, 14, 90, 103, 182, 188
Job descriptions, 85
Job enrichment, 135–136
Job market, changing, 265, 266
Job satisfaction, 58
  "human relations" theory and, 177, 178
  mentors and, 121
  organizational climate and, 100
  technological change and, 222
Job seeking, 5, 62–63
  "cold calls" in, 67–68
  want/classified ads and, 67, 68, 71, 194–195
Job sharing, 237
Job/work security
  adaptation and, 12
  automation and loss of, 7–8
  Herzberg's motivation theory and, 135
Joe Camel, 206, 218
"Joining," 165, 179
Journal keeping, 46, 55

Kahn, R. L., 132, 146, 181
Katerberg, C. A., 118, 125
Katz, D., 132, 146, 181
Kelman, H. C., 100, 103, 128, 137, 142, 146
Kerlinger, F. N., 217, 232
Killmann, R., 138, 139, 146
King/queen mentors, 120
Klassen, M., 248, 252
Kleinfield, N. R., 254, 255, 269
Know-how, 163
Knowledge. *See also* Organizational knowledge
  adaptation and, 40
  change and, 214, 217, 220
  client analysis and, 4
  communication and, 18–22
  communication dialogue and, 4, 27–28
  computers and, 40
  content research and, 4, 16–22, 39
  decision making and, 18
  homophily and, 31
  information vs., 40
  leadership and, 163

  organizational, 21–22
  perceptions and, 21, 273. *See also*
    Perceptions
  selectivity and, 20
  "storehouse of," 16
  types of, 22–25
  usable, 179
Knowledge bank, 21
Knowledge base, 21–22, 47, 56
  change and, 217
  informal, 57
Known groups, 48, 53, 55, 230
Kollath, M. L., 261, 269
Kouzes, J. M., 34, 37, 163, 192, 212
Koys, D. J., 201, 212
Kram, K. E., 117, 118, 125
Krantzler, M., 256, 269
Kreps, G. L., 91, 103, 138, 146, 158, 167
Krupp, Sherman, 169, 180, 189
Kubler-Ross, E., 256, 269

Laboratory experiments, 48, 49, 55
Laissez-faire leadership, 159
Language, 29. *See also* Messages
  internationalism and, 249
  non-discriminatory, 247
  power and, 247
  reacting to, 112, 114
  on résumés, 75
Language intensity, 113
Laser printers, 43
Laws, 192, 197, 210, 275
  equity and, 208
  privacy, 207
Lawsuits, 201. *See also* Legal concerns; Torts
  defamation, 202, 204
  discrimination and, 234, 236
  ethics and, 209
  sexual harassment, 241
  systems theory and, 182–183
  wrongful termination, 201–202, 204
Layne, S. P., 197, 200, 201, 212
Layoffs, 66, 106
  discrimination and, 234
  downsizing and, 257
  firing and, 201, 257
  professional conduct and, 201
  therapy groups and, 153
  today vs. previously, 254–255

Leaders, 169
  appointed vs. emergent, 155
  characteristics of admired, 192–194
  groupthink and, 156
  ideal, 160
Leadership
  apprenticing for, 105–125
  characteristics of, 163
  communication cues and, 112–116
  empowerment and, 163–165
  groups and, 147–148, 157–165
  individuality and, 105–125
  management as, 158–159
  styles/models of, 107, 159–163, 165
  systems theory and, 185
  task groups and, 155
  TQM and, 187
  of work groups, 147–148, 157–165
Leadership adaptability, 161–163
Leadership contingency, 160–161
Leap, T. L., 246, 252
Learning, 16
  communication and, 19–20
  communication dialogue and, 26–29
  research and, 21
Lectures, 19
Legal concerns. *See also* Laws; Lawsuits
  ADA and, 248–249
  consciousness-raising groups and, 153
  change and, 214
  daily, 203–208
  firing and, 202
  general, 207–208
  hiring and, 194, 197
  internationalism and, 278
  sexual harassment and, 242
Legalistic culture, 94
Legitimate power, 137, 142
Letters, etiquette and, 211
Letters of recommendation, 259, 260
Lewis, Robert, 262, 266, 269
LEXIS/NEXIS, 42, 207
Liaisons, 98, 99
Libraries (electronic), 42–43
Lifestyle, perceptions and, 32–33
Lifetime career/employment, 172, 173, 185
Likert, R., 160, 167
Lincoln, Y. S., 59
Linder, B. C., 244, 252

Lindsay, L. L., 186, 225, 227, 229, 230, 232, 249, 252
Line functions, 87
Linkages, 97–100
Lippitt, R., 159, 167
Listening
  active, 130
  communication cues and, 112
  male vs. female behavior and, 245
  motivation and, 132
  persuasion and, 274–275
  quality circles and, 230
  supervision and, 130
Literature review, 25, 41–44, 228
Lobbying, 219
Locke, E. A., 177, 189
"Lone eagle/loner," 118, 119
Long-term thinking, 186, 193, 218, 219, 224
  structural change and, 226
Louis, M. R., 267, 269
Low-verbal personality, 109
Lower-level management
  groups and, 148
  leadership and, 157
Loyalty, 11
  customer, 209, 224
  leadership and, 163
Lynch, Richard, 80, 82

Machiavelian personality, 109
Machine theory, 172–173
Magazines
  careers/job seeking and, 66
  content research and, 4, 19, 42, 93
Mail questionnaires, 52
Maintenance roles, 111
Malden Mills Industries, Inc., 11–12
Management
  administration and, 148
  changes in theories of, 214
  communication dialogue and, 39
  communication roles and, 97
  economic knowledge and, 23
  evaluation and, 231
  future of, 276–278, 279
  of groups, 169
  "human relations" theory and, 178
  "human resources school" of, 160
  leadership as, 158–159

Management *(Continued)*
  lower-level, 148, 157
  middle. *See* Middle management
  new theories of, 180–187
  post-World War II, 7
  professional conduct and, 191–192
  shareholders and, 11
  supervision vs., 128, 157–158
  theories of. *See* Theories
  upper. *See* Upper/top management
  workers and, 11
Management Communication Style
    (MCS), 165
Management levels
  flattening of, 97
  motivation and, 136
Manipulation, 140
Manley, W. W. II, 204, 206, 212, 248, 252
Manning, P. K., 228, 232
Manufacturing organizations
  "human relations" theory and, 178
  scientific managment and, 176
March, James G., 169, 180, 189,
    194, 212
Marketing, 11, 206–207
  communication dialogue and, 39
  rhetoric in, 26
Marketing research, 22
"Marketing wars," 184
Markets, sub-sectors of, 25
Maslow, Abraham, 127, 132–134, 142,
    146, 177
Masterson, J. T., 152, 167
Matarazzo, J. D., 89, 103
Mausner, B., 134, 146
Mayo, Elton, 176–179
McAdams, T., 248, 252
McCain, T. A., 34, 37
McCarthy, J., 247, 252
McCormick, M., 59
McCroskey, J. C., 20, 30, 34, 37, 89, 104,
    108, 125, 128, 130, 142, 143, 146,
    154, 157, 160, 165, 167
McGregor, Douglas, 160, 167, 178, 189
MCS. *See* Management Communication
    Style (MCS)
Mead, G. H., 86, 103
Measurement, validity and, 56–57

Media malfunctioning, 29
Meditation, 263
Medium (for message), 28, 29
Memory
  computer, 173
  perceptions and, 17–18, 19
  selectivity and, 20
Men/males
  communication by, 245
  homophily and, 30
  mentors and, 118, 119
  sexual harassment and, 243–246
Mental illness, 258, 259
Mentor-to-friend mentors, 120
Mentoring, 106, 107, 116–123, 256
  communication dialogue and, 39
  dysfunctional, 124
  formal vs. informal, 117, 118, 121
  leadership and, 163
  professional conduct and, 191
  teamwork and, 149
  types of, 119–121
Meritor Savings Bank v. Vinson, 241
Message management, 277
Message overload, 97. *See also* Information
    overload
Message/communication flow, 46,
    164–165, 178
Messages, 3, 274–275. *See also* Language
  behavioral alteration techniques (BATs)
    and, 143–145
  "boomerang" by, 114
  communication cues and, 112–115
  communication dialogue and, 4
  in communication model, 28–29
  computers and, 264
  content analysis of, 54–55
  "core," 29
  critical, 112
  evaluation of, 29, 35, 140
  leadership and, 163
  motivation and, 127, 141–145
  negative, 112
  nonverbal, 114–115
  relationships and, 35
  responding to, 112
  systems theory and, 185
  verbal, 112–114

Metric system, 184
Metzger, N. J., 255, 269
Meyer, P., 51
Middle management
    change and, 168–169
    groups and, 148, 152
    leadership and, 157
    mentors and, 122
    professional conduct and, 191–192
    task changes and, 222
Middle of the road leadership, 160
Miller, D. L., 100, 103
Miller, G. R., 112, 113, 125
Miller, M. L., 228, 232
"Mini-audit," 53
Minority persons, 6, 220, 233–252
Mission, 169
    language and, 247
    motivation and, 145
    organization culture and, 247
Mission statement, 44
Mobil, 214
Models. *See also* Theories
    change, 216
    communication, 26–29, 136–145, 174
    contingency, 160–161
    influence, 142
    leadership, 160–161
    participant-observation, 55
    role. *See* Role models/modeling
    separation, 256
Modems, 43
Mohan, M. L., 100, 103
Molloy, J. T., 78, 82, 210, 211, 212
Monitoring, by computer, 176
Monroe, C., 202, 212
Moorman, R. H., 242, 252
Morale, 11, 100, 153
Moreau, D., 71, 79, 82
Morgan, G., 89, 104, 138, 146, 169, 170, 171,
        176, 177, 189
Morse, Samuel F. B., 173–174
Motivation, 126–128, 131–146
    communication cues and, 113
    conflict and, 138, 140, 154
    equilibrium and, 179
    external vs. internal, 132
    in future, 270

Herzberg's two-factor (motivation-hygienic)
        theory of, 134–136, 142
Homans' exchange theory of, 137, 140, 141,
        142, 144
"human relations" theory and, 177
and implementing change, 227
individualized, 131
knowledge and, 18
leadership and, 165
Maslow's hierarchy of needs and,
        132–134, 142
mentors and, 119
personality and, 119
power and, 131, 138
professional competence and, 193
supervision and, 136
systems theory and, 185
TQM and, 187
Motivation-hygienic theory, 132, 134–136
Motivator factors, 134–136, 144
Moussavi, F., 248, 252
Mouton, J., 160, 167
Multigroup communication, 158
Murty, K. S., 89, 103
Myths, 91

Nadler, B. J., 76, 82
NAFTA. *See* North American Free Trade Agree-
        ment (NAFTA)
Nationality/national origin, 153, 234
Nebergall, R. W., 125
Needs, 142, 192, 194, 275
Needs hierarchy, 132–134
Negative entropy, 181, 185
Negative feedback, 28, 174–175
Negative messages, 112
Negentropy, 181
Negotiating, 245, 257, 272
Networking/networks. *See also* Computer net-
        works
    careers/job seeking and, 68
    centralized vs. non-centralized, 150–152
    formal, 97
    in future, 278
    informal, 89, 98–100
    "human relations" theory and, 177, 179
    systems theory and, 185
    types of group, 149, 150–152

Neutral feedback, 28
Neutrality, 140
"New Organizations," 1–14, 254,
        270–279
  adaptation by, 4, 10, 214
  communication knowlege in, 4
  culture of, 236–240
  discrimination and, 234, 251
  future of, 276–278
  harassment and, 251
  non-specialization in, 185
  old vs., 5
  principles of, 11
  privacy regulations and, 207
  researching in, 38–59
  stress in, 263
New products, 11
New/neophyte employees, 84–101. *See also*
        Socialization
  anticipation and, 84–94
  bottom-line orientation and, 106
  etiquette toward, 210
  identification and, 100–101
  organizational culture and, 89
  orientation for, 84–85
Newsletters (in-house), 101, 249
Newspapers
  careers/job seeking and, 67
  content research and, 4, 19, 42, 93
Niche, 4
Noe, R. A., 118, 125
Noise, 28, 29, 174, 179
Non-profit organizations, 2, 22, 23
Nonjudgmental climate, 140
Non-specialization, 185
Nonverbal codes, 28, 29, 114–115
Nonverbal communication, 29. *See also* Body
        language; Eye contact
  communication cues and, 112, 114–116
  employment interview and, 79–80
  focus groups and, 53–54
  internationalism and, 249, 250
  leadership and, 107
  listening and, 130
  male vs. female, 245
Norms, 84, 88–89, 100, 276
  behavioral alteration techniques
        (BATs), 144
  rules as, 90

North American Free Trade Agreement
        (NAFTA), 220
Notes, etiquette and, 210

Objectives. *See also* Goals
  career, 76–77
  multiple, 2
  and types of organizations, 1–2
O'Brien, T., 264, 269
Observation, 46–47
  careers/job seeking and, 65
  formal vs. informal, 46–47, 57
  participant-, 46, 48, 55–56, 57
  problem definition and, 228
  in time-and-motion studies, 172
  validity and, 56–57
Occupational Safety and Health Act, 205
Ogden, C. K., 112, 125
Oil companies, 23, 215, 219
On-the-job training, 131, 192
Open communication, 97
  legal issues and, 208
  quality circles and, 230
"Open door" policy, 97
Open relationships, 160
Open system, 181, 184
Opening phase, 154
Operational definitions, 54
Organisms (in "human relations" theory),
        177, 178
Organizational change, 11. *See also* Change
  adaptation to, 4, 10. *See also* Adaptation
  assessing, 230–231
  communication and, 11, 214
  implementing, 227–230
  types of, 215–227
Organizational chart, vertical, 225
Organizational climate, 89, 100. *See also* Cul-
        ture (of organization)
  leadership and, 159, 165
  "warm and fuzzy" syndrome and, 223
Organizational communication, 2, 35. *See also*
        Communication
  adaptation and, 214
  change and, 214
  communication dialogue and, 4
  future of, 276–278
  hierarchical levels of, 158
  leadership and, 107

new (modern), 3
new theories of, 180–187
participant-observation and, 55
patterns of, 46, 53, 98
preparing for, 60–82
problems in, 46, 90, 127
process of, 275–276
professional conduct and, 190–212
Organizational knowledge, 21–22
Organizational performance
  informal observation and, 57
  vision and, 169
Organizational structure
  anticipation and, 87–91
  change in, 225–227
  formal vs. informal, 87–91
  researching, 92–94
Organizational view, 169
Organizations
  control by, 40, 41
  defined, 1
  "entrepreneurial," 87
  evolving of American, 5–10
  "excellent," 4
  hierarchical vs. horizontal, 128, 129
  line vs. staff functions of, 87
  new (modern). *See* "New Organizations"
  norms of, 84, 88–89, 90, 100, 144, 276
  old, 5–10, 106
  post-World War II, 6–7
  roles in. *See* Roles
  rules of. *See* Rules
  separation from, 253–269
  types of, 1–2
Orientation
  bottom-line, 106
  communication, 158
  of dialogue, 39
  of goals, 148
  job, 222
  leadership and, 159
  for new employees, 84–85
  personality, 110–111
  problem, 140
  problem solving and, 157
  research, 217, 218
  security, 172
  task, 107, 113, 148, 160–161, 162
Ouchi, William, 127, 136, 146, 185

Oversocial personality, 109
Overt subcodes, 114, 115
Overtime, 11
Owners, 23

Pace, R. W., 89, 103, 108, 125
Packaging, 54
Paraphrasing, 157
Parent mentors, 120
Part-time workers, 237, 250
Participant management, 136, 179
Participant-observation, 46, 48, 55–56, 57
  new/neophyte employees and, 89
  organizational change and, 231
Participative decision making, 159, 179
Partners, dislike for working as, 35
Part-time workers, 11
Passive stretches, 263
Patents, 206
Patton, M. Q., 230, 232
Pay. *See also* Compensation; Salary; Wages
  discrimination and, 234
  motivation and, 131
Pearce, W. B., 3, 14, 47, 59, 35, 37
Pentagon, 7
People, concern for, 160
"People factor," 158
Pepper, G. L., 89, 103, 234, 252
"Perceived similarity," 30
Perceptions, 17–18, 19
  age groups and, 32–33
  change and, 217, 220
  communication and, 21
  communication audit and, 46
  conflict and, 154–155
  credibility and, 34
  homophily and, 30–31
  and implementing change, 230–231
  intent and, 29
  knowledge and, 21, 273
  motivation and, 132
  of power, 137, 138–139
  selectivity and, 20, 273
  sexual harassment and, 241–242, 244
  subcodes and, 115
Perfect Interview, The, 78
Performance
  organizational, 57, 169
  self-assessment of, 12

Performance evaluations, 11, 197, 199–200, 235
"Performance strategy," 180
Perinbanayagam, R. S., 86, 104
Perot, Ross, 159
Personal computers. *See also* Computers
  change and, 216, 217
  clerical staffs and, 7
  research and, 40
Personal information manager (PIM), 278
Personality, 107
  conflict and, 139
  constructivist vs. proceduralist, 119
  groups and, 157
  mentors and, 119
  motivation and, 132
  orientation of, 110–111
  personnel changes and, 222–225
  professionalism and, 193
  roles and, 111, 116
  types of, 108–110
Personnel changes, 222–225, 272
  structural change and, 225, 226
Persuasion, 25, 26, 28
  communication cues and, 112
  male vs. female behavior and, 245
  motivation and, 136
  with social and task messages, 274
Peter Principle, 122
Peters, Tom J., 4
Peterson, R. B., 244, 252
Phatic listening, 130
Phillips, G. M., 255, 269
Photocopiers, 216
Physical appearance, 68, 78, 115
Physical attraction, 34
Physical-economic school, 177
Physiological needs, 132, 133
"Piecemeal" work, 135
Piecework, 172
Piggybacking, 229
PIM. *See* Personal information manager (PIM)
"Planned obsolescence," 185–186
Planning
  careers/job seeking and, 63, 65–68
  communication dialogue and, 39
  economic knowledge and, 23

Policies, 66, 87, 92
  in bureaucracy, 173
  drug and alcohol, 204
  grievance, 244
  Herzberg's motivation theory and, 135
  hiring, 197
  internationalism and, 249
  research questions and, 44, 47, 48
  sexual harassment, 244
  termination, 201
Political correctness, 210, 247, 275
Political knowledge, 23–24, 25
Politics
  ADA and, 248–249
  change and, 214, 218–219
  communication cues and, 113
  homophily and, 31
  perceptions and, 32–33
  power and, 138
Polls, 4, 52, 53
Pollution, 219
"Poor attitude," 235
Populations, 50–51, 54
Positive feedback, 28, 175
Posner, B. Z., 34, 37, 163, 192, 212
Powell, J. L., 29, 37
Power, 127
  bases of, 137, 140
  behavioral alteration techniques (BATs) and, 144
  communication cues and, 114, 115, 116
  conflict and, 138, 140
  language and, 247
  leadership and, 160
  motivation and, 131, 136, 137–140, 142
  supervision and, 130–131
  systems theory and, 182–183
"Power brokers," 225
"Power plays," 86
Pragmatic syndrome, 224
Prediction, 40, 41, 56, 106
  change and, 220
Preponent needs, 132, 134, 142, 144
Primary groups, 176–177
Primary sources, 56
Printers, 43
Prioritizing, 278

Privacy, 194, 204, 208
  computers and, 207
  disciplinary interviews and, 202
  in future, 278
  secrecy vs., 209
Problem analysis, 228
Problem orientation, 140
Problem solving
  groups and, 152, 157
  and implementing change, 227, 229, 230
  process of, 227, 229
Proceduralists, 119, 120
Procedures, 87, 92
  bureaucracy and, 172
  internationalism and, 249
Process-oriented goals, 148
Processes
  leadership and, 148, 163
  goals as, 273
Product quality, 205
Product recall, 209
Product-oriented goals, 176, 180
  leadership and, 148
Production, concern for, 160
Production component, 87
Productivity, 101
  Hawthorne Effect and, 176
  "human relations" theory and, 177
  involuntary termination and, 258
  Japanese, 185
  new vs. old culture and, 240
  technological change and, 222
Professional competence, 192–203
Professional conduct, 190–212
  advertising and, 206–207
  in employee evaluations, 197, 199–200
  in firing, 200–202
  "Golden Rule" in, 197, 202
  in hiring, 194–197, 198, 211
  involuntary termination and, 260
  marketing and, 206–207
Professionalism, 193–194
Profit, 9, 271
  diversity and, 31
  exchange theory and, 140–141
  free enterprise and, 8, 10
  homophily and, 31
Profit-making organizations, 2, 22, 23
Profit sharing, 153

Programming, 173
"Programs," 180
Promotions
  in bureaucracy, 173
  discrimination and, 234
  and individual goals, 9
Provisionalism, 140
Public relations, 206, 219, 223
Public safety, 204
Punishment, 138, 142, 143–144

Qualitative research/analysis, 45, 47, 55–56, 228
  communication audit and, 46
  content analysis and, 54, 55
  focus groups and, 53
  and implementing change, 230
  observation and, 47
Quality circles, 136, 187, 230, 231
Quantitative research/analysis, 44–45,
    47, 48–55
  communication and, 179
  communication audit and, 46
  content analysis and, 54, 55
  and implementing change, 230
  observation and, 47
  reliability and, 56
  validity and, 56
Questionnaires, 52, 54
Quid pro quo harassment, 240
Quill, The, 43

Race, 234, 240
Racial harassment, 236, 246–247
Radical (role), 100
Railroads, 21
Rancer, A. S., 153, 167
Random assignment, 50
Rasberry, R. W., 186, 225, 227, 229, 230,
    232, 249, 252
Raven, B., 137, 146
Re, E. D., 208, 212
Readers Guide to Periodical Literature, 42
Ready, Aim, You're Hired, 80
Realistic personalities, 110
Receiving, 28, 29, 174
Recognition, 177
Recognition needs, 135
Redundancy, 175
Reece, B. B., 206, 212

Re-educational classes, 153
Reengineering, 163, 250
Reengineering the Corporation, 2
Referent power, 137, 142
Reflective thinking, 227, 279
Refrigerator companies, 184
Rehabilitative programs, 204, 258, 260
*Reinventing Leadership: Strategies to Empower
        the Organization*, 163
Relational leverage, 202
Relationship orientation, 161, 162
Relationships
    communication climate and, 140
    episodes and, 3
    "human relations" theory and, 177
    informal communication and, 98
    messages and, 35
    open, 160
    primary groups and, 176–177
    separation and, 255, 256
    structural change and, 226
    supervision and, 128
    workgroups and, 180
Relaxing posture, 263
Reliability, 56, 57
Religion, 153
    discrimination and, 249
    homophily and, 31
Religious knowledge, 24, 25
Reorganization, 225
Replacement units, 172
Research, 38–59, 223
    change and, 220
    computers and, 20, 21, 40–43
    content. *See* Content research
    formal vs. informal, 4, 22. *See also* Formal
        research; Informal research
    initiating, 41–47
    interpreting, 47
    marketing research, 22
    mentors and, 119
    primary vs. secondary sources of, 56
    problem analysis and, 228
    problem definition and, 228
    professional competence and, 193
    quantitative vs. qualitative, 44–45. *See also*
        Qualitative research/analysis; Quantita-
        tive research/analysis
    reason for, 40–41

Research and development, 11
Research methods, 44–56
Research orientation, 217, 218
Research questions, 44, 52
Research triangle, 46
Resistance points, 141
Resource referrals, 236–237
Resources, 10
Respect, 210
Responsibility
    behavioral alteration techniques (BATs), 144
    discrimination and, 235
    ethics and, 209
    "human relations" theory and, 177, 178
Responsibility needs, 135, 142
Restructuring, 163
Retirement, 221, 251, 257
    of baby boomers, 263
    early, 256, 260–263
    involuntary, 260–262
    mandatory, 250
    voluntary, 262–263
    working after, 264–266
Re-transmitting, 28–29
Return on investment, 23
Review, literature, 25, 41–44, 228
Revolutions, 23
"Revolving door," 86
Reward power, 137, 138, 142
Rewards
    behavioral alteration techniques (BATs) and,
        143–144
    exchange theory and, 137, 140–141
    "human relations" theory and, 177
    job enrichment and, 135, 136
    motivation and, 135, 136, 142
    professionalism and, 194
    scientific managment and, 177
Reynolds, R. J., 218
Rhetoric/persuasion, 25, 26. *See also*
        Persuasion
Rhodes, John, 13
Rhodes Company, 13
Richards, I. A., 112, 125
Richards, P., 261, 269
Richmond, V. P., 30, 37, 89, 104, 128, 130,
        142, 143, 146, 154, 157, 165, 167
Rifkin, J., 5, 8, 14, 255, 269
Rightsizing, 225, 234, 250

Rimer, S., 255, 269
Risk
  knowlege and, 18
  leadership and, 163
Ritualistic culture, 94
Robots/robotics, 7, 272
Roebuck, J. B., 89, 103
Rogers, Everett M., 89, 98, 104, 184, 189, 214,
    216, 227, 228, 232
Role models/modeling, 118, 144
  leadership and, 164
  mentors as, 118
Roles, 3, 90, 91, 98, 100
  group, 153–154
  motivation and, 132
  new vs. old culture and, 230–240
  participant-observation and, 55
  personality and, 108, 111, 116
  professional competence and, 193
  supervision, 131
  types of organizational, 111
  work group, 94–97
Roosevelt, Eleanor, 159
Rosenfeld, P., 82
Routines, 90, 91, 238–240
Rowland, M., 262, 269
Rubin, B. D., 182
Rudolph, E., 100, 104
Rules, 91
  enforcement of, 132
  motivation and, 132
  new vs. old culture and, 238–240
  new/neophyte employees and, 87
  participant-observation and, 55
  scientific management and, 173
Rumors, 89, 93, 113
Résumés, 62–63, 68, 69, 71–77, 82
  cover letters and, 68, 69–71

Safety
  alcohol and drug addiction and, 204
  workplace, 205
Safety needs, 132, 133, 142
Salary. *See also* Compensation; Pay; Wages
  benefits and, 238
  in bureaucracy, 173
  discrimination and, 235
  Herzberg's motivation theory and, 135
Salary negotiation, 80

Sampling, 45, 50–52, 54
Sampling error, 51–52
Scandura, T. A., 118, 121, 124
Schockett, M. R., 118, 125
Schrode, W. A., 248, 252
Schwartz, K., 234, 252
Schwartz, R. D., 45, 59
Scientific management, 169–176
  "human relations" theory vs., 177
  new vs. old culture and, 239
  systems theory vs., 184
  time-and-motion studies in, 170, 172,
    173, 175
  TQM vs., 187
SEC. *See* Securities and Exchange Commission
    (SEC)
Sechrest, L., 45, 59
Secondary sources, 56
Secord, P., 3, 14
Securities and Exchange Commission (SEC),
    207, 258
Security (of information), 207, 278
Security needs, 132, 133
Security-oriented worker, 172
Seductive manipulators, 120
Selection
  in hiring, 195–197
  of solutions, 229
Selective exposure, 273–274
Selectivity, 20
Self-actualization, 133–134, 144, 179
Self-centered roles, 111
Self-concept, 86–87
Self-development, 164, 165
Self-esteem, 143. *See also* Esteem needs
Self-fulfilling prophecy, 111
Self-initiated change, 214
Self-promoter mentors, 120
Self-respect, 86, 201
"Selling," 165, 179, 272
Seminars, employee-spouse, 101
Sender, 27–28
Seniority, 11, 173
Sensitivity, 245, 251, 274
Separation (from organization), 253–269
  involuntary, 255, 258–263
  types of, 257–264
  voluntary, 263–264
Sexism, 245

Sexual harassment, 205, 240–246, 275
  nonsexual harassment vs., 248
  perspectives on, 242
Shannon, Claude, 174, 175, 189
Shareholders, 11
Sheets, P., 111, 124
Shell, 214
Sherif, C. W., 125
Sherif, M., 125
Shimanoff, S., 114, 125
Short- vs. long-term thinking, 185–186, 218
Shrode, W. A., 204, 206, 212
Simon, Herbert A., 169, 179, 180, 189,
    194, 212
Skills, 12
  analyzing, 63–65
  communication. *See* Communication
      skills
  entrepreneurial, 267
  involuntary termination and, 258
  new, 267
Small groups, 16, 169, 179–180
  adaptation to, 148, 149
  and implementing change, 227
  leadership and, 107
  roles in, 94–95
Smeltzer, L. R., 246, 252
Smircich, L., 89, 94, 104
Smith, W. S., 94, 104, 227, 228, 232
Snydermann, D. B., 134, 146
Sociability, 31, 35
Social attraction, 35
Social change, 214, 217, 221–222
  technological change and, 221–222, 254
Social group, 153
Social interaction, 273–275
Social issues
  ADA and, 249
  communication cues and, 113
  of "New Organizations," 278
  perceptions and, 32–33
Social knowledge, 24–25
"Social man," 179, 180
Social messages, 274
Social needs, 133, 135, 177
Social personalities, 110
Social power, 137
Social responsibility, 153
Social subcodes, 114, 115

Socialization, 83–104, 275, 276
  adaptation and, 246, 276
  anticipation phase in, 84–94
  communication cues and, 112
  communication roles and, 96–97
  encounter phase in, 94–100
  harassment and, 246
  identification phase in, 100–101
  informal observation and, 57
  internationalism and, 278
  leadership and, 106
  linkages and, 99
  mentoring and, 116–123
  motivation and, 142
  phases of, 91
  power and, 142
  professional conduct and, 191, 192
  separation and, 255
Sociological group, 30
Sociometrics, 179
Software, 43
Soviet Union, 6
Span of control, 97
Spanish-speaking workers, 220. *See also*
    Hispanics
Spatial subcodes, 114, 115
Specialization, 6
Spontaneity, 140, 157
Spy systems, 178
Stacks, D. W., 19, 43, 45, 47, 59, 62, 78,
    82, 131, 132, 138, 144, 146, 159,
    167, 185, 189, 211, 217, 245, 252
Staff function, 87
Standardization process, 170
Standards
  involuntary termination and, 258
  leadership and, 164
Stano, M., 199, 200, 212
Startup costs, 23
Statistics, 45, 46
  error and, 51–52
  reliability and, 56
Status
  communication cues and, 114,
      115, 116
  motivation and, 136, 142
  nonverbal communication and, 274
  quality circles and, 230
  supervision and, 130–131

Steelworkers, 6, 7
Stereotypes
    gender, 241
    homophily and, 31
    internationalism and, 250
    personality and, 222
    roles and, 90, 95
    sexual harassment and, 243
Stewart, C. J., 77, 82, 202
Stockholders, 7, 225
Stogner, Camille, 255
Stohl, C., 89, 104
Stories, 91
Stress
    downsizing and, 226, 263
    and implementing organizational change,
        225, 226, 231
    leadership and, 163
    occupation and, 266
    relieving, 263
    social change and, 221–222
    structural change and, 225
    technological change and, 221–222
Stress interview, 79
Strikes, 23
Strodbeck, F., 157, 167, 179
Subcodes, 114–115
Subgroups, 225
Subsystems, 181, 182
Suggestion boxes, 178
Sullivan, G. M., 246, 252
Summarizing, 157
Superiority, 140
Supervision, 126–131, 136–146, 148
    in future, 278
    groups and, 151
    Herzberg's motivation theory
        and, 135
    management vs., 128, 157–158
    motivation and, 136
    sexual harassment and, 243
Supportive climate, 140, 142
    consensus and, 156
    leadership and, 165
Suprasystem, 181, 182
Surveys, 4, 48, 50–52, 55
    focus groups vs., 53
    informal, 57
    organizational change and, 231

System, defined, 181
System 1/2/3/4 model (of leadership),
        160, 165
Systematic actions, 234
Systems theory, 179, 181–185

Tannen, D., 245, 252
Taping, 173
Tardiness, 235
Task attraction, 35, 142
Task changes, 217, 222, 224
Task groups, 152, 155
Task incentives, 132
Task information, 92
Task leadership, 160
Task messages, 274
Task requirements, 159
Task roles, 111
Task-oriented goals, 148
Task-oriented communication, 113
    leadership and, 107
    scientific management and, 172
Task-oriented leadership, 160–161, 162
Taxes, 7–8, 218
Taylor, Frederick, 169, 189
"Team player," 119
Teams, 149. *See also* Groups; Small groups;
        Work groups
    professional competence and, 193
    leadership of, 160
Teamwork, 147
    advancement and, 149
    leadership and, 164
Technological change, 214, 216–217, 219
    downsizing and, 263
    social change and, 221–222, 254
    task change and, 222
Technology, 214
    adaptation and, 272
    bean-counting syndrome and, 223
    communication and, 11
    content research and, 93
    in future, 277, 278
    investing in, vs. people, 11
Tedeschi, J. T., 82
Telemarketing, 239
Telephone companies, 226
Telephone etiquette, 211
Telephone surveys, 52

Television
  cable, 226
  content research and, 19, 43, 93
  interactive, 221, 277
"Telling," 165, 179
Temporary workers, 11
Tepper, B. J., 118, 125
Termination, 201–202, 203, 258–260. *See also*
      Firing; Layoffs
Texaco, 214, 236
Thaves, B., 8
Theory X/Y, 160, 165, 178–179, 185–186
Theory Z, 127, 136
Theories
  behavioral alteration techniques (BATs), 128,
      142–145
  change in management, 214
  Herzberg's two-factor (motivator-hygiene),
      134–136, 142
  Homans's exchange theory, 137, 140–141,
      142, 144
  "human relations," 169, 176–179, 184
  influence, 128, 137, 142
  information, 173–176
  machine, 172–173
  Maslow's hierarchy of needs, 132–134, 142
  new management, 180–187
  systems, 179, 181–184
  transactional, 136
Therapy group, 153
Thill, V., 77, 82
Third world, 220
Thomas, K., 138, 139, 146
Thriving on Chaos, 4
Time-and-motion studies, 170, 172, 173, 175
Tobacco companies, 206, 218
Tobacco smokers, 248
Top management. *See* Upper/top management
Top-down management, 3
Torts, 207
Total Quality Management (TQM), 136,
      186–187, 230
Townsend, Robert, 163, 167
Toxic substances, 205
TQM. *See* Total Quality Management (TQM)
Trade secrets, 206
Training, 25
Transactional theory, 136
Transmitting, 28, 174, 176. *See also*
      Re-transmitting

Trial and error, 18–19
Triangulation, 45, 54
Tripp, T. M., 212
Trust. *See also* Fiduciary relationships
  in companies, 236
  leadership and, 160, 162
Trustworthy, 260
Typewriters, 184, 216

Uchitelle, L., 254, 269
Uncertainty, homophily and, 30
Uncertainty reduction, 255
Understanding, 40, 45, 46
  communication cues and, 112
  motivation and, 142, 145
  needs and, 134
  persuasion and, 274
  quality circles and, 230
Unions, 7, 23
United States
  in future, 277
  post-World War II, 6
United States Steel (USS), 6
Upper/top management
  change and, 169
  communication and, 3
  groups and, 148, 152
  as individuals, 16
  leadership and, 157
  mentors and, 122
  professional conduct and, 191–192
  structural change and, 226
  task change and, 222
Upward communication, 97
  "human relations" theory and, 178, 179
  leadership and, 165
  scientific managment and, 176
Upwardly mobile personality, 108
USS. *See* United States Steel (USS)

Validity, 56–57
Values, 153, 180, 275
  homophily and, 30
  identification with organizational,
      100, 101
  professional conduct and, 192
  research questions and, 44, 48
Valujet, 209
Van Maanen, J., 228, 232
Variables, dependent vs. independent, 49–50

Verbal codes, 28, 29
    nonverbal vs., 114
Verbal communication
    communication cues and, 112–114, 116
    employment interview and, 78–79
    focus groups and, 53–54
    internationalism and, 249–250
    leadership and, 107
Vertical communication, 225. *See also*
        Downward communication; Upward
        communication
Vertical organizational chart, 225
Videotapes, content analysis and, 55
Violation of public policy, 201–202
Vision
    "common," 193
    communication and, 169
    credibility and, 34
    leadership and, 163
    professional competence and, 193
Voice, 115, 274
Voluntary separation, 263–264

Wabba, M. A., 134, 146
Wages. *See also* Compensation; Pay; Salary
    for part-time and temporary workers, 11
    post-World War II, 7
    scientific management and, 173
Wal-Mart, 249
Wall Street Journal, 43, 66, 93
"Warm and fuzzy" syndrome, 223–224
Warner, D. M., 248, 252
Waterman, R. H., Jr., 4
Watson, K., 146
Web sites, 42, 43, 66
Webb, E. J., 45, 59
Weber, Max, 87, 104, 170
Weick, Karl, 108, 111, 125
Weiner, Norbert, 173, 189
Western Electric Company, 176
Wheel network, 150, 151
Whistle blowing, 202
White, R., 159, 167
White-collar employees, 106, 170, 238–240
White knight mentors, 120
Wiens, A. N., 89, 103
Willis, S. L., 192, 193, 212
Wilmot, W., 111, 125, 138, 146
Wireless communications, 226
Womach, D. F., 153, 167

Women/females, 186, 233–252
    communication by, 245
    consciousness-raising groups and, 153
    demographic change regarding, 220
    homophily and, 30
    mentors and, 118, 121
    World War II and, 6, 7
    sexual harassment and, 240–246
Work groups. *See also* Groups; Small groups;
        Teams; Teamwork
    "human relations" theory regarding, 177
    leadership of, 147–167
    relationships in, 180
"Work itself," 135, 177
Workers. *See also* Employees
    in future, 277
    management and, 11
    part-time and temporary, 11
    post-World War II, 6–8
    security-oriented, 172
Workforce
    demographic changes in, 220–221
    diversity of, 249, 254
    internationalism and, 249
    women and minorities in, 233–252
Working conditions, 205
    Herzberg's motivation theory and, 135
    motivation and, 131–132
Working relationships, 177. *See also*
        Relationships
Workplace
    goal orientation in, 271–273
    human factors in, 248–251
    internationalism in, 249–250
    social interaction in, 273–275
Workplace safety, 205
Workplan, 177
World Wide Web (WWW), 41–42, 43
    etiquette and, 211
    social changes and, 221
Wright, D. W., 67, 72, 82, 152, 167
Written communication, 172, 173
Wrongful termination/discharge,
        201–202, 204
WWW. *See* World Wide Web (WWW)

Y network, 150, 151

Zander, A., 149, 167
Zimmerman, R. A., 237, 252, 201–202, 204